New Testament Theology and its Quest for Relevance

New Testament Theology and its Quest for Relevance

Ancient Texts and Modern Readers

By Thomas R. Hatina

BLOOMSBURY
LONDON · NEW DELHI · NEW YORK · SYDNEY

Bloomsbury T&T Clark

An imprint of Bloomsbury Publishing Plc

50 Bedford Square
London
WC1B 3DP
UK

175 Fifth Avenue
New York
NY 10010
USA

www.bloomsbury.com

First published 2013

© Thomas R. Hatina, 2013

All rights reserved. No part of this publication may be reproduced or transmitted in any form or by any means, electronic or mechanical, including photocopying, recording, or any information storage or retrieval system, without prior permission in writing from the publishers.

Thomas R. Hatina has asserted his right under the Copyright, Designs and Patents Act, 1988, to be identified as Author of this work.

No responsibility for loss caused to any individual or organization acting on or refraining from action as a result of the material in this publication can be accepted by Bloomsbury Academic or the author.

British Library Cataloguing-in-Publication Data
A catalogue record for this book is available from the British Library.

ISBN: HB: 978-0-567-53396-8
PB: 978-0-567-65471-7

Library of Congress Cataloging-in-Publication Data
A catalog record for this book is available from the Library of Congress.

Typeset by Fakenham Prepress Solutions, Fakenham, Norfolk NR21 8NN

CONTENTS

Introduction 1

Part one: New Testament theology in theory 11
1 What is New Testament theology? 13
2 Foundationalist flaws 43

Part two: New Testament theology in practice 81
3 New Testament theology and the history of biblical interpretation 83
4 Foundationalist structuring of New Testament theology 119
5 Dialectical structuring of New Testament theology 139

Part three: New Testament theology in a pluralistic age 175
6 Religion and theology: The new conversation 177
7 New Testament theology as a dialectical process: An exercise in mythmaking 209

Concluding reflections 241

Bibliography 253
Author Index 269
Scripture Index 275

Introduction

The problem of relevance

I begin with an autobiographical note that helps to explain the purpose of this book. Since my initial exposure to the discipline of New Testament theology as an undergraduate student, I was intrigued by the many interpretative questions it raised, not only within its own boundaries, but also in relation to other fields such as history, literary criticism, sociology, psychology, history, politics, philosophy, and especially religious studies. Perhaps this is one of those happy hazards of a liberal arts education. But the overarching question that persisted, and frustratingly so with each passing lecture and assigned reading, concerned the relevance of two thousand-year-old writings in today's world. How does one establish what is and is not relevant in the New Testament? How does one communicate the ancient ideas, presented in an alien language, alien time, and alien culture to a post-Enlightenment audience? Stemming from this pre-occupation was a host of related questions concerning the theological unity of the New Testament, the nature of history and methods of interpretation. These questions were foundational because if suitable answers could not be offered, in my mind one could not even speak of a New Testament theology. And if one could not speak of a New Testament theology, the consequences for Protestantism (or at least many of its denominations) seemed dire. When push came to shove, I did not even have a definition for "suitable". Some of my professors tried to justify the unified nature of the New Testament and its relevance through grand metanarratives, worldviews, pet doctrines, or what they considered to be the human condition. Others argued for theological disunity while at the same time using in the same breath the terms "New Testament" and "theology", both of which, as we will see later, imply unity and relevance on some level.

Years later, when I began to teach, and thus urgently needed to clarify the varied approaches to unity and relevance (or lack thereof), I came to the resolution that the discipline of New Testament theology has been suffering from a kind of identity crisis that is rooted in a very old problem, namely the relationship between objective and subjective knowing. Using terms that are more amiable to the field, the problem lies in the relationship between theology and history, or faith and reason, or meaning and fact. Although most New Testament theologians have viewed the scriptures as authoritative, and thus relevant for today (in widely varying degrees), the interplay between the so-called "original" meaning and the meaning for today has been the source of much debate and consternation—to a level that was not envisioned by the founders of the discipline. So the overarching problem in the field of New Testament theology is the bridging of the two thousand-year-old gap—no small feat. On the one hand, historical integrity must be maintained, yet on the other, today's Christians, living in a vastly different world, seek meaning from these ancient texts.

My journey thus far has taken me to the realization that we must first step back and assess the chasm from both sides. When this is done, it is easy to see how, like modern Christians, the New Testament writers were primarily governed by a quest for and/or a legitimization of contemporary meaning and identity in the face of competing religious options. Stepping back a little further, I have found it advantageous to situate the problem of New Testament theology within the larger field of religious studies. Not only has this perspective provided for a clearer understanding of Christianity as a whole, but it has influenced the way I understand the language of the New Testament and what its writers and earliest audiences were attempting to be and to do.

This book is intended to serve as a methodological introduction to the field of New Testament theology aimed at a range of readers—undergraduate and Seminary students, clergy and the layperson interested in the relevance of scripture. It is not a New Testament theology. It is intended to be a guide which aims to help readers understand how the practitioners in this discipline have wrestled with the relationship between historical reconstruction (i.e. description) of the New Testament and its interpretation (i.e. normativity) in the modern world.[1] Many excellent introductions to New Testament theology have been written from which I continue to learn, as is evident throughout this book. In attempting to make this book fresh, I have tried to carve out a niche that emphasizes the discipline's enduring quest for normativity. In doing so, I have tended to give more weight to the role of the reader as has been the practice in contemporary literary theory —be it the individual, group or entire ecclesia—instead of the intent of the author or the text as the locus of meaning in the interpretative process.[2]

The study is divided into three parts. In the first part, readers are introduced to New Testament theology's identity crisis and its attempt to arrive

---

[1] I use the terms "normative" and "normativity" throughout the book to refer to relevance or the act of making the text relevant in the context of modern readers. It is also synonymous with the act of interpretation.

[2] In comparison to, say, the recent introduction by Dan O. Via—who focuses on "how to identify and articulate theological meanings found in the New Testament, whether one is dealing with a small text, a large text, or the whole of the New Testament canon"—in *What is New Testament Theology?* (Guides to Biblical Scholarship; Minneapolis: Fortress Press, 2002) 4.

at a definition of the discipline. The second part of the book explores how New Testament theology has been practised within the intellectual movements that have been called modernist and postmodernist. The third part is an attempt to lay the groundwork for doing New Testament theology in today's pluralistic culture. It is an attempt to re-direct (or perhaps rescue) a discipline that has traditionally not engaged with the mainstream academy. Running through this third section is a proposal that New Testament theology should be informed by the academic study of religion *before* attempts at theologizing take place. It is not too much of a stretch to say that the future of Protestantism, as we have known it, is at stake.

As I see it, the Christian belief in the New Testament as a (sacred) collection of sacred texts that still speak to the human condition after almost 2000 years is not the problem today. The belief in the sacredness or inspirational quality of scripture, be it the Bible, the Qur'an or the Vedas, is not even a matter of historical or rationalistic testability. The problem lies in *how* the New Testament is communicated and integrated within both the broader Christian community and modern Western culture, which is on the one hand secularized, yet on the other hand accommodates religious plurality. Grasping the tensions of our times is vital if New Testament theology is to have a viable voice in broader society. Understanding one's target audience is indispensable in any interpretative task. It's one thing to formulate a New Testament theology within the "safe" context of like-minded believers where interpretative methods are rarely challenged and where social and theological views rarely clash. In such cases, a New Testament theology often functions to support and even legitimize the ideology of its own group regardless of external critique, even from other Christian traditions and denominations. But it is an entirely different enterprise when a New Testament theology is intentionally formulated to interact within an inter-faith dialogue in mainstream culture where it is much more vulnerable to critique.

So what does our cultural context look like? By "culture" I am referring to North Atlantic Western culture (Europe, Canada and the United States), which identifies itself historically with Latin Christendom, yet has become very suspicious and in some cases even antagonistic toward the institutionalism of its religious heritage. One does not have to travel too far in Europe to notice that its beautiful churches suffer from a lack of attendance on Sundays. Nor does one have to engage in many political and religious conversations in the pubs and cafés to realize that Christianity is kept at an intentional distance. Statistically, regular church attendance in Canada has not fared much better.[3]

---

[3] On the state of religion in Canada, see Peter C. Emberley, *Divine Hunger: Canadians on Spiritual Walkabout* (Toronto: HarperCollins, 2002). Though the numbers have changed since the publication, the same conclusions stand.

The past is the sediment of the present. Despite their involvement in religious communities, most people would still identify themselves as "cultural Christians", even though society has moved in secular directions. At the same time, immigration from non-Western countries over the last few decades has led to a religious mosaic throughout Western society. For example, it has been repeatedly reported over the last few years in the British media that in England more Muslims regularly attend mosques than Christians regularly attend churches. Thus, we are in an age where "official" secularism has accommodated religious pluralism. The United States is an anomaly with its sizeable Evangelical constituency, numbering some 69 million in 2007, according to MarketResearch.com, the world's largest and continually updated market research company. It was not that long ago when suburbia was synonymous with the American ideal, where family roles, religion and the state were in step with one another.[4] Despite the mutual support that each one of these has provided for the other—even as it is attempted to be lived out today by a number of people devoted to an Evangelical lifestyle and religious nationalism—the triad fell victim in the turbulent 1960s to the crisis of authority brought about by the sexual revolution, the civil rights movement, feminism and the Vietnam war, to mention but a few. Assault on those who hope to maintain and/or rescue the "ideal" interconnection of the nuclear family, religion and the state, as has been propounded by the Moral Majority in the 1980s, for example, has shown no signs of receding. Although the Moral Majority movement has lost its national influence, the relationship between religion and the state has remained strong. The religious rhetoric and god-talk in recent election campaigns is a prime example. There are no signs on the horizon that this kind language is on the decline. To exclude the topic of religion from the campaigns of either party would probably have a negative impact at the polls. The American electorate still wants their candidates to be people of faith—particularly of a Protestant sort.

If a New Testament theology is to have a meaningful voice in mainstream North Atlantic Western culture, then it must be formulated in such a way that it can respectfully and intelligently interact with both secularism and religious pluralism. Both of these are, of course, immense topics that have been approached from a variety of perspectives, and we certainly cannot do them justice here, but a brief description should be helpful. Beginning with secularism, one of the most thorough and insightful treatments is presented

---

[4] The high point of this three-tiered social structure was post-World War II America. Charles Taylor writes in *A Secular Age* (Cambridge, MA: Belknap Press, 2007), "The family was the matrix in which the young were brought up to be good citizens and believing worshippers; religion was the source of the values that animated both family and society; and the state was the realization and bulwark of the values central to both family and churches." This was all the more underscored politically in the cold war since American freedom was in conflict with "Godless communism" (506).

by Charles Taylor. In attempting to understand what it means to say that we live in a secular age, Taylor is guided by the question, "why was it virtually impossible not to believe in God in, say, 1500 in our Western society, while in 2000 many of us find this not only easy, but even inescapable?"[5] Taylor, like Max Weber before him, argues that over the span of five hundred years we have passed from a view of the world that was "enchanted" to one that is "disenchanted". What he means by this is that the enchanted world of our predecessors fused the natural world with divine purpose and action to the extent that natural and personal disasters as well as prosperity and progress (say, agriculturally or medically) were viewed as acts of God. The fusion also extends to the social sphere whose authority structure (e.g. legal, moral and political) was viewed as divinely sanctioned. In the enchanted world, meaning was understood as being present in objects and/or agents independent of us. The individual was "porous" in the sense that she or he was vulnerable to agents (e.g. spirits) and/or objects (e.g. relics) by virtue of their intrinsic causal power.[6] The distinctions between sin and sickness and health and holiness were often blurred. In other words, that which makes one holy was often the same force that made one physically well. Absolution, for instance, was believed to clear up certain physical and emotional conditions. The Lateran and other councils warned against using ordinary medicine in place of spiritual remedies, and forbade the sick from visiting infidel doctors (e.g. Jews).[7] By contrast, today we make distinctions that were unthinkable in CE 1500. Most people today do not view natural events as direct acts of God. Our societal structures are democratic with many more built-in accountability and human rights variables that have emerged out of past human struggle against traditional authoritative structures. Today, meaning is viewed as stemming from the mind in the sense that events and objects awaken a variety of responses in us based often on past experiences. Even religious belief today is situated within a plurality of options that are constantly bumping up against one another. As a result, doubt, argumentation for or against faith, and even mediating explanations are part of the contemporary life of faith. Just as today's alternatives were unthinkable in 1500, so it is unthinkable that the secularism of Western culture might return to its enchanted roots.[8] This, in a nutshell, is what Taylor means by secular. Yet, the spiritual fervour has not diminished. If anything, many baby-boomers and their children are pursing personal spiritual instincts

---

[5] Taylor, *A Secular Age*, 25.
[6] See also Stanley J. Tambiah, *Magic, Science, Religion, and the Scope of Rationality* (Cambridge: Cambridge University Press, 1990); Stephen Wilson, *The Magical Universe: Everyday Magic and Ritual in Pre-Modern Europe* (London: Hambledon & London, 2004).
[7] Taylor, *A Secular Age*, 39.
[8] Taylor, *A Secular Age*, 25–89.

and interests, usually apart from institutions. In this sense the postmodern reaction to the rationalism, materialism and institutionalism continues.[9]

In the broader context of our secular society, religious pluralism has found a thriving home, which is another indicator that the spiritual climate has not waned. This potentially bodes well for the relevance of New Testament theology in our culture. But the pluralistic context has a significant impact on how that theology is formulated and communicated. If New Testament theology is to have a voice, we can no longer assume a posture of "business as usual" which assumed that competing religions are inferior and held to the standard of one religion.[10] In order for meaningful communication to take place, common ground and common media are essential. All voices need to be respected, heard, and understood on as much of an egalitarian level as possible. Otherwise, any meaningful communication is ineffective. Our secular culture with its promotion of religious plurality should not be disparaged as if the "good old days" somehow promised a better way of life. I regard the challenges all around us as an auspicious time to rethink how the New Testament is read. It will no longer suffice simply to pronounce a condemnation or *fatwa* against any group that does not share the same belief. History continues to instruct us that we cannot have peace in the world without peace among religions.

The way forward, in my opinion, is not to begin with *theology*, but to begin with the phenomenon of *religion*. What I mean by this is that scripture texts must first be understood as religious texts that use religious language, mythical narration, and historicizing techniques for religious purposes such as legitimization of beliefs, self-identity, and the formation of ideology. This does not discredit their value as sacred texts in any way. Quite to the contrary, understanding scripture texts as religious texts helps to identify their quality and purpose, and prevents the often problematic and sometimes dangerous confusion that scripture texts trump all forms of knowledge because they convey the mind of God in contrast to the mind of humanity. An example of this kind of confusion is particularly visible today in some forms of Evangelical Christianity and radical Islam. In the former, the book of Genesis, for instance, is treated as a scientific textbook on geology, biology, chemistry, anthropology and climatology, to name but a few. In the process science is confused with religion. Apart from misunderstanding the genre of Genesis within the context of Ancient Near East creation stories, the book's primary religious value is ignored, and thus locked in the past. A similar interpretative phenomenon is seen in radical

---

[9] On the resurgence of spirituality in contemporary American culture, see Wade Clark Roof, *Spiritual Marketplace: Baby Boomers and the Remaking of American Religion* (Princeton: Princeton University Press, 1999).

[10] An insightful study and critique of how Christianity has assumed dominance in comparative religions is Jonathan Z. Smith, *Drudgery Divine: On the Comparison of Early Christianities and the Religions of Late Antiquity* (Chicago: Chicago University Press, 1994).

Islam, which reads the Qur'an literally as a monolithic cultural manifesto. To use one example, the treatment of women in seventh- and eight-century Arab culture is viewed as the standard for the present. The potential danger in treating scripture in non-religious ways is that its relevance is threatened with change. As the scientific, literalist reading of Genesis continues its losing battle with the sciences, it will eventually, and ironically, lose its religious value as well. In the West, we have seen this increasing lack of confidence in the Bible for quite some time. Once again, the problem can be reduced to a premature theologizing with no accountability sought from the study of the nature of religion. What is more, it is a theologizing that has a remedial understanding of the discipline of theology.

In the context of the Christian religion, the New Testament is, of course, not competing with other sacred texts for an audience. Together with the Jewish Bible, and in some traditions the deutero-canonical books, it forms the sacred scriptures. But appreciating the New Testament as religious writings (i.e. in the context of the study of religion) significantly impacts how they are theologized and ultimately unified. When the New Testament writers are read comparatively alongside their Jewish and Greco-Roman contemporaries, considerable parallels and even borrowing is observed. Nascent Christianity, though unique in its claim to the messiahship and resurrection of Jesus, nevertheless expresses itself in the cultural beliefs, mores and language of its time. When the comparison is extended to world religions, again very interesting parallels have emerged that have begged explanations from the social sciences and literary arts, as well as theology. Some of the more glaring similarities have to do more with process than content, such as myth-making, historicizing, ritualizing, self-legitimizing, and transitioning towards ideology. It is also widely observed that religions necessarily use non-literal language (even if it is not understood as such within a given religion), such as metaphor and symbol, in order to express imaginatively meaning that often requires the bridging of heaven and earth. When the New Testament is approached from these observations it prevents an over simplified literalism and orients it in the context of a religious purpose, which in my opinion allows the writings to take on a sacred role that transcends culture and generational change, while at the same time eliminating the fear of cultural and scientific advancement. The constant is found in addressing the question "What does it mean to be human?" Ultimately, an appreciation of religion forces the Church to ask two foundational questions in the formation of a New Testament theology: What is the purpose of the New Testament? And how should we interpret it as a divine message for our time?

A final introductory note: while the definition of New Testament theology is discussed in the first chapter, a preliminary explanation of how it compares to other theological disciplines should clarify its distinctiveness from the outset. The study of theology since the enlightenment has been divided into various sub-categories, such as systematic theology, philosophical theology, natural theology, historical theology, spiritual theology, moral theology, applied theology, feminist theology, liberation theology, ecumenical theology, black theology and biblical theology—and many more can be added. New Testament theology, like its counterpart, Old Testament theology, has traditionally been understood as a sub-category of biblical theology. While all the above wear the same "theology" label, the differences with regard to methods, presuppositions, foci, and limitations are vast. To simplify the matter, most contemporary mainstream theologians would still argue that theology proper is best represented by systematic theology or as it is sometimes called "dogmatics". It is the umbrella category under which all the others can be placed. The term "systematic" should not be pushed to its end so as to denote a rigid structure, but simply indicates that the program of theology is to bring coherence and clarity to all its constituent parts together with all human knowledge derived from all the other disciplines. While it is oriented towards contemporary questions and issues, it is always rooted in its own religious tradition, be it Roman Catholicism, Eastern Orthodoxy or Protestantism. Theology continually mediates between culture and the significance of religion within that culture. If the theologian assumes a classical notion of culture (i.e. universal and permanent), then theology is regarded as a permanent achievement that engages in discourse about its own nature. But if the theologian assumes an empirical notion of culture (i.e. in constant flux), which is more common today, then theology is regarded as a discipline concerned with process, change and method.[11] In other words, one of the larger questions it poses is "In the quest for wholeness, how can theology unify our growing knowledge in the sciences with the revealed truths of scripture and tradition?"

There has been considerable discussion whether New Testament theology and Old Testament theology should be separate disciplines or united under the broader discipline of biblical theology. While the entire canon must inevitably be incorporated into a broader Christian theology, and certainly plays a huge role in the compositional history of the New Testament writings, I side with the view of G. B. Caird who argues that expertise in both testaments after the Enlightenment is an impossibility. While Caird admits that the pre-critical readings of the Old Testament through the lenses of the New have contributed theological insight, some of which may have been regrettably lost, far more insight over the last two centuries has been gained by studying the Old Testament on its own.[12] The Old Testament forever remains part of the Christian canon, but that does not mean that we silence what those ancient writers had to say to the audience in their own

---

[11] Bernard Lonergan, *Method in Theology* (Toronto: University of Toronto, 1990) xi.
[12] G. B. Caird, *New Testament Theology* (Oxford: Clarendon Press, 1994) 24–5. For an alternative that challenges the division between the testaments, see Brevard S. Childs, *Biblical Theology of the Old and New Testaments: Theological Reflection on the Christian Bible* (Minneapolis: Fortress Press, 1992).

day. The problem in a nutshell is that if we apply historical analysis to the Old Testament as we do to the New, we do not end up with a unified canon. If we read the Old in light of the New, we sacrifice the historical analysis of the Old, and end up with a Christianized Old Testament that has little to say for itself in its own right.[13]

---

[13] See the discussion of the issues in Scott J. Hafemann, ed., *Biblical Theology: Retrospect and Prospect* (Downers Grove: InterVarsity Press, 2002); John Barton, "Biblical Theology: An Old Testament Perspective," in *The Nature of New Testament Theology* (ed. Christopher Rowland and Christopher Tuckett; Oxford: Blackwell Publishing, 2006) 18–30; Mogens Müller, "Neutestamentliche Theologie als Biblische Theologie: Einige grundsätzliche Überlegungen," *New Testament Studies* 43 (1997) 457–90. On attempts to unify the testaments, see Francis Watson, *Text and Truth: Redefining Biblical Theology* (Edinburgh: T & T Clark, 1997).

PART ONE

New Testament theology in theory

1

What is New Testament theology?

Two perspectives

The identity crisis

New Testament theology has played a substantial role in both the popular and academic spheres. It has been the focus of college and university courses. It has served as the larger idea which has given the particularities of exegesis its purpose. It has served as the foundation for denominational distinctions. It has served as the basis for church life. It is a pillar for evangelism. And it has continued to be profitable for Christian publishers. So, it is very much alive, but is it well?

What is "New Testament theology?" At first glance this question appears to be easily answered. Some might say that it is simply the theological or religious (used synonymously) ideas found in the New Testament writings. Others might respond by saying that it is the authoritative repository of "essential" Christian teaching, apart from later doctrinal formulations. Still others might say that it is the teachings of Jesus—or at least that which is grounded in the teachings of the historical Jesus—such as the kingdom of God. While these kinds of brief answers are not incorrect, they are incomplete. In fact, to assume that New Testament theology is simply associated with the religious content of the corpus we call "the New Testament" is to omit much of what New Testament theology has sought to accomplish. Since its inception approximately two and a half centuries ago, New Testament theology has certainly dealt with the religious content of the New Testament, but more overtly it has been concerned with *how* the religious content is to be identified, understood and interpreted within its own historical context and in the present. It is the issues associated with the question of *how* rather than the question of *what* which have primarily contributed to the difficulty since its inception of defining New Testament theology as a discipline.[1] The

---

[1] On the difficulty of defining New Testament theology, see Hendrikus Boers, *What is New Testament Theology?* (Guides to Biblical Scholarship; Philadelphia: Fortress Press, 1979) 9–14.

question of *how* New Testament theology is to be understood and done is essentially a hermeneutical one, meaning that it is a product of particular interpretative methods, structures and sets of assumptions that stem from the person who attempts to formulate a New Testament theology. When we read the New Testament, we do not find a New Testament theology within it. We find theological language, reflection and faith conviction, but no unified theology. New Testament theologies are books written by modern scholars attempting to describe and/or prescribe the religious teaching in the New Testament, as they see it or want to see it.

In the broadest terms possible, the discipline has suffered from an identity crisis because its practitioners have written their New Testament theologies differently from one another. This diversity should come as no surprise given that the New Testament is on the one hand a collection of ancient texts that are culturally and linguistically alien to our culture, yet on the other hand these texts are believed to be religiously authoritative by some two billion Christians around the world. Thus defining the discipline has proven to be quite difficult. While it is a little more firm than trying to nail jelly to a wall, an overview of the possibilities will nevertheless lead many students to echo Peter Balla's resignation that there is no correct definition that captures the character of New Testament theology.[2]

The definitions that have emerged have mostly focused on the historical-hermeneutical divide. In other words, some have argued that New Testament theology is primarily a historical enterprise that seeks to understand the so-called original meaning of the text, authors or traditions (such as the historical Jesus) behind them. Others have argued that it is primarily a hermeneutical discipline that focuses on the meaning of the text (and/or the traditions behind it) for today. Still others have argued that it is a combination of these, in varying degrees of balance. As a result, a common way of explaining the discipline has been to divide its practitioners into their respective camps, be they termed historical/hermeneutical, objective/subjective, or modernist/postmodernist. A recent example of such categorizing is found in Dan Via's excellent introduction wherein he presents three established approaches: (1) "New Testament Theology as a Historical Project," (2) "New Testament as Historical and Hermeneutical," and (3) "New Testament Theology as Hermeneutical: Postmodernism."[3]

The difficulty with these categories is that history and hermeneutics can easily be perceived as exclusive of one another. Apart from a handful of practitioners such as William Wrede who advocates the historical approach (discussed below) and Francis Watson who advocates the hermeneutical approach (though not mentioned by Via), I cannot escape the nagging

---

[2] Peter Balla, *Challenges to New Testament Theology: An Attempt to Justify the Enterprise* (Peabody: Hendrickson, 1997) 240, 250.

[3] Dan O. Via, *What is New Testament Theology?* (Guides to Biblical Scholarship; Minneapolis: Fortress Press, 2002).

observation that the vast majority of New Testament theologians that Via places in each of his three categories inevitably incorporate both the historical and hermeneutical approaches. The differences are actually differences of degree, not of kind. Via uses A. K. M. Adam as an example of a recent scholar who might fit within his third category, but here too Via admits that Adam is not denying the need for historical criticism, despite his severe curtailing of its authority.[4] When the sampling is broadened, Via's all too common division does not take into account the prevalent interplay between hermeneutics and history, especially in German scholarship.[5]

As is discussed more fully below, the title "New Testament theology" necessarily includes both elements. While an alternating emphasis on the one over the other is an expected result of a healthy tension, the exclusion of one at the expense of the other only results in devaluing both. For example, in postmodern literary criticism, arguments in support of objective historical knowledge have been severely critiqued, and in many cases rightly so. The roots of New Testament theology in Enlightenment rationalism have also been well exposed. But the historical nature of the New Testament documents cannot at the same time be discarded. If nothing else, we would have no way of even reading these documents if it were not for the historically oriented study of ancient texts. Since the New Testament was originally written in a popular Greek, which today is a "dead" language, a postmodern (or strict hermeneutical) approach would have no translation available to it and could not engage in its hermeneutical exercises. Even in the midst of our postmodern awareness that language is indeterminate and not a fixed set of signs that correspond to reality, English translations, on which most literary critics depend, are constrained by the historically oriented disciplines of philology and lexical semantics which depend on contextual and comparative usage of the language in literature contemporary with the New Testament. It is one thing for English speaking readers to creatively "play" with English translations, but it is quite another matter when a critic's reading is sensitive to the original language of the

---

[4] Via, *What is New Testament Theology?* 102–3. A. K. M. Adam, *Making Sense of New Testament Theology: Modern Problems and Prospects* (Studies in American Biblical Hermeneutics 11; Macon, GA: Mercer University Press, 1995).

[5] The most recent works include, Klaus Berger, *Theologiegeschichte des Urchristentums* (Tübingen: Francke, 1994); Joachim Gnilka, *Theologie des Neuen Testaments* (Freiburg: Herder, 1994); Hans Hübner, *Biblische Theologie des Neuen Testaments* (3 vols.; Göttingen: Vandenhoeck und Ruprecht, 1990–95); Walter Schmithals, *The Theology of the First Christians* (trans. O. C. Dean Jr; Louisville: Westminster John Knox, 1997); Peter Stuhlmacher, *Biblische Theologie des Neuen Testaments* (2 vols.; Göttingen: Vandenhoeck und Ruprecht, 1992, 1999); Georg Strecker, *Theology of the New Testament* (trans. M. E. Boring; Louisville: Westminster John Knox, 2000); Ferdinand Hahn, *Theologie des Neuen Testaments* (2 vols.; Tübingen: Mohr Siebeck, 2002); Ulrich Wilkins, *Theologie des Neuen Testaments* (5 vols.; Neukirchen-Vluyn: Neukirchener, 2002–); Udo Schnelle, *Theology of the New Testament* (trans. M. Eugene Boring; Grand Rapids: Baker Academic, 2009).

text. While imaginative readings that reflect on who we are as readers can be insightful, it is frankly alarming how some current literary approaches to the New Testament exclude any serious discussion of the text in its original language.[6] So we find ourselves in the overlap of modernity and postmodernity.

Before proceeding further, it may be helpful to say a few words about "postmodernity" or "postmodernism"—contemporary labels that have been applied to almost every aspect of our culture and have been the topic of countless books and articles. Usually, "postmodernity" is used to refer to a specific historical period, whereas "postmodernism" is used as a reference for our cultural reflection or thinking. Echoing Terry Eagleton, the distinction between the two terms "seems to me useful, but it is not one which I have particularly respected in this book."[7] These labels are used to refer to a way of thinking about reality and our way of comprehending it. As the terms suggest, they convey a direct reaction to the ideals of modernism which emerged during the European Enlightenment (approx. CE 1650–1800). One of the main ideals of modernism was the strong optimism that objective knowledge/truth can be achieved through proper scientific method and reasoning. The subjective and objective aspects of knowing were believed to be distinct. In other words, the subject can know and verify the reality, its mechanisms, and even its grand narrative, within which he or she participates. Much more will be said about modernity in the third chapter. Postmodernity, which began to emerge in the early part of the twentieth century, and came into its own in the 1960s, is a way of thinking that challenges modernity's optimism of attaining objective knowledge, authority, foundations and absolutes. It subsumes the objective into the subjective, claiming that knowledge is reduced to a series of unstable contingencies that interact with one another without an identifiable, agreed upon or privileged foundation for truth.[8]

But is the inevitable critique of modernity to be understood as a distinct era of cultural thinking, apart from postmodernity? This question has been the source of much debate. Because many philosophers have found it exceedingly difficult to define "postmodernity" and have even questioned whether it really exists, they have argued for its connection with modernity. For example, Matei Calinescu views postmodernity as an extension of

---

[6] See, for example, the essays in Janice Capel Anderson and Stephen D. Moore, eds, *Mark and Method: New Approaches in Biblical Studies* (Minneapolis: Fortress Press, 1992).

[7] Terry Eagleton, *The Illusions of Postmodernism* (Oxford: Blackwell Press, 1997) vii–viii.

[8] See A. K. M. Adam, *What is Postmodern Biblical Interpretation?* (Guides to Biblical Scholarship; Minneapolis: Fortress Press, 1995). A helpful summary of the shift from modernity to postmodernity in theological studies is provided by David Tracy, "Theology and the Many Faces of Postmodernity," in *Readings in Modern Theology: Britain & America* (ed. Robin Gill; Nashville: Abingdon Press, 1995) 225–35.

modernity, calling it "the face of modernity".⁹ Timothy Reiss understands it as the culture's hidden discourse that emerges when the dominant discourse (modernity) is unable to explain reality.¹⁰ In one of the most telling examples of the problem of defining postmodernity, Dan Via quotes from a *New York Times* interview with the frequently hailed proponent of postmodernity, Richard Rorty.¹¹ When asked by the interviewer what some of the loftiest overrated ideas are today, Rorty responded,

> The first thing that comes to mind is post-modernism. It's one of these terms that has been used so much that nobody has the foggiest idea what it means. It means one thing in philosophy, another thing in architecture and nothing in literature. It would be nice to get rid of it. It isn't exactly an idea; it's a word that pretends to stand for an idea. Or maybe the idea that one ought to get rid of is that there is any need to get beyond modernity.¹²

Throughout the book I will use the label "postmodern" to represent the reaction to classical modernism. However, with Rorty and others, I do not attribute to it a uniqueness that has somehow succeeded modernism. While retaining the label is important, it is best viewed as an extension of modernity. And if postmodernity does exist, it is best understood as existing in an overlap with modernity. However we understand this overlap, we remain in an era of suspended tension between the objective and the subjective claims to truth.

Returning to the historical work of William Wrede, I hesitate to place him fully within the discipline of New Testament theology, for which I anticipate criticism.¹³ Although he has been influential due to his attempt to carry out a New Testament theology solely from an "objective" historical perspective, with no regard for canonicity, inspiration or ecclesiastical

---

⁹ Matei Calinescu, *Five Faces of Modernity: Modernism, Avant-garde, Decadence, Kitsch, Postmodernism* (Durham: Duke University Press, 1987) 265–78. Some have preferred to see modernity resuming its upper hand. See, for example, Jürgen Habermas, *Philosophical Discourse of Modernity: Twelve Lectures* (trans. Frederick Lawrence; Cambridge, MA; The MIT Press, 1987).

¹⁰ Timothy J. Reiss, *The Discourse of Modernism* (Ithaca: Cornell University Press, 1982) 378–82.

¹¹ Via (*What is New Testament Theology?* 124) quotes from Richard Rorty, "Lofty Ideas that May be Losing Altitude", *The New York Times* B 13:3, November 1, 1997.

¹² See also the criticisms in Ihab Hassan, *The Postmodern Turn: Essays in Postmodern Theory and Culture* (Columbus: Ohio State University Press, 1987); Robert P. Scharlemann, ed., *Theology at the End of the Century: A Dialogue on the Postmodern* (Studies in Religion and Culture; Charlottesville: University Press of Virginia, 1990); Eagleton, *The Illusions of Postmodernism*.

¹³ William Wrede, "The Task and Methods of 'New Testament Theology,'" in *The Nature of New Testament Theology* (ed. Robert Morgan; Studies in Biblical Theology 2.25; London: SCM Press, 1973) 68–116.

authority—which he regarded as subjective categories—his approach today is well within the study of Early Christian religion instead of theology. One of the most successful attempts to carry out Wrede's project is Gerd Theissen's much more appropriately entitled *A Theory of Primitive Christian Religion*.[14] Wrede carried the rationalist pursuit of objective knowing to its conclusion and in the process demonstrated that a strict historical approach results in the fragmentation of early Christian thought and the undermining of New Testament theology. Wrede's insistence that historical study purge itself from theological interests captured considerable interest in the larger field of biblical studies and makes him an influential figure to this day in both positive and negative ways. On the positive side, he successfully demonstrated how and why a rigorous historical method should be carried out apart from faith assumptions. A few, such as Krister Stendahl and James Barr, have continued to maintain that the task of biblical theology (Old and New Testament) is strictly historical and linguistic, thus descriptive, leaving the so-called prescriptive or hermeneutical issues to the systematic theologian who has the requisite philosophical and theological knowledge.[15] But on the negative side, his results led to the realization that New Testament theology, if it is to be given the name *theology*, requires a goal that aims beyond a disinterested concern for historical knowledge. Even Wrede himself, recognized that the label "New Testament theology" was inappropriate for his approach, though it did not stop him from using it.[16] Furthermore, it has increasingly been demonstrated how the approach of Wrede and his followers suffers from the delusion of historical objectivity, which will be taken up more fully in the next chapter.[17]

Two definitions

Instead of the standard historical-hermeneutical divide, I follow Gerhard Ebeling's two definitions of "biblical theology" since they are still relevant and better suited to introduce students to the problem of the discipline of

---

[14] Gerd Theissen, *Eine Theorie der urchristlichen Religion* (Gütersloh: Gütersloher Verlagshaus, 1999). It has been published in English under the title *The Religion of the Earliest Churches: Creating a Symbolic World* (trans. J. Bowden; Minneapolis: Fortress Press, 1999).
[15] Krister Stendahl, "Biblical Theology, Contemporary", in *The Interpreter's Dictionary of the Bible* (ed. G. A. Buttrick; Nashville: Abingdon Press, 1962) 1.418–32; *ibid*, "Method in the Study of Biblical Theology", in *The Bible in Modern Scholarship* (ed. J. P. Hyatt; Nashville: Abingdon Press, 1965) 196–216; James Barr, *The Concept of Biblical Theology: An Old Testament Perspective* (Minneapolis: Fortress Press, 1999) 202–4, 258–42.
[16] Wrede, "The Task and Methods of 'New Testament Theology'", 116.
[17] Mark Cousins, "The Practice of Historical Investigation", in *Post-Structuralism and the Question of History* (eds D. Attridge et al.; Cambridge: Cambridge University Press, 1989) 126–36.

New Testament theology. The first definition of New Testament theology is that it is "a study of that theology which is exclusively *found in* or *limited to* the New Testament". I refer to this definition as the "foundationalist" view. The second is that it is "a study of that theology which is *based upon* or *rooted in* or *in accordance with* the New Testament". I refer to this second definition as the "dialectical" view. Both are developed in considerable detail below.[18] These two definitions are well suited to speak to the modern religious divide in contemporary Christianity where on the one side New Testament theology is so historically oriented that it risks sacrificing relevance; and on the other side it is so oriented towards relevance that it sacrifices its original message.

Neither one of Ebeling's two definitions necessarily denies the authority of the scriptures. Neither necessarily denies the inspiration or sacredness of the scriptures, though they may be understood differently. Both recognize the importance of careful exegesis as a path to theology.[19] Both have emerged out of and continue to be practised within the Protestant tradition. And both attempt to solve the seemingly insurmountable problem of bridging the past and the present—a problem that is well articulated by Dan Via.

> Those scholars who understand New Testament theology as a strictly historical project but also maintain the authority of the New Testament for the continuing life of the church over the centuries create a two-part configuration that lacks a connector. The anomaly of their position is that, given their historical approach, they do not develop a hermeneutical vocabulary and conceptuality to represent the theological meanings of the New Testament in such a way that these meanings could address the present moment as a summons that could or should be listened to as compelling and authoritative. That is, the claim of authority is not supported by hermeneutical-theological discourse, a discourse that would demonstrate why the New Testament message should be grasped as taking priority over the understandings of reality today.[20]

The primary difference between the two meanings is not found so much in their aims, but in the way each attempts to fulfill those aims.

This is a crucial distinction that is often missed in the public sphere and mainstream media when the Bible is brought into social or political debate. For example, during the 2008 CNN/Youtube Republican Primaries debate, a questioner asked the candidates if they believe every word in the

---

[18] See Gerhard Ebeling, "The Meaning of 'Biblical Theology'", *Journal of Theological Studies* 6 (1955) 210–25. Also in *Word and Faith* (London: SCM Press, 1963) 79–97.
[19] See the insightful comments in Leonhard Goppelt, *Theology of the New Testament. Volume 1* (ed. Jürgen Roloff; trans. John E. Alsup; Grand Rapids: Eerdmans, 1981) xxv.
[20] Via, *What is New Testament Theology?*

Bible.[21] The answers varied, but none of the candidates pointed out that the question is meaningless at best and forces a false dichotomy at worst. The dichotomy implied in these kinds of questions is that if another person does not subscribe to the same (often literalist) interpretation, they obviously do not regard the Bible as sacred or as God's word. The difficulty of justifying one interpretive approach over another is certainly an immense task, and I address it to some degree below, but what is important to point out here is that whatever the approach, it is necessarily formulated outside of the Bible and imposed upon it. There is no explicit hermeneutical key mandated in the Bible, though a text which might be read in this way is John 5.39 where Jesus says to the Jewish religious leaders, "You search the scriptures because you think that in them you have eternal life; it is these that testify about me." Although the saying concerns the Jewish scriptures and not the New Testament, it gives us some idea of how the Johannine Christians, at least, understood the purpose of scripture, which had an enormous effect on its interpretation. This text certainly does not advocate a literalist interpretation. There is no doubt that in the story, Jesus and the Jewish religious leaders shared the belief that the scriptures were sacred. Neither is chastising the other for a low view of scripture. Instead, what emerges is that two people can share the same belief that the Bible is God's word, but they can differ tremendously in how they appropriate it in their lives. The better question in the Republican debate would have been: "If you believe the Bible to be a sacred book, how do you interpret it?" Or, "What do you see its overall purpose to be?" In other words, the question should have addressed the issue of meaning.

One further consideration: if we view the New Testament as the canonical source for formulating New Testament theology, we are immediately confronted with the problem of the first half of the Christian canon, the Old Testament. For this reason, many have called for a biblical theology that includes both the New and Old Testaments.[22] This is certainly a valid and ideal appeal, but in practice it is difficult to achieve, though it is an acknowledged deficiency of this book. In today's academic environment, the vast majority of biblical scholars specialize not only in one of the two Testaments, but in individual books and/or genres (such as the historical narrative, wisdom literature and poetry in the Old Testament; and the Gospels or Epistles in the New). By contrast, a history-of-religions approach, such as that of Wrede, need not worry about what is or is not canonical since all relevant texts are brought into play without a commitment to a theological hierarchy in the exegesis.

---

[21] St. Petersburg, Florida, November 28, 2007.
[22] E.g. Brevard S. Childs, *Biblical Theology of the Old and New Testaments: Theological Reflection on the Christian Bible* (Minneapolis: Fortress Press, 1992). Stuhlmacher, *Biblische Theologie des Neuen Testaments*.

The foundationalist view

Again, the first definition which Ebeling offers, and one that resonates with most New Testament theologians in the history of the discipline, is that it is "a study of that theology which is exclusively *found in* or *limited to* the New Testament with little or no regard for later interpretations or traditions". This definition stems directly from the inception of the discipline, which was initiated by a search for a "pure" theology that has not been "distorted" by traditions and doctrines. It is, so to speak, a building of a theology from the ground up. The underlying premise is that if a "pure," unified theology, solely derived from scripture, can be found, then it alone becomes the standard for Christian belief and practice. A few scholars who reflect this approach have advocated that the foundation should even be pushed further back to the historical Jesus, as he might be reconstructed from the canonical material.[23]

The foundationalist view, which limits the data in the formation of theology to the canonical collection of texts, has been called (sometimes incorrectly) descriptive, historical, objective or text-based (and the like) because the primary task has been concerned with understanding the New Testament writings within their historical and literary contexts. Based on this understanding various attempts at structuring early Christian beliefs have been proposed in order to isolate a New Testament theology. This has often resulted in attempts to justify historically (or "objectively") unification or cohesion among the ideas expressed by the New Testament writers. It is the act of structuring or systematizing the writings that is then called New Testament theology. Whatever the particular agenda and whatever the structuring, the textual and historical boundaries are regarded as sufficient parameters in the formulations of theological and even doctrinal norms. Inevitably, this view abruptly bumps up against and potentially displaces systematic theology or dogmatics.

I do not intend to suggest that the foundationalist view has no interest in normativity. Rather, the focus on the historical meaning of the text overshadows the *means to* normativity. While it is true that many foundationalist New Testament theologians are strictly concerned in their research to represent accurately early Christian beliefs and practices (i.e. what the text *meant*), guided by the intentions of the authors and/or the texts, they would nevertheless resonate with the traditional assumption that the scriptures are relevant for Christian life and practice in all generations.[24]

---

[23] E.g. Joachim Jeremias, *The Parables of Jesus* (trans. S. H. Hooke; New York: Scribner, 1963, revised 1972); ibid, *New Testament Theology* (trans. J. Bowden; New York: Scribner, 1971).

[24] Robert Morgan, "Can the Critical Study of Scripture Provide a Doctrinal Norm?" *Journal of Religion* 76 (1996) 207.

Foundationalists have frequently advocated New Testament theology as the basis for preaching, missions and evangelism. In this regard, Wrede was correct in saying, though simplistically, that "anyone who accepts without question the idea of the canon places himself under the authority of the bishops and theologians of those centuries."[25] I say "simplistically" because he did not indicate a proficiency in the function of tradition in the development of religions nor did he discuss phenomenologically the connection to the scriptures that believers have experienced for centuries. The residual effect when history is prioritized over normativity is an increased blurring of the theological message(s)/meaning(s) of the New Testament with our present culture.[26]

For a number of scholars, the normative element is assumed to be embedded in the canonical text. I offer a couple of examples that have been the source of considerable controversy in the recent past: eternal punishment and homosexuality. Many conservative biblical scholars who approach New Testament theology in a foundationalist manner have argued that since some of the New Testament writers convey a strong belief in eternal punishment meted out in a location called hades, hell or *gehenna*, modern Christian belief needs to maintain this conviction as well. The locus of meaning clearly resides in the intent of the author, and/or the text and its historical context. Those who advocate a dialectical approach (defined below) question the relevance of such a belief in modern Western culture, arguing for instance that (1) the apocalyptic worldview within which the New Testament was written is not necessarily Christian, (2) the fear which the belief generates is psychologically harmful, and (3) the division of humanity into the categories of the saved and the condemned has historically incited bigotry, hatred and violence. The locus of meaning in this case resides in the reader and his or her context. What is interesting is that both sides of the debate utilize historical criticism to support their position.

The same can be seen with regard to references in the New Testament to homosexuality. The foundationalist position regards texts like Rom. 1.27–28 as ethically normative for all generations.[27] Proponents of this view would hold that if Paul were listing examples of acts of unrighteousness today, he would have listed them in the same way; whereas the dialectical reading would place considerably more weight on recent research in biology, psychology and sociology before making a normative statement. Thus proponents of this view might be more apt to say that if Paul were

---

[25] Wrede, "The Task and Methods of 'New Testament Theology'", 71.
[26] This was one of Rudolf Bultmann's key observations in formulating his New Testament theology. Bultmann wanted to find the "kernel" of the New Testament apart from the trappings of the apocalyptic worldview in which it was preached.
[27] See the discussion in Richard B. Hays, *The Moral Vision of the New Testament: A Contemporary introduction to New Testament Ethics* (New York: HarperCollins, 1996) 379–406.

discussing the unrighteous condition of humanity today, he would not include homosexuality as an example.

Since an exhaustive survey of all New Testament theologians who can be aligned with the foundationalist approach is beyond the scope of this book, a few examples of their attempts to bridge past and present meanings may be helpful. The first two examples represent what I would call mainstream foundationalism, whereas the last three examples, which are given more attention, are representative of the recent Evangelical resurgence in New Testament theology, which is more overtly oriented towards normativity. In keeping with the broader divisions of our study, the focus here is on how these practitioners identify New Testament theology. In the second section, the focus is on the varied structures that both the foundationalist and dialectical approaches have generated.

G. B. Caird

The British scholar G. B. Caird carefully employs the historical method to uncover what the New Testament writers meant.[28] Uncovering the "original" meaning is vital for Caird because his quest is guided by the belief that the New Testament is the final revelation for the church in all generations.[29] More specifically, his historical method is governed by an assumption that the revelation resides in the *intention* of the New Testament writers.[30] Thus the task of New Testament theology is to recover their thoughts. Caird admits that some subjectivity creeps into descriptive history, but considers it unavoidable. A hermeneutical approach is chastised for fear that it will distort the *intended* meaning of the texts. Yet at times his attempt to verify historically coherence among the New Testament writers, along with continuity between the historical Jesus and the church's portrayal of Jesus, is influenced by an incarnational theology.[31] In this, the link between the past and the present is difficult to grasp, since the historically reconstructed meaning is at the same time the contemporary meaning.

Georg Strecker

A second example is the comprehensive work of the German scholar Georg Strecker who grounds his approach thoroughly in the historical method.[32] His engagement with parallel ideas in non-canonical and non-Christian sources, which is masterfully done, contributes to insightful exegetical

---

[28] G. B. Caird, *New Testament Theology* (ed. L. D. Hurst; Oxford: Clarendon Press, 1994).
[29] Caird, *New Testament Theology*, 1–4, 421–2.
[30] Caird, *New Testament Theology*, 422–3.
[31] Caird, *New Testament Theology*, 423–4.
[32] Strecker, *Theology of the New Testament*, 20–1.

outcomes. While his New Testament theology is primarily oriented towards the disclosure of the so-called "original" meaning of the texts, his belief that the New Testament is the authoritative source for the church today does not allow him to leave those meanings in the past. Thus his exegetical results are transferred into present-day existential concerns in the context of faith; though once again, laudable intentions to make the New Testament relevant without a developed hermeneutical connecter leave his otherwise excellent treatment incomplete.

I. Howard Marshall

A third example is the recent work of I. Howard Marshall who has become deeply influential within evangelical biblical scholarship. While rightly advocating that the content of a New Testament theology should emerge from the New Testament and not non-canonical writings, his perception of the canon as containing a common theme apart from other Christian writings of the day is historically difficult to sustain. He writes, "there is a manifest unity of theme about the New Testament writings in that they are all concerned in one way or another with Jesus and the religion that developed around him." Marshall admits that they do not say the same thing about this theme, but "Nevertheless, a corpus of writings with the same central theme must constitute a legitimate object of study."[33] Marshall also bases his restriction on the view that the New Testament writings "constitute virtually the whole of the surviving Christian literature of the first century, although some of the apostolic fathers (*1 Clement*, *Didache*) probably belong to this period.... The basic distinction between first- and second-century Christian literature remains a valid one, even if the boundary is not sharply defined except by canon makers."[34]

Marshall's attempt to unify the New Testament theologically is certainly laudable, but the problem is that while most, if not all, of the New Testament can be dated to the first century, this kind of historical reasoning cannot be sustained as an objective basis for restricting New Testament theology to the canon. If the criterion is age, then are Paul's writings of more value than, say, John's Gospel, which may even have been edited in the early part of the second century? Since Marshall sees value in mining the sources that lie behind the New Testament, such as the historical Jesus, Q and non-literary material, how does a New Testament theology treat potential divergence between these source materials and the final form of the New Testament? Also, of what value are first-century non-canonical Christian writings? In the end, legitimizing the New Testament as the

---

[33] I. Howard Marshall, *New Testament Theology: Many Witnesses, One Gospel* (Downers Grove: InterVarsity Press, 2004) 19–20.
[34] Marshall, *New Testament Theology*, 19.

source for New Testament theology cannot be sustained on historical or objective grounds. Ultimately, one has to rely on the subjectivity of the Church's decision-making processes and one's own decision to follow in the tradition and grant the writings a unique status. Finally, like other foundationalists who emphasize the historical component, and believe that the New Testament is relevant for today's Christians, Marshall in the end is left with a high degree of uncertainty as to how his main theme finds meaning in our culture.[35] As an evangelical, he would say that we participate in and personally experience the same central theme of the good news of Jesus, but this osmosis-like connection with the past begs all sorts of hermeneutical questions.

Frank Thielman

The most recent example is that of Frank Thielman's comprehensive volume that covers the theological ideas in every writing of the New Testament. Thielman serves as a good example of a foundationalist because he writes from a devout Reformed perspective that values its doctrinal tradition. From the Preface onward, Thielman is lucid in presenting his belief that all of the twenty-seven books of the New Testament are theologically unified "when read sympathetically".[36] By "sympathetically", Thielman means that they should be read (and in his terms "want to be read") from "the perspective of a Christian faith that acknowledges them to be the Word of God".[37] In the attempt to achieve a unified theology, Thielman divides the New Testament into three parts and treats each as a unified theological unit: The Gospels and Acts, the Pauline Letters (including the disputed ones), and the non-Pauline letters, together with Revelation. At the beginning of each unit, he introduces their coherent and unifying theological elements. The rationale for the division is based on a rather odd canonical chronology that seems to be influenced by Patristic apologetics. He begins with the Gospels because they are concerned with the life of Jesus. He follows with the Pauline and non-Pauline letters because they focus on combating the "heresy and persecution in the developing church".

At the same time, Thielman is sensitive to the historical context of these writings. In fact, his method throughout the book falls well within traditional historical criticism. But he vehemently argues against the division between theology and history—as it has been implemented by Wrede and later Heikki Räisänen—claiming that one's faith in the scriptures as the Word of God does not cripple historical investigation. While he is correct to

---

[35] Marshall, *New Testament Theology*, 43–6.
[36] Frank Thielman, *Theology of the New Testament: A Canonical and Synthetic Approach* (Grand Rapids: Zondervan, 2005) 9.
[37] Thielman, *Theology of the New Testament*, 9.

admit that every historian conveys his or her own perspective, he immediately follows this admission by saying that the New Testament theologian "proclaims the perspective of the texts, but that does not mean that he or she is any less a historian for doing so".[38] The implication is that if one believes the New Testament to be the Word of God, one has much more of a vested interest in preserving the history of those texts because they are the objects of faith. He goes on to say that "The uninterested party is rarely the best candidate for discovering the truth about any issue."[39] One is, however, hard-pressed to understand why the empathy is one sided.[40] Does Thielman imply that Christians are at a disadvantage for understanding the sacred writings of other religions, which not only includes distant texts like the Qur'an and the Vedas, but more familiar texts like the Torah, the Dead Sea Scrolls or the Gnostic writings? As an aside, I am curious what he thinks of Western justice systems wherein magistrates attempt to weigh evidence in an unbiased manner. Nevertheless, pushing the confidence level further, Thielman gives the impression that the New Testament theologian can achieve objective results through the historical method when acting from the perspective of faith. He writes, "New Testament theologians who work within and for the church hope to hear the text rather than echoes of their own voices because they believe the perspective of the text, and not their own presuppositions, should shape the identity of the church."[41] While discounting what he calls the "subjective and myopic" approaches of those who attempt to find a "canon within a canon" (i.e. a hermeneutical principle whereby one part of scripture guides the interpretation of whole), Thielman ironically advocates his own in the form of theological themes within a threefold structure of the New Testament. The intention to eliminate a so-called "canon within a canon" is certainly honourable, but in the practice of Christianity (and all religions claiming sacred writings) this has not as yet been achieved in a unanimous way.

The primary distinction that Thielman draws is between the Christian believer, who is truly a New Testament theologian, and the unbeliever, who is primarily interested in studying the history of early Christianity. On the one hand, one can understand the distinction because definite perspectives are strongly conveyed by each side. On the other hand, the distinction is far too simplistic. We have no way of assessing fairly the spiritual condition of scholars like Wrede or Räisänen. Nor should they be clumped into the same spiritual category. Such an assessment borders not only on a discrimination that demeans the individuality of the other, but does not appropriately assess research on its own merits in its distinct contexts.

---

[38] Thielman, *Theology of the New Testament*, 32.
[39] Thielman, *Theology of the New Testament*, 33.
[40] On the attitude of the scholar, see Heikki Räisänen, *Beyond New Testament Theology: A Story and a Program* (London: SCM Press, 2000, 2nd edn.) 176–8.
[41] Thielman, *Theology of the New Testament*, 34.

Who is and is not a Christian is an exceedingly difficult determination to make. In addition, questions like "What is Christian?" and "What is it about the New Testament that is Christian?' have been underlying quests of New Testament theology. Today, given what we know about the function of language and ideology, the term "authority" of, say, the canon allows for a range of meanings. Who decides on *the* meaning? Historically, prior to the canonization of the writings, groups that identified themselves as Christian held a variety of beliefs about the canon, Christ and the meaning of salvation. Moreover, Thielman appears to associate New Testament theology with a certain way of interpreting the texts. The text itself, for Thielman, already contains the meaning for us to discover. As interpreters, he claims, we have to place ourselves under its authority. This noble-sounding statement, however, is a veil that achieves nothing except the postponing of the quest for meaning.

The confusion between the historical and the hermeneutical reaches its pinnacle in Thielman's book, and because of that it becomes a valuable example of how each is compromised when distinctions are not developed. To claim that the New Testament theologian should not rely on his or her own presuppositions but on the text represents the sentiment that has brought New Testament theology to the brink of collapse. Thielman's form of neo-rationalism is in theory identical to the traditional historical-critical approaches of his nemesis, Wrede, who would also insist on the suspension of presuppositions in order to find the "true" meaning of the text. Both also share an underlying fideism that governs their exegesis. For Wrede, it is a belief that the New Testament is not a theologically unified collection; and for Thielman it is a belief that the New Testament contains no contradictions. It is unfortunate that he did not interact with New Testament theologians, such as A. K. M. Adam and Dan Via (not to mention contemporary literary and hermeneutical critics such as Roland Barthes, Michel Foucault, Stanley Fish and Hans Georg Gadamer), who have addressed this confusion. Thielman's rationale for his threefold division is a fine example of how both the historical and the normative are compromised, for the division is neither historically nor theologically supported. For instance, the Gospels, while focusing on the life of Jesus, are just as concerned with the social conflicts that take place in the evangelists' communities as Paul's letters. With no serious discussion of their genre, one gets the impression that they are viewed as historical accounts. In short, an unsupported genre is assumed. Thielman also uses terms like "heresy" and "orthodoxy" in the context of first- and second-century Christianity, but as so many historians have pointed out, if we want to be faithful to the sociopolitical context of nascent Christianity, such terms are anachronistic and unnecessarily devalue the non-canonical writings and the canonical process.[42]

---

[42] See Jonathan Z. Smith, *Drudgery Divine: On the Comparison of Early Christianities and the Religions of Late Antiquity* (Chicago: Chicago University Press, 1994).

Peter Balla

Finally, we need to say something about Peter Balla's work because he clearly articulates the fear of conservative historical critics that a hermeneutical or dialectical approach can potentially distort the revelation contained in the New Testament. For Balla, historical criticism is an indispensable tool for describing the theology in the New Testament.[43] But unlike Wrede's focus on the breadth of early Christian belief, with no prescriptive element, Balla's historical method, which is limited to Christian beliefs about God in the canon, has an ulterior motive despite his affirmations that New Testament theology should not be normative or hermeneutically centred. Throughout the book, Balla's so-called objective historical approach is guided by the theological presupposition that the New Testament affirms its own unique authority and that it should be studied as a canon. He goes so far as to claim that some of the writers believed that they were writing canonical documents.[44] In addition, Balla's historical approach does not demonstrate, but is guided by the belief that the New Testament conveys a unified and non-contradictory theology.[45] Dan Via aptly expresses the overall internal conflict: "In view of Balla's clear highlighting of this particular configuration it seems not amiss to hold that he makes a tacit claim for the normativity of New Testament theology."[46] If Via is correct, and I believe he is, then the connecter between past and present meaning, for Balla, is conflated into the original intentions of the New Testament writers.

The historical Jesus as foundation

Those who look behind the New Testament to find the historical Jesus as the basis for revelation, and thus the locus which binds past and present meaning, can also be placed within the foundationalist category. Scholars like Oscar Cullmann, Joachim Jeremias and most historical Jesus scholars use historical criticism to peel back the early Christian interpretations to reconstruct the teachings, acts and self-identity of Jesus. Once the rigorous historical programme is exhausted and a confident (seemingly objective and not theologically influenced) reconstruction of the so-called "facts" is crafted, the hermeneutical potential of the reconstruction is mined. The New Testament primarily serves as the gateway to authority, and not as an authoritative interpretation. The reconstructed Jesus becomes the ultimate authority for theology and thus the connector bridging past and present.

---

[43] Balla, *Challenges to New Testament Theology*, 20–2.
[44] For example, Balla, *Challenges to New Testament Theology*, 84–6, 113–16.
[45] Balla, *Challenges to New Testament Theology*, see chapter 2.
[46] Via, *What is New Testament Theology?* 45.

What authority is specifically attributed to him, however, is rarely if at all developed. On what basis should Jesus be relevant? The assumption of relevance surely presupposes prior interest. Thus the major problem in this approach is that once again, despite the intentions to be objective and to release Jesus from religious bias, the reconstruction is guided by prescriptive concerns. And the more that one seeks to make the historical Jesus relevant for our day, the more one runs the risk of a revisionist/prejudiced history.

For example, it has become fashionable in recent years to reconstruct Jesus as a non-eschatological figure whose preaching of the kingdom of God does not include an imminent apocalypticism. Instead, the apocalyptic expectations in some of the Synoptic accounts are attributed to later followers of Jesus. Thus Jesus emerges as a social and political (passive) revolutionary or activist, calling for social justice reform in the midst of an economic and religious oppression of fellow peasant Jews.[47] Such a portrayal easily conforms to our concerns for equality, social justice and suspicions of institutions and authority figures, at least in academia. By contrast, those who argue that Jesus was an eschatological figure who was immersed in the early Jewish apocalypticism of, say, John the Baptist, the Essenes or the writer of Enoch, may be inclined to take future kingdom of God sayings at face value. Yet in the process they have a more difficult time asserting relevance since our worldview is so different, and since apocalyptic predictions attributed to Jesus in the Gospels were to be fulfilled in "a generation".[48] Albert Schweitzer's call for an apocalyptic and thoroughly Jewish (not Christian or Hellenistic) Jesus perceptively recognized that it led to the irrelevance of his kingdom message for modern Christians.[49]

So, whether it is the New Testament itself, the original writers' intentions or the reconstructed Jesus, the prioritization of historical criticism serves as the common denominator for foundationalist formations of New Testament theology. The major problem, as we have seen in the examples, is that historical criticism cannot be cleanly separated from hermeneutical concerns. Nor can it deliver the once promised coherent and "pure" theology. It cannot operate as the foundational interpretative principle because the kind of objectivity that has been assumed only leads to the discipline's demise. Without deep-seated faith assumptions, we cannot even speak of a "New Testament", let alone "theology". To push the matter

---

[47] See, for example, Marcus J. Borg, *Conflict, Holiness and Politics in the Teachings of Jesus* (Harrisburg, PA; Trinity Press International, 1998); John Dominic Crossan, *The Historical Jesus: The Life of a Mediterranean Jewish Peasant* (New York: HarperCollins, 1991).

[48] For example, Dale C. Allison, *Jesus of Nazareth: Millenarian Prophet* (Minneapolis: Fortress Press, 1998); Bart D. Ehrman, *Jesus: Apocalyptic Prophet of the New Millennium* (Oxford: Oxford University Press, 1999).

[49] Albert Schweitzer, *The Quest of the Historical Jesus: A Critical Study of Its Progress from Reimarus to Wrede* (3rd edn; trans. W. Montgomery; London: Adam & Charles Black, 1954) 349–64.

further, since the canonizing of the New Testament writings is the product of the Church, the Protestant experiment of deriving theology solely from scripture requires some prior commitment to early ecclesiastical decisions. In this, there is truth in the dictum that "all good Protestants must first be good Catholics."

The dialectical view

The second definition sounds similar, but conveys a significant shift from the first. In contrast to a "a study of that theology which is exclusively *found in* or *limited to* the New Testament with little or no regard for later interpretations or traditions", it is defined as "a study of that theology which is *based upon* or *rooted in* or *in accordance with* the New Testament". It is certainly a theology that takes the scriptures seriously, but it recognizes that its formulation, structuring, and attempts at unifying the New Testament into doctrinal norms are highly influenced by external factors (e.g. cultural, existential, literary, social-scientific, biological, environmental or even theological systems) that continually intersect and contribute to our understanding of humanity and the world. It is, so to speak, a building of a theology from the top down.

The dialectical view has been called normative, subjective, prescriptive, or existential (and the like) because its primary aim is not reconstructive, but interpretative.[50] Often this approach to New Testament theology is informed by the Church, some valued tradition, prevailing philosophy or cultural mores. Thus it tends to be more dialectical in the (ongoing) formulation of a theology rather than building its theology solely from scripture in a foundationalist manner, or in a vertical direction from the ground up, so to speak. It has been said that the dialectical view is much more interested in what the New Testament text *means* rather than what it *meant*.[51] This distinction is helpful as long as it does not omit the original assumption of the foundationalist view that scripture alone conveys divine meaning not only to the first-century Christians, but for all Christians.[52] The distinction also implies that the dialectical view is only interested in current meaning, which as we shall see below is not the case. The statement is correct,

---

[50] I make a distinction between exegesis, which is historical in its orientation, and interpretation, which is normative. Although the two are related since all historical inquiry has a subjective element, their methods and rules of evidence diverge.
[51] E.g. Krister Stendahl, *Meanings: The Bible as Document and as Guide* (Philadelphia: Fortress Press, 1984).
[52] See the critique of Stendahl's distinction in Ben C. Ollenburger, "What Krister Stendahl 'Meant'—a Normative Critique of 'Descriptive Biblical Theology'", *Horizons in Biblical Theology* 8 (1986) 61–98.

however, in clarifying where each view places the locus of meaning (i.e. where meaning is ultimately determined).

To clarify, the emphasis on normativity does not indicate that the dialectical view is not interested in historical research. In fact, it was the strict use of historical criticism that has significantly contributed to the formation of this view, especially through the influence of Wrede. While praising Wrede for his rigorous historical method, a number of New Testament theologians recognized that exclusive use of his method leads to the disintegration of the canon and the fragmentation of its books. If New Testament theology were to follow Wrede's programme, it probably would have died a long time ago, since it contained no cohesive element or connector that justified the religious value of the ancient writings for today. Moreover, as Albert Schweitzer recognized almost a century ago in his critique of the Jesus biographies of the nineteenth century, claims to objectivity are always guided by subjective factors. Those who would align themselves with the dialectical view likewise advocate a rigorous engagement with historical method, but the goal is not the retrieval of what people once believed, nor is it oriented towards the unification of those ancient beliefs. Rather, the goal is relevance. In assuming that the New Testament is authoritative for all generations of Christians, the historical tools are used to discern how the canon might speak to today's vastly different culture. To this end, the historical-critical method has been beneficial, for it demonstrates how different ancient beliefs and practices were from our own. Putting the problem in the form of a question, the dialectical theologian asks, "How does one utilize historical criticism within an interpretative programme that seeks to make the New Testament theologically relevant?"

A dialectical approach does not attempt to formulate a universal, a final or a complete theology, such as a doctrine or creed. Instead, the result is further dialogue. As each generation wrestles with its Christian identity in the face of new issues, it converses with the scriptures both historically and hermeneutically to provide provisional answers to new questions. As John Macquarrie observes, New Testament theology should not be regarded as a branch of systematic theology, but as a special way of considering theological questions. Along with historical theology, it is for Macquarrie part of the first strand in theological studies. Like other disciplines, New Testament theology (along with Old Testament theology) can be used to inform systematic theology.[53] A helpful comparison of this kind of theological dialogue is rabbinic Judaism whose writings are filled, not with doctrinal or creedal statements, but with dialogue, albeit heated at times, that represents varied interpretations of scripture.

The point of historical research is that it is ordered to normative ends beyond the contextual boundaries of the Bible. The text is in dialogue, so

---

[53] John Macquarrie, *Principles of Christian Theology* (2nd edn; New York: Charles Scribner's Sons, 1977) 40.

to speak, with the interpreter and his or her context. When the dialogue is complete, the individual interpreter or the interpretative group (e.g. ecclesiastical traditions and denominations) becomes the final arbiter, or the locus of meaning, in deciding how it is (or is not) relevant for contemporary religious life and practice.

Another way of speaking about this distinction is in terms of "worlds", as it is sometimes found in literary studies. There is a "world" *behind the text*, which concerns the intent of the author and/or editor(s) (whose identity in many ancient writings is difficult to ascertain) of a New Testament writing. There is a "world" *in* (or *of*) *the text*, which has to do with the written text itself apart from the intent of the author or editor(s). And there is a "world" *in front of the text*, which is concerned with the reader and his or her own context. A caveat: in some circles this last "world" is identified with the potential influences of a text, and not as I am using it here to refer to the "world" of the reader who imposes his or her context, and thus confers meaning, onto the text. Literary theorists, such as Roland Barthes, Michel Foucault and Stanley Fish, have been particularly influential in arguing that interpretation is determined in the world of the reader. Walter Ong summarizes Barthes' position this way:

> For all texts have extratextual supports. Roland Barthes... has pointed out that any interpretation of a text has to move outside the text so as to refer to the reader: the text has no meaning until someone reads it, and to make sense it must be interpreted, which is to say related to the reader's world—which is not to say read whimsically or with no reference to the writer's world. One might describe the situation this way: since any given time is situated in the totality of all time, a text, deposited by its author in a given time, is *ipso facto* related to all times, having implications which can be unfolded only with the passage of time, inaccessible to the consciousness of the author or author's coevals, though not necessarily absent from their subconscious.[54]

When we ask the question, "Where is the locus of meaning in a New Testament theology to be found?" how might we answer? Does it reside primarily at the level of the writer, the text or the reader? The foundationalist view has variously focused on the world of the author and/or the world of the text; whereas the dialectical view has focused on the world of the reader. These distinctions have weighty implications for Christian theology as a whole because they have a bearing on the locus of the Holy Spirit and ecclesiastical authority, raising questions such as, "Can we really have an inspired text without an inspired interpreter?" or "What

---

[54] Walter Ong, *Orality and Literacy: The Technologizing of the Word* (London: Routledge, 1982) 159.

difference does an inspired text make without an inspired interpreter?" In the foundationalist view, divine inspiration is limited to the authors and/or texts, and has been the norm in the Protestant tradition; whereas the dialectical view extends the possibility of inspiration to the reader (namely the Church), which is more consistent with the Catholic and Orthodox traditions. An overlap is sometimes encountered in liturgical Protestant traditions, such as Anglicanism and Lutheranism.

Once again, a few examples of prominent New Testament theologians who can be placed in the dialectical camp may be helpful.

Rudolf Bultmann

Without question, the name that has been synonymous with attempting to make the message of the New Testament relevant for contemporary culture is that of Rudolf Bultmann. His contribution to the field of New Testament theology has been immense and continues to be influential. Some have even called him the most important New Testament theologian of the twentieth century—and rightfully so.[55] While Bultmann's method and structure are discussed in chapter five, a brief description of his approach provides a vivid example of how a current hermeneutic determines meaning and relevance. Bultmann recognized that the historian cannot escape the so-called hermeneutical circle, meaning that all attempts at finding an objective past contains the subjective point of view of the historian. But the subjective feature was not regarded as a detriment to the quest for objective knowing. Rather, it was viewed as a benefit. Since no one can disclose the full reality of the past, the acknowledgement of subjectivity (and hence the recognition of a limited point of view) allows us to engage personally with selected parts of the past.[56]

Through rigorous historical criticism, Bultmann concluded that both Paul (the founder of Christianity) and John took existing Gnostic mythological stories of salvation, stripped away the parts that were no longer accepted, and Christianized them by placing Jesus at the centre of salvation.[57] Bultmann called this early Christian practice "demythologization", and it in turn, he proposed, should serve as a prescription for contemporary Christian readings of the New Testament. Thus we need to peel back what we today consider the mythical features of the New Testament, and apply its message anew. For Bultmann, the apocalyptic worldview in which the

---

[55] E.g. John R. Donahue, "The Literary Turn and New Testament Theology: Detour or New Direction?" *Journal of Religion* 76 (1996) 251.
[56] Rudolf Bultmann, *History and Eschatology: The Presence of Eternity* (New York: Harper Collins, 1962) 115–22.
[57] Rudolf Bultmann, *Theology of the New Testament* (2 vols; trans. Kendrick Grobel; New York: Charles Scribner's Sons, 1951, 1955).

New Testament was written and in which Jesus proclaimed the end of the age is not our worldview, though the gospel message remains. At the root of this message, or *kerygma* as he called it, is the human liberation from the anxieties and structures of the "world", by which he meant society's status quo herd mentality, and a complete reliance on the security of God found in the freedom of the community of believers which does not place such burdens on fellow members.[58] Historical inquiry, according to Bultmann, reveals that the theological thoughts in the New Testament writings

> *be conceived and explicated as thoughts of faith*, that is: *as thoughts in which faith's understanding of God, the world and man is unfolding itself*—not as products of free speculation or of a scientific mastering of the problems involved in "God", "the world", and "man" carried out by the objectifying kind of thinking.[59]

In other words, it is through rigorous historical inquiry that faith is freed from any one historical context or cultural paradigm. The history peels back the cultural constraints and requires the nature of faith as an independent response to a call that transcends historical knowledge.[60] As a result, Bultmann's insight can be extended to every age. In our own, he would undoubtedly say that we should ask whether the overlapping modernist and postmodernist view of the world is likewise necessarily Christian prior to the formulation of any theology.

So, in Bultmann's dialectic between the past and the present, his historical programme is consciously guided by an attempt to understand the deep-seated sense of what it means to be human (called existentialism) or as he sometimes calls it, "the act of living". His anthropological quest defines true existence as the redeemed life in Christ, which releases us from worldly pressures to conform. True redeemed existence, which is the life of faith, opens itself to a radical openness to God that leads to courageous action. Analogous to our contemporary situation is Jesus' *call to decision* as the kingdom of God approaches.[61] And each generation must meet the call in its own context, using its own culturally conditioned language and imagery. For Bultmann's generation it was the oppressive regime of the Nazis, the horrors of war and the post-war desolation of Germany. Bultmann writes, "The theological thoughts of the New Testament can be normative only insofar as they lead the believer to develop out of his faith an understanding

---

[58] Rudolf Bultmann, "The New Testament and Mythology", in *Kerygma and Myth* (ed. H.-W. Bartsch; trans. R. H. Fuller; London: SPCK, 1954) 20–2.
[59] Bultmann, *Theology of the New Testament*, 2.237. Italics are his.
[60] Edgar Krentz, *The Historical-Critical Method* (Guides to Biblical Scholarship; Philadelphia: Fortress Press, 1975) 30–1.
[61] Bultmann, *Theology of the New Testament*, 1.9.

of God, the world and man in his own concrete situation."[62] Historical inquiry, as important as it is for Bultmann, always stands in the service of interpretation, not the reverse, stemming from the presupposition that the New Testament has "something to say to the present"[63].

John R. Donahue

Followers of Bultmann have tended to be less optimistic about an objective retrieval of the past. Since the advancement of postmodern literary studies, social scientific criticism, and the new historicism, to which Bultmann, who died in 1976, was only partly privy, emphasis has all the more been placed on the interpreter's point of view as the connector between past and present. In the end, how much Bultmann actually differed from his followers on the relationship between subjective and objective components in the practice of history is still a source of debate. One of these followers is the Jesuit scholar John R. Donahue, who is representative of a still small group of Catholic biblical scholars engaging New Testament theology.[64] Donahue wrote two important articles that have advanced Bultmann's quest for relevance beyond existentialism. In the first article, he conveys his indebtedness to Edward Schillebeeckx's prioritization of experience in Christian faith and theology.[65] Schillebeeckx writes, "Christianity is not a religion which has to be believed, but an experience of faith which becomes a message, and, as an explicit message, seeks to offer a new possibility of life experience to others who hear it from their experience of life."[66] Although Schillebeeckx intends this approach to serve as a prolegomenon to systematic theology, Donahue adopts it for the practice of New Testament theology. According to Donahue, modern readers of the New Testament can bridge the divide between past and present meaning by looking to early Christian religious experiences as the model, analogy, or a voice that creates awe, wonder, imagination and motivation for the life of faith today. Beginning with religious experience as a connector between the past and present Christian condition, Donahue uses social-scientific and literary criticisms, with the aid of rhetorical criticism, to lay bare the so-called "religious power" that the early Christian texts conveyed and continue to convey. In a concise and

---

[62] Bultmann, *Theology of the New Testament*, 2.238.
[63] Bultmann, *Theology of the New Testament*, 2.251.
[64] Among Catholic attempts at forming New Testament theologies, Donahue includes liberation theologians (normally omitted in surveys of New Testament theologies) such as Jon Sobrino, *Christology at the Crossroads* (Maryknoll, NY: Orbis, 1978) and Juan Luis Segundo, *Jesus of Nazareth Yesterday and Today* (3 vols; Maryknoll, NY: Orbis, 1984–6).
[65] John R. Donahue, "The Changing Shape of New Testament Theology", *Theological Studies* 50 (1989) 314–35.
[66] Edward Schillebeeckx, *Interim Report on the Books Jesus and Christ* (New York: Crossroad, 1981) 50.

lucid conclusion, Donahue calls for a way forward: "Since biblical theology has always been the child of the marriage of reigning exegetical methods to theological questions of a given period, there is every hope that today's emerging methods and shifting paradigms will be the parents of tomorrow's comprehensive NT theologies."[67]

In his second article, which provides a helpful survey of current literary movements in New Testament studies from formalist to postmodern approaches, Donahue attempts to demonstrate that the way forward in New Testament theology is by combining the insights gained from New Historicism and rhetorical criticism. New Historicism's dismantling of the traditional divide between literature and history, its distinction between language and reality, and its focus on the interpreter together with rhetorical criticism's focus on the art of persuasion "offer the best combination for historical research (not guided by theological interests), a literary sophistication, and concern for religious experience which can give a new direction to New Testament theology"[68]. All along, Donahue follows Bultmann's sentiments that the New Testament is an expression of faith experience that every generation must renew for itself.

A. K. M. Adam

In one of the most acute critiques of the modernist hold on New Testament theology, A. K. M. Adam aggressively tips the scale by placing much more weight on the hermeneutical side.[69] He is severely critical of historical criticism as a foundational method for formulating a New Testament theology because (1) it is incapable of validating its own assumed pre-eminence over and against other approaches, (2) it is ordered simply to description and not prescription, which is vital for theology, and (3) its conclusions often mirror prior theological convictions. Despite the call for exegesis, historical critics are never freed enough from themselves with regard to interest and purpose and thus fall victim to *eisegesis* ("a reading into the text").[70] Adam, however, does not call for historical criticism's demise, but he endeavours to demonstrate that its preoccupation with reconstruction, systems, chronology, strictures of reason, delusions of progress and the cult of expertise through which and wherein the hallmark of truth has been baptized is not necessary. The quest to "make sense" of the New Testament, which is the primary task of New Testament theology,

---

[67] Donahue, "The Changing Shape of New Testament Theology", 335.
[68] Donahue, "The Literary Turn and New Testament Theology", 273.
[69] A. K. M. Adam, ed., *Handbook of Postmodern Biblical Interpretation* (St. Louis: Chalice Press, 2000); *What is Postmodern Biblical Interpretation?* (Guides to Biblical Scholarship; Minneapolis: Fortress Press, 1995); *Making Sense of New Testament Theology*.
[70] Adam, *Making Sense of New Testament Theology*, 171.

need not resign itself to an interpretative authority that is ordered to the excavation of so-called "original" meanings.[71] If there is a main problem, it is historical criticism's philosophical basis in modernism's delusion that "proper" method leads to objective truth. For New Testament theology, this translates to the insistence "upon historical inquiry as an indispensable guide to legitimate interpretation of the ancient Bible".[72]

In *Making Sense of New Testament Theology*, Adam begins by drawing a "composite portrait" of modernity which he describes as being "(1) committed to novelty and progress and opposed to tradition; (2) particularly concerned with questions of chronology; (3) committed to a rationalized scholarly practice; and (4) intellectually elitist and antipopulist".[73] He then shows how contemporary New Testament theologies, even those that have been critical of historical criticism (such as the work of Elisabeth Schüssler Fiorenza), are still entrenched in the assumptions of modernism. In attempting to provide an alternative, Adam lays out the landscape of postmodernity as a further diagnosis and critique of modernity with an aim to show that foundationalist New Testament theologies are beyond quick fixes and minor adjustments. For Adam, the very ground of New Testament theology needs to change. However, he does not fully subscribe to the postmodern mandate as a replacement for fear of falling back into modernism's criteria and procedures.[74] Instead, he calls for a "nonmodern" New Testament theology, which prioritizes the reader as the ultimate authority that attempts to "make sense" of or bring understanding to the text. Influenced by literary theorists such as Jonathan Culler and Jeffrey Stout, and the hermeneutics of Martin Heidegger, Adam calls for a ground to New Testament theology that recognizes the human need to overcome what he calls the *alienness* of texts and bring them into familiar territory through terms that are more familiar to us as contemporary interpreters.[75]

Adam's approach is not without criteria that evaluate the validity of one New Testament theology over and against another. His criteria appear to provide a means of "legitimately" bridging the past and the present. These he divides into *general* and *local* criteria. I will only summarize the former, given its direct bearing on our comparison of the foundationalist and dialectical approaches in this chapter. In opposition to those who would follow Wrede, one general criterion is that a New Testament theology must focus on the theological character of the New Testament. Another is that the theology which is imposed upon the New Testament, whether it homogenizes the various voices or not, should "appeal to general criteria

---

[71] Adam, *Making Sense of New Testament Theology*, 170–81.
[72] Adam, *Making Sense of New Testament Theology*, 212.
[73] Adam, *Making Sense of New Testament Theology*, 47.
[74] Adam develops his understanding of postmodernity in his *What is Postmodern Biblical Interpretation?*
[75] Adam, *Making Sense of New Testament Theology*, 174.

of aesthetic judgment".[76] An example of aesthetic judgment, provided by Adam, is Luther's (mis)reading of Romans and Galatians. Since Luther's reading of these epistles eclipsed the original meaning to such an extent that it generated new insights and enthusiasm among his audience and fierce reaction among his opponents, we can call it a truly creative act that falls among the criteria of aesthetics. Ethical and political criteria of the dominant social group are also in play for Adam. He observes that while one can reasonably argue for a New Testament theology that insists on the subjugation of women, based on numerous patriarchal texts, such a theology would not only be irrelevant but offensive to the dominant culture. A final criterion is simply called a "theological criterion". What Adam means by this is that broad theological frameworks that are considered orthodox or heterodox determine the end results of a New Testament theology.[77] What emerges from these criteria is that communities play a vital role in determining how the scriptures are relevant.

While Adam argues against historical criticism's right to be a pre-eminent tool, he sees it as one of several legitimate tools that plays a significant role in keeping particular theological positions honest. As Adam puts it, "history must take a place among the various other interpretative interests jostling for influence on the interpreter, and sometimes it will attain more influence than others."[78] So how does Adam bridge the past and the present? Simply put, the interests of the reader and/or his community determine what the text means. However, the method with its varied criteria of legitimacy is far from simple.

Adam's appropriation of postmodernist hermeneutics is certainly refreshing and much needed. He is part of a still minor force that has launched similar arrows into the modernist behemoth, but it is unlikely that his will be fatal. One of the main reasons for this prediction is that while the criticisms are valid, a suitable alternative is still awaited. Adam is correct to say that the reader attributes sense to the New Testament, but can we say that the text itself has no role in the interpretative process? While I would agree that authorial intention is not accessible to us, formalist literary critics who focus on the text and its structures and sequences, as opposed to its pre-history, have repeatedly shown through, say, narrative criticism of the Gospels and rhetorical criticism of the epistles, that they emit a *sense* which is widely accepted and that is not necessarily theological. Here I invoke Donahue. In short, while we certainly impose upon the text, we cannot dismiss the phenomenon that the text also imposes upon us. Moreover, the dethroning of historical criticism is warranted, and certainly Adam would agree with Dan Via that the New Testament is a historical text claiming a

---

[76] Adam, *Making Sense of New Testament Theology*, 184.
[77] Adam, *Making Sense of New Testament Theology*, 187.
[78] Adam, *Making Sense of New Testament Theology*, 188.

historical revelation. Adam is also instructive in pointing out that *interpretation* (in the exegetical sense) differs from *understanding* in much the same way that Via argues for the distinction of history and theology since each is ordered to its own inquiry with its own rules of evidence and criteria of evaluation.[79]

Conclusion

The major differences between the two definitions of New Testament theology can be summarized as follows. (1) The foundationalist position, which has predominated in (though not exclusive to) evangelicalism, has assumed that a coherent and unified New Testament theology can be formulated using only historical criticism; whereas the dialectical position, which has dominated in mainline Protestantism, has assumed that a coherent and unified New Testament theology *cannot* be formulated strictly on the basis of historical criticism. (2) In the foundationalist view, the coherence is already embedded in the text—a theology exclusively *found in* or *limited to* the New Testament; whereas in the dialectical view the coherence is found external to the text—a theology *based upon* or *rooted* in the New Testament. (3) In the foundationalist position the formulation of a New Testament theology is guided by the intention of the texts and/or their authors (or the historical Jesus); whereas in the dialectical position the theology is guided by the ever-changing intentions of the reader. (4) The foundationalist position tends to operate from the past to the present; whereas the dialectical position tends to operate from the present to the past. (5) The foundationalist position tends toward authoritative theological propositions; whereas the dialectical view tends toward provisional conclusions oriented towards ongoing dialogue. (6) Using the terminology of a "connector", in the foundationalist view the connecting element that binds past meaning and present meaning is assumed to be found in the New Testament (be it the historical Jesus, the text or its authors); whereas in the dialectical view the connecting element consciously resides in the one formulating a New Testament theology. (7) In the foundationalist position, the tendency is to view the Church as the product of the New Testament which was later canonized on the basis of its *recognized* authority; whereas in the dialectical view, the tendency has been to regard the New Testament writings and their canonization as the product of the Church which *invested* particular authority in the writings. Finally, (8) the foundationalist position tends to cohere with the idea that religion changes culture; whereas the dialectical position tends toward the reverse. These eight distinctions are intended to serve as helpful tendencies

---

[79] Via, *What is New Testament Theology?* 104–5.

that characterize the two positions, but they cannot be extended to every practitioner equally.

It is easy to see how each side could be critical of the other. Foundationalists are suspicious of hermeneutical approaches that might distort the "original" meaning of the New Testament writings and overall unity of the canon, but in the process revelation in the present can be overlooked. One can easily imagine statements directed against the dialectical view such as "a hermeneutically driven New Testament theology runs the risk of deciding what is and is not relevant in the scriptures", or "who decides what is and is not revelation?" From the other end of the spectrum, those who would align themselves with the dialectical view might fear that the New Testament would continue to slide into irrelevance in modern mainstream culture. Some might even fear that in the interest of relevance, the foundationalist view could easily advocate a social framework that closely reflects the social and cultural particularities of the New Testament, in much the same way that the Qur'an is interpreted in the more extreme forms of Islam.

How we approach New Testament theology is not simply an academic exercise, but has political, social and ethical implications. We live in a religiously charged world where the interface between religion and politics is alive and well. In the United States, for instance, religious language continues to be used in the public sphere. As an example, during the 2008 Primaries, the Republican candidate Governor Mike Huckabee advocated changing references to life and marriage in the US Constitution so that they might conform to his reading of the Bible. Huckabee stated, "[Some of my opponents] do not want to change the Constitution, but I believe it's a lot easier to change the constitution than it would be to change the word of the living God, and that's what we need to do is to amend the Constitution so it's in God's standards rather than try to change God's standards."[80] In addition to "God's standards", the common use of the adjective "biblical" in popular speech among Christians requires definition. What is it that the Christian user truly means by it? Is he or she advocating social change that strictly *conforms* to the New Testament, or is he or she proposing social change that is *in conversation* with the New Testament? The distinction appears slight, but the implications are socially significant.

While there are substantive differences between the two definitions of New Testament theology, there are also similarities. In the broadest sense, both views see the New Testament as an authoritative source for constructing New Testament theology. Both views share an interest in maintaining the relevance of the scriptures. Both seek to be sensitive to the exegetical task. And both recognize that at the heart of relevance is the need for a connector that bridges the past and the present.

So which of the two views of New Testament theology is more suited to interact with the issues of our pluralistic society? In the next two chapters,

---

[80] From NBC News' *First Read* (firstread.msnbc.msn.com/), January 15, 2008.

I will address the deficiencies of the foundationalist view and suggest a provisional agenda for a dialectical New Testament theology.

Discussion questions

1. Should New Testament theology be primarily a historical or hermeneutical discipline?
2. Where does the authority of interpretation reside—in the intentionality of the author, at the level of text or in the reader?
3. How might one's belief in the inspiration of scripture impact on the definition and function of New Testament theology?
4. Is it necessary to unify theologically the twenty-seven writings of the New Testament?
5. What role might the historical Jesus play in the formation of a New Testament theology?
6. Since the first-century culture in which the New Testament was written is so different from our own, how do we determine what is of universal significance?

2

Foundationalist flaws

The problems of a traditional New Testament theology

Since theological pursuit is oriented towards relevance, it must always take the posture of a perpetual student, navigating between the sacred and secular realms in search of unifying meaning. In my estimation, the future of New Testament theology depends on the development of the dialectical position. The foundationalist approach has placed, and continues to place, too much confidence in the historical-critical method as a means for attaining meaning. The problem is that the method has no inherent means, or connector, that bridges the enormous gap between ancient texts and contemporary meaning. As James M. Robinson states in a very insightful article, Wrede's historical programme should have once and for all dispelled this confidence.[1] Robinson goes on to say that many of the New Testament theologies that were written after Wrede have attempted to make the historical programme relevant, but they only succeeded in showing what early Christians, conditioned by a culture and modes of thought that are foreign to our own, once thought. Putting the unresolved problem in the form a question, we can ask along with Bultmann the inescapable and penetrating question, "Is the worldview within which the New Testament was written necessarily Christian?" Those who advocate a dialectical position answer "no" and thus are more deliberate in selecting parts of the New Testament that are suited to interact with our North Atlantic Western secularism and religious pluralism. The connector bridging the gap between past and present is more hermeneutically developed because the locus of meaning lies in the reader instead of the text or authorial intention. Yet a

---

[1] James M. Robinson, "The Future of New Testament Theology", *Religious Studies Review* 2 (1976) 17–18.

reader-oriented New Testament theology is, of course, not without its own problems, as we shall see below. Nevertheless, if New Testament theology is to survive as a legitimate discipline, and have a respected voice in today's marketplace of ideas and beliefs, it needs to incorporate the hermeneutical, meaning-making dimension much more aggressively. In today's religiously charged world, foundationalist approaches in all monotheistic religions are viewed with suspicion—sometimes warranted and other times not. Nevertheless, our age is increasingly recognizing that the problems with religion (and associated negative perceptions) do not lie in the texts themselves, but in their interpretations. The rest of this chapter discusses the problems of the foundationalist approach and in turn sets the stage for a provisional agenda for a dialectical approach.

The problem of objectivity

Competing truth claims

If New Testament theology is to survive as a viable and relevant discipline for both the Church and the broader culture (participating in inter-faith dialogue), it needs to adopt a self-critical posture and recognize not only its current intellectual isolation, even in the field of religious studies; but its own identity crisis which, as we said, is rooted in a confusion between objective and subjective knowing. This crisis has affected the discipline's task, method and goal.[2] Too often Protestant biblical theologians have assumed that their constructs of New Testament theology can be objectively verified or somehow represent an early orthodoxy that is theologically unified. This is partly understandable when the theologian is, so to speak, preaching to the converted. Groups sharing common ideological convictions are less likely to evaluate their own truth claims and the methods that support them. The proverbial hermeneutical circle of attempting to prove what one already knows to be true is easily recognizable within groups that define themselves religiously because religious conviction as opposed to philosophical conviction tends to be more emotionally and relationally rooted at the deeper level of identity and social belonging. Moreover, religious convictions are usually much more bulky due to their doctrinal and narratological (i.e. the salvation history metanarrative) constructs. As a result, critique is often met with a higher degree of emotion (e.g. sadness, fear, anger, frustration), sometimes resulting in hostility, ostracism or

---

[2] Frank J. Matera, "New Testament Theology: History, Method, and Identity", *Catholic Biblical Quarterly* 67 (2005) 1–2. For descriptions and evaluations of current problems in biblical and New Testament theology, see James Barr, *The Concept of Biblical Theology* (Minneapolis: Fortress Press, 1999).

actual physical violence. But when religious groups interact seriously with competing truth claims and methods in tolerant pluralistic settings, their subjectivity, and hence their notion of a "pure" theology, becomes more apparent to themselves which, in turn, allows for a more balanced interplay between objective and subjective knowing. The pursuit of a "pure" theology or universal truth becomes multi-dimensional, overwhelming and, for some, impossible to attain.

At the same time, our pluralistic culture provides for an optimistic setting where fair evaluation of religious truth claims can occur. For much of the last five hundred years Latin Christendom has not had this opportunity. Instead, it has often suffered from violence that stemmed from the battle of only two truth claims, Protestant and Catholic. This phenomenon was already observed by Voltaire who commented that England during the Enlightenment period was unusually a nation of many faiths, but only "one sauce". His dry humour poignantly conveyed the merits of religious pluralism over that of one or two religions in society: "If there were only one religion in England, there would be danger of despotism, if there were only two they would cut each other's throats; but there are 30, and they live in peace."[3]

The clash between objective and subjective knowing will be familiar to anyone who has studied the humanities and social sciences. For those who have no familiarity with this clash, the problem stems from the question "how do we know what we know?" In the philosophical field called epistemology ("the study of knowledge"), the relationship between the knower (the subject) and that which is known (the object) has been the traditional aim of study. During our so-called postmodern period, which has reacted against modernism's confidence in attaining objectivity through "proper" reasoning and scientific method, the subject/object distinction has become especially pronounced.[4] In a nutshell, it has shone much needed light on the one making an assertion of objective knowledge, illuminating such factors as the interpreter's values, metaphysical beliefs, social conditions, apologetic aims, evaluations of evidence, understanding of language and its relation to reality and overall interpretative methods. The distinctions between facts and values, along with facts/events and their meaning/interpretation, have made it much more difficult (some would say impossible) to verify truth claims. As a result, analyses of truth claims have come to include analyses of the claimant. In my estimation, the criticisms of postmodernity levelled against objective truth claims since the 1960s have provided welcome

---

[3] A. Potter, "Respect All and Trust No One: Life in a Multi Culti World", *Maclean's* (November 27, 2006) 13.

[4] The term "postmodernity", encountered frequently in contemporary culture, has been much debated. For an accessible treatment, see Fredric Jameson, *Postmodernism, or The Cultural Logic of Late Capitalism* (Post-Contemporary Interventions; Durham, NC: Duke University Press, 1991).

correctives, but they have not resulted in the elimination of modernity. The hard sciences, such as chemistry and biology, are still essentially modernist. And in the social sciences, scholars unanimously espouse negative value statements about tragic events, such as the Holocaust, Soviet gulags, the Rwandan genocide and the 9/11 terrorist attack. Postmodernity's unveiling of the so-called "myth of Truth" has resulted in its participation in the so-called "myth of liberation". On the one hand, we have become increasingly aware of the strengths and weaknesses of each, but on the other hand we are currently left with little option but to abide with the tensions. In the study of religion, and Christian theology in particular, issues relating to the possibility of objective knowing and the subjective impact on that knowing have been insightfully presented by Martin Heidegger, Hans-Georg Gadamer, Richard Rorty, Paul de Man, Paul Ricoeur, Stanley Fish, Jean–François Lyotard, Roland Barthes and Jacques Derrida, to name a few of the most influential thinkers. Though varied in their methods, arguments and conclusions, they all share a common scepticism towards the modernist optimism that objective knowledge can be attained through "proper" method and structure.

New historicism

Most foundationalists have also not interacted with the major movement made popular in the last thirty years called New Historicism. Emerging principally in the field of Renaissance literary studies through the work of Stephen J. Greenblatt, New Historicism is not so much a theory, method, ideology or a mapping of some new territory, but a strategy of reading that is mindful of the cultural imprints embedded in all texts from the past.[5] Thus texts from the past are viewed as reflections of their culture, not simply the vehicle to that culture. This means that the so-called retrieval of the *authentic* past is impossible. All we have are scattered cultural fragments that are the by-products of unconscious representation. Definitions of the movement have been difficult to pin down because New Historicism consists of a synthesis of questions that have to do with perspective. Nevertheless Hunter Cadzow is helpful in defining it as "an array of reading practices that investigate a series of issues that emerge when critics seek to chart the ways texts, in dialectical fashion, both represent a society's behaviour patterns and perpetuate, shape or alter that culture's dominant codes".[6]

---

[5] The origin of the movement is often credited to Stephen J. Greenblatt, *Renaissance Self-Fashioning: From More to Shakespeare* (Chicago: University of Chicago Press, 1980)
[6] Hunter Cadzow, "New Historicism", in *The Johns Hopkins Guide to Literary Theory and Criticism* (ed. Michael Groden and Martin Kreiswirth; Baltimore: Johns Hopkins University Press, 1994) 535.

Greenblatt has been particularly critical of the assumption of the "old historicism" that history is an ordered process, that historians must be value-neutral in attaining objectivity, and that historians must venerate the past that they are studying, which was often done from the perspective of "high culture". For Greenblatt, the focus is on the particulars of history and its cultures—its obscurities, anomalies, tensions, conflicts, generational differences, economic contrasts, and so on. Values are not always neutral, nor can they be. Creativity can emerge from both acceptance and dissonance.[7] As post-structuralists have done, New Historicism problematizes the traditional distinctions between history and literature, claiming that historical writing gives the impression of the actual, but is in reality culturally contingent in all its dimensions.[8] Unlike the modernist view of history, New Historicism gives far more attention to the varied contingencies of culture without attempting to fit them into grander structures, like a philosophy of history. Brian Rosenberg explains,

> Its understanding of context, however, distinguishes it dramatically from older forms of historical criticism, since it imagines not a monological, objectively verifiable past reflected in unified works of literature, but a past of competing voices, values and centres of power whose meaning is constructed, not discovered by the interpretative critic or historian.[9]

New Historicism is particularly important for biblical studies because it addresses the modernist historical practices that have traditionally assumed objectivity in historical retrievals. In especially historical Jesus research and New Testament theology, which are oriented towards a recovery of the past, it raises the important problem of identifying what we mean by "history". Only a handful of biblical scholars, however, have attempted to interact with the challenges that the movement continues to pose.[10]

---

[7] Stephen J. Greenblatt, *Learning to Curse: Essays in Early Modern Culture* (London: Routledge, 1990) 164–9.

[8] Greenblatt (*Learning to Curse*, 13–14) writes, "One of the principal achievements of post-structuralism has been to problematize the distinction between literary and non-literary text, to challenge the stable difference between the fictive and the actual, to look at discourse not as a transparent glass through which we glimpse reality but as the creator of what Barthes has called the 'reality effect.'"

[9] Brian Rosenberg, "Historicizing the New Historicism: Understanding the Past in Criticism and Fiction", *Modern Language Quarterly* 50 (1989) 376.

[10] See, for example, John R. Donahue, "The Changing Shape of New Testament Theology", *Theological Studies* 50 (1989) 314–35; Stephen D. Moore, "History After Theory? Biblical Studies and the New Historicism", *Biblical Interpretation* 5 (1997) 289–99; Clive Marsh, "Quests of the Historical Jesus in New Historicism", *Biblical Interpretation* 5 (1997) 403–37; A. K. M. Adam, *What is Postmodern Biblical Interpretation?* (Guides to Biblical Scholarship; Minneapolis: Fortress Press, 1995); Gina Hens-Piazza, *The New Historicism* (Guides to Biblical Scholarship; Minneapolis: Fortress Press, 2002).

The subjectivity of scripture

When it comes to scripture (and all texts for that matter), all interpretative approaches are formed externally and imposed upon it. The historical-critical method, which has attempted to disclose the "original" meaning of texts in their original language and social setting, has been the choice of foundationalists since the beginning of New Testament theology. The problem, however, has not been the method in and of itself, but the confidence expressed by its practitioners who assumed that its proper use leads to objective interpretation. While the method is still in use, its value lies in data collection and evaluation, not in constructs of meaning.[11] Using a simplistic distinction, it has certainly been successful in unveiling what the ancient texts probably *meant*, but it remains poorly suited to the larger task of what the text *means*. Moreover, it is ill suited to uncover the cultural influences and unconscious motives of the historian in his or her search for what the text meant. The chasm between past data and present meaning is often bridged via terms like "application", but unfortunately is rarely evaluated critically.

The same phenomenon occurs at the authorial level. Even historical critics must admit that the phenomenon of ancient retelling, writing and rewriting was a highly selective process where not all of the so-called facts mattered.[12] Writers were very selective in their creation of narrative worlds wherein the facts were recreated, reinterpreted, added and omitted. The narrative not only gives meaning to the facts, but it determines what indeed is a fact.[13] Every writer thus becomes the primary authority for determining meaning. But every writer is also a reader. Consider Mark, our earliest Gospel. Not only does Papias (second century bishop of Hieropolis), our earliest extant commentator on Markan authorship, tell us that the evangelist did not compose his Gospel in chronological order,[14] but there is also good evidence today that the Gospel may have been performed orally

---

[11] Mark Cousins, "The Practice of Historical Investigation", in *Post-Structuralism and the Question of History* (ed. D. Attridge et al.; Cambridge: Cambridge University Press, 1989) 126–36.

[12] Walter Ong, *Orality and Literacy: The Technologizing of the Word* (London; Routledge, 1982).

[13] Christian Smith, *Moral, Believing Animals: Human Personhood and Culture* (Oxford: Oxford University Press, 2003) 66.

[14] According to Eusebius (*Ecclesiastical History* 3.39.15), Papias (c. 120 CE) writes, "And this is what the elder said, 'Mark, who became Peter's interpreter, accurately wrote, though not in order, as many of the things said and done by the Lord as he had noted. For he neither heard the Lord nor followed him, but afterwards, as I said, he followed Peter who composed his teachings in anecdotes and not as a complete work of the Lord's sayings. So Mark made no mistake in writing some things just as he had noted them. For he was careful of this one thing, to leave nothing he had heard out and to say nothing falsely.'" Translation is taken from Robert A. Guelich, *Mark 1–8.26* (WBC 34A; Dallas: Word, 1989) xxvi.

several times in slightly different versions prior to its final composition.[15] Apart from the problem of Mark's genre, which most would agree is not ancient history, these two points show how the incessant quest for meaning affects the entire story of Jesus. Matthew's reading of Mark leads to a reinterpretation of Mark not only on the broader narrative level such as the characterization of Jesus, but in individual episodes and sayings. Carrying the chronology forward, the reading of Matthew by Irenaeus in the second century results in other new interpretations.[16] The process repeats itself with every new reading because meaning and relevance are the prime motivators, especially in the reading of religious texts.

In fact, when we examine how individual New Testament writings became authoritative in early Christianity, prior to their official canonization in the late fourth century, the reasons are not what we might deem objective. While there was wide disagreement among those who called themselves "Christian", this does not preclude today's belief in scripture's unique divine quality or inspiration, yet this quality is not accessible objectively. It is a faith position shared by fellow devotees and lies in the subjective realm. The same can be said of all faiths that profess sacred texts. The Muslim does not derive from the New Testament the same kind of personal meaning as does the Christian. Conversely, the Christian does not find the same meaning in the Qur'an as does a Muslim. Sociologically speaking, the authority of determining what is and is not scripture among the world religions is derived and maintained subjectively. Devotees *make* the writings scripture in every generation. Thus the interpretative authority seems always to lie in the realm of the reader.

The historical? Jesus

The same problem confronts those who want to base their hermeneutical programme on the historical or pre-Easter Jesus. Joachim Jeremias, who entitled this kind of endeavour *New Testament Theology*, understood his historical quest as a search for theological authority that spans the distance of time.[17] Although most historical Jesus scholars would not consider their work to be classified as New Testament theology, the reverse has not always been the case. The assumption among many historical Jesus scholars has been that a rigorous historical programme can yield objective results, but

---

[15] Joanna Dewey, "The Gospel of Mark as an Oral-Aural Event: Implications for Interpretation", in *The New Literary Criticism and the New Testament* (ed. E. S. Malbon and E. V. McKnight; JSNTSup 109; Sheffield: Sheffield Academic Press, 1994) 145–63. On oral performance in the ancient world, see *Orality and Literacy*.
[16] D. Jeffrey Bingham, *Irenaeus' Use of Matthew's Gospel in* Adversus Haereses (Traditio Exegetica Graeca 7; Leuven: Peeters, 1998).
[17] Joachim Jeremias, *New Testament Theology* (trans. J. Bowden; New York: Scribner, 1971).

as has been the case in traditional exegesis, historical quests have led to differing conclusions, which demonstrates that the pursuit of historical knowledge is not a disinterested one. As we see in both progressive scholarship represented by John Dominic Crossan, Marcus Borg and Richard Horsley, and more conservative scholarship represented by N. T. Wright, John Meier and James D. G. Dunn, theological and political assumptions play a role in what kind of Jesus one reconstructs. I do not mean to indicate that these scholars use the same methods—they do not. For example, I consider Crossan's preliminary step of evaluating what constitutes a credible historical source (though we disagree on some of the particulars) superior to Wright's hypotheses-verification model which attempts to use the sources selectively in support of hypotheses. My point, which echoes Elisabeth Schüssler Fiorenza's outstanding analysis of the politics of interpretation in current Jesus research, is that deeper assumptions affect historical outcomes.[18] In conservative scholarship one of these assumptions is that the historical Jesus closely resembles, if not parallels, the interpretations of him in the New Testament. Thus the authority or locus of meaning lies in the canonical writings (or writers). In progressive scholarship, which tends to extend the sources beyond the canon and is more critical of the historical value of the Synoptic Gospels, the locus of authority is the reconstructed Jesus who is not necessarily tied to New Testament interpretations of him. Quite often, Jesus is freed to subvert and correct later interpretations of him. In recent years, reconstructions of Jesus have tended to be anti-institution, anti-establishment, anti-power and pro-social justice. No matter what one's theological leanings are, since facts alone do not convey meaning, Albert Schweitzer's critique of the subjective reality in any reconstructive effort remains relevant.[19]

Once again, we are back to the so-called "world" *in front of the text* as the locus of authority. It is always the reader or interpreter that gives authority to the text of the New Testament, its authors or the historical Jesus. In every historical endeavour, the historian must enquire retrospectively about the ultimate value of his or her work. One final remark: while it is important to recognize the dichotomies between the subjective and objective, especially when trying to make sense of New Testament theology, at the same time a strict contrast cannot adequately represent our conscious and, perhaps even more telling, subconscious cognitive processes.[20] Far more complex than simple binary oppositions, these are neither static

---

[18] Elisabeth Schüssler Fiorenza, *Jesus and the Politics of Interpretation* (New York: Continuum, 2000).
[19] Albert Schweitzer, *The Quest of the Historical Jesus: A Critical Study of Its Progress from Reimarus to Wrede* (3rd edn; trans. W. Montgomery; London: Adam & Charles Black, 1954).
[20] Heikki Räisänen, "Comparative Religion, Theology, and New Testament Exegesis", in *Challenges to Biblical Interpretation: Collected Essays 1991–2001* (ed. H. Räisänen; Biblical Interpretation Series 59; Leiden: Brill, 2001) 211.

nor punctiliar, but instead represent a range of possibilities within a wide spectrum of significance.

The problem of language

While many students are aware that the problem of subjectivity lies subtly below the surface for all of us, by contrast the nature of language and its relation to objectivity is less familiar. This lack of familiarity is apparent among many who espouse the foundationalist view. Foundationalists have been consistently negligent in describing the limitations not only of language in general, but religious/mythical language in particular. Yet the last half-century or so of literary theory and criticism has influenced a number of biblical scholars, particularly in the study of Old Testament poetry and narrative as well as the study of the Gospels. But surprisingly it has had little impact on the field of New Testament theology, despite a few voices calling for adherents. One of the earliest of these voices was that of Norman Perrin, who argued that a New Testament theology hermeneutically based on a linguistic philosophy is a viable route that would lead to relevance.[21] Unlike Bultmann's demythologizing which sought the kernel of the Christian message, Perrin sought to decipher the symbolic retelling of Jesus by the New Testament writers. These symbolic retellings were the earliest appropriations of Jesus' teachings and acts. Despite varying symbols and systems, Perrin argued that they should serve as a model for modern appropriation. Since Perrin, significant work has taken place, but it has not infiltrated what might be called mainstream New Testament studies, which remains a relatively traditional field.[22]

---

[21] See especially, Norman Perrin, *Jesus and the Language of the Kingdom: Symbol and Metaphor in New Testament Interpretation* (Philadelphia: Fortress Press, 1976); idem, *Rediscovering the Teaching of Jesus* (New York: Harper & Row, 1967). Perrin's theory of symbol is influenced by Paul Ricoeur, *The Symbolism of Evil* (trans. E. Buchanan; Boston: Beacon Press, 1969) and Philip E. Wheelwright, *Metaphor and Reality* (Bloomington: Indiana University Press, 1962). See also Paul Ricoeur "Biblical Hermeneutics", *Semeia* 4 (1975) 29–148.

[22] On contemporary approaches that take the philosophy of language into account, see, for example, A. K. M. Adam, *Making Sense of New Testament Theology: Modern Problems and Prospects* (Studies in American Biblical Hermeneutics 11; Macon, GA: Mercer University Press, 1995); John R. Donahue, "The Changing Shape of New Testament Theology", *Theological Studies* 50 (1989) 314–35. The following provide a helpful foundation for the literary study of the Gospels: Frank Kermode, *The Genesis of Secrecy: On the Interpretation of Narrative* (Cambridge, MA: Harvard University Press, 1979); Petri Merenlahti, *Poetics for the Gospels? Rethinking Narrative Criticism* (Edinburgh: T & T Clark, 2002). For a more traditional approach see Kevin J. Vanhoozer, *Is There Meaning in this Text? The Bible, The Reader, and The Morality of Literary Knowledge* (Grand Rapids: Zondervan, 1998); *First Theology: God, Scripture and Hermeneutics* (Downers Grove: InterVarsity Press, 2002). In the end, however, both books fall into the same postmodernist trap from which he wants to extricate

When addressing the topic of language, two problems immediately rise to the surface. The first is that the meanings we derive from language (texts or otherwise) are culture specific. Despite the proposals that we all participate in a so-called "general hermeneutics", this too is culturally determined, but on a wider scale. All hermeneutical endeavours, from the origin of a writing to its reception, are guided by interests which are often determined by the community of which the reader is part.[23] In a recent volume on New Testament theology, Philip Esler has argued for the importance of the community in the interpretative process.[24] This can be construed as an example of a "general hermeneutics" within Christianity. Esler's community includes a broad connection between the intention of the author, the text and later Christian readers/hearers. Meaning is understood as an imprint by the author onto the text that is comprehended by the reader. In one respect, Esler's aim is to show how all the components in the communication process which have been divided by postmodern critics can be re-integrated as a community within a theological schema that is rooted within Chalcedonian Christianity (namely, Trinitarian and Catholic) from within which the Holy Spirit is operative from Jesus to the early church, to canonization, to the councils, to the modern interpreter. From the start of the book Esler's agenda is lucid. He writes, "... my intention in writing is an avowedly theological one. I wish to promote a specifically Christian rationale for reading the New Testament that is related to its role in speaking of God's ongoing relationship with human beings and the cosmos."[25] Esler is correct to say that the New Testament is primarily the interest of communities, be they small or large, like the Catholic Church. Meaning, however, is nevertheless imposed onto the text, especially in a self-avowed theological reading. The pressing problem is that there is no homogeneous or static state of language. Stanley Fish perceptively described the flux in which readers will rightly notice similarities with the salient criticisms of the New Historicism:

> Language does not have a shape independent of context, but since language is only encountered in contexts and never in the abstract, it always has a shape, although it is not always the same one. The problem with this formulation is that for many people determinacy is inseparable

---

himself. Each serves as an example of ideological justification and language/meaning control, but this time it is partisan to a Reformed theology speech-act theory and Trinitarianism. A recommended introduction to the use of symbol and metaphor in the Bible is Pierre Grelot, *The Language of Symbolism: Biblical Theology, Semantics, and Exegesis* (trans. C. R. Smith; Peabody: Hendrickson, 2006).

[23] See Frank Kermode, "Institutional Control of Interpretations", in *The Art of Telling* (ed. Frank Kermode; Cambridge, MA; Harvard University Press, 1983) 168–84.

[24] Philip F. Esler, *New Testament Theology: Communion and Community* (Minneapolis: Fortress Press, 2005).

[25] Esler, *New Testament Theology*, 1.

from stability: the reason that we can specify the meaning of a text is because a text and its meanings never change. What I am suggesting is that change is continually occurring but that its consequence is never the absence of the norms, standards and certainties we desire, because they will be features of any situation we happen to be in.[26]

A distinction should be made here between the reconstruction of a text and its interpretation or meaning (used synonymously). For example, scholars may share the same reconstruction of the infancy accounts of Matthew and Luke, agreeing, say, on its indebtedness to scriptural allusion, on the genre, on the intended audience, and on its connection (or lack thereof) with the rest of the narrative. But they will often disagree on what the account means. Meanings are determined by reading communities, as many literary theorists have cogently argued. Individual interpreters reflect their allegiances to their communities, even subconsciously, and thus share in their ideological programmes. So we can say that language elicits a common *reconstruction* since we all share in an ability to communicate with one another through it, but we cannot say that it elicits the same *meaning*, or understanding, for all of us. The conflicts often appear at the ideological level, which has no external criterion for evaluating what is and is not the "correct" meaning. Applying this to New Testament theology, Adam narrows the issue to a single question:

> The pivotal question here, however, is not whether there is good reason for pursuing New Testament theology as a distinctly modern enterprise; the question is whether any other sort of New Testament theology is legitimate. The answer to that question is, "Yes, for those interpreters who do not grant primary allegiance to the interpretives of modernity."[27]

Quite bluntly, there are no transcendent rules or criteria for judging interpretations.

If this is the case, since foundationalist approaches do not have an inherently built-in self-reflection that is sceptical of absolutes, they are at a considerable hermeneutical disadvantage in benefiting from ideologically different readings, such as Marxist, feminist, or otherwise. The usual response to these varied readings is one of suspicion that current ideological impositions on the biblical text manipulate its (true?) meaning. But is such a critique itself free from ideological boundaries, reading communities, interests and impositions? Of course not—foundationalist readings are just as ideologically bound, often using the "old" historicism to legitimize

---

[26] Stanley Fish, *Is There a Text in the Class: The Authority of Interpretive Communities* (Cambridge, MA: Harvard University Press, 1980) 268–9.
[27] Adam, *Making Sense of New Testament Theology*, 178.

dogmatic assumptions. While there is no intrinsic problem in taking this approach as long as it is self-aware, it does not guarantee the objective meaning of the text's language. Once again, I defer to Adam who writes, "the historical-critical effort to allow the otherness of the text to speak most often (if not always) results in a sort of self-effacing ventriloquism, where we are asked to believe that the text itself is speaking, but we always hear the interpreter's voice."[28]

The second problem, being a narrowing of the first, is that amid attempts to formulate a consistent theology, religious language in the New Testament has tended to be understood propositionally and literally instead of metaphorically and imaginatively. In some conservative circles, propositional readings are directly tied to radical theories of inspiration, which claim that every word in the Bible was dictated by God. For those steeped in Enlightenment rationalism, the language in the Bible directly represents historical and spiritual reality. One often hears an aphorism like, "God has given humanity a clear revelation." But if the Bible is so clear why is there so much diversity among Christians in the world?

Belief in a God that reveals himself is certainly not the issue. The problem is that the principles of rationalism underlying such theories have been imposed without the benefit of understanding the nature of religion and the language it uses both to describe and interpret transcendent realities and inward experiences. More is said about this in chapter 6, but for now it is important to note that any religion which addresses belief in a non-material reality, be it a deity, spirits, heaven and hell, an inward spiritual life is limited to material, temporal, finite, and culturally conditioned language, which is our only frame of reference. If language operates through comparison and contrast, how do we "literally" describe the eternal, post-mortem existence, or the infusion of the divine into the human? Like other religions attempting to give expression to the content of belief, early Christians necessarily used symbol, metaphor, narrative and poetry, all of which were accessible to them in their own culture. Unique language—whatever that is supposed to be—would not have been comprehended. Moreover, religious language is not descriptive in the scientific sense, but is oriented towards meaning. It is not clinical psychology, anthropology, geology or cosmology, to name but a few. The religious experiences recorded by early Christians always convey meaning, and it is that meaning which takes on a metaphorical expression. This, however, does not mean that the original writers or hearers always understood it metaphorically. An apocalyptic view of the world or a three-tiered universe, consisting of earth, heaven and hell, or a belief that illness is caused by demons, affects whether or not one understands language about such beliefs as literal or metaphorical. Experience simply found its expression in the language of the culture. Nor does it mean that we have to

---

[28] Adam, *Making Sense of New Testament Theology*, 181n. 28.

suspend belief in the supernatural, but it does mean that we would probably use different language to express such beliefs.

Consider, for example, the ascension of Christ in Acts 1. Whatever the original experience, it was recorded by Luke using the language found in similar stories of ascension in Greco-Roman and Jewish stories of great men, such as Moses, Enoch, Elijah, Apollonius, Heracles, Ganymedes, Romulus and Augustus.[29] All these stories, including Luke's, assumed a cosmology that usually divided the world into three levels. The present level of daily life was sandwiched between the world of death and punishment below and the world of divine bliss above. So how should we read the ascension today? If we approach the vignette as a literal occurrence and omit the conventional ancient cosmology and comparative stories of ascension, then we transfer Luke's culture-specific language into our own culture. This, however, raises all sorts of scientific questions that did not appear to arise in the ancient world. For example, how does a body (let alone a resurrected one) defy gravity? Many have seen the television programme *Mindfreak*, in which the illusionist Chris Angel levitates himself and others, but is this the same thing? How is it that a cloud can envelop someone? Is Jesus still ascending? Given what we know today about cosmology, if Jesus is travelling at the speed of light, he would not even be halfway through the Orion Arm of our Milky Way galaxy, which is 80,000 to 100,000 light years in diameter at its main disk, composing 200–400 billion stars. Where is he going? If his resurrected body was somehow absorbed into spirit, how can he be ubiquitous if he is fleshly? But metaphorically, we can read the ascension story, sometimes called a "supernatural abduction", as an early Christian testimony of Jesus' righteousness and/or deification. It is, in short, language that tries to bring together heaven and earth. The challenge for the contemporary reader is: What form does our religious language take? Once again, we are faced with the problem of meaning.

Mysticism, which penetrates the most profound parts of religion, is a helpful analogy of how language is woefully inadequate to describe and interpret religious experience. Janet Martin Soskice insightfully writes,

> We discover perhaps to our surprise that the Christian mystic of all theists is most likely to be a realist, aware of the presence and reality of God, yet aware at the same time of the inability of human speech and thought to contain Him. To make sense of her experience the mystic has recourse to figures and images. Compelled by the strength of experience (or by religious superiors) to give an account of it, she does so in the

---

[29] See Hans Conzelmann, *Acts of the Apostles* (trans. J. Limburg, A. T. Kraabel and D. H. Juel; Hermeneia; Philadelphia: Fortress Press, 1987) 7; C. K. Barrett, *The Acts of the Apostles* (ICC; Edinburgh: T & T Clark, 1994) 81–2. On the ascension and deification of Augustus, see Ittai Gradel, *Emperor Worship and Roman Religion* (Oxford Classical Monographs; Oxford: Clarendon Press, 2002) ch. 12.

language of her time and tradition, using the language, perhaps, of Aquinas, or Cassian, or St. Paul. But beneath this is the bedrock of her experience and it is here that her reference is grounded for those who take her account as authoritative.[30]

For Soskice, the symbolic language is bound to the reality it symbolizes, unlike the idealist position which substitutes symbol for reality.[31] In, say, Jacques Derrida's famous view of language, the only reality is the text (or symbol) because we cannot determine an absolute without it. The meaning we give to language is, for Derrida, determined on the plane of language whereby one meaning is separated from another. Ultimate meaning is forever deferred or delayed. We cannot get past language to describe another reality.[32] Here the experiences of other mystics are often expressed in silence, because even symbol is regarded as a limiting or controlling element of the encounter.

The problem of unity

Canons within the canon

The main reason why New Testament theologies have differed so much over the years is due to the fact that the New Testament is not a single book expressing a unified and consistent plot, characters, crisis, resolution or theme. While Jesus can be said to be the main character (though even here some may argue that it is God in some writings, the Holy Spirit in others, and one or two of the Apostles in still others), too many theological nuances and differences are found in the canonical corpus. As Ernst Käsemann has famously said, "the New Testament canon does not, as such, constitute the foundation of the unity of the Church. On the contrary, as such (that is, in its accessibility to the historian) it provides the basis for the multiplicity of the confessions."[33] Attempts at unification have often resulted in one part of the New Testament—be it a theological theme, a writer or a writing—dominating the interpretation of the other parts. A sort of canon

---

[30] Janet Martin Soskice, *Metaphor and Religious Language* (Oxford: Clarendon Press, 1985) 152.
[31] She refers to the insightful discussion in A. Léonard, "Studies on the Phenomena of Mystical Experience", in *Mystery and Mysticism: A Symposium* (A. Plé et al.; London: Blackfriars, 1956) 108.
[32] E.g. Jacques Derrida, *Speech and Phenomena* (trans. D. Allison; Evanston: Northwestern University Press, 1979) 129–41. See also his *Of Grammatology* (trans. G. C. Spivak: Baltimore: Johns Hopkins University Press, 1980).
[33] Ernst Käsemann, *Essays on New Testament Themes* (trans. W. J. Montague; London: SCM Press, 1964) 103.

within a canon emerges. The process of unification, and hence the search for the overriding meaning of the New Testament, requires that the data be subjected to a method of interpretation by which it can be prioritized, organized and deciphered. Unity requires the prior imposition of a theology or some other controlling element. Roy Harrisville and Walter Sundberg rightly observe that

> Awareness of the disunity of the biblical canon and the multiplicity of biblical theologies has led to the increasing tendency to shy away from confident use of the Bible as the principal source for theological judgment. Many have come to realize that what we have in theology is not the "use" of scripture but, as David H. Kelsey points out, the "uses" of scripture by various theologies. These "uses" neutralize each other.[34]

Literary critics have long pointed out that texts cannot exist apart from interpreters; otherwise they would be reduced to meaningless symbols on a page. Hermeneutics not only brings attention to the many contextual features associated with a written text such as genre, audience and purpose; but also discloses the perspectives and presuppositions of the reader who seeks to interpret the written text in his or her own context. Structuring such a New Testament theology is a topic to which two chapters are devoted in this book. For now, in order to appreciate initially the varied interpretations that have resulted in various New Testament theologies, consider the differing approaches by George Eldon Ladd and N. T. Wright. Both scholars are conservative Protestants and both well recognize the diversity of thought in the New Testament; and yet, they differ in their approach, and predictably in their conclusions. Ladd, in his *A Theology of the New Testament*, tends to regard the eschatological reading of the kingdom of God as central. While not overt, Ladd favours the teachings of Jesus in the Synoptic Gospels, which provide the hermeneutical key for the rest of the New Testament. On the other hand, Wright, in his as yet incomplete multi-volume work *Christian Origins and the Question of God*, advocates the theme of "Christ and his church as the reconstitution of Israel" as the controlling theme. It is interesting to see how this theme, which is present in Wright's earlier work on Paul, has found its way into the first three volumes, especially the volume on Jesus. The result is that Paul's thinking about Jesus Messiah as the representation of Israel becomes the key for understanding the message of the Gospels.[35]

---

[34] Roy A. Harrisville and Walter Sundberg, *The Bible in Modern Culture: Theology and Historical-Critical Method from Spinoza to Käsemann* (Grand Rapids: Eerdmans, 1995) 11. The quotation is from David H. Kelsey, *The Use of Scripture in Recent Theology* (Philadelphia: Fortress Press, 1975).
[35] N. T. Wright, *The New Testament and the People of God* (Christian Origins and the Question of God 1; Minneapolis: Fortress Press, 1992); *Jesus and the Victory of God* (Christian

The assumption that the New Testament can, and indeed should, be unified into a single theology stems from three interconnected presuppositions. The first is that early Christianity, or at least the "proto-orthodox" Christianity represented in the canonical writings, is a monolithic religion.[36] Although divergences are recognized, such as among the Gospels, they do not threaten broader theological ideas, especially in relation to the identity, teachings and work of Christ. It is assumed that differing Christological accounts can be harmonized or rendered "non-contradictory" if they appear paradoxical. The second presupposition is that "proper" method, which in the case of many New Testament theologians has been historical criticism, will result in a unified authoritative theology which is assumed to take precedence over all doctrinal formulations. Historical-critical results that have countered a unified theology of the New Testament have tended to play a peripheral role, have been deemed suspect, or at worst have been completely ignored. One such example is the baptism of Jesus in the Gospel of Mark. Exegetical studies that have concluded that Mark's Jesus is baptized for the forgiveness of sins—lending itself to an adoptionist Christology (namely, that God adopted Jesus as his son) in contrast to the Synoptic counterparts—are generally massaged or harmonized by New Testament theologians who aim for consistency. On an epistemological level, the formulation of a theology based entirely on a historical-critical interpretation of the New Testament has resulted in an optimism that objectivity should not only be the goal, but can be reached. The final presupposition that has been instrumental among practitioners who seek to unify the New Testament is the inspiration of scripture. In its most simplistic and perhaps extreme form, it is assumed that since God is directly involved in the composition of the NT, through human agency, all twenty-seven writings must be consistent and unified. No doubt God is pleased to be a modernist!

The implications of a non-unified New Testament for Protestantism have proven costly. Even though historical criticism was successful in justifying emancipation from ecclesial control, its unfettered proliferation has succeeded in endangering the continued existence of its founding tradition. In asserting its reliance on the perspicuity of the Bible, and not on theologically guided multi-layered ecclesiastical interpretations and

---

Origins and the Question of God 2; Minneapolis: Fortress Press, 1997); *The Resurrection of the Son of God* (Christian Origins and the Question of God 3; Minneapolis: Fortress Press, 2003). Wright's early ideas on Paul, which are influential in his later works, are collected in his *Climax of the Covenant: Christ and the Law in Pauline Theology* (Minneapolis: Fortress Press, 1993).

[36] The term "proto-Orthodox" is used to distinguish the groups of Christians in the first three centuries, and which eventually became the dominant group. See, for example, Bart D. Ehrman, *The New Testament: A Historical Introduction to the Early Christian Writings* (4th edn; Oxford: Oxford University Press, 2008) 398–401.

traditions, Protestantism unknowingly set itself up for a crisis that would lead to exponential divisions, with each denomination claiming its own "clear" reading. The so-called founding "protest" or "reform" is today more directed at other Protestant groups than at Roman Catholicism. The unfettered historical study of the Bible, which found its climax in the early twentieth century, led to a dissatisfaction by some Protestant scholars, like Karl Barth and Rudolf Bultmann, who called for a renewed integration of theology into the interpretative process.[37] In attempting to convey the relevance of the scriptures, both scholars acutely recognized that a purely historical approach created not only a fragmented Bible, but a dangerous disconnect between the academy and the church. The fragmentation pitted one historical result over and against another at the exclusion of what each called the reality of God in the scriptures. For Barth especially, historical criticism, while useful, was subservient to the inspiration of scripture, which was the ground of unity.[38] A rigorous debate about the relationship between theology and historical criticism has not abated in scholarly circles.

Inspiration

This final presupposition of a unified New Testament is the most pervasive because it has a direct impact on how exegesis is performed and what its results turn out to be. A view of inspiration that assumes a thoroughly unified New Testament corpus is suspect of, or does not allow the possibility of, discrepancies at the exegetical (i.e. historical) level. In radical forms such as the verbal-plenary theory of inspiration, which is about a hundred years old, every word of scripture in the original documents (none of which are extant) is believed to be dictated by God. Proponents of this view will certainly object to my use of "dictated", but whether it is a verbal dictation, some kind of telepathic communication, a movement of the heart, or a feeling, the result is the same: the words that were used are the words God wanted. These same proponents may also find my use of the term "radical" objectionable. However, when compared with other theories, it has been well established that this is a relatively recent one held by a minority of Christian theologians and biblical scholars. One of the problems which has emerged from this view is that the human element (even if affirmed), characterized by literary artistry, freedom, imagination, creativity and limitations of ability and knowledge has been downplayed or overshadowed. Scripture in all practicality is turned into a mechanized, dictated writing that has dropped from heaven for the purpose of empowerment through a process of mining for propositions. This radical

---

[37] See the discussion in Stephen Neill and Tom Wright, *The Interpretation of the New Testament, 1861–1986* (Oxford: Oxford University Press, 1988).
[38] Harrisville and Sundberg, *The Bible in Modern Culture*, 12–13

theory of inspiration, however, does little justice to the literary forms and socio-religious processes in the composition of these early Christian texts. Moreover, it does not take into account the sociological processes in the formation of religions, the early Christian quest for meaning over historical reconstruction, early Christian and Hellenistic understanding of the term "inspiration" (*theopneustos*), first-century Jewish and Christian use of scripture, the function of social memory and retelling in oral cultures, and the hermeneutical assumptions of the modern post-Enlightenment exegete. What we have here is an example of how a cultural framework—in this case rationalism—gives expression to what is and is not Christian. These are just a few criticisms of a theory that does not emerge out of scripture, but is placed *a priori* onto it. Much, of course, has been written in this regard.[39] The past century has witnessed an especially angry debate among Protestant groups as to which theory of inspiration is best. The result has been anything but a consensus or even a compromise.

Yet no theory is found in the New Testament. Even 2 Tim. 3.16, which is often cited as "proof" of inspiration, cannot be regarded as a theory; nor can it exegetically be applied to the New Testament. In the context of the epistle, it is a reference to the Jewish scriptures, probably the Septuagint at that. What is more, since the term *theopneustos* is only used once in the New Testament (which is called a *hapax legomenon*), it is very difficult to ascertain its meaning. When the word is divided into its two parts, we end up with "God" (*theos*) "breath/spirit" (*pneustos*). But what does this mean? And should we even divide it in this way? After all, English compound terms like "butterfly" cannot be divided like this if their compound meaning is to be preserved. Scholars who devote their attention to understanding this term in its Patristic and Hellenistic contexts, where it was used with more frequency, have noticed that its primary reference is to teaching that is considered orthodox or consistent with a prior received tradition.[40]

An instructive example of how diversity in the New Testament is acknowledged on the one hand, but due to a unifying presupposition grounded in a radical view of inspiration, is completely avoided on the other, is found in Leon Morris' *New Testament Theology*. In support of his view that all of the New Testament writers believed in the divine nature of Jesus, Morris writes, "And, although not all writers have such a succinct way of putting it as John ('the Word was God'; 'My Lord and my God'), all see Jesus as more than a mere man."[41] Apart from the Johannine corpus and a few scattered possibilities, Morris' view is difficult to support, especially

---

[39] See Paul J. Achtemeier, *Inspiration and Authority: Nature and Function of Christian Scripture* (Peabody: Hendrickson, 1999); James Barr, *Holy Scripture: Canon, Authority, Criticism* (Philadelphia: Westminster Press, 1983).
[40] Achtemeier, *Inspiration and Authority*.
[41] Leon Morris, *New Testament Theology* (Grand Rapids: Academic Books, 1986) 330.

in monotheistic Jewish contexts of the earliest Christians. For example, can we say for sure that Mark understood Jesus to be Yahweh? Jesus certainly does the work of God, is the agent of God, and announces and enacts the kingdom of God, but is he presented as God? If so, how does one understand Jesus being baptized for the forgiveness of sins (Mark 1.4, 9-11) or Jesus' cry of dereliction "My God, my God, why have you forsaken me?" (Mark 15.34)? Is Jesus presented more as a prophet or Davidic king? Is the title "son of God" used to refer to his divine nature or to subvert the Roman emperor, who was also declared a divine son, a saviour, and one who brought good news?[42] The issues are much more complex than Morris lets on.

Having said that, the inspiration of scripture is a vital and cherished Christian belief that need not be limited to any one theory. After all, can anyone say with certainty how God exactly reveals himself in/through/by the scriptures? For instance, one could just as well argue that the diversity in the New Testament writings is a result of divine inspiration which discourages us from attempts to systematize and control revelation; concluding that God may have wanted dialogue about the diversity, as is the case in rabbinic Judaism. Whatever the theory and its inherent circularity, it must be derived from the scriptures, even if they diverge.

Generally speaking, among those Protestant denominations where the scriptures are believed to be unified on historical grounds and which serve as the only source for Christian theology (which goes beyond the intentions of the first Reformers who recognized the importance of ecclesiastical tradition), Old and New Testament theologies, as unifying programmess, become the final goal of exegesis. In turn, the theologies become the interpretative paradigms for exegesis, and so on. The rationalist undercurrents to this approach are still with us largely in North American Evangelical circles where objectivity in the reading of scripture is assumed to be attainable through "proper" interpretative techniques. Students in a number of Evangelical institutions are trained in the historical-critical method and the original biblical languages so that they might be adequately equipped to interpret the scriptures "properly" and apply them to their lives. The key criterion for assessing a "correct" exegesis is its degree of consistency with the rest of scripture. If a Pauline text is interpreted in a way that contradicts or is inconsistent with, say, a similar passage in Matthew's Gospel, the exegete's results are deemed more suspect than those resulting in consistency or harmony. In essence, an unspoken biblical theology which functions as a unifying paradigm is usually operative prior to the exegete's initial opening of his or her lexicon or commentary. The result is a kind of

---

[42] See for example, the Priene Inscription (9 BCE), which refers to Caesar Augustus as a saviour, son of a god, and his birth as "gospel". Cf. Mark 1.1 and 15.39. See the summary of titles applied to the emperors in Craig A. Evans, *Mark 8.27–16:20* (WBC 34B; Nashville: Thomas Nelson, 2001) lxxxi–xciii.

individualistic empowerment and sophist-like confidence in the belief that "correct" method leads to "correct" interpretation. The circularity of such a process becomes obvious when one attempts to observe the phenomenon from an external, pluralistic vantage point. What one observes is a built-in problem: as one tries to unify the New Testament, one runs the risk of muting biblical texts.[43]

Another difficulty which proves challenging is the meaning of unity. Some hold to an understanding of unity that includes internal contradictions and a scepticism about an author's creative role in the establishment of a coherent governing purpose, whereas others assume an understanding of unity wherein conflicting data can be harmonized or synthesized in accordance with an overriding purpose cleverly orchestrated by an author. In the latter case, unity is sometimes supported by appealing to numerous redaction-critical studies that have revealed pervasive unifying features. Unity may also find its basis in underlying theological opinions about, say, the nature of the Gospels. If, for example, one assumes that God is also involved in the production of the Gospels' narrative form, coherence of purpose must also be assumed, even if it cannot be immediately perceived.[44] What clearly emerges from these varied positions is that the meaning of unity is itself not unified.

The problem of displacing dogmatics

For many Protestants, the slogan *sola scriptura* (scripture alone), which conveys the idea that Christian theology emerges only from the Bible, and not from philosophy, tradition or official ecclesiastical teachings, called "dogmatics" (or systematic theology), is foundational. An example of a current practice of *sola scriptura* is the Mennonite Brethren Biblical Seminary in Fresno, California, which has not traditionally offered courses in systematic theology or dogmatics (in contrast to Mainline Protestant, Catholic, or Orthodox schools), but instead offers courses devoted to the study of Old and New Testament theologies. But can this kind of biblical theology omit dogmatics? In keeping with what has been said about the subjective/objective problem, biblical theology's independence from, and displacement of, dogmatics is, in my estimation, incapable of being supported.

In its favour, the detachment from dogmatics has certainly provided a much-needed critique of elaborate philosophical explanations of so-called

---

[43] Steven J. Kraftchick, Charles D. Myers, Jr, and Ben C. Ollenburger, eds, *Biblical Theology: Problems and Perspectives. In Honor of J. Christiaan Beker* (Nashville: Abingdon, 1995) 8.
[44] See the discussion on differing positions in Moore, *Literary Criticism and the Gospels*, 35–6.

Christian mysteries, such as the incarnation. A *sola scriptura* approach has also kept in check the encroachment of dogmatics on exegesis.[45] And further, a *sola scriptura* approach can be an agent of change, which is vital for the survival of all religions, because it is able to challenge oppressive, intolerant and unjust ecclesiastical norms and mores by subjecting them to new interpretations of the ancient text.[46] There is no denying that a *sola scriptura* approach brings more accountability to the discussion. It has sometimes been said that the best critique of the Church is still the gospel.

On an individual level, the primacy of *sola scriptura* (exegesis) over dogmatics can lead to a weakening or dismantling of cherished theological ideas. Most professors who teach religious studies in confessional institutions have encountered a so-called "crisis of faith" when exegetical results have contradicted the students' theological (i.e. dogmatic) convictions. I have especially encountered this in courses on the historical Jesus and the Gospels. Often the "crisis" has actually been a vital stepping-stone, not a stumbling-stone, in the development of one's identity (which is a key component of religion) because it allows the student to re-examine the positive and negative aspects of the traditions within which he or she was raised.[47] This is not a "loss of faith" as it is sometimes perceived; though it may well be a loss of rationalistic certainty, which is disguised as faith. Often the problem in these circles when students are exposed to critical scholarship is that they are confronted with the realization that reason cannot *prove* their faith. They begin to realize that their faith is grounded in God. Often such "crisis" events are the first time that students are free to think independently and creatively, and recognize that faith need not, and should not, be static or controlled by rationalism. This prospect is exciting for some and frightening for others.

To claim, however, that the study of the Bible should lie strictly within its own purview raises immense problems. For one, without the benefit of dogmatics, the foundationalist view would have no scriptural canon with which to work. To put it differently, it would have to remove the words *New Testament* from its formation of a theology. While certain New Testament writers gained authority fairly early on, such as Paul and the evangelist Matthew, one is hard-pressed to demonstrate that even these Christian writers were viewed on the same level in the first century and across the Roman empire as were the Jewish scriptures. The idea of a New Testament canon is foreign to the New Testament itself. In other words, there is no writer in the New Testament who posits that the twenty-seven

---

[45] See Walter Brueggemann, *Theology of the Old Testament: Testimony, Dispute, Advocacy* (Minneapolis: Fortress Press, 1997) 726–8.
[46] Heikki Räisänen, *Beyond New Testament Theology: A Story and a Program* (2nd edn; London: SCM Press, 2000) 156–9.
[47] See Klaus Berger, *Hermeneutik des Neuen Testaments* (Gütersloh: Gütersloher Verlagshaus G. Mohn, 1988) 186–8.

writings are to be viewed as sacred scripture alongside the Jewish scriptures. It is surprising to many lay people when they discover that it was not until CE 367 that we first find a list of canonical writings (compiled by Athanasius, the bishop of Alexandria) that consists of the twenty-seven books we now call the New Testament. This collection was finally authorized at the Council of Hippo (CE 393) and the Council of Carthage (CE 397). The compilation of lists of authoritative Christian writings was not new to the fourth century. Since the second century, a variety of groups calling themselves Christian compiled their own lists that included various writings—some that are in the New Testament and others that are not, such as the *Shepherd of Hermas* and the *Epistle of Barnabas*.[48]

Another major problem in displacing dogmatics with a foundationalist biblical theology is that it leaves no room for theories of divine inspiration, which are the property of dogmatics. I have already explained how a theory of inspiration can be used as a unifying principle that affects exegesis. And since no theory appears in the New Testament, nor is there any mention that the twenty-seven books are sacred, one needs to be imposed upon it. Thus a foundationalist view must assume a dogmatic basis before it even begins.[49] Such theories, however, are not arbitrary, but have been formulated over long periods of time, through much debate, within contexts of worship and Christian practice, as was the case with the canonical process. Jaroslav Pelikan's developmental formula still echoes in my ears. In a course that I took from him a number of years ago on statements of faith in the Reformation period, he repeatedly stated the principle of doctrinal development: "*lex orandi* always precedes *lex credendi*" ("the law of prayer always precedes the law of creed"). This principle would suggest that during the two and a half centuries of canonical development, a New Testament theology would have been impossible. All that one could say with historical confidence is that early Christian groups had their own theologies, some of which were consistent with each other and others were not.

---

[48] For a clearly written introduction to the formation of the New Testament canon, see Harry Gamble, *The New Testament Canon: Its Making and Meaning* (Philadelphia: Fortress Press, 1985). For a more advanced treatment, see Bruce M. Metzger, *The Canon of the New Testament: Its Origin, Development and Significance* (Oxford: Clarendon Press, 1987). On the political influence in the formation of the canon, see David L. Dungan, *Constantine's Bible: Politics and the Making of the New Testament* (Minneapolis: Fortress Press, 2006).

[49] Gerhard Ebeling, "The Meaning of 'Biblical Theology'", in *Word and Faith* (London: SCM Press, 1963) 89.

The problem of the diversity of early christian thought

One could say that the Protestant experiment of building a theology solely from scripture, as the truest expression of revelation, has been too successful, though not in the results for which it originally hoped. The reliance on historical-critical exegesis as an isolated method that promised objectivity has actually undermined the quest for a New Testament theology. The major problem for the foundationalist view is that the historical-critical method over the last two centuries has successfully demonstrated not that the writings of the New Testament are unified, but that they diverge from one another, and at times intentionally so. These writings represent early Christian groups whose beliefs differed on significant matters such as ethnicity, religious experience, eschatology, Christology, ecclesial authority and the Jewish law, to mention but a few. This is a crucial observation, which has not been given enough attention by many New Testament theologians.[50] While on the one hand it is understandable, given theology's predisposition for unification, on the other hand, the initial step in formulating a New Testament theology should be an assessment of the sources one is attempting to unify or bring into some kind of coherence.

Attempts at unifying the New Testament can best be understood when the diversity of the writings is appreciated. Another way of looking at this process is to back up, so to speak, and first lay bare the New Testament material from a distance, as it were, before it is subjectively reconstructed into a theology. Such a task is beyond the aim of this book, since this is not a New Testament theology, but a sampling of the diversity of early Christian thought is offered here to demonstrate that a foundationalist view creates more problems than it solves. Moreover, recognizing the diversity within first- and second-century Christianity is not new. It was articulated in an influential way approximately one hundred and fifty years ago by Ferdinand Christian Baur (1792–1860), who argued that earliest Christianity was shaped by the division between Pauline and Petrine Christianities.[51] In the early part of the twentieth century, Walter Bauer (1877–1960) further challenged the prevailing assumptions of first-century theological unity by arguing that historians can no longer use terms like

---

[50] Once again, I recommend the discussion of "differences" in any comparative approach in Jonathan Z. Smith, *Drudgery Divine: On the Comparison of Early Christianities and the Religions of Late Antiquity* (Chicago: Chicago University Press, 1994).

[51] Ferdinand Christian Baur, *The Church History of the First Three Centuries* (trans. Allan Menzies; 3rd edn; London: Williams and Norgate, 1878. Original German publication in 1853); "[ET] The Christ Party in the Corinthian Church, The Conflict Between Petrine and Pauline Christianity in the Early Church, the Apostle Peter in Rome", *Tübinger Zeitschrift für Theologie* 4 (1831) 61–206.

"orthodoxy" and "heresy" in historical reconstructions of earliest Christian thought.[52] For many historians standing on the shoulders of Bauer, "orthodoxy" and "heresy" were viewed as more appropriate categories from the council of Nicea (CE 325) onward.[53]

Three specific problems emerge with the attempt to formulate a theology using the historical-critical method. First, the New Testament is not a single, organized treatise. There is no writing within it that can be called a theology, if we understand theology as a unification of thought that is appropriated. Neither is the New Testament as a canonical corpus a theology, even though it contains theological language and reflection. Creedal statements like Thomas' confession to the risen Christ "My Lord and my God" in John 20.28 is not yet theology, but it is theological reflection using theological language.

Second, what emerges from historical and literary studies is that there are several theologies at play in the New Testament. For example, Jesus' preoccupation with the kingdom of God in the Synoptic Gospels (Matthew, Mark and Luke) is of little concern to the Johannine Jesus.

And third, historical study has not determined where the centre of a New Testament theology should reside. Is the centre to be found in the historical Jesus, Paul, the Gospels, or in the traditions they used? This problem has led to a variety of proposals and even divisions among scholars, pastors and denominations.

It is to the diversity of early Christian thought that I now turn with the intention of providing samples of data that historical, literary, social-scientific criticisms have succeeded in unfolding. This can be called the "raw material" with which any New Testament theology needs to work. The main point that I wish to communicate through these various examples of diversity is that the formation of a New Testament theology on historical grounds is far more complex than it has often been made to appear. Harmonizations and claims of coherence require verification and cannot simply be asserted because they are found within the canon. Any formation of a New Testament theology must include the aim of each writer (if indeed this is possible to recover), his social circumstances, the genre in which he writes and traditions that he uses. Each of these must be given close attention, lest we commit ethical violations in accepted processes of research.

While early Christian thought may be rooted in the historical Jesus of Nazareth who ministered to fellow peasant Jews in the late twenties of rural Galilee within the religious context of Judaism before the emergence

---

[52] Walter Bauer, *Orthodoxy and Heresy in Earliest Christianity* (trans. Philadelphia Seminar on Christian Origins; ed. R. A. Kraft and G. Krodel; Philadelphia: Fortress Press, 1971).
[53] On evaluations of Bauer and others, see James D. G. Dunn, *Unity and Diversity in the New Testament: An Inquiry into the Character of Earliest Christianity* (2nd edn; London: SCM Press, 1990).

of Christianity, it is not limited to Jesus' teachings. Rather, early Christian thought as it appears in the New Testament largely represents early Christian interpretations of Jesus' teachings, actions and identity after his death. These interpretations were communicated by various individuals and groups that identified themselves as followers of Jesus the Christ. Scattered across the Empire, they interpreted their new found faith within a variety of ethnic settings, religious contexts, political conflicts and economic strata. Limiting these early Christians at this point just to the New Testament, we can divide them into two categories: those that are detectable in the New Testament, usually in hostile terms; and those that are represented by the New Testament writers.

Diversity among Christians detected in the New Testament

With respect to the former, the New Testament writers make mention of several groups who believed that Jesus was the Messiah or unique agent of God, but were at odds with some of their views on such topics as ethics, salvation, ritual, the nature of God and apostolic authority. One example is that of the Judaizers, Jewish Christians from Palestine who advocated, in contrast to Paul, that Gentile converts were required to undergo circumcision and obey the dietary laws as they were prescribed in the Torah. They believed that these and other legal requirements functioned as the boundary markers that identified the people of God. The Galatian Christians, who were apparently susceptible to the teachings of the Judaizers, were warned by Paul not to abandon the gospel that he originally preached to them. The Corinthian Christians seem also to have been influenced by Judaizers, but the issues in 2 Corinthians have more to do with justifying Paul's apostolicity. In 2 Corinthians, Paul's apostolic authority seems to be challenged by a group of Jewish Christians who have again followed Paul and attempted to undermine his teachings. A considerable amount of ink has been spilt over the past two centuries in the attempt to identify the Judaizers, be they members of one group or several. One of the most common proposals has been that they were Jerusalem Christians, perhaps led by James or Peter.

Several examples of groups who followed Jesus have been detected in the Gospel of John and the epistles of John. In the Gospel, Raymond Brown has detected three groups of Christians distinct from the Johannine community: Christian Jews within the synagogues, Jewish Christians who left the synagogues to form their own churches, and Jewish Christians represented by the Twelve (especially Peter, Philip and Andrew).[54] More recently, some

---

[54] Raymond E. Brown, *The Community of the Beloved Disciple: The Life, Loves, and Hates of an Individual Church in New Testament Times* (New York: Paulist Press, 1979) 71-88.

scholars have argued that an early Gnostic Christian group can also be detected. Elaine Pagels, for example, has suggested that John's Gospel and the epistles appear to be responding to a Gnostic group that followed Jesus, but denied that he actually came in the flesh—much like the later Docetists who believed that Jesus only appeared to be physical, but in actuality was a spirit. On the basis of the numerous similarities between the Gnostic *Gospel of Thomas* and John's Gospel, Pagels proposes that the Johannine community was partly in conflict with the so-called Thomas Christians. Thus John's statements about Jesus coming in the flesh and his use of Thomas' confession after touching the risen Christ are intended to counter the Gnostic claims. Similar statements about Jesus coming in the flesh in other New Testament texts (e.g. 1 Tim. 3.16) have led some to believe that Gnostic influences within nascent Christianity were more widespread than once thought.[55]

Synoptic Gospels scholars who accept the Two-Source theory—that Matthew and Luke used Mark and a sayings source called Q (for the German "*Quelle*" meaning "source")—have pointed to what might be the oldest detectable Christian group. No list of examples is ever complete without their mention. The hypothetical Q document (often called the Q Gospel), dated to the CE 40s, is often attributed to the first generation of Christians who led an itinerant existence. As wandering prophets, they aimed their mission at the Jews in Palestine. According to Ulrich Luz, after the failure of the mission to Israel and the devastation caused by the Jewish War, the community settled in Syria, where it received significant theological inspiration from the community associated with the Gospel of Mark. It was at this point that it oriented its efforts towards the Gentile mission, as it was eventually recorded at the end of Matthew's Gospel (28.16-20).[56] If the reconstruction of the Q Gospel is correct, then its omissions in comparison to the Synoptic Gospels may be indicative of their beliefs. Two of the more glaring omissions are an infancy account and a resurrection account. The aim of the Q Gospel (as is the case in the *Gospel of Thomas*) seems to have been the preservation of sayings attributed to Jesus, and not what is the central message in Paul's letters (which are the earliest extant Christian writings), namely the cross and resurrection of Jesus. Social historians who have attempted to trace the development of early Christian thought by isolating various early Christian groups and their beliefs have commonly referred to the earliest groups of disciples as the *Jesus Movement*, though the use of the term "movement" is not intended to convey the common

---

[55] Elaine Pagels, *Beyond Belief: The Secret Gospel of Thomas* (New York: Random House, 2003). See also, Udo Schnelle, *Antidocetic Christology in the Gospel of John: An Investigation of the Place of the Fourth Gospel in the Johannine School* (trans. Linda M. Maloney; Minneapolis: Fortress Press, 1992).

[56] Ulrich Luz, *Studies in Matthew* (trans. Rosemary Selle; Grand Rapids: Eerdmans, 2005) 7-8.

connotation that it contained strictly charismatic and anti-institutional tendencies.[57]

Overlapping the *Jesus Movement* was a more structured push for the establishment of churches beginning in Jerusalem and Judea and extending into Syria and Asia Minor (the so-called Gentile churches). These early churches, however, should not be equated with buildings designated for communal worship, as they are today. They should instead be viewed as communities consisting of people from varied social and ethnic backgrounds who expressed a common belief in Jesus as Messiah and saviour within a shared geographical area. In fact the earliest church building discovered by archaeologists, in the town of Dura in Eastern Syria, dates to the middle of the third century. Communal worship and fellowship in the first century would have been held in people's homes—so-called "house churches". Many Christians today are surprised to hear that the church in Corinth, for example, with all its problems and vulnerabilities according to 1 Corinthians, would have consisted of approximately fifteen people in the middle of the first century. Interaction among early communities in different cities was limited. While they may have been founded by common itinerant prophets or teachers, such as the Apostle Paul or John the Elder, they each retained their autonomy and essentially developed on their own, interacting with and being influenced by local religious ideas and customs. On occasion, interchurch relations were strained, as is indicated by the admonishment directed at the Asian churches in Revelation. On other occasions relations with fellow members who held differing ideas were severed, as may be the case in John the Elder's warning (in 3 John) to a certain Gaius about Diotrephes, an alleged ambitious upstart who disregarded the teachings of the Johannine community.

This religious diversity and "in-house" conflicts were not unique to nascent Christianity. Early Judaism, out of which Christianity emerged, was likewise far from being monolithic in its religious beliefs and practices. The Roman Jewish historian Josephus, the Dead Sea Scrolls and the Pseudepigrapha have been very valuable literary sources that show the diversity and conflicts among Jewish groups in the first century, most notably the Pharisees, Sadducees, Essenes and Samaritans. As is the case with rival religious groups sharing a common ancestry, each claimed a superior status, belief system, ritual practice, interpretation of the scriptures and direct lineage to a foundational figure, such as Moses or Abraham. Given this diversity, it has become fairly common among biblical scholars to speak of Judaisms and Christianities, instead of a monolithic Judaism and Christianity.

---

[57] Ekkehard and Wolfgang Stegemann, *The Jesus Movement: A Social History of Its First Century* (trans. O. C. Dean, Jr.; Minneapolis: Fortress Press, 1999) 187.

Diversity among Christians represented by the New Testament

When attention is turned to the beliefs of Christians represented by the New Testament, we are on firmer historical ground, but we find no less diversity. This should come as no surprise when the occasion for the composition of the writings is considered. They were written during the second half of the first century, over approximately a fifty-year period, primarily in Asia Minor and Syria, by Jewish Christians (except perhaps for Luke) who were attempting to legitimize their new-found faith in Jesus as God's Messiah in response to mostly Jewish, and some Roman, opposition. As is the case with all nascent religions, formulations of belief needed to draw on existing language, symbols, myths, rituals, worship practices and authoritative texts and traditions. The culture was the cradle. Since the Greco-Roman world accommodated numerous religious and philosophical traditions, one of them being Judaism, the options for expressing the content of early Christian faith were immense. Even the Judaism of this period, which was the primary source of influence for earliest Christian theological expression, took on various nuances across the Empire, some of which were considerably influenced by Hellenism.[58] Inscriptions and the location of synagogues in Roman cities have suggested that Jewish participation in mainstream culture was also varied. In some places, like Ephesus and Sardis, there is evidence that Jews participated fully in civic life, even at the administrative levels. In another example, prime reserved seating in the theatre at Miletus is inscribed "Place of the Jews, who are also called 'God-fearers'",[59] whereas in other places, like Rome during the time of Claudius, they were banished. In Ostia Antica, as a further example,

---

[58] When the archaeological data and the major early Jewish written sources are studied critically—namely Apocrypha, Pseudepigrapha, Josephus, Philo, the Dead Sea Scrolls and the Mishnah—they reinforce the view that Judaism from ca. 330 BCE to CE 200 cannot be regarded as a monolithic religion. Jewish religious life and belief varied considerably. As a result, scholars often speak of multiple Judaisms that are too divergent to be seen as simply variations of a single pattern. For example, Jewish writings from both Palestine and the Diaspora exhibit diverse understandings of common religious rituals and concepts. Topics such as eschatology and the Messiah only appear in some texts. Even the basic rite of circumcision is used and interpreted differently in the Hebrew Bible, Paul, 1 Maccabees, Josephus and Philo. The Hellenistic period was especially conducive to diverse development. See Jonathan Z. Smith, *Imagining Religion: From Babylon to Jonestown* (Chicago Studies in the History of Judaism; Chicago: University of Chicago Press, 1988); George W. E. Nickelsburg, *Ancient Judaism and Christian Origins: Diversity, Continuity, and Transformation* (Minneapolis: Fortress, 2003); Randall A. Argall, Beverly Bow and Rodney A. Werline, eds, *For a Later Generation: The Transformation of Tradition in Israel, Early Judaism, and Early Christianity* (Harrisburg PA; Trinity Press International, 2000).

[59] Adolf Deissmann, *Light from the Ancient East: The New Testament Illustrated by Recently Discovered Texts of the Graeco-Roman World* (trans. L. R. M. Strachan; New York: George H. Doran Co., 1927; reprinted by Hendrickson, 1995) 451–2.

the synagogue ruins are located well outside the city, which may indicate exclusion or sectarianism. Dating the construction of ancient synagogues, which were more like community halls and not like modern places of worship, has been controversial, but their proximity (or lack thereof) to the cities and their temples nevertheless indicates degrees of integration within Greco-Roman culture.

"God-fearers", gentile converts to Judaism who did not undergo circumcision, were an important group in Christianity's transition from a Jewish context to the broader Hellenistic one. During Paul's missionary travels, his rejection by Jews in synagogue contexts would have inevitably put him into contact with God-fearers.[60] According to the book of Acts (which along with Luke, may have been written by a God-fearer), several God-fearers were receptive to the Christian message because it claimed to be the fulfilment of Judaism.[61] Their Jewish interests along with their deep-seated Hellenistic traditions provided yet another religious context for the expression of nascent Christianity. Historically and sociologically, it should come as no surprise that the variety of cultural influences led to a variety of interpretations and expressions of Christianity during its vulnerable infancy.

Differences among the canonical Gospels

So what kind of diversity do we find in the New Testament writings? A comprehensive answer would take us far afield and is beyond the scope of this book, but some examples are necessary for appreciating the New Testament as the raw material for the formulation of a theology. One of the clearest ways of demonstrating some of the diversity is by carefully comparing the four Gospels. Since, at the popular level of religious worship, most Christians do not read the Gospels comparatively, the events that are narrated are often harmonized and rolled into one overarching story. In a real sense, the four Gospels are turned into one Gospel, which in turn is no longer canonical. This practice has occurred ever since the four Gospels were regarded authoritatively. One of the most well-known harmonizing practices in the early church was that of Tatian's (CE 110–180) *Diatessaron* (lit. "through [the] four [Gospels]") which forced all the Gospels into one chronological, historical and theological mold. Ancient practices of harmonizing the Gospels were often conducted for apologetic and theological reasons. Apologetically, the church leaders (since most laypersons were illiterate) needed to respond to the inconsistencies in the four accounts

---

[60] John Dominic Crossan and Jonathan L. Reed, *In Search of Paul: How Jesus's Apostle Opposed Rome's Empire with God's Kingdom. A New Vision of Paul's Words & World* (New York: HarperCollins, 2004) 34–41.
[61] John Nolland, *Luke 1–9.20* (WBC 35A; Dallas: Word Books, 1989) xxxii–xxxiii.

pointed out by opponents. Theologically, the early Christian hermeneutic was oriented toward Christological consistency and doctrinal/ethical formulation, and thus what we call historicity was simply subsumed into whatever reconstructions were needed at the time.

Today, in our highly literate culture, most Christians read the Gospels vertically instead of horizontally, which is easy to do since they are placed sequentially in a codex (or book). One begins with Matthew and ends with John. By the time all four are completed, the stories have rolled into one. The problem is amplified when the reading programme is governed by a quantitative rather than a qualitative agenda such as the so-called "one year" Bible reading programme. Harmonizing practices also appear in popular expressions of Christian faith, such as Nativity scenes in plays and on Christmas cards and calendars where Matthew's infancy account is blended with Luke's. In films such as *King of Kings* (1961), *The Greatest Story Ever Told* (1965), *Jesus Christ Superstar* (1973), *Jesus of Nazareth* (1977) and the more recent *The Passion of the Christ* (2003), the harmonizing of the Gospels is even more noticeable. Mark Goodacre provides a telling example from a scene in *Jesus Christ Superstar* where Mary Magdalene is characterized as a prostitute who anoints Jesus before his death and is then opposed by Judas who complains about the cost of the anointing oil. This scene draws together the following elements from all four Gospels: (1) the anonymous woman who anoints Jesus' feet in Mark 14 and Matthew 27, (2) the anonymous woman "sinner" who anoints Jesus in Luke 7, (3) the name "Mary, called Magdalene" in Luke 8.2, (4) Mary of Bethany who anoints Jesus in John 12 and (5) Judas who complains about the anointing (likewise in John 12). Watching this one scene on a cursory level gives no indication of the sources used.[62]

When the Gospels are read horizontally—that is, alongside one another in a comparative way—they appear in an entirely different light. They certainly contain similarities. All four Gospels, for example, are narratives that share a common plot, antagonists, protagonists, climax and resolution. All have Jesus as their main character and hero, who is portrayed as the Messiah, son of God, deliverer of God's people and the prophet predicted in the Jewish scriptures. All of them include Jesus' teaching about redemption, salvation and discipleship. All of them portray Jesus as performing miracles. And all of them describe his passion—his trial, suffering, death and eventual resurrection (though Mark is subtle). Yet alongside the similarities, numerous differences emerge, not only in emphasis, but in what is meant and signified by Jesus' messianic identity, role, death and resurrection.

Among the Synoptic Gospels, which share the same basic chronology, emphasize the kingdom of God, and contain many common events and

---

[62] Mark Goodacre, *The Synoptic Problem: A Way Through the Maze* (The Biblical Seminar 80; London: Sheffield Academic Press, 2001) 13–14.

sayings, divergences in meaning are everywhere. Each evangelist omits material found in the other two. Each contains unique incidents. Some of the shared events are put in a different order, such as the last two temptations of Jesus in Matt 4.5-11 and Luke 4.5-13. Also some sayings of Jesus are placed in entirely different contexts. Take for example, the saying "No one can serve two masters; for either he will hate the one and love the other, or he will be devoted to the one and despise the other. You cannot serve God and mammon." In Matthew (6.24), the saying is found in the context of the Sermon on the Mount, but in Luke (16.13), it appears verbatim in the context of parables narrated much later in the story. The three evangelists also emphasize different themes, most notably in their portrayals of Jesus. To mention a few, in Mark, Jesus appears as the concealed Messiah who alone preaches the kingdom of God (in contrast to Matthew where the disciples also preach it). In Matthew, Jesus is portrayed as a new Moses who brings the correct interpretation of the Law. In Luke, Jesus is portrayed as a rejected prophet who is concerned with the welfare of social minorities and outcasts. In Mark, the earliest of the three, the resurrection account is subtle and incomplete when compared with the other two Gospels, which raises the question of how Mark understood it.

One of the most glaring omissions in Mark is the birth and infancy account. Did Mark not know this tradition? If he knew of it, did he not believe it? When Luke and Matthew's infancy accounts are compared, there are clear similarities, such as the same parents of Jesus, Bethlehem as the location of the birth, and a supernatural conception involving the same divine source. Some of the tensions can also be conflated with little effort, such as Matthew's account of the angel telling only Joseph about the virginal conception and Luke's version where Mary is the only one told. Many of the other differences are, however, much more difficult and even impossible to conflate. Take, for example, the sequence of events beginning with the annunciation. In Matthew, the reader is led to believe that the annunciation to Joseph (1.18-25) takes place in Bethlehem since this is the only location mentioned in the immediate context (2.1). In Luke, the annunciation takes place while Mary and Joseph are in Nazareth (1.26-27), which in Luke's account even appears to be their home, given that Mary returns "to her house" (1.56) after visiting Elizabeth. In Matthew, the Magi find Mary and Jesus in a house (2.11), not a stable as in Luke, which presumes that they are settled in a permanent residence. In contrast to Luke, Matthew does not imply that Jesus was newly born, which fits Herod's killing of children under two years of age. Luke has no Magi and Matthew has no shepherds. The travel sequence in each account likewise cannot be reconciled with that of the other. Luke has the family travelling from Nazareth (their home) to Bethlehem to fulfil the census requirement, and then peacefully back to "to their own city Nazareth" after the baby is presented in the Temple. In Matthew, the geographical movement is the opposite. The family travels from Bethlehem, Joseph's home, to Egypt, for which there is no time in Luke's plot, and then to Nazareth, the family's new home. There is no mention in Matthew of a birth during a quick local trip. There is also no mention of returning back to Nazareth. Matthew narrates that the family "settled in a city called Nazareth" (2.23), the same word used later in the narrative to refer to Jesus' first visit to Capernaum (4.13).[63]

When John is brought into the picture and compared with the Synoptics, the divergences escalate. Whether the Johannine evangelist knew the Synoptic tradition, and thus intended the differences, or had no knowledge of the other Gospels continues to be debated. But this is not the issue before us. What the differences make clear is that a unified New Testament theology is far more complicated than is sometimes indicated. John's presentation of Jesus is completely different. He is portrayed as the incarnate pre-existent Word of God whose speeches and miraculous deeds ("signs") focus on his divine identity and intimate relationship with the Father, which he publicly communicates. Yet as a divine figure, he is still subordinate to God. John's focus is not on Jesus' preaching of the kingdom of God, messianic concealment, the Mosaic Law, or social justice. Instead, the focus is on belief in Jesus as the Christ and son of God who has come in the flesh. Without drawing out each occasion where John differs from the Synoptics, a list should suffice to show John's uniqueness. The following are in no particular order.

(1) Only John has Jesus cleansing the temple at the beginning of his ministry, rather than at the end. In the Synoptics, the temple action constitutes Jesus' *last* public act; yet in John it his *first*. In the Synoptics, it is met with fierce opposition, and even a call for his death (Mark 11.18). In John there is no repercussion. Instead, the event is spiritualized and used to forecast Jesus' resurrection.

(2) In John, Jesus dies on the day of preparation, and not on the Passover as the Synoptics record. In John 18.28 the crucifixion takes place on 14 Nisan, the day before Passover. In the Synoptics (Mark 14.12) the last supper (which was the Passover meal) and the crucifixion occurred on 15 Nisan. Again, it is interesting how John tends to spiritualize the event by having Jesus die on the "day of Preparation for Passover, at noon" (19.14) which corresponds to the time of the killing of the sacrificial animals.

---

[63] These and other differences are discussed in more detail in Raymond E. Brown, *The Birth of the Messiah: A Commentary on the Infancy Narratives in the Gospels of Matthew and Luke* (2nd edn; New York: Doubleday, 1993). On the diversity, distinctions and similarities throughout the Synoptics, see Robert H. Stein, *The Synoptic Problem: An Introduction* (Grand Rapids: Baker, 1987); Pheme Perkins, *Introduction to the Synoptic Gospels* (Grand Rapids: Eerdmans, 2007). See also the highly controversial view that the Synoptics are based on eyewitness testimony in Richard Bauckham, *Jesus and the Eyewitnesses: The Gospels as Eyewitness Testimony* (Grand Rapids: Eerdmans, 2006).

(3) In John, the Baptist repudiates any identification with Elijah (John 1.21a), but in the Synoptics Jesus is identified as an Elijah figure (Matt. 11.14; 17.10-13; Luke 1.17).

(4) In John, Jesus teaches in extended sermons rather that in short parables. There are no kingdom parables in John.

(5) In John, Jesus is confessed as Messiah from the beginning of his ministry (1.41), but in the Synoptics this confession comes later in the story (Mark 8.27-30) and marks the turning point of his ministry.

(6) In John, both the disciples and Jesus publicly declare his exalted identity. In the Synoptics, neither Jesus nor his disciples speak publicly about his exalted status during his lifetime. His true identity is revealed in snippets: in private epiphanies, at his baptism, to the inner circle at his transfiguration and in Peter's confession. In Mark especially, his messianic identity is intentionally secretive.

(7) In John, Jesus is presented as more divine than human. It has commonly been said that in comparison to the Synoptic portrayals, the Johannine Jesus "hardly touches the ground". His divine status is regularly acknowledged and occasionally recognized by other characters, which may explain why the fourth Gospel contains no actual baptism, transfiguration or temptation. These accounts may not have been viewed as necessary because Jesus' entire mission seems to be presented as an epiphany.

(8) In John, Jesus never casts out demons.

(9) In the Synoptics, Jesus espouses the causes of the poor and the oppressed, but in John he has nothing to say about them.

(10) In John, there is no Lord's Supper prior to his death. While many have argued that John 6 is based on Eucharistic celebrations, the chronology and event are significantly different from that of the Synoptics.

(11) In the Synoptics, Jesus' primary opponents are the Sadducees, Pharisees, scribes and Herodians; whereas in John, they are called "the Jews" and "the world".

(12) In the Synoptics, Peter is the most prominent of the apostles, whereas in John the "beloved disciple" takes the lead role.

(13) In John, Jesus does not pray the "Lord's Prayer".

(14) In John, the disciples are not sent out on a mission during Jesus' lifetime. Instead, he sends them after the resurrection.

When the rest of the New Testament is brought into the comparison, the differences escalate. Some of them are theologically significant. For example, many biblical scholars have observed that Jesus' teachings differ significantly from that of the Apostle Paul. Whereas Jesus (of the Synoptic tradition) is concerned with teaching about the kingdom of God, Paul has little to say about it—or, for that matter, the entire so-called earthly ministry of Jesus. Instead, Paul focuses on the effects of Jesus' death and resurrection. This difference has led to many theologians raising the question whether it is Jesus or Paul who should be credited for the beginning of Christianity. Is the Jesus of the Synoptic tradition, or even the reconstructed historical Jesus, still situated well within Judaism instead of nascent Christianity, or is he the first Christian, so to speak? Another significant theological divergence has to do with the meaning of Jesus' death. Mark, for example, understands the death as a pattern of faithfulness for all followers; whereas Hebrews understands it as a sin sacrifice. It is no wonder that differing theories of atonement find support in the New Testament. The role of women in the fledgling Christian communities also varies, sometimes in the writings of the same author. The early writings of Paul, for instance, appear to be much more relaxed about leadership positions for women than the later writings—if we assume that the two correspondences to Timothy are Pauline. Nevertheless, several studies have shown that women appear to lose authority as Christian communities become more institutionalized.[64] The role of the Jewish law also varies. Matthew, for instance, appears much more traditional than does Paul. As a final example, consider the differing views on the role of government or governing officials. In Romans 13.1-2, Paul leaves little, if any, room for resisting authority when he writes, "Every person is to be in subjection to the governing authorities. For there is no authority except from God, and those which exist are established by God. Therefore whoever resists authority has opposed the ordinance of God; and they who have opposed will receive condemnation upon themselves." Luke, however, implies that God (and hence his followers) subverts social structures. When some of the disciples are arrested for not complying with a ban on their Christian teaching, Luke writes,

> When they had brought them, they stood them before the Council. The high priest questioned them, saying, "We gave you strict orders not to continue teaching in this name, and yet you have filled Jerusalem with your teaching and intend to bring this man's blood upon us." But Peter

---

[64] Elisabeth Schüssler Fiorenza, *In Memory of Her: A Feminist Theological Reconstruction of Christian Origins* (New York: Crossroad, 1983); Karen Jo Torjesen, *When Women Were Priests: Women's Leadership in the Early Church and the Scandal of Their Subordination in the Rise of Christianity* (San Francisco: HarperCollins, 1993); Ross Kraemer and Mary Rose D'Angelo, eds, *Women and Christian Origins* (Oxford: Oxford University Press, 1999).

and the apostles answered, "We must obey God rather than men" (Acts 5.27-29).

While these and many other variances in the theological thinking among the New Testament writers can be explained (not necessarily harmonized) by appealing to their immediate social contexts, they nevertheless raise enormous problems for the foundationalist approach to the formation of a New Testament theology.

Diversity beyond the New Testament

Diversity in early Christian thought extends beyond the New Testament, though unfortunately a number of the early extracanonical writings are no longer extant. Some may have been incorporated into other writings (such as Q was incorporated into Matthew and Luke), others disappeared due to lack of interest, and still others were destroyed by rival Christian groups which were more dominant. The destruction was particularly intense when in CE 380 Emperor Theodosius made Christianity the official state religion of the Empire and outlawed all theological thinking that deviated from one version of the faith as it was expressed in the council of Nicea.[65] Not all of the writings that deviated from the official theology were destroyed, however. Lists of early Christian extracanonical writings within the first hundred years of Christianity, say up to CE 130, will vary from scholar to scholar, but a helpful (perhaps generous) sampling is provided in Bart Ehrman's *The New Testament and Other Early Christian Writings: A Reader*,[66] which has become the standard text for introductory courses on Christian origins and the New Testament in North American colleges and universities. Ehrman includes the *Gospel of Thomas*, the *Gospel of Peter*, the *Infancy Gospel of Thomas*, the *Secret Gospel of Mark*, the *Unknown Gospel* (Papyrus Egerton 2), the *Gospel of the Ebionites*, the *Gospel of the Nazareans*, the *Gospel to the Hebrews*, the *Acts of Paul and Thecla*, 1 Clement, the *Didache*, the letters of Ignatius to the Ephesians, Magnesians, Trallians, Romans, Philadelphians, Smyrneans, Polycarp, the letter of Polycarp to the Philippians, the *Letter of Barnabas*, the *Preaching of Peter*, the *Fragments of Papias*, the *Shepherd of Hermas* and the *Apocalypse of Peter*.[67] In addition,

---

[65] Recent studies suggest that it was Theodosius, not Constantine, who made Christianity the state religion. Harold A. Drake, *Constantine and the Bishops: The Politics of Intolerance* (Ancient Society and History; Baltimore: Johns Hopkins University Press, 2000); Elizabeth Depalma Digeser, *The Making of a Christian Empire: Lactantius and Rome* (Ithaca: Cornell University Press, 2000).
[66] Bart D. Ehrman, *The New Testament and Other Early Christian Writings: A Reader* (Oxford: Oxford University Press, 1998).
[67] For a critical translation and discussions of these and other extracanonical texts, see Edgar Hennecke and Wilhelm Schneemelcher, eds, *New Testament Apocrypha* (2 vols.;

the variance in early Christian thought is preserved (though negatively) in a number of early Church Fathers and apologists (e.g. Justin Martyr and Irenaeus) who argued against the beliefs of rival Christian groups.

New Testament theologians do not usually incorporate extracanonical writings or the ideas they contain into the constructs of their New Testament theologies. But when they do, they tend to be consulted more by those who view New Testament theology as a dialectic. Among foundationalists, these writings are generally ignored. I am in agreement that the focus of New Testament theology should be on the canonical writings. Yet, if we are intent on calling it "theology", the extracanonical writings should nevertheless play an important role in the study of early Christian religion, which in turn should inform New Testament theology. Omission of extracanonical writings short-changes theology and does not allow it to fulfil its unifying role because it cuts itself off from the larger early Christian religious context which gives meaning to terms and concepts, and provides for the possibility of reconstructing rival groups. Furthermore, understanding the varied Christian trajectories provides for patterns of development, which in turn shed light on influences and syncretism with non-Christian religions.

The relationship between canonical and extracanonical writings has been an important topic in historical Jesus research and has provided significant insights into our understanding of early Jewish and Christian thought. While most historical Jesus scholars agree that Mark is the earliest canonical Gospel, a few—such as John Dominic Crossan, Helmut Koester and Ron Cameron—have argued that Mark is antedated by some extracanonical (or so-called Apocryphal) Gospels, which in some cases contain material that was used by the four evangelists.[68] Most often discussed are *Papyrus Egerton 2*, which consists of five small codex fragments that resemble the Synoptics and John, the *Gospel of Thomas*, which contains a list of 114 sayings of Jesus, the *Gospel of Peter*, which abruptly begins its Synoptic-like narrative with Jesus' trial, and the *Gospel of the Hebrews*, which was originally a syncretistic Jewish-Christian, Matthew-like narrative of which only a few quotations survive in early church writings. The parallels between Mark and extracanonical Gospels are extensive and the debate over their chronological order and relationship has not been resolved.

---

trans. R. McL. Wilson; revised edn; Louisville: Westminster John Knox, 1991–2). On the production and circulation of early Christian texts, see Harry Y. Gamble, *Books and Readers in the Early Church: A History of Early Christian Texts* (New Haven: Yale University Press, 1995).

[68] John Dominic Crossan, *The Birth of Christianity: Discovering What Happened in the Years Immediately After the Execution of Jesus* (New York: HarperCollins, 1998); Helmut Koester, "Apocryphal and Canonical Gospels", *Harvard Theological Review* 73 (1980) 105–30; Ron Cameron, "Thomas, Gospel of", in *Anchor Bible Dictionary* (ed. David Noel Freedman; New York: Doubleday, 1992) 6.535–40.

The implication for historical Jesus research is that the earliest layer of sources, and possibly the most reliable, may or may not contain Mark. And if Mark is dependent on some of these sources, its value as a historical source becomes more limited.[69] This would suggest (as with Q) that earliest Christian thought is not necessarily represented in the canonical writings. Whether this is the case or not, a New Testament theology which is informed by this kind of history of religions research would be more sensitive to the dynamics of influence, development, syncretism and omission. It would also have to wrestle with the idea that inspiration and the authoritative status of the canonical writings is not an instantaneous event, but a process that leads to recognition. If this is the case, then most New Testament theologies would be rooted in Christian thought that is at least one generation removed from Jesus. This, in turn, again raises the question whether or not the historical Jesus was the founder of the Christian religion. Is it more correct to call him the first Christian, or did he remain a Jew who did not intend to start a new religion? Building a New Testament theology only on the canonical documents leaves the process incomplete and artificial. It is essential to recognize the maxim that religion must inform theology.

Conclusion

When the problems associated with the foundationalist position are viewed cumulatively, the confidence that was so pervasive in the history of New Testament theology in its search for a "pure" theology is, in my estimation, misplaced. If exegesis is equated with the historical-critical approach, it cannot be the sole instrument for formulating a unified New Testament theology. Exegetical practice since the Enlightenment has actually succeeded in demonstrating the reverse. While on the one hand it has shown theological coherence among the writings, on the other it has equally demonstrated that reconstruction leads to fragmentation. Moreover, exegesis has shown itself incapable of establishing a theory of interpretation. It is ordered to reconstruction and data-mining, not meaning. While normativity is important to foundationalists, their hesitation towards the imposing of external ideas or paradigms onto the New Testament for fear of losing the revelation contained in the writings comes at the expense of relevance.

When the foundationalist position is subjected to literary criticisms and theories that are often associated with postmodernity, an equally challenging problem arises. Since the modernist ideas about history, language, authorial intention and objective truth claims—all of which are still advocated by

---

[69] A helpful list of parallels between Mark and extracanonical sources is provided by Evans, *Mark 8.27–16.20*, xxxii–xxxiv.

foundationalists—are being understood in new ways in the humanities and social sciences (especially the study of religion), foundationalists are left in the unenviable position of arguing for their position against the informed consensus of these respective fields.

If the discipline of New Testament theology is to survive and contribute to both the Church and our broader pluralistic culture, its quest for relevance needs to be approached not from the bottom up, but from the top down in a dialectical way.

Discussion questions

1. Discuss the implications of Rudolf Bultmann's observation that "The worldview within which the New Testament was written is not necessarily Christian."
2. Is an objectively verifiable New Testament theology possible? If so, what would constitute evidence?
3. In the formation of a New Testament theology, is it possible to avoid the proverbial hermeneutical circle, which is the attempt to prove what one already knows to be true?
4. Foundationalist approaches to New Testament theology have utilized historical-criticism as the method of choice for uncovering what the original text meant. But is historical criticism simply a data-mining tool or can it be used to uncover the relevance of the New Testament?
5. What is the relationship between a historical fact and its meaning?
6. Should the religious language in the New Testament be understood propositionally and literally or metaphorically and imaginatively?

PART TWO

New Testament theology in practice

3

New Testament theology and the history of biblical interpretation

No introduction to the discipline of New Testament theology is ever complete without an explanation of its origins. Situating the rise of the discipline within its cultural context is an effective means of appreciating the aims and issues that have emerged since. There is no shortage of excellent historical surveys of the discipline. A few are very detailed in tracing the discipline's practitioners and development, such as Heikki Räisänen's *Beyond New Testament Theology*, Leonhard Goppelt's two volume *Theology of the New Testament* and Gerhard Hasel's *New Testament Theology*.[1] The last two remain an invaluable Who's Who encyclopedic resource. Since most surveys have their niche, my objective in this chapter is to survey the history of biblical interpretation with the purpose of developing an appreciation for how truly unique New Testament theology is in the history of Christian biblical interpretation and how it has been subversive in relation to established ecclesiastical power structures.

Many of the current issues in New Testament theology have their roots in the distant past, so understanding its foundational context as a branch of nascent critical biblical studies is vital. Unfortunately, the broader field of biblical studies is often misunderstood and mistrusted by many Christians who perceive the academic study of scripture as having a counterproductive

---

[1] Heikki Räisänen, *Beyond New Testament Theology: A Story and a Programme* (2nd edn; London: SCM Press, 2000); Leonhard Goppelt, *Theology of the New Testament. Volume 1: The Ministry of Jesus in its Theological Significance* (trans. John E. Alsup; ed. Jürgen Roloff; Grand Rapids: Eerdmans, 1981); *Theology of the New Testament. Volume 2: The Variety and Unity of the Apostolic Witness to Christ* (trans. John E. Alsup; ed. Jürgen Roloff; Grand Rapids: Eerdmans, 1982); Gerhard F. Hasel, *New Testament Theology: Basic Issues in the Current Debate* (Grand Rapids: Eerdmans, 1978); Robert Morgan, "Introduction: The Nature of New Testament Theology", in *The Nature of New Testament Theology* (ed. Robert Morgan; Studies in Biblical Theology 2.25; London: SCM Press, 1973) 1–67.

agenda to the enhancement and understanding of faith. Appreciating the common origins of biblical studies and New Testament theology goes a long way in curtailing the overall confusion and potential hostility or intolerance towards their current practice. While some biblical scholars have advocated an anti-Christian agenda, the overwhelming majority in the last two hundred years have attempted to make Christianity relevant to an ever-changing world.

In the previous chapters, I have mentioned several times in passing that the discipline of New Testament theology began in the Enlightenment period and that its effects have been with us ever since. In order to convey how transformative the Enlightenment truly was for the interpretation of the Bible, the first part of this chapter traces various approaches to the Bible before the Enlightenment.

Before the Enlightenment

Interpretation in early Judaism and Christianity

For much of Christian history there was no biblical or New Testament theology as we know it today. Earliest Christianity as it is expressed in the New Testament writings developed its theological thinking through interpretative methods that were very different from current approaches in New Testament theology. Since most of the earliest Christians were Jewish, common interpretative methods circulating in the Judaisms of the first century transitioned seamlessly into nascent Christianity. Early Jewish interpretation is most well known for its midrashic approaches. The aim of *midrash* (Hebrew for "commentary")—which is related to the verb *darash*, meaning "to search"—was essentially to contemporize the scriptures so that they might suit the needs of the present situation, be it legal, political, cultural or religious. The underlying assumption was that scripture conveys a fluidity of meaning for all generations and for all circumstances of life. Some midrashic interpretations appear to have established themselves as favoured community readings and became inseparable from their scriptural sources. Midrashic readings did not merely interpret scripture to legitimate new ideas like proof-texting might be done today, but shifts in popular socio-religious identity and practice were at times actually incorporated into varied versions of scripture.

Midrash was practiced in two general ways called *Halakhah* and *Aggadah*. *Halakhah* ("way of going"), or *Halakhic* midrash, refers to interpretations of scripture that are oriented towards meeting legal or ethical concerns. These often take the form of minor explanations or adjustments of biblical law. For example, the Septuagint (LXX), which is a Greek translation of the Hebrew scriptures that was used more than any other version by the New Testament writers, contains numerous legal changes that presumably reflect the social conditions among the Jewish populace in Alexandria between the third and first centuries BCE. Assuming that the Septuagint translators used a Hebrew source that reflects the Masoretic Text (MT), which is the standard source for the Jewish Bible and the Christian Old Testament in Western Christianity, consider the following comparisons that reflect existing social shifts in legal thinking.[2] The first example is a familiar text to most people:

> MT Gen. 2.2: And *on the seventh day* God finished his work that he had done, and he rested on the seventh day from all his work which he had done.[3]

> LXX Gen. 2.2: And God finished the works that he had done *on the sixth day* and rested on the seventh day.

The slight shift from God finishing his work on the seventh day to the sixth day may well reflect a more established Sabbath in Alexandrian Judaism. As an aside, the NIV translators use "by the seventh day" which creatively harmonize both versions, though they do not reflect either one.

The second example expresses shifts in ritual legal practice enforced by the religio-political establishment. Lev. 24.7 concerns weekly bread offering, whereas Deut. 26.12 advocates a tithing that can be compared to our taxation system:

> MT Lev. 24.7: and you shall put pure frankincense with each row

> LXX Lev. 24.7: and you will add to the offering pure frankincense and salt

> MT Deut. 26.12: When you have finished paying all the tithe of your increase in the third year, the year of tithing, then you shall give it to the Levite, to the stranger, to the orphan and to the widow, that they may eat in your towns and be satisfied.

> LXX Deut. 26.12: When you have finished paying all the tithe of the produce of your land in the third year, you shall give the second tithe to the Levite...

There are numerous examples like this spread throughout the legal texts in early Judaism.

---

[2] Examples are taken from Anthony Tyrrell Hanson, *The Living Utterances of God: The New Testament Exegesis of the Old* (London: Darton, Longman and Todd, 1983) 11–18.
[3] Revised Standard Version.

Early Christian Jews like Mark, Matthew and Paul express even greater shifts in legal and ethical thinking.[4] In Mark 7, for instance, Jesus is portrayed quite radically when he challenges prevailing biblical dietary laws by pronouncing that all food is clean. In Matthew, one need not look any further than the sermon on the mount (chapters 5–7) to see legal and moral shifts, though they are not to the same degree as in Mark. And in Paul's rethinking about Judaism in, say, Galatians, he radically calls for an abandonment of circumcision for Gentile converts to Christianity, which he regards as the fulfilment of Judaism and the culmination of Israel's history. This shift is particularly radical because it takes aim at Jewish identity as it is rooted in the establishment of a perennial covenant between God and Abraham, Israel's founding patriarch. Genesis 17.14 uses the words of God to establish clearly the boundary that divides God's people from the rest when it stipulates, "But an uncircumcised male who is not circumcised in the flesh of his foreskin, that person shall be cut off from his people; he has broken my covenant."

Aggadah ("narrative"), or *Aggidic* midrash, likewise aims to make scripture relevant to its new social contexts, but instead of addressing legal and moral issues it explains scriptural narratives through legendary enlargements or even the rewriting of scripture itself in a kind of expanded paraphrase. In a sense, it engages in the retelling of biblical stories events, or persons with a theological, ethical, or political aim. For example, the *Testament of the Twelve Patriarchs* (second–first century BCE) is regarded as a midrash on Genesis that intends to make the case for Levi as the ruling tribe during the reign of John Hyrcanus. Likewise, *Jubilees* (second century BCE) rewrites Genesis and Exodus as a protest against the Hasmonean princes. *Joseph and Aseneth* (first century BCE–second century CE), on the other hand, is a lengthy expansion on a single verse, explaining how it came to be that a righteous Israelite like Joseph could ever have married Aseneth, the daughter of Potiphera, the pagan Priest of On (Gen 41.45).

Examples also abound on a smaller scale where specific texts are newly explained. For instance, in contrast to Genesis, *Wisdom* (first century BCE) represents Jacob as an innocent character when he fled after deceiving his brother over obtaining the blessing from Isaac. *Wisdom* 10.10 reads, "Wisdom rescued from troubles those who served her. When a righteous man fled from his brother's wrath, she guided him on straight paths; she showed him the kingdom of God, and gave him knowledge of angels; she prospered him in his labours, and increased the fruit of his toil." One of the tendencies in *Aggadic* midrash is to cast characters from the distant biblical past in the role of saints. Especially helpful examples of *Aggadah* are found

---

[4] A highly recommended introduction to early Christian interpretation is Craig A. Evans, *Ancient Texts for New Testament Studies: A Guide to the Background Literature* (Peabody: Hendrickson, 2005).

in the Targums (lit. "translations"), which were Aramaic paraphrases of the Jewish scriptures written down as early as the second century CE. One such Targumic expansion is Gen. 22.10 which concerns the near sacrifice of Isaac by Abraham. The italicized portion is the midrashic enlargement.

MT Gen. 22.9-10:
Then they came to the place of which God had told him; and Abraham built the altar there and arranged the wood, and bound his son Isaac and laid him on the altar, on top of the wood. [10] Abraham stretched out his hand and took the knife to slay his son. [11] But the angel of the Lord called to him from heaven and said, "Abraham, Abraham!" And he said, "Here I am."

Targum Neofiti Gen. 22.10:
Abraham stretched out his hand and took the knife to slay his son *Isaac. Isaac answered and said to his father Abraham: "Father, tie me well lest I kick you and your offering be rendered unfit and we be thrust down into the pit of destruction in the world to come." The eyes of Abraham were on the eyes of Isaac and the eyes of Isaac were scanning the angels on high. Abraham did not see them. In that hour a Bath Qol* [voice from heaven] *came forth from the heavens and said: "Come, see two singular persons who are in my world; one slaughters and the other is being slaughtered. The one who slaughters does not hesitate and he who is being slaughtered stretches out his neck."*[5]

Many have observed that some of the Gospel accounts are best explained as *Aggadic* midrash as well. If we assume the common view that Matthew and Luke independently used Mark along with the hypothetical source Q, then some of the additions and expansions in Matthew and Luke can potentially be midrashic. For instance, only Matthew and Luke contain the infancy accounts of Jesus. Though they differ in numerous places, they both extensively use scripture and cognate traditions to explain theologically the meaning of Jesus' humble birth for the good of humanity.[6] At the other end of the story, the passion accounts in Matthew and Luke are much more extensive than that of Mark, again containing numerous scriptural citations and allusions that are used to explain the significance of Jesus' suffering, death and resurrection. In Q, which would have consisted of a list of sayings by Jesus much like the *Gospel of Thomas*, there is no passion account. When later writings contain expansions that heavily rely on scriptural quotations

---

[5] Translation is from Martin McNamara, *Targum Neofiti 1: Genesis* (The Aramaic Bible 1A; Collegeville: Liturgical Press, 1992) 117–18.

[6] On the midrashic function of the infancy account in Matthew, see Robert H. Gundry, *Matthew: A Commentary on His Handbook for a Mixed Church under Persecution* (Grand Rapids: Eerdmans, 1994, 2nd edn).

or allusions, scholars debate the compositional sequence. Which came first in the composing of the Gospel, the quotation from scripture or the Gospel narrative that contains it? In other words, were some of the sections in the Gospels, like the infancy accounts and portions of the passion accounts, composed as enlargements of scripture, or were the scripture texts embedded after the accounts were written? Some of the texts point more clearly in one direction than the other. For instance, John's passion account reflects the former. Unlike the Synoptic tradition wherein Jesus dies on Passover, John has Jesus die on the day of preparation for Passover at the same time that the sacrificial animals were beginning to be slaughtered (18.28; 19.14). In addition, John connects Jesus' death to the preparatory mandates in Exodus. Commentators usually explain that the summary of Jesus' execution in John 19.36 ("For these things came to pass to fulfil the Scripture, 'no bone of his shall be broken'") is taken from Exod. 12.46 ("You shall not break any of its bones") which is part of a list of regulations for the preparation of the paschal victim.[7] For John, since Jesus was the Passover sacrifice, it is no surprise that in the narrative he should die at the same time as the sacrificial animals. As Frank Kermode puts it, "the typology came to be understood as chronology."[8] John's midrash is not unique to early Christian thought. The same idea is found in Paul's interpretation of Jesus' death when he writes in 1 Cor. 5.7 that "Christ our Passover also has been sacrificed."

A third common form of interpretation was called *pesher* ("meaning"). Unlike the seamless expansions and alterations of scripture in *Aggadah* and *Halakhah*, *pesher* distinguishes itself as an explicit commentary on scripture. This form of interpretation is commonly associated with the Essenes, a Jewish group that is usually connected with the Qumran community and the writing of the Dead Sea Scrolls. The Essenes at Qumran were an apocalyptic sect that awaited the imminent coming of God and the accompanying final battle between the righteous and the wicked, or, as they put it, the sons of light and the sons of darkness. The primary aim of *pesher* was to show how scripture points prophetically to the end of the age in which the Essenes believed themselves to be. *Pesher* commentary operated from the perspective of two principles: (1) prophetic scripture refers to the end times, and (2) the present era is the end times. Thus persons and events in the scriptures were connected, sometimes in an allegorical fashion, with persons and events contemporaneous with the Qumran community. Since Moses and David, for example, were prophetic figures for the Essenes, all of their teachings were believed to be ultimately directed at the Qumran community. The following example is typical. In a *pesher* on Habakkuk (1QpHab), the original lament and outrage by the prophet

---

[7] E.g. Brown, *The Gospel According to John XIII–XXI* (The Anchor Bible 29A; New York: Doubleday, 1970) 555–8.
[8] Frank Kermode, *The Genesis of Secrecy: On the Interpretation of Narrative* (Cambridge, MA: Harvard University Press, 1979) 93.

at the destruction caused by the Chaldeans is interpreted by the Essene commentator several centuries later as a lament and outrage directed at the Temple establishment. The reference to the Chaldeans becomes a code word for the *Kittim*—which many scholars understand as the Romans—who are viewed as the instruments of God's judgement against the corrupt Temple leadership in Jerusalem.

> MT Hab. 1.4, 6:
> So the law becomes slack
>   and justice never prevails.
> The wicked surround the righteous—
>   therefore judgment comes forth perverted...
> For I am rousing the Chaldeans,
>   that fierce and impetuous nation,
> who march through the breadth of the earth
>   to seize dwellings not their own.
>
> 1QpHab. 1.10–13:
> "Therefore Law declines, [and true judgment never comes forth" (Hab 1.4a). This means] that they rejected God's Law [... "For the wicked man hems in] the righteous man" (Hab 1.4b). [The "wicked man" refers to the Wicked Priest, and "the righteous man"] is the Teacher of Righteousness.
>
> 1QpHab. 2.10–15:
> "For I am now about to raise up the Chaldeans, that br[utal and reckle]ss people" (Hab. 1.6a). This refers to the Kittim, w[ho are] swift and mighty in war, annihilating [many people, and ...] in the authority of the Kittim and [the wicked...] and have no faith in the laws of [God].

The New Testament writers were no strangers to *pesher* interpretation, but it is not used nearly as often as *Aggadah* and *Halakhah*. When it does occur, it tends more towards allegory. Unlike at Qumran where the fulfilment is found in the sect, in early Christianity it is found in the person of Jesus, around whom the early Christian sects were formed. Paul's interpretation of Deut. 30.12-14 in Rom. 10:6-8 is a case in point.

> Deut. 30.11-14:
> Surely, this commandment that I am commanding you today is not too hard for you, nor is it too far away. It is not in heaven, that you should say, "Who will go up to heaven for us, and get it for us so that we may hear it and observe it?" Neither is it beyond the sea, that you should say, "Who will cross to the other side of the sea for us, and get it for us so that we may hear it and observe it?" No, the word is very near to you; it is in your mouth and in your heart for you to observe.

Rom. 10.5-9:
Moses writes concerning the righteousness that comes from the law that "the person who does these things will live by them." But the righteousness that comes from faith says, "DO NOT SAY IN YOUR HEART, 'WHO WILL ASCEND INTO HEAVEN?'" (that is, to bring Christ down) "or 'WHO WILL DESCEND INTO THE ABYSS?'" (that is, to bring Christ up from the dead). But what does it say? "THE WORD IS NEAR YOU, ON YOUR LIPS AND IN YOUR HEART" (that is, the word of faith that we proclaim); because if you confess with your lips that Jesus is Lord and believe in your heart that God raised him from the dead, you will be saved.

In comparison to our own day, those who have read Hal Lindsay's bestseller *The Late Great Planet Earth* or watched the television evangelist Jack van Impe (both being representative of contemporary doomsday prophets who read the Bible in light of the latest headlines) should find *pesher* sounding very familiar—and indeed they would be correct to do so.

Midrashic and *pesher* interpretation in early Judaism and Christianity should not be thought of as falsehoods or lies as we use the categories today. While some of the expansions of scripture, especially in *Aggadic* midrash, may well have been recognized as "stretches" of past stories, especially among dissenting groups, they were by and large believed to be factual and meaningful. The use of the term "ancient fiction" also does not capture the midrashic aim, for fictional narratives in the ancient world were not versions of prior events or factual persons. In short, unlike midrash, they were not referential.[9] The aim of midrash was simply to make scripture relevant to ever changing circumstances and culture. Since scripture was believed to be God's revelation, it was able to address every new situation.

When compared to the breadth of early Judaism, the most distinctive feature of early Christian interpretation of scripture, and hence the formulation of new theological thinking, was its Christological focus.[10] In other words, the basic early Christian hermeneutic was that the Jewish scriptures pointed to, foretold or in some sense illumined Jesus' identity, teachings and actions. Typology has often been viewed as the key hermeneutical principle whereby Jesus is assumed to parallel and fulfil prominent biblical figures and events. In short, it was believed that what God did in the past, through figures like Moses, Israel and David, he does in the life of Jesus, though in a complete sense. Theology at this point was not derived from a historical or a literalist reading of scripture, but out of a concern for what those scriptures meant in light of the Christ event.

---

[9] David Konstan, "The Invention of Fiction", in *Ancient Fiction and Early Christian Narrative* (Society of Biblical Literature Symposium Series 6; ed. Ronald F. Hock, J. Bradley Chance and Judith Perkins; Atlanta: Scholars Press, 1998) 8.
[10] Donald Juel, *Messianic Exegesis: Christological Interpretation of the Old Testament in Early Christianity* (Philadelphia: Fortress Press, 1988).

In addition to the numerous quotations and allusions from the scriptures in the New Testament, many of which contain introductory formulas that draw direct parallels between Jesus and the borrowed texts, we are fortunate to have preserved a few explicit references to the Christological hermeneutic. For example, in John's Gospel, during an exchange with antagonistic Jewish religious leaders (called "the Jews"), Jesus validates his superior authority by claiming that the scriptures point to him. In 5.39 he tells the leaders, "You search the scriptures because you think that in them you have eternal life; it is these that testify about me", and further in 5.46, Jesus reiterates, "For if you believed Moses, you would believe me, for he wrote about me." These statements provide clear insight into how the Johannine Christians, who claimed to be guided by the Holy Spirit (literally the *paracletos* promised by Jesus in chapters 14–16), appropriated scripture in the formation of their theological thinking. Another example of a window into early Christian interpretation is found in Luke's story of the travellers on the Emmaus road and their encounter with the risen Christ. When Jesus is eventually recognized by the two travellers, the narrator summarizes, "Then beginning with Moses and with all the prophets, he explained to them the things concerning himself in all the scriptures" (Luke 24.27). A third example is found in 1 Cor. 15.3-4, which has often been regarded as part of a very early creedal statement. Here Paul connects the gospel of salvation from sin with the scriptures, which he understands to foreshadow or foretell the means through which the good news is accomplished, namely the death and resurrection of Jesus. He writes, "For I delivered to you as of first importance what I also received, that Christ died for our sins according to the scriptures, and that he was buried, and that he was raised on the third day according to the scriptures." It is not at all clear to which text Paul is referring or whether he has in mind the entire biblical story, but it is unquestionably clear that the ultimate purpose of the scriptures is to convey that Jesus is the Christ.

What is important to notice is that the earliest Christians were not concerned with literal interpretations or historical reconstructions of their scriptures, but with the way in which the scriptures provided meaning to a newly experienced spiritual reality. How the Christological hermeneutic came to be formed is a matter of anthropological and sociological debate, but phenomenologically early Christianity was founded on the claim that Jesus was raised from the dead. Claims of visions of Christ and experiential encounters with the risen Christ in the post-biblical period abound, especially in the context of commemorative meals.[11] Scripture texts were frequently taken out of their original literary contexts as if they were

---

[11] See the illuminating study of Jesus visions, past and present, in Phillip H. Wiebe, *Visions of Christ: Direct Encounters from the New Testament to Today* (New York: Oxford University Press, 1998).

isolated units that collectively addressed a climactic Christology within a salvation history. The same can be said about the early Christian interpretations of Jesus' life and teachings.

A deliberate separation between faith and historical fact, salvation history and history, theology and history, or faith and reason as we have come to know these in the post-Enlightenment age appear to have been nonexistent. If anything, theology and what we call history appear to have been unified in a way that the former gave direction to the latter. That which occurred in the past was divinely orchestrated to give shape and meaning to the present because it was believed that the purpose and goal of history has been revealed. Like their contemporaries in other religions, the early Christians developed their theological thinking from the perspective of faith and imaginative retellings of the past and not the reconstruction of events. Truth was baptized by present meaning, not the critical evaluation of the past. In the Gospels, for example, the pre-Easter Jesus is combined with the post-Easter Jesus. Thus in the narratives he is identified as Messiah, son of God and Lord, which are titles that would have emerged organically from the Easter experiences. Jesus' sayings, especially in John, have been viewed by many modern scholars as reflections of beliefs among early Christians who would have imaginatively appropriated and contemporized them to meet specific ends. Historical events were not omitted, but they were metaphorized for the primary purpose of proclaiming and strengthening faith that the crucified Jesus was raised from the dead and will come in glory to judge the world.

Early Christian groups that are not represented in the New Testament were no different in appropriating the scriptures and the traditions of Jesus for their own theological benefit, though some who had a disdain for the God of Israel because he differed morally from Jesus (e.g. Marcion) or because he created the material world which was considered to be the curse of fallen spirit beings (i.e. Gnostic groups) had little reason to use the scriptures apart from in an antagonist way.

Interpretation in the patristic and medieval era

During the Patristic and medieval periods, Christian interpretations of both Old and New Testaments followed their predecessors in not developing theologies derived from historicized or literal readings. This period of Christian history is often associated with doctrinal formulation and their related crises and controversies. It is also marked by a higher degree of influence from Hellenistic philosophy, which is not unusual, given that the Christian intellectual centres were now in Romanized urban settings outside of Palestine. Scripture was usually appropriated for doctrinal ends and regularly taken out of its original literary and historical contexts. For the Church Fathers, the present meaning of scripture and its relation to the future had as its starting point the literal sense, which concerned itself with the text's past ("original") meaning, but was not governed by it. The dominant non-literal meaning was always related to what can be called the proto-orthodox confession of faith which had at its centre the paschal mystery of Christ's life, death, resurrection, and his imparting of new life upon all followers who in turn form the communal life of the Church. These two elements, the mystery of Christ and the communion of the one Church, which together formed the life of salvation, served as the inspired precondition for the discovery of deeper meaning in the inspired texts. Since the life of salvation was believed to cover the entire span of human existence, scripture was applicable to all facets of life.[12]

In the early monastic communities, the hermeneutic was likewise conditioned by the culture—often the solitude of the desert—but unlike the Fathers' emphasis on right belief, monasticism was guided by an intense drive towards perfecting the life of holiness. Certain social pronouncements, like the call to sell everything and give the proceeds to the poor (Matt. 19.21) and the admonition to not harbour anger past sunset (Eph. 4.25), were pivotal hermeneutical keys that provided meaning to the rest of scripture.[13]

Since both the text and the interpreter were believed to be inspired, the prevalent use of potentially unfettered allegory was controlled by the so-called "common faith" (*Quod ubique, quod semper, quod ab omnibus creditum est,* "What has been believed everywhere, always, and by all").[14] As a result, dissenters from the "common faith" who argued for their theological positions from a more literal sense, could easily be challenged and opposed, as we see among proponents of the Alexandrian school, such as Origen, Ambrose, Hilary and Augustine.

A helpful example of interpretation that was guided by doctrinal concerns associated with the "common faith" is the phrase "God is spirit" in John 4.24. The phrase functions in the Gospel's literary setting as a contrast between the new worship which the Johannine Jesus institutes and the old worship which is legitimized by sacred places, namely Jerusalem for the Jews and Mount Gerizim for the Samaritans. But during the controversies of the second and third centuries, the phrase was used to demonstrate the divine substance of the Father and the divine element in

---

[12] Jaroslav Broz, "From Allegory to the Four Senses of Scripture Hermeneutics of the Church Fathers and of the Christian Middle Ages", in *Philosophical Hermeneutics and Biblical Exegesis* (ed. Petr Pokorny and Jan Roskovec; WUNT 153; Tübingen: Mohr Siebeck, 2002) 304–7. On the principles of Patristic theology and hermeneutics, see Angelo Di Berardino and Basil Studer, eds, *History of Theology 1: The Patristic Period* (trans. M. J. O'Connell; Collegeville, MN: Liturgical Press, 1997).

[13] Douglas Burton-Christie, *The Word in the Desert: Scripture and the Quest for Holiness in Early Christian Monasticism* (Oxford: Oxford University Press, 1993) 18–23.

[14] Edgar Krentz, *The Historical-Critical Method* (Guides to Biblical Scholarship: Philadelphia: Fortress Press, 1975) 6–7.

the Son. Tertullian, influenced by Stoic materialism, argued that the "spirit" is the total corporeal substance of the Father within which the Son participated (*Adversus Praxean* 7.8; 8.4; 9.2). Together with texts like John 10.30 ("I and the Father are one"), Tertullian argued that the Father and Son, each separate persons, share in the same substance. Origen, on the other hand, interpreted both texts in a dynamic manner, arguing that "God is spirit" because he leads to and brings about new life (*De Principiis* I 1.1–2; *Commentary on John* 13.21–3) and that the unity of the Father and the Son refers to their common purpose or will.[15] The term "spirit" (*pneuma*) was so charged with philosophical baggage that it easily led to readings of New Testament texts that were novel. During the Arian controversy, when attention turned to the Holy Spirit, John 4.24 was used to demonstrate the divinity of the third hypostasis of the Trinity.[16]

Contrary to several contemporary historical critics who have faulted the Fathers for reckless and uncontrolled readings of scripture, Patristic exegesis was not an exercise simply in theological fantasy nor did it lack a method.[17] Much like their apostolic predecessors—who, by the way, are rarely faulted for their method—Patristic interpreters of the Bible assumed that revelation was not restricted to historical events and that scripture was not regarded as a surviving record of those events that needed to be reconstructed. In other words, scripture was not viewed as the means to truth; it was the truth because it was assumed to be the language of God. For many Fathers, like Origen and Gregory of Nyssa, the meaning of scripture was considered to be the door to eternity.[18] Thus interpretation was a spiritual encounter that involved the subjection of the intellect and the emotions. Origen is typical when he writes that the reader who subjects himself to scripture will discover that "his mind and his feelings will be touched by a divine breath and he will recognize that the words he is reading are not utterances of man but the language of God".[19] Origen was convinced that scripture was able to enlighten people at various stages of spiritual development.

Interpretations varied depending on which side of a theological controversy one was defending. It is not unusual to find the same text used on both sides of an argument or controversy in order to make a mutually

---

[15] Manlio Simonetti, *Biblical Interpretation in the Early Church: An Historical Introduction to Patristic Exegesis* (trans. John A. Hughes; Edinburgh: T & T Clark, 1994) 122, 124, 129. Simonetti cites Tertullian, *Adversus Praxean* 7.8; Athanasius, *De Sententia Dionysii* 15; Ps.-Athan. *Ctr. Apoll.* I 6.
[16] Simonetti (*Biblical Interpretation in the Early Church*, 122) cites Epiphanius, *Ancoratus* 7.70; Basil, *Adversus Eunomium* III 3; *De Spiritu Sancto* 18.47; 19.48.
[17] J. J. O'Keefe and R. R. Reno, *Sanctified Vision: An Introduction to Early Christian Interpretation of the Bible* (Baltimore: Johns Hopkins University Press, 2005) 114–39.
[18] Broz, "From Allegory to the Four Senses of Scripture Hermeneutics of the Church Fathers and of the Christian Middle Ages", 307.
[19] Origen, *On First Principles*, 4.1.6. Taken from O'Keefe and Reno, *Sanctified Vision*, 116.

exclusive point. In addition to finding supporting scripture texts, doctrinal rivals attempted to re-appropriate each other's favourite texts in an effort to weaken their opponents' positions.[20] One of the most influential crises that led to the development of an elaborate interpretive agenda was the Marcionite controversy in the second century. Marcion, a wandering Gentile Christian prophet and philosopher, maintained that Paul is the truest Apostle because his preaching sets the gospel of Christ over and against the Jewish Law. For Marcion and his followers, there were immense differences between what Jesus preached and what the Jewish scriptures teach, especially concerning the nature of God. Marcion argued, using historical and moral persuasion, that the God of the Old Testament is vengeful and violent. He punishes disobedience, demands retribution, slaughters the enemies of Israel and commands his people to make slaves of women and children from among the peoples they conquer. The God of Jesus, on the other hand, extends mercy and forgiveness even to Gentiles, and commands people to love their enemies. In addition to influencing early formations of canonical lists of Christian writings among Marcion's many opponents, proto-orthodox Christian groups were also forced to respond by providing their own interpretations of the scripture texts that Marcion used. The hermeneutical divergences became an important factor in the demise of the Antiochan School of interpretation, which prided itself on literal reading.[21] At the same time it spawned the development and popularity of the Alexandrian School, which was known for its allegorical readings. The latter would win the day for the next thirteen hundred years.

Often called the "fourfold sense", appeal to the multi-layered or polysemous meaning of scripture became a broadly established interpretative practice until the Reformation period when it was challenged for its lack of attention to the so-called "original" meaning intended by the New Testament writers.[22] One of the overarching features inherent in the polysemous approach was the theological unification of the New Testament—and the whole Bible for that matter. Its engagement with scripture was not unlike what is found in most religions that make use of canonical texts, namely the process of legitimizing existing belief on the

---

[20] Simonetti, *Biblical Interpretation in the Early Church*, 126.
[21] The Antiochan school is well known for its literal exegetical approach through the work of scholars like Theodore of Mopsuestia, but it did not deny that scripture had a spiritual sense as well. Its reputation for literalism emerged in part from its need to respond to the monophysite belief that Christ had only one nature (divine), as opposed to the Chalcedonian council which argued for two natures (divine and human).
[22] The term "polysemous meaning", as Northrop Frye uses it (*Words with Power: Being a Second Study of The Bible and Literature* [New York: Viking Penguin, 1990] 16), allows for more breadth than the usual reference to the fourfold senses of scripture. In addition to being called the "fourfold sense", it was also called the "four understandings", "four ruling principles", and "four rules of interpretation." See Henri de Lubac, *Medieval Exegesis. Volume 1: The Four Senses of Scripture* (trans. Mark Sebanc; Grand Rapids: Eerdmans, 1998) 16–17.

basis of an authoritative past. Since the ultimate author was believed to be the Holy Spirit, the scriptures were assumed to be full of divine mystery, transcending the surface meaning, and thus had the ability to communicate various aspects of truth. At the same time, the single divine author allowed for the belief that the scriptures are ultimately unified in their message. The unity of even the most divergent texts lay in the subjectivity of the interpretative approaches. Ironically, the Reformation and post-Reformation movements that challenged the validity of Catholic polysemous interpretations in favour of a single, unified, historical and objective interpretation only succeeded in establishing principles that would eventually lead to the fragmentation of the scriptures and the Protestant movement itself, since no unified historical reading has yet been unanimously accepted.

The conclusions that have been consistently reached over the last fifty years—at least in philosophy, linguistic theory and literary studies—indicate that written texts are much more pliable and open to a plurality of meaning than was once thought. While we cannot retreat to the fourfold sense in the same way that it was understood in the ancient world, the contemporary idea of a polysemous meaning inherent in written texts has more in common with ancient hermeneutics than with the monolithic assumptions that have emerged in Protestantism between its inception and the Enlightenment period. In the following lengthy excerpt from a Pontifical Biblical Commission document, the Catholic Church, unsurprisingly, has recognized the insufficiency of a monolithic hermeneutic (often characterized as the historical-critical method) and capitalized on the similarities between ancient and modern polysemous hermeneutics.

> The contribution made by modern philosophical hermeneutics and the recent development of literary theory allows biblical exegesis to deepen its understanding of the task before it, the complexity of which has become ever more evident. Ancient exegesis, which obviously could not take into account modern scientific requirements, attributed to every text of Scripture several levels of meaning. The most prevalent distinction was that between the literal sense and the spiritual sense. Medieval exegesis distinguished within the spiritual sense three different aspects, each relating, respectively, to the truth revealed, to the way of life commended and to the final goal to be achieved. From this came the famous couplet of Augustine of Denmark (thirteenth century):
> *Littera gesta docet, quid credas allegoria,*
> *Moralis quid agas, quid speres anagogia.*[23]
> In reaction to the multiplicity of senses, historical-critical exegesis adopted, more or less overtly, the thesis of the one single meaning: a text

---

[23] Translated, *The literal teaches facts; the allegorical, what you are to believe; the moral, what you are to do; the anagogical, what you are to hope for.*

cannot have at the same time more than one meaning. All the effort of historical-critical exegesis goes into defining *the* precise sense of this or that text as seen within the circumstances in which it was produced.

But this thesis has now run aground on the conclusions of theories of language and of philosophical hermeneutics, both of which affirm that written texts are open to a plurality of meaning.[24]

Although Patristic approaches were deeply rooted in the earliest Christian interpretations of the Jewish scripture, their methods were not always the same. Church Fathers quantitatively enlarged the testimonies of the New Testament writers and developed their methods, primarily, as we already mentioned, for apologetic reasons.[25] Allegory became a primary hermeneutical principle. The most well known representative of its application was Origen, whose chief influence came not from the earliest Christian writers but from the broader Greek philosophical tradition, and particularly from Philo of Alexandria.[26] While Patristic interpretation as a whole assumed that the meaning of scripture extends beyond the literal sense, there was not a unanimous view on how many senses there actually were. Many, however, agreed on three or four—the second of which became the most popular among the Medieval successors of the Fathers, partly due to Augustine's preference for four in his influential work *De doctrina Christiana*.

Throughout the Patristic and Medieval periods the following four senses of scripture stemmed from six contextual principles which Jaroslav Broz, following the work of Innocenzo Gargano, summarizes as "(1) *Ecclesia legit et tenet* (The Church reads and preserves [the Scripture and its interpretation]); (2) the context of the community and its liturgy; (3) the context of tradition; (4) the sacramental dimension; (5) the simultaneity of mystery; and (6) the uniform character of the Bible."[27]

The first of the four senses of scripture is referred to as the "literal sense" because its aim is to disclose the historical meaning intended by the author.[28] But the conclusions need not necessarily correspond to a faith position or doctrine. Having said that, it should be kept in mind that at this point in time theology and exegesis were not clearly separated. Exegesis was the task

---

[24] Joseph A. Fitzmyer, "The Interpretation of the Bible in the Church", in *The Pontifical Biblical Commission Document: Text and Commentary* (Rome: Pontifical Biblical Commission, 1995) 117–18.

[25] Broz, "From Allegory to the Four Senses of Scripture Hermeneutics of the Church Fathers and of the Christian Middle Ages", 302–3.

[26] Broz, "From Allegory to the Four Senses of Scripture Hermeneutics of the Church Fathers and of the Christian Middle Ages", 305.

[27] Broz, "From Allegory to the Four Senses of Scripture Hermeneutics of the Church Fathers and of the Christian Middle Ages", 308.

[28] An excellent introduction to the fourfold sense of scripture is found in Michael Casey, *Sacred Reading: The Ancient Art of Lectio Divina* (Liguori: Triumph, 1996) 51–7.

of the theologian, and so the "historical" reading was already coloured by Christian faith.[29] Even though the term "literal" or "historical" was not always agreed upon, the common foundational hermeneutical premise was that the two Testaments were theologically unified because they were both written by the same divine author. The patristic and medieval interpreters considered this sense to be operative at the level of the intellect, and as such it formed the foundation for the other, more prescriptive, senses.

Like their early Protestant predecessors, many biblical scholars today who employ the historical-critical method limit their interpretations to the literal in search of *the* single "correct" meaning. In some ways the pre-Reformation understanding of the literal sense, as in the case of Augustine who is widely adopted by the Reformers, is closer to more recent literary approaches because it allowed for the possibility of more than one literal meaning. For example, contemporary scholars acknowledge that the Gospel of Mark may be guided by one of at least three possible programmatic verses at the beginning of the story. Some, like Joel Marcus, argue that the phrase "the way of the Lord", which is part of the quotation from Isa. 40.3 in Mark 1.3, guides the journey of Jesus.[30] Others, such as Craig Evans, argue that it is Mark's incipit (opening line or title: "The beginning of the gospel of Jesus Christ, the son of God...")[31] that provides the main clue to the evangelist's purpose. I have, for example, argued that Mark's story of Jesus is guided by Jesus' programmatic announcement in 1.15 that the kingdom of God has come.[32]

The other three senses are interpretative approaches that aim at retrieving the revelation that lies beneath the surface of the texts where rich spiritual insights for every generation abide. Without assuming any particular order, the first of these is the "Christological sense" which has also been called the "allegorical sense". As a conscious reading from a theological perspective, its aim was to find the Christian meaning of salvation in otherwise unrelated Old Testament texts for the purpose of building the believer's faith. Michael Casey speaks of this sense as an approach that is guided by the believer's response to experienced grace. The entire Bible is viewed as a story of humanity's fall and restoration. The Christological sense applies the experienced restoration in Christ to the entire story. Thus, for example, the disobedience of Adam and Eve in Genesis is read in the light of Easter.[33] For the modern reader the conclusions that were sometimes reached seem

---

[29] de Lubac, *Medieval Exegesis. Volume 1*, 67–74; Susan K. Wood, *Spiritual Exegesis and the Church in the Theology of Henri de Lubac* (Edinburgh: T & T Clark, 1998) 35–6.
[30] Joel Marcus, *The Way of the Lord: Christological Exegesis of the Old Testament in the Gospel of Mark* (Louisville: Westminster John Knox Press, 1992).
[31] Craig A. Evans, *Mark 8.27–16:20* (WBC 34B; Nashville: Thomas Nelson, 2001) lxxxi–xciii.
[32] Thomas R. Hatina, *In Search of a Context: The Function of Scripture in Mark's Narrative* (JSNTSup 232; SSEJC 8; London: Sheffield Academic Press, 2002).
[33] Casey, *Sacred Reading*, 57.

bizarre, but it should be kept in mind that similar allegorical readings of scripture are also found in some passages of the New Testament, such as Romans 4 and Hebrews 11.

The second of the theological senses is the "behavioural sense" or as it has been sometimes called the "tropological sense" (from the term "trope" which is used for a figure of speech that stands for something other than its literal meaning). This approach was prized among the monastic communities because its aim was to shape moral character so that it might be Christ-like. This reading of scripture focused on activating the conscience so that over time the believer embraced the need for daily reformation of character that would eventually guide his or her life by a desire to obey God. Casey points to several texts which were used to legitimize this approach, such as Luke 11.28 where Jesus says, "Blessed are those who hear God's word and keep it", and James 1.22-25 where the writer says that Christians are called to be "doers of the word and not hearers only".[34] More recently, Stephen Fowl has advocated a similar kind of interpretative approach. Ongoing frustration with the incessant need to uncover the "correct" interpretation among contemporary biblical scholars, Fowl argues against the assumption that written texts contain a single meaning. Instead, he proposes that interpretation should embrace the varied interests of readers. One such interest that he puts forth is a Christian one, asking "What is a Christian reading?" His response is that it is a reading that nurtures communal life among Christians and leads to increasingly deeper devotion to God.[35] Along similar lines of thinking, Edward Schillebeeckx asks whether orthopraxy (right-doing) provides meaning and validity to orthodoxy (right-thinking). He asks: Can we really understand the significance of the radical teaching of the Sermon on the Mount if we don't attempt to live it?[36]

The last of the theological senses is usually called the "mystical sense" or the "anagogical sense" because its aim is to lead the reader into a deeper life of communion with God through prayer. The reading process becomes the means through which the relationship with God is deepened because, as Casey writes, the word speaks to our spirit, penetrates the innermost level of our being to the point of our personhood, and "we become aware that the Word is no longer an intermediary between us and God; we experience the Word as person."[37] Some scripture texts, like John's Gospel, were viewed as particularly conducive to this deepest of the theological senses. Others have described the anagogical senses as a mystical reading from the

---

[34] Casey, *Sacred Reading*, 57–8.
[35] Stephen E. Fowl, "The Role of Authorial Intention in the Theological Interpretation of Scripture", in *Between Two Horizons: Spanning the New Testament and Systematic Theology* (ed. Joel B. Green and Max Turner; Grand Rapids: Eerdmans, 2000) 71–87.
[36] See Edward Schillebeeckx, *The Understanding of Faith: Interpretation and Criticism* (London: Sheed & Ward, 1974) 63–70.
[37] Casey, *Sacred Reading*, 57.

perspective of the final consummation of history in Christ when the Church will be unified. Henri de Lubac argues that there were two anagogical senses: one referring to the eschatological age when Christ returns, and the other referring to reading as contemplation. According to de Lubac, these were complementary, since the Church in heaven is connected to the Church on earth.[38]

Bringing the four senses together, a simple yet helpful example is the use of "Jerusalem" in the scriptures. According to the literal sense, Jerusalem refers to the physical city in the Middle East. According to the Christological sense, Jerusalem refers to Christ or the Church. According to the behavioural sense, it refers to the individual Christian. And according to the mystical sense, it refers to the eschatological kingdom of God, the New Jerusalem, which can already be experienced in part.[39] As an analogy, Casey uses the now famous illustration of three persons witnessing a man jumping off a bridge, originally used by Bishop Fulton Sheen in the 1950s (from the television series *Life is Worth Living*). In an attempt to interpret the event, the first witness, a physicist, speaks about the cause of death in relation to the victim's speed, acceleration and impact. The second witness is a psychologist who tries to explain the event in light of the victim's inner motivations and unconscious processes. Finally, the third witness, a priest, interprets the event through the prism of ethics and theology. The point of all this is that, as in the fourfold approach to scripture, different perspectives or questions affect how texts or events are interpreted.

Interpretation in the Reformation era

Contrary to popular belief, the Reformation was not unique in its emphasis that all theology should stem from scripture. Prior to the Reformation it was unanimously held that scripture, as the ground of all theology, contains all necessary revelation for salvation. On this issue, the main difference was a hermeneutical one. The Catholic Church overtly maintained that the scriptures needed to be interpreted by tradition because it is in the Church where one finds "Scripture's pithy core of mystical meaning hidden as by a veil beneath its letters".[40] Among the Reformers, the hermeneutic was guided by a search for the so-called "original" or historical/literal meaning since the Church was viewed as a fallible institution. In the process, of course, the Reformers could not free themselves of their own traditions and anti-Catholic bias.

Many of the interpretative approaches of the Reformers were practised in their expositional commentaries on biblical books, which seem to have

---

[38] Wood, *Spiritual Exegesis*, 44–5.
[39] Wood, *Spiritual Exegesis*, 25.
[40] de Lubac, *Medieval Exegesis. Volume 1*, 26.

been the preferred genre of the day. The commentaries primarily contained exegeses with a focus on textual study that aimed at the legitimization of Protestant theologies and political structures in contradistinction to the imperialism of Roman Catholicism. Other treatises that contained exegeses were also polemical. For example, many of Luther's non-commentary writings were written specifically against opponents such as Johann Eck, Ulrich Zwingli and Desiderius Erasmus.[41]

Also contrary to popular belief, many of the early Reformers were familiar with the Church Fathers and the medieval scholastic theologians and often included their interpretations alongside their own. The traditional drawing of clean lines of separation between the Reformation and either the Middle Ages or the Renaissance (as if it was a shift from pre-critical to critical exegesis), or between the Reformation and the subsequent era were not present in the sixteenth century. In his survey of recent literature on the history of biblical interpretation in the Reformation period, Richard Muller observes that it is impossible to locate a sudden shift in interpretative method in the Reformation period. Even though major Reformation figures like John Calvin and Martin Luther give primacy to the literal sense, their theological intrusions into exegesis have much more in common with Patristic and medieval biblical interpretation than with the Enlightenment or today's historical-critical approach. This is particularly evident in the postulate that the literal sense is guided by the intentions of the divine author. Since the primary author of scripture is God, the two Testaments are integrated, whereby the Old prefigures the New and the New fulfils the Old, which inevitably results in a literal sense that incorporates allegory.[42] For example, in Calvin's understanding of the literal sense, not only do the prophecies in the Hebrew scriptures coincide with Christ's announcement of the kingdom of God, they include prescription for Christian belief and morality. Thus his understanding of the literal sense includes elements that one finds in the fourfold sense, but it is not equated with it.[43]

Although there appears to be much more continuity between the Reformers and their predecessors than was once thought, at the same time the discontinuities that made the Reformation foundational for Protestantism should not be overlooked. One of the shifts that occurred

---

[41] Hans J. Hillerbrand, *The Protestant Reformation* (New York: Harper & Row, 1968) 87.
[42] Richard A. Muller, "Biblical Interpretation in the Era of the Reformation: The View From the Middle Ages", in *Biblical Interpretation in the Era of the Reformation: Essays Presented to David C. Steinmetz in Honor of His Sixtieth Birthday* (ed. Richard A. Muller and John L. Thompson; Grand Rapids: Eerdmans, 1996) 8–13. See also the essays in David C. Steinmetz, ed., *The Bible in the Sixteenth Century* (Second International Colloquy on the History of Biblical Exegesis in the Sixteenth Century; Durham NC: Duke University Press, 1990).
[43] Richard A. Muller, "The Hermeneutic of Promise and Fulfillment in Calvin's Exegesis of the Old Testament Prophecies of the Kingdom", in *The Bible in the Sixteenth Century* (ed. David C. Steinmetz; Second International Colloquy on the History of Biblical Exegesis in the Sixteenth Century; Durham NC: Duke University Press, 1990) 68–82.

was that the spiritual meaning of scripture was now assumed to be located entirely in the literal sense. Another shift was the assumption that the meaning of scripture could be distinguished (though rarely separated) from its traditional significance.[44] The shift to a literal and more independent exegesis was directly connected to the rise of philological, syntactical and rhetorical interests in Renaissance humanism. Although the Vulgate was not absent, the Reformation period was marked by a focus on studying the scriptures in their original languages.

By drawing on both the medieval and the Renaissance exegetical heritage, the Reformation provided a stimulating and fresh context wherein challenges to existing approaches to scripture could be synthesized with new readings or even rejected. None of this, however, could have been attained were it not for specific social factors. The first is the underlying political will of city-state princes in various regions of Europe to be emancipated from Rome. Political emancipation was directly connected with exegetical emancipation. And once the challenge to ecclesiastical authority was planted, it would never by uprooted. Independence of thought would find its initial climax in the Enlightenment. The second factor was the broad interest in recovering the classical and biblical past among humanist scholars, such as Erasmus. The third important factor was the invention of the printing press, which allowed for unprecedented dissemination of knowledge and more efficient means for political assembly, leading to broad and organized resistance movements.

Emancipation from the ecclesial authority of Rome came at a hefty price. The less uniform interpretations of the sixteenth and seventeenth centuries led to and legitimized severe conflicts within Protestantism that eventually led to divisions between state churches and non-state splinter churches. Another way of looking at these divisions (which is particularly helpful for understanding the subterranean foundations of New Testament theology) is to view them as conflicts between the Protestant dogmatic or scholastic theology of state churches and a fledgling "biblical theology" as it was initially forming itself among the Anabaptists (also called the Radical Reformers) in the sixteenth century, and then especially within German Pietism a century later. As the first Reformers sought to emancipate themselves from Rome by appealing to scripture, so the Anabaptists and the Pietists subsequently sought to emancipate themselves from the established Protestant Orthodoxy by likewise appealing to scripture, though they utilized a more literalist and proof-texting hermeneutic. For example, unlike the early Reformers, these splinter groups had little desire to include the Fathers, such as Augustine, into their apologetic. Also, unlike the Protestant state churches, the establishment of dogma was not a priority. Interpretation was controlled by the leaders of the splinter groups. Their

---

[44] Muller, "Biblical Interpretation in the Era of the Reformation", 14.

back-to-the-Bible approach had an immense influence on the emergence and legitimacy of "biblical theology" as a discipline. What was originally a reactionary proof-texting tool against the dogmatics of Protestant Orthodoxy eventually became its rival discipline. Anton Friedrich Büsching (1724–93) is often credited for fusing elements of Pietism and rationalism in elevating the new discipline, which he called "biblical theology", from its subsidiary level to a rival of the prevailing dogmatics.[45]

These early conflicts led to an escalation of divisions among newly formed denominations, each clinging to its own distinctives as the truest expression of faith. Since each group claimed to have the correct interpretation, each tended to separate itself from, and even demonize, groups who held rival interpretations. A familiar sociological pattern is at play in the formation of these new groups: a common opponent (be it a person, a practice or an idea) tends to bind members of any social group, and members of groups who have split from larger associations tend to lose their sense of objectivity and self-accountability. Power and control shifts. Since the Reformation, countless Protestant groups have forged statements or confessions of faith which function not only as formulations of "true theology", but also serve as identity boundary markers that distinguish them from their rivals. The result of these statements of faith historically has been that they excluded more people (i.e. other Christians) than they have included. Over the last two hundred years, we have also witnessed in North America the proliferation of sectarian Protestant groups, such as Jehovah's Witnesses, who have systematically rejected any value in religious pluralism or benefit in being accountable to mainstream Christianity.[46] Their emancipation, however, has led to social isolation and irrelevance.

Yet an interesting trend has been occurring in recent years among younger Evangelicals in North America. Church attendees under twenty-five years of age are beginning to distance themselves from denominational titles like Baptist, Mennonite, Evangelical Free or Church of God. From my discussions with hundreds of undergraduate Evangelical students over the past ten years, from various parts of North America, the vast majority does not find denominational affiliation significant. In fact, they innocently convey a hope of Christian unification and are more accepting not only of pluralism within Christianity, but pluralistic culture in general.

---

[45] Hasel, *New Testament Theology*, 20. Anton Friedrich Büsching, *Dissertatio inauguralis exhibens epitomen theologiae e solis literis sacris concinnatae* (Göttingen, 1756); idem, *Epitome Theologiae* (Lemgo, 1757); idem, *Gedanken von der Beschaffenheit und dem Vorzug der biblisch-dogmatischen Theologie vor der scholastischen* (Lembgo, 1758).
[46] On religious sectarianism, see Bryan R. Wilson, *The Social Dimensions of Sectarianism: Sects and New Religious Movements in Contemporary Society* (Oxford: Clarendon Press, 1990).

The Enlightenment period

The Enlightenment period, or as it is sometimes called the "age of reason", the "age of science", or the "age of modernity", is the cradle for New Testament theology—not to mention a host of other modern disciplines such as modern biblical studies, comparative religion, psychology, anthropology, sociology and the modern sciences.[47] Although the exact dating of this period is debated, many historians locate its beginning in the first half of the seventeenth century. Some have pointed to its scientific cause through the work of Francis Bacon (1561–1626) whose implementation of the scientific method has gained him a reputation as the father of technological culture. But Bacon's use of experimentation in his scientific method did not arise in a vacuum. Almost a century earlier Nicolaus Copernicus (1473–1543) had already discovered that the earth was not at the centre of the universe. Copernicus' observations formed a considerable challenge to the Church's medieval three-storied cosmology that consisted of three levels of existence: the earth, heaven above and hell below. Contemporaneous with Bacon, Galileo (1564–1642) explained the movement of planets on the basis of mathematical equations in contrast to the Church's explanation that planetary bodies are guided by their inner purposes. The net effect was significant because it demonstrated that mathematics, not the Church, was the purest means of attaining knowledge. Although the Church did not have an official cosmological dogma, its claim to authority on scientific matters was considerably weakened and even became distrusted.

Others have pointed to the Enlightenment's philosophical cause initiated primarily by the philosopher René Descartes (1596–1650), who is often touted as the father of modern philosophy. Descartes was instrumental in shifting epistemological authority from the Church to the individual by attempting to demonstrate that one could argue to God via reason alone, which was believed to be more certain than empirical observation or ecclesiastic tradition. In attempting to discover what we can know for sure, he grounded his method of inquiry in mathematics. Instead of leading to scepticism, doubt served as the first principle of all reasoning. For when the mind doubts everything, Descartes reasoned, the only thing that remains certain is the doubter. Doubt, as an act of thinking, results in the certainty of existence. As a summary statement, Descartes postulated the now famous adage *cogito ergo sum* ("I think, therefore I am"). This began a quest for truth that replaced divine revelation with the reasoning subject as the starting point for philosophy.

---

[47] On the origins of the use of the term "Enlightenment", see James Schmidt, "Introduction: What Is Enlightenment? A Question, Its Context, and Some Consequences", in *What Is Enlightenment? Eighteenth-Century Answers and Twentieth-Century Questions* (ed. James Schmidt; Berkeley: University of California Press, 1996) 1–44.

Still other historians have pointed to its political cause, namely the Peace of Westphalia (1648), which marked the end of the Thirty Years' War. Often called Europe's first world war, it was in reality a series of violent conflicts among rival Christian groups. It was initiated by the Habsburg conquest of Bohemia and eventually spread into a Pan-European power struggle. When it was over, portions of Europe were devastated. The battles over doctrinal supremacy resulted in religious exhaustion and scepticism. The post-war years saw the rise of private, even secretive, assemblies that offered substitutions for traditional religious rituals and allowed for political dialogue outside bureaucratic institutions.[48] One of the most influential political writings that emerged in the aftermath of the war was Baruch Spinoza's *Tractatus Theologico-Politicus* (1670). Spinoza argued that if such wars are to be averted in the future, religious conviction must give way to the sensibility of human reason as the better option to guide the future of humanity. While the Bible was still of great value to Spinoza, he advocated an interpretation that is guided by a philosophy of nature derived from the common ideas of humankind regardless of religious conviction, instead of an interpretation grounded in theology which, as was evident from the war, aims to secure obedience and piety.[49]

The end of the Enlightenment is usually dated at the end of the eighteenth century with the publication of Emmanuel Kant's *Critique of Pure Reason* (1791), wherein many of the philosophical problems raised by his predecessors were synthesized. Kant's syntheses have formed much of the framework for contemporary philosophy.[50] In short, it lasted one hundred and fifty years, yet brought about a paradigm shift in Western thought from the so-called pre-critical era to the critical era which has been with us ever since. It has irretrievably altered the way that we think about ourselves, culture, nature and religion.

Foundational principles of the Enlightenment

Understanding the foundational principles of the Enlightenment period not only provides a context for appreciating the rise of New Testament theology, but also allows students of the Bible to appreciate the perspective of modern biblical scholarship, which has been shaped over the last two

---

[48] Schmidt, "Introduction: What Is Enlightenment?" 2–6. See also Richard van Dülman, *The Society of the Enlightenment: The Rise of the Middle Class and Enlightenment Culture in Germany* (trans. Anthony Williams; Cambridge: Polity Press, 1992).
[49] Krentz, *The Historical-Critical Method*, 14. On the importance of Spinoza, see also Leo Strauss, *Spinoza's Critique of Religion* (New York: Schocken Books, 1965); Yirmiyahu Yovel, *Spinoza and Other Heretics* (Princeton: Princeton University Press, 1989).
[50] James M. Byrne, *Religion and the Enlightenment: From Descartes to Kant* (Louisville: Westminster John Knox Press, 1997) 4.

hundred years. Historians have offered a variety of combinations, but most include four principles that together formed a unified consciousness.[51]

The first of these is the principle of reason. Extrapolating from what has been said above about Bacon's scientific method and Descartes' deductive reasoning, the Enlightenment period is particularly renowned for its optimistic emphasis on human rational capability. Early on Descartes' followers split into two groups: (1) those who wanted to maintain the consistency between the truth of reason and the truth of the scriptures in an effort to rescue the latter, and (2) those who saw that truth is found through reason. The latter, however, gained ascendency.[52] Since the human mind was believed to be itself governed by order and structure, it was naturally enabled to know the order and structure of the world around it. All that was needed was proper method. Thus truth was believed to be recoverable through the exercise of method and structure. Experimentation in science and the application of mathematics were particularly instrumental in determining what constitutes revelation. Prior to the Enlightenment, the order of knowing was reversed. Reason was utilized in the service of revelation and faith. Among the Scholastic theologians, like Thomas Aquinas, reason was a tool for gaining understanding of revelation and faith and for deflecting objections to them. Anselm's well-known maxim "I believe in order that I may understand" is often used as a succinct representation of the order of knowing in the pre-Enlightenment period.

The second principle is "nature" or "natural law", which appeared to have been buzz words of the day. Closely connected to the principle of reason, Enlightenment thinking removed God as the direct cause of the mechanisms of the universe and replaced him with the natural laws that he created. Order in the universe was present because it was designed by an orderly God. As a result, nature became an important means of revelation. If one could discover how nature followed laws (hence "natural law"), one could gain insight into the creative mind of God. Since nature was governed by extrinsic laws and not the inner purposes of objects, predictability served as an epistemological foundation upon which scientific measurement could be based. The climax was probably reached in the work of Isaac Newton (1642–1727) who argued that the universe was an orderly machine that followed observable laws established in the properties of particles. Eventually, some radicalized this idea to the point of equating truth and reality with that which could be measured or empirically tested. This quest, termed "natural theology", extended even to the realm of ethics. It was argued that since natural laws emerge from God's laws, all of life should be governed by them. Ethical statements found in scripture, especially the Ten

---

[51] I include four of the five principles summarized in Stanley J. Grentz and Roger E. Olson, *20th-Century Theology: God and the World in a Transitional Age* (Downers Grove: InterVarsity, 1992) ch. 1.
[52] Krentz, *The Historical-Critical Method*, 13.

Commandments and the teachings of Jesus, were still valued as revelatory, but they were evaluated on the basis of natural law. Again, reason, not the ecclesia, became the final arbiter of truth. It is important to clarify that the locus of the division was not between scripture and reason or nature, but between one kind of interpretation of scripture and another. As a revelatory source, scripture remained authoritative for most Enlightenment thinkers. Miracles and other supernatural events, however, did not fare so well because they were viewed as being contrary to the laws of nature, or as the empirical philosopher David Hume (1711–76) put it, the "law of probability". Hume argued that "since no testimony of any kind of miracle has ever amounted to a probability, much less a proof," no such testimony could "act as the foundation of a system of religion".[53]

The third principle is the elevation of human individuality or autonomy in relation to ecclesiastical and state control of knowledge. Some also called this the principle of scepticism. The anti-Papal sentiment that was widespread throughout much of northern Europe during the Reformation era spread to a general suspicion of dogma and ecclesiastical views (even Protestant ones) during the Enlightenment. In academia, religious authorities were no longer viewed as experts on external claims of truth, such as in the natural sciences and philosophy. Compliance with the traditional teachings of Rome, the various expressions of Protestantism, or even the Bible itself no longer played an important epistemological factor in reaching conclusions. Since individual reasoning was optimistically elevated to the level of the ecclesia's reasoning, individuals were free, and in some circles encouraged, to test all truth claims, even those that claimed to speak for God. The Enlightenment provided the opportunity for individuals to think for themselves and to look within themselves in their pursuit of truth. This was a considerable shift from previous thinking. Prior to the Enlightenment, individuals gained importance from their role within the story of God's activity in history as it was told by the Church. After the Enlightenment, individual thinkers determined the role of God in the light of their own life stories. Hermeneutically, the idea of God's position in the heavens directly influencing or controlling the events on earth, as it was represented in medieval art and some Greco-Roman myths, was replaced by the idea that God is influential in the world of human affairs, namely ethics. The shift from ecclesiastical control to individual autonomy is famously symbolized in Fyodor Dostoevsky's story of the "Grand Inquisitor", wherein a controlling and zealous cardinal is visited by Jesus and chastised for curtailing freedom of thought at the expense of the Church's "truth." In response to Jesus, the cardinal critically exclaims,

> Instead of taking over men's freedom, you increased it still more for them! Did you forget that peace and even death are dearer to man

---

[53] David Hume, *Hume on Religion* (ed. R. Wollheim; New York: Meridian, 1963) 222–3.

than free choice in the knowledge of good and evil? There is nothing more seductive for man than the freedom of his conscience, but there is nothing more tormenting either. And so, instead of a firm foundation for appeasing human conscience once and for all, you chose everything that was unusual, enigmatic and indefinite, you chose everything that was beyond men's strength, and thereby acted as if you did not love them at all—and who did this? He who came to give his life for them! Instead of taking over men's freedom, you increased it and forever burdened the kingdom of the human soul with its torments. You desired the free love of man, that he should follow you freely, seduced and captivated by you. Instead of the firm ancient law, man had henceforth to decide for himself, with a free heart, what is good and what is evil, having only your image before him as a guide—but did it not occur to you that he would eventually reject and dispute even your image and your truth if he was oppressed by so terrible a burden as freedom of choice?[54]

The final principle is progress. As new approaches to old quests yielded startling results in the sciences and the humanities, the social outlook was optimistic. All was moving onward and upward. Some, like the English scientist and philosopher Joseph Priestley (1733–1804), viewed their era as an unprecedented time of improvement, arguing that the advancements in science, government, law, commerce, religion and even happiness must be the result of a benign divine providence.[55] The scientific method was believed to be the vehicle of progress that could change the world for the better. But the attainment of new knowledge was never an end in and of itself. Its ultimate goal was the happiness, freedom and rational development of humanity. On the political level, it was no accident that the French and American revolutions produced collective documents, like their constitutions, that were representative of the social posture of progress. Politically and legally, the rights of individuals were significantly elevated beyond the "collective good" of the feudal systems of the Middle Ages and the bureaucratic city-state monarchism of the Reformation era. Democracy, political freedom, egalitarian constitutions that guaranteed individual rights, and emancipation from ecclesiastical and state controls were hallmarks of progress.[56]

Each of these principles has brought advancements that are enjoyed in many parts of the developed world today. Many historians, however, have also noted the negative effect of the Enlightenment, such as the domination of nature which has led to our environmental crisis, totalitarian regimes which have reacted to the unrestricted capitalism of the industrial period,

---

[54] Fyodor Dostoevsky, *The Brothers Karamazov* (trans. Richard Pevear and Larissa Volokhonsky; Everyman's Library 70; New York: Alfred A. Knopf, 1992) 254–5.
[55] Byrne, *Religion and the Enlightenment*, 8–9.
[56] Schmidt, "Introduction: What Is Enlightenment?" 11–15.

Colonialism which legitimized the domination of non-Western people groups, strict materialism which has led to a crisis in ethics, and the focus on individual rights at the expense of the rights of the community.[57]

Protestant Christianity and the Enlightenment

The Enlightenment has forever altered how scholars approach the Bible. Emancipated from the dominance of ecclesiastical interpretation of the Bible, traditional readings and applications were reformulated and even discarded. The shift significantly affected religious belief. Perhaps the most fundamental hermeneutical shift was that reason and nature—understood as conveying revelation when "proper" method was employed—became the arbiters of what was considered revelatory in the Bible. During the Enlightenment, the distinction was presented as one between "natural religion", which assumed that belief in God and his disclosing of moral laws could be attained through reason, and "revealed religion", which referred to truth in the Bible. Those portions of the Bible that were no longer relevant or contravened reason were ignored or rejected. These usually consisted of supernatural events that did not coincide with the divine construct of "predictable" nature. However, since most Enlightenment thinkers believed that Christianity was the most reasonable of religions, they held the Bible in very high esteem, especially in the formation of ethical systems. As a result, religion was not regarded as a relationship with the divine or as a belief system, but as a basis for morality.

One of the chief intellects who spawned the view that the superiority of Christianity lay in its ethics was the empirical philosopher John Locke (1632–1704). In his *Essay on Human Understanding* (1690) and *The Reasonableness of Christianity as Delivered in the Scriptures* (1695), Locke argued that reason is a "natural revelation".[58] In a revolutionary thesis, Locke argued that when Christianity rids itself of dogmatic baggage, it emerges as the most reasonable expression of religion. Locke's argumentation contributed to the rise of deism, which became a popular alternative to theological orthodoxy among intellectuals. Today, deism is often associated with some of the American founding fathers like Benjamin Franklin (1706–90) and Thomas Jefferson (1743–1826). Deists believed that God created the universe and the natural laws that govern it, but He is not directly involved in its ongoing operation. God was completely transcendent. The God of deists has often been compared to a watchmaker who makes a watch, winds it up, and then lets it run its course. The Bible was used to sanction a reasoned moral system—a kind of supplement

---

[57] On modern critiques of the Enlightenment, see the discussion and bibliography in Schmidt, "Introduction: What Is Enlightenment?" 1.
[58] Krentz, *The Historical-Critical Method*, 16.

that consisted of an important historical stage in human development. Thus the entirety of the Bible was not regarded as the infallible record of divine revelation for all generations.[59] Jesus' life and moral teachings were especially attractive for deists. As an example, in Thomas Jefferson's now famous account of Jesus' life, he rejects Jesus' divinity and the Gospels' supernatural events. For Jefferson, Jesus was "A man, of illegitimate birth, of a benevolent heart... enthusiastic mind, who set out without any pretensions of divinity, ended in believing them, and was punished capitally for sedition by being gibbeted according to Roman law."[60]

Not all intellectuals, however, accepted Christianity as the most reasonable of religions. Unlike the deists and theists, this period in intellectual history is also regarded as the dawn of aversion towards religion in general, again based on reason.

In spite of its moral attraction, many Enlightenment thinkers of varied ideologies began to study the Bible as an ancient artifact in much the same way that other ancient writings were studied. The Biblical books and their assumed authors were situated in their historical contexts so that the message of each book was not primarily, if at all, viewed as an intended witness for the modern reader, but as a reflection of its own time and culture. The immense accumulation of historical and literary data quickly led to new theories on authorship, purpose, meaning and compositional history of biblical books, challenging many of the well-established ecclesiastical views in the process. For example, among the more well-known shifts in thinking which have remained current, the book of Isaiah was regarded as a composite of at least two authors, the Jesus of history was distinguished from the Jesus of the Gospels, and the compositional sequence of the Synoptic Gospels which traditionally placed Matthew first in the order was up for debate. In New Testament studies the emphasis clearly lay in the search for the historical, or as it was understood, the factual. Historical inquiry also led to conclusions that challenged the unity of the Bible. Some scholars began to publish findings that pointed out contradictions among the Gospels and between Jesus and Paul.

But the age of reason and liberation had its limits. Such views were often expressed cautiously due to the fear of retribution from ecclesiastically controlled institutions, such as universities and parliament. In the seventeenth and eighteenth centuries, professors who espoused what we might call progressive views about Christianity still feared loss of employment, social ostracism and even imprisonment. One such example is the case of John Toland (1670–1722) who may have been the first academic to argue that the supernatural events contained in the Gospels were borrowed from

---

[59] See the discussion in Werner G. Kümmel, *The New Testament: The History of the Investigation of Its Problems* (Nashville: Abingdon, 1972) 51–72.
[60] From T. Jefferson, *Thomas Jefferson's Life of Jesus: Bicentennial Edition* (Springfield: Templegate, 1975) 388.

paganism. Authentic Christianity, for Toland, did not lie in miracle or events of mystery, but lay instead in the daily practice of life that is guided by reason. Toland's aim in his *Christianity Not Mysterious* (1696) was not only to show how Christianity was the most reasonable of religions when stripped of the supernatural accounts, but he was intent on rescuing Jesus from the confines of mystery and dogma. Reaction to Toland's ideas was immediately hostile. The British Parliament ordered that Toland be arrested and that all copies of his book be burned.[61] Another example of how fear was prevalent in the academic scene is that of Hermann Samuel Reimarus (1694–1768) who is often credited for the beginning of the historical quest for Jesus. Reimarus made a sharp distinction between the Jesus of history and the Christ of faith, arguing that Jesus' teachings are distinct from those of his disciples. Based on Gospel events like Jesus' royal arrival into Jerusalem and sayings like the cry of dereliction (Mark 15.34//Matt 27.46), Reimarus argued that the Jesus of history never intended to suffer and die on the cross, but intended to liberate Israel from bondage and establish an earthly kingdom wherein he would reign as a kingly messiah. Unfortunately, according to Reimarus, Jesus' hopes were frustrated and he died in disappointment. However, throughout his career as professor of Oriental Languages in Hamburg, Reimarus exhibited the demeanour of orthodoxy while intentionally keeping his views private for fear of losing his employment.[62] Eventually, after his death, his ideas were published.[63] Both Toland and Reimarus serve as important examples of how biblical scholars attempted to formulate new theologies based on either select scripture texts or reconstructions of Jesus, and in each case apart from ecclesiastical tradition.

Not all academics adopted a progressive approach to biblical interpretation. The Enlightenment also saw a rigorous response from conservative academics and especially the clergy who vehemently wanted to preserve the unity of the Bible and the coherence between the Jesus of history and the Christ of faith. Ironically, such attempts, which also resulted in theologies based strictly on the Bible and critical of ecclesiastical tradition, utilized the same rationalistic principles. The results, however, were quite different. What was "reasonable" to one group may not have been reasonable to another. While the same rationalist principles were used by conservative proponents in response to their adversaries, the real challenge lay in the attempt to justify the Bible's unity. Since reason and the historical method

---

[61] From C. Bennett, *In Search of Jesus: Insider and Outsider Images* (New York: Continuum, 2001) 91–2. John Toland, *Christianity Not Mysterious* (reprint; London: Routledge, 1995).
[62] Peter Hans Reill, *The German Enlightenment and the Rise of Historicism* (Berkeley: University of California Press, 1975) 162–3.
[63] One of his most important writings, published in 1778, was "On the Intentions of Jesus and His Disciples" (fragment 7), reprinted in Charles H. Talbert, ed., *Reimarus: Fragments* (trans. R. S. Fraser; Lives of Jesus Series; Philadelphia: Fortress, 1970).

were viewed as the means to truth and meaning on both sides of the divide, it was employed to show that the Bible is indeed the inspired Word of God. In the process, articles of faith were blurred with scientific certainty, and fact was confused with meaning. Too often the clerical response led to condemnation and a failed opportunity to embrace and interact with cultural change—the results of which have been with us ever since.[64] James Byrne reflects,

> What is perhaps the tragedy for Christianity is that in its attempts to respond to many of the—often shallow—attacks it endured, its intellectuals too often resorted to condemnation. The Enlightenment's avowal of the freedom to investigate all subjects, to bracket authority in the name of inquiry, and its insistence on secular thinkers' independence from religious interference all came across to religious leaders and many theologians, otherwise well-disposed towards innovative thinking, as simply an attack on the foundations of religion as such. Of course in some cases this is precisely what it was, but the inability of so many theologians, bishops and elders to see the potential for theological development in the new ideas of the time meant that Christian thinking often stood still while the modern world was formed about it.[65]

The rise of historical criticism, together with antagonism toward ecclesiastical tradition, led to the quest for a "pure" Christian theology based on scripture which was termed "biblical theology", with its subordinate fields of Old and New Testament theologies. So what is the historical-critical method? The earliest applications can be traced to the 1655 publication of Isaac de la Peyrère's *The Pre-Adamites*, wherein it is scientifically argued that Adam cannot be the first man, and to the 1678 work of the French Catholic priest Richard Simon (*Histoire critique du Vieux Testament*) wherein the Old Testament is treated as a historical document composed and edited over a long period of time by numerous authors, instead of divinely orchestrated unity.[66] The earliest full expression of the historical-critical method has been traced to Barthold Georg Niebuhr's *History of Rome* (1811–12), which is claimed to be the first work that critically evaluates the value of sources in the reconstruction of history. In his attempt to separate what he called poetry and falsehood from truth, Niebuhr's reconstruction posed two influential questions—"What is the evidence?" and "What is the value of the evidence?"—that were inevitably applied to the Bible and have remained with us ever since.[67]

---

[64] See the summary issues in Mark Noll, "Evangelicals. Creation and Scripture: Legacies from a Long History", *Perspectives on Science and Christian Faith* 63.3 (September 2011) 147–58.
[65] Byrne, *Religion and the Enlightenment*, 26.
[66] Byrne, *Religion and the Enlightenment*, 11–12.
[67] Krentz, *The Historical-Critical Method*, 22–3.

Historical criticism, as it emerged from scientific inquiry, was primarily a data-mining method, and thus poorly suited to provide meaning. Its similarity to the scientific method is inescapable. As O'Keefe and Reno write,

> Modern science developed methods, not to get beyond or behind the natural world but to see *into* it. An evolutionary biologist wishes to explain fossil data rather than discern or interpret what the data might represent. The data are what matter most; data cannot be a means or medium for something more important. The hallmark of modern science, experimental method, serves this goal. It brings the data into focus as the control upon scientific theory.[68]

One of the areas of study where this has been particularly noticeable is in historical Jesus research which also arose alongside the rise of the natural sciences. Not only did Jesus research attempt to apply the same method, but participated in the same discourses of domination. Politically motivated and engineered interpretations did not disappear with the call to science or objectivity.[69]

The historical-critical method as it was applied to the early formation of biblical theology was not strictly a single approach, but a variety of approaches that have common principles. Edgar Krentz' description of the historical-critical method can be summarized as containing the following principles:[70]

(1) It tries to read scripture within its historical, cultural and linguistic context, utilizing linguistic and comparative tools.

(2) It seeks to interpret scripture without the aid of church traditions or doctrines.

(3) It claims to achieve a distance between interpreter and text, which leads to objectivity.

(4) It often tries to rule out the divine as a causal factor in history.

(5) It is primarily descriptive.

(6) It often uses the New Testament as a window for reconstructing earliest Christianity.

(7) It usually presupposes a single meaning.

(8) It often assumes authorial intention.

(9) It seeks to uncover the "facts" which supposedly lie behind the myths of the day.

---

[68] O'Keefe and Reno, *Sanctified Vision*, 117.
[69] Elisabeth Schüssler Fiorenza, *Jesus and the Politics of Interpretation* (New York: Continuum, 2001) 16–20.
[70] Krentz, *The Historical-Critical Method*.

The rise of the discipline of New Testament theology

The quest for purity

The rise of New Testament theology is contingent upon the long-held Protestant conviction that the Bible alone in its literal, or historical, sense reveals God's will for humanity. The belief that the New Testament can communicate God's revelation afresh to each new generation has been a foundational assumption underlying the intense study that has taken place since the Reformation. N. T. Wright sums it up well:

> This belief grows out of the ineradicable Christian conviction, held from very early times, that being Christian means, among other things, living, believing and behaving in some sort of continuity, in principle demonstrable, with the New Testament.... This belief gained additional momentum as a result of the Protestant Reformation, when the principle of *sola scriptura* was articulated, placing the Bible (and, *de facto* at least, the New Testament in particular) in the position of supreme authority. Reading the New Testament, it has always been felt within Protestantism, is where the Christian begins, and in doing so he or she is equipped, challenged, reinforced, given a basis for belief and life.[71]

As a discipline, New Testament theology emerged during this period of Protestantism's deliberate quest for a historically recoverable "pure" Christianity that was not tainted by centuries of ecclesiastical tradition. It was indeed an age of great optimism in the recovering of the past. In contrast to Roman Catholic formulations of dogma which placed emphasis on tradition as expressed in councils, creeds, liturgy and ecclesial interpretations of scripture, the search for a "pure" theology among Enlightenment Protestant scholars focused solely on the scriptures, the Old and New Testaments apart from the so-called Apocrypha. While Roman Catholic scholars of the day understood tradition as a derivative of scripture interpreted through the lenses of theological and philosophical thought throughout the centuries, and while Orthodox theologians likewise applied a mystical/platonic hermeneutic (though largely unscathed by Western modernist trends), their Protestant counterparts sought to bypass the long ecclesiastical tradition which they regarded as a kind of contaminant. For Protestants all literature apart from the Bible, be it the writings of the Church Fathers, saints, ancient philosophers or Greco-Roman and Jewish myths,

---

[71] N. T. Wright, *The New Testament and the People of God* (Christian Origins and the Question of God 1; Minneapolis: Fortress Press, 1992) 19.

was regarded as radically inferior, yet the method that was used to interpret these was also applied to the Bible. "Pure" dogma according to many of these Protestants could only be discovered through a historical-critical interpretative process that aimed at disclosing the original meaning and authorial intent of scripture. Exegesis through the historical-critical method was used in the service of New Testament theology and was distinguished from dogmatic or systematic theology, which was regarded as less certain and subject to cultural, historical, philosophical and geographical currents and ever shifting contexts. For many Protestant scholars of the day, the true, pure and unchanging revelation of God was believed to reside in scripture and was able to be retrieved through "proper" exegetical method. This became the early aim of New Testament theology. The early practitioners argued that only after the formulation of a pure New Testament theology should one begin to construct a dogmatic or systematic theology that concerned itself with the formulation and prescription of doctrines such as the nature of God, original sin or salvation. In sum, the sequence was becoming clear: New Testament theology was dependent on exegesis, and dogmatics was dependent on New Testament theology.

But the historical-critical search for a "pure" theology brought with it a lasting and an insurmountable problem: namely the problem of meaning. If, as classical Protestantism insisted, scripture contained one literal meaning which historical inquiry was to disclose definitively, what was to be the corrective should disagreements emerge about what is and is not part of the "pure" theology? Moreover, what if historical inquiry should lead to a conclusion that subverted accepted doctrines? What was to be the role of historical criticism? Was it to show that the scriptures convey a pure and unified theology in a literal sense? Or was it to select only those parts that contained so-called timeless truths? Was it ordered to ethics or metaphysics, or both? Was it to be used in support of established faith, in support of reform, or in support of subverting Christianity altogether? Hypothetical questions became all too real and ultimately led to the realization that the quest for meaning could not be answered by historical-critical inquiry alone. When wide-ranging disagreements began to emerge among exegetes who relied on the same historical method, it was realized at the beginning of the twentieth century that a certain degree of subjectivity guided how the objective tool was used.

Founding fathers

Most modern historical surveys of the formative years of the discipline give credit to numerous scholars, especially in German universities, for their influential contributions. Mention of a few is a must. In addition to Anton Friedrich Büsching's success in elevating what he termed "biblical theology" to the level of a rival to dogmatics, Johann Solomo Semler (1725–91) and

Johann Philipp Gabler (1753–1826) stand out as chief catalysts. Under the influence of Richard Simon, Semler's contribution lay in his carefully argued distinction between the Word of God and the Bible. Not everything in the Bible was considered to be inspired, revelatory or, as he put it, the Word of God. In a four-volume treatise (*Treatise on the Free Investigation of the Canon*, 1771–5), Semler aimed to convince his readers that the Bible must be viewed as a historical collection of writings and as such must be studied exegetically like any other historical writing. He argued that the task of biblical theology cannot be anything but a historical discipline which poses a direct challenge to traditional dogmatic theology.[72] It is in the work of Semler where much of the hermeneutical groundwork is historically formed for the foundationalist approach to New Testament theology as it was presented in the first chapter.

Johann Philipp Gabler is often credited for making the most decisive and lasting contribution to biblical theology. His far-reaching impact did not, however, come by means of a detailed and premeditated volume on the subject, but quite innocently by means of an inaugural lecture at the University of Altdorf on 31 March 1787. Hasel writes, "This year marks the beginning of biblical theology's role as a purely historical discipline, completely independent from dogmatics."[73] Gabler believed that the New Testament was the clearest source for obtaining hope of salvation. The problem was that the Church had clouded its clarity through centuries of improper exegesis that was guided by theological interests and not the recovery of the "pure" revelation. Like his predecessors, Gabler separated biblical theology, which he viewed as the historical pursuit for the unchanging "pure" revelation, from that of dogmatic theology, which he regarded as a culturally conditioned practice that seeks to address the changing circumstances of every generation, much like other "human" disciplines. Ideally, for Gabler, biblical theology should make dogmatics more certain. Gabler writes,

> There is truly a biblical theology, of historical origin, conveying what the holy writers felt about divine matters; on the other hand there is a dogmatic theology of didactic origin, teaching what each theologian philosophizes rationally about divine things, according to the measure of his ability or of the times, age, place, sect, school, and other similar factors.[74]

Gabler's attempt to recover the "pure" revelation is based on three methodological assumptions. First, the assumption of authorial intention allows Gabler to focus on what the ancient writers thought about divine

---

[72] Hasel, *New Testament Theology*, 20–1.
[73] Hasel, *New Testament Theology*, 22.
[74] Gabler's address is translated by John Sandys-Wunsch and Laurence Eldredge, "J. P. Gabler and the Distinction Between Biblical and Dogmatic Theology: Translation, Commentary, and Discussion of his Originality", *Scottish Journal of Theology* 33 (1980) 137.

things. Second, Gabler advocated the necessity of a comparative approach whereby the individual ideas of the writers could be collected and compared. And third, he proposed that the comparative analysis of the ideas should be evaluated for their value in the formation of Christian doctrine. For Gabler, the overriding criterion for determining what is "pure" revelation in the New Testament was content specific; that is, if a text pertained to the topic of salvation, it was deemed a "pure" revelation and hence relevant for Christian theology.[75]

Gabler's influence soon led to the first publication of a New Testament theology entitled *Biblische Theologie des Neuen Testaments* by Georg Lorenz Bauer, who was professor of philosophy and Oriental languages, also at the University of Altdorf. Not only does he apply "reasoned" historical criticism to the New Testament, but he moves beyond his predecessors to include issues of philosophical and religious import that continue to be discussed today.[76]

Conclusion

On the one hand, the rise of biblical theology as a counter to pre-existent ecclesiastical authority is not new. In this sense, one is tempted to redefine New Testament theology altogether as a subcategory or movement in the study of the history of biblical interpretation, since turning to the scriptures in protest against existing religious power structures is as old as the scriptures themselves. Pointing out how opposing groups misinterpret the common sacred writings in the process of legitimizing one's own group is likewise an ancient practice that continues to this day. Also not new is the reading and applying of the scriptures within each new generation and shift in cultural thinking. The rapid change that has been seen in biblical interpretation from the beginning of the Reformation to the end of the Enlightenment only reflects the rapidity of cultural change that took place in this relatively short period of time.[77] Whether it is John Chrysostom's attempt to justify anti-Semitism, the medieval Church's justification of the crusades, Luther's appeal to drop James from the canon, the Deists' attempt to demonstrate the reasonableness of select texts, or Jerry Falwell's explanation of the 9/11 terrorist attacks as the result of sin perpetuated by the "ACLU, abortionists, feminists, gays and the People For the American

---

[75] See a similar summary in Hasel, *New Testament Theology*, 23.
[76] Hasel, *New Testament Theology*, 24–5. Georg Lorenz Bauer, *Biblische Theologie des Neuen Testaments* (2 vols; Leipzig: Bengandschen, 1800–02).
[77] On the frequent shifts in biblical interpretation, see John Sandys-Wunsch, *What Have They Done to the Bible? A History of Modern Biblical Interpretation* (Collegeville: Liturgical Press, 2005).

Way",[78] the legitimizing function of the scriptures has always resided in the collective belief that they are relevant. Every interpretative movement or collective has its own canon within a canon that affects how the balance of the Bible is read. What is relevant seems always to be understood through the lenses of shifting social paradigms. It is not so much that the Bible (or even religion) is the cause of cultural change; rather it is the reverse.

On the other hand, biblical theology is a unique endeavour in the history of biblical interpretation. Its reliance on the historical-critical method displaced centuries of polysemous readings of the Bible. Preoccupation with the historical agenda brought with it issues that were unprecedented. Not all parts of the Bible were valued equally or regarded as inspired. The question of what is and is not relevant for modern society consumed New Testament theologians for much of the twentieth century. And its antithesis towards ecclesiastical tradition and dogmatics raised it to a level of great prominence in the last two hundred years of Protestant thought. Historical interpretation of the Bible was fused with an emphasis on the moral and practical function. The result was a new approach to Christian doctrine, known as "neology", which equated the historically derived "biblical revelation" with the rationalistically derived "natural revelation".[79] For the first time in the history of biblical interpretation, the Bible's function in Christianity came perilously close to obsolescence because its relevance in "modern" culture was increasingly viewed as a tangential affirmation from ancient times of what was already discovered by reason.

Discussion questions

1 How do the interpretive methods of the earliest Christian writers differ from today's foundationalist and dialectical New Testament theologians?

2 How might a polysemous approach to biblical interpretation affect the development of a New Testament theology?

3 When attempting to formulate a New Testament theology, should the interpretative process prioritize the question "What really happened?" or "What did it mean?"

4 What are the underlying assumptions in a "literal" interpretation of the New Testament?

5 How should the discoveries in the sciences and social sciences since the Enlightenment influence the interpretation of scripture and the formation of a New Testament theology?

---

[78] From the 13 September 2001 edition of *The 700 Club* television programme.
[79] Schmidt, "Introduction: What Is Enlightenment?" 7.

4

Foundationalist structuring of New Testament theology

Although the beginning of the discipline of New Testament theology can be traced to the second half of the eighteenth century, it is the twentieth century that has seen the most creativity in the structuring of New Testament theologies. The aim of each structure is to present a coherent and organized understanding of early Christian thought. Some are more overt than others in presenting that thought in a relevant way. It is important to reiterate that each structure is a modern scholarly construct. New Testament theologies are books written by modern scholars who impose upon the ancient texts contemporary configurations. The structures presented in this chapter and the next should not be viewed as clear divisions, since some practitioners can be placed in more than one category. They do, however, represent the general tendencies in the field today.

Before proceeding to classify these structures, some mention should be made of their relationship to Gerhard Ebeling's two definitions of New Testament theology that were presented in the opening chapter. In review, the first definition which Ebeling offers, and one that resonates with most New Testament theologians in the history of the discipline, is stated as "a study of that theology which is exclusively *found in* or *limited to* the New Testament with little or no regard for later interpretations or traditions". I referred to this as the "foundationalist" view of New Testament theology since the theology is (believed to be) formed from the ground up, so to speak. This understanding stems directly from the inception of the discipline which was initiated by a search for a "pure" theology that can be found and derived solely from scripture. This "pure" theology alone becomes the standard for Christian belief and practice. In an effort to extend this datum as far back as possible, a few scholars have even insisted that the point of reference is the historical Jesus.

The second definition may seem similar, but conveys a significant shift from the first. It is defined as "a study of that theology which is *based upon* or *rooted in* the New Testament". I referred to this as the "dialectical" view since it begins forming a theology (or theological dialogue, to be more precise) from the top down, so to speak. In other words, it assumes the necessity of imposing external categories upon the formation of a New Testament theology. Structures rooted in this second definition are taken up in the next chapter.

Within the last century, New Testament theologies have usually been structured in one of five ways. These are identified as the chronological approach, the author-by-author approach, the salvation-history approach, the dogmatic approach and the existentialist approach.[1] In presentations of New Testament theologies that adopt a chronological and author-by-author structure, one finds its practitioners comfortably allying themselves with the foundationalist definition, meaning that reconstruction or exegesis leads to interpretation. These two structures are the focus of this chapter. Whatever impositions are placed upon the text (and indeed many are) are minimized, shrugged off as necessary, or ignored. These structures reflect classic modernism. A common belief that underlies these structures is that revelation resides in the *intention* of the New Testament writers. The task of the New Testament theologian is thus to present systematically the thinking of the ancient writers to a modern audience of believers. This process often assumes that relevance is automatically conveyed because both the scriptures and the believer share in the presence of the Holy Spirit. But this pneumatic connection between the text and reader should not be confused with the Catholic understanding of the Holy Spirit's role in the Church as the guiding interpreter through ecclesiastical structures like the Magisterium, creeds and councils. In Protestantism, the interpreter may claim the Holy Spirit as well, but it is on an individual level. This topic certainly requires much more development than can be offered here, but in a rather simplistic way a major distinction between Catholic and Protestant *collective* interpretations of the Bible can be summed up in this way: Catholics claim an inspired ecclesial interpretation of an inspired text; whereas Protestants claim a non-inspired individual interpretation of an inspired text.

Understanding how scholars structure their New Testament theologies is tantamount to understanding how the discipline is "practised". Structuring is very effective in controlling how the text is read and prescribed. For example, proposing a central message or even a central figure (e.g. Jesus or Paul) in the New Testament creates a hermeneutical key, or a canon within the canon, that has implications for the interpretation of the balance of the writings. Even when the same structuring is followed, this issue alone has generated ongoing debate with varied conclusions. Nevertheless, structuring is impossible to avoid if the aim of New Testament theology moves

---

[1] Some of these categories are taken from G. B. Caird, *New Testament Theology* (Oxford: Clarendon, 1994) 8–14. Caird's list of structures consists of the dogmatic, chronological, kerygmatic and author-by-author approaches.

beyond a description of early Christian thought towards a unification and prescription of that thought.

The chronological approach

Aim

More than any of the other approaches, the Chronological (or Historical) approach has the most nuances, though all of them have the historical reconstruction of the development of early Christian thought as their central goal. Once again, it is important to note that the reconstruction tends to be conflated with interpretation. Often associated with the History-of-Religions school, the advocates of a chronological structure have argued in response to dogmatic theology that the New Testament is not a theologically unified corpus, but a collection of diverse ideas that must be studied as a developmental history of early Christian ideas and beliefs. Although such studies have been called "New Testament theology", strictly speaking it does not resemble "theology" at all. Rather, it is better termed the study of early Christian thought, with subtle challenges to dogmatics thrown into the mix. The chronological approach usually has taken the form of structuring the New Testament writings chronologically so as to trace the streams and shifts in earliest Christian thought which have at their root underlying influences, either from early Judaism or the Greco-Roman culture. Many have advocated that the chronology of the New Testament exhibits a shift of influence from the former to the latter. Tracing the diversity in New Testament thought into the second century, a synthesis begins to emerge in "early catholic" Christianity under the leadership of bishops like Irenaeus, who is often touted as the father of unity in the developmental process. Critics of the synthesis point out that it comes at a weighty price, arguing that the diversity in the New Testament must take precedence over syntheses.

Among the nuances, three approaches to the chronological structuring of the New Testament have been common. First, those who opted for a recovery of the "oldest" representation of Christian thought have tended to focus on the influences of early Judaism in either earliest Christian tradition or in the teachings of the historical Jesus. The oldest traditions were often regarded as the foundational ones. Others sought to compare the varied ideas in the New Testament with similar ideas in contemporaneous religions in the hope of recovering the truly distinctive features of Christianity. This approach required one to ascertain the dating and socio-religious context of each New Testament writing. Still others started with the entire developmental process of the New Testament and attempted to discover common truths, usually of an ethical nature.

Chronological structuring was particularly common in the first half of the twentieth century when large amounts of data about different expressions of early Judaism and Greco-Roman religion and society were being collected. All of the data provided wide-ranging options for contexts wherein individual New Testament writings could be located. Many of these proposals were formed on the basis of reconstructed conflicts that the early Christians were facing. Paul's letters and the Gospels, for example, were increasingly viewed as apologetic responses directed at either divergent Christian groups or Jewish groups.

Practitioners

The chronological approach was very popular from the latter part of the nineteenth century to the middle of the twentieth. Newly discovered archaeological, literary and philological data provided for a variety of reconstructed contexts wherein the New Testament was interpreted, which quickly resulted in debates about not only the validity of the new data, but the reconstructed contexts themselves. For example some, like Adolf Deissmann, utilized papyri and epigraphic evidence that post-dated the New Testament. Others, like Birger Gerhardsson, used rabbinic material to reconstruct first-century Palestine. Others still, like Wilhelm Bousset, relied on Hellenistic religions to understand Christological titles, such as "Lord". It was a period that saw no shortage of reconstructions ranging from Pharisaic Judaism to Jewish apocalypticism to the Greco-Roman mystery religions.

Among more recent of the chronological approaches, Werner Kümmel's outstanding *The Theology of the New Testament According to its Major Witnesses* should serve as an example of this approach on any list. At the beginning of his treatment, Kümmel articulates his approach in this way: "I shall attempt to set forth the preaching of Jesus, the theology of Paul against the background of the primitive community, and the message of Christ in the Gospel of John, in their essential features, and, on the basis of this presentation, to inquire about the unity which is exhibited in these forms of proclamation."[2] In developing his structure, Kümmel assigns a chapter to each phase of his reconstruction of a New Testament chronology. In the first chapter, which treats the preaching of Jesus according to the Synoptic Gospels, the teachings of Jesus prior to the resurrection are placed at the foundational level of his New Testament theology in order to show that the Proclaimer became the one proclaimed. In chapter two, Kümmel turns to "the faith of the primitive community" which is grounded in the belief in the resurrected Christ. Chapter three is about Paul and the transition from

---

[2] Werner Kümmel, *The Theology of the New Testament According to its Major Witnesses: Jesus-Paul-John* (trans. John E. Steely; Nashville: Abingdon, 1973) 18.

Palestinian Christianity to Gentile Christianity. The final chapter in the chronology focuses on the theology of the Johannine Writings, which reflect a later development of Christianity wherein the historical Jesus is fused with the saving activity of Jesus as God's Christ. Although Kümmel does not shy away from divergences of ideas and certainly accepts fragments in the development of early Christian thought, his overall aim is to show that on the key theological issues, such as the eschatological salvation in Christ, the major early Christian witnesses exhibited a unified belief. Unlike many of Kümmel's predecessors and peers who proposed a similar approach, the diversity, for example, among Jesus, Paul and John, is only viewed as peripheral. Kümmel firmly advocates that a historical-critical approach, when practised from the perspective of faith within the context of the Church, will yield the same unified message to the contemporary reader as it was conveyed and understood by the first audiences. The message is "that Jesus God, the Lord of the world, has come to us. But this coming of God can become a personal reality for us only if we so allow ourselves to be grasped by God's love that has come to us in Jesus Christ that we become new persons."[3]

A second example of a chronological structure is Joachim Jeremias' *New Testament Theology*, which was originally intended to be the first of two volumes, but the second was never completed.[4] Jeremias' approach is essentially an attempt to reconstruct the theology of the historical Jesus whose authority transcends that of the canon. In exploiting the famous distinction between *ipsissima vox Jesu* (the voice of Jesus, namely his message) and *ipsissima verba Jesu* (the words of Jesus), Jeremias was intent on presenting the voice of the pre-Easter Jesus to a modern audience. He writes, "Our faith is a return to the actual living voice of Jesus. How great the gain if we succeed in rediscovering here and there behind the veil the features of the Son of Man! To meet with him can alone give power to our preaching."[5] For Jeremias, the voice of Jesus conveys the message that he is the bringer of God's salvation, which is grounded in the love of God for sinners. As such, argues Jeremias, Jesus correctly anticipated (in the light of Isaiah 53 and Zech. 13.7) the obligation to take on the necessary suffering and eventual death for the sake of his people. Jeremias' method for reconstructing the message of the historical Jesus is based partly on Norman Perrin's famous criterion of dissimilarity which states that the sayings and themes of Jesus that find no parallel in Judaism and the early church are most likely derived from the pre-Easter period. Admitting that the criterion is biased towards originality, Jeremias also proposes that the sayings of Jesus be evaluated according to their "language and style". This is to say

---

[3] Kümmel, *The Theology of the New Testament*, 333.
[4] Joachim Jeremias, *New Testament Theology: The Proclamation of Jesus* (trans. J. Bowden; London: SCM Press, 1971).
[5] Jeremias, *New Testament Theology*, 114.

that those sayings in the Synoptics that exhibit an Aramaic origin should likewise be deemed early.[6]

For Jeremias, there is much more consistency in the developmental process from the pre-Easter Jesus to the proclamation about Jesus in the apostolic age than many of his critics would permit.[7] According to Jeremias, the early church embraced and proclaimed the message of the pre-Easter Jesus with much less creativity than was commonly ascribed. Whatever *could* be ascribed to Jesus, *should* be. In fact, Jerermias has been criticized for letting his theology dictate the conclusions of his historical reconstruction. On a more basic methodological level, Hasel correctly wonders why in the light of the momentous debate about whether or not the historical Jesus should be part of any New Testament theology, Jeremias has not justified his foundational assertion. As Hasel states, there is no question that the proclamation of Jesus constitutes the *foundation* of New Testament theology, but there is a question whether that proclamation should be *part* of that theology.[8]

Evaluation

The longevity of the chronological approach has brought with it a host of long-standing criticisms that penetrate the heart of a foundationalist approach to New Testament theology. Thus the evaluation here is disproportionately more extensive than those below. The first problem that has often been raised is the formulation of a chronology. Most scholars today would agree that a general working chronology begins with the historical Jesus in the late 20s CE, continues with Q (a hypothetical sayings source common to Matthew and Luke) in the 40s, Paul from the late 40s to the mid-60s, Mark just prior to or just after 70, Matthew and Luke in the 80s, John in the 90s, and ends with the remaining documents written in the last quarter of the first century. While this chronology is generally proposed, it is by no means agreed upon. For example, while most Johannine scholars date the Gospel and the Epistles in the 90s, the tenacity of the arguments for a much earlier dating of the Fourth Gospel, proposed a number of years

---

[6] Jeremias, *New Testament Theology*, 2–3.

[7] See the discussion of Kümmel and Jeremias in G. Hasel, *New Testament Theology: Basic Issues in the Current Debate* (Grand Rapids: Eerdmans, 1978) 102–11.

[8] Hasel, *New Testament Theology*, 110–11. On the role of the historical Jesus in New Testament theology, see the differing viewpoints in Robert Morgan, "The Historical Jesus and the Theology of the New Testament", in *Studies in Christology in Memory of G. B. Caird* (ed. L. D. Hurst and N. T. Wright; Oxford: Oxford University Press, 1987) 187–206; and Christopher Tuckett, "Does the 'Historical Jesus' Belong within a 'New Testament Theology'?" in *The Nature of New Testament Theology: Essays in Honour of Robert Morgan* (ed. Christopher Rowland and Christopher Tuckett; Oxford: Blackwell, 2006) 231–47.

ago by John A. T. Robinson, continues to thwart a consensus.[9] Another example is the recent challenge to the Q hypothesis, which, if correct, would place Paul at the chronological forefront in the New Testament.[10] Hebrews, Revelation and the Timothy correspondences also continue to be debated, ranging from the mid-60s to the end of the first century. Moreover, form and source critics have been very effective in demonstrating that the writers incorporate theological material, like creeds (e.g. in 1 Corinthians 15) and hymns (e.g. in Philippians 2) that may be considerably older.

The second problem is related to the first. Discrepancies in dating not only play havoc with any theory of straight-line development, but also create potential frustration in locating the writings, their traditions and their theological ideas in specific cultural/religious contexts, such as Hellenistic Judaism, Palestinian Judaism or Greco-Roman religions. For instance, if John was written early, do the titles he attributes to Jesus, like "Word", "Son", or "Paraclete" reflect a Palestinian, Alexandrian or Ephesian context, to mention just a few? Since words derive their meanings from contextual usage, the titles can potentially incorporate different nuances depending on the audience he is targeting.

Moreover, similarities of terms and even concepts do not necessarily constitute causal links. For instance, when theologically loaded titles like "son of God" appear in both an early writing like Mark and a later writing like John, a causal connection cannot be assumed. In Mark's context, the title can be used to convey Jesus' royal status and in the process subverts the Roman Emperor and his role as the bringer of peace and salvation. In John, it appears to convey Jesus' filial relationship to the Father. With regard to larger themes or theological ideas, we can no longer assume that the New Testament conveys an unbroken development from a so-called "low" Christology which supposedly arose in early Jewish Christian settings to a "high" Christology which developed later in Hellenistic settings. Greek categories are no longer viewed as expressing "higher" concepts than Jewish categories. An example that has often been used to confront a straight-line development is the hymn in Phil. 2.5-11 which many scholars think predates the letter to the Philippians. While most scholars believe that the hymn was an insertion, they are uncertain whether it originated with Paul or whether it was borrowed. If the letter was written while Paul was in prison, which could be in CE 53–55 in Ephesus, CE 57–59 in Caesarea or as late as CE 61 in Rome, the hymn could have been in use as early as the CE 40s. Even if it did originate with Paul, the so-called "high" Christology, which is reminiscent of what we find in John at the end of the first century, disrupts the traditional understanding of the development. While there

---

[9] John A. T. Robinson, *The Priority of John* (London: SCM Press, 1985).
[10] See, for example, Mark Goodacre, *The Synoptic Problem: A Way Through the Maze* (London: Sheffield, 2001).

is little debate that theological ideas developed over the span of the first century of Christianity, and have continued to do so ever since, the main point is that the streams of development are notoriously difficult to track. Ideas are unpredictable and rarely develop in a straight line. Though an idea is recorded, its oral history is difficult to trace, and its initial reception varies widely until it is eventually synthesized with more widespread beliefs, often many years later. For instance, it would be interesting to step back in time and ask the author of Mark, or the author Q, or even Jesus himself, if they endorse the Christology in Phil. 2.5–11 (or John's prologue, or the Nicene Creed, and so on).

A third problem concerns the relationship between a hypothetical structure and the canon. If a New Testament theology is to be chronological in its structure, two questions arise. First, do the earlier writings or the reconstructed teachings of Jesus convey more authority or theological precedent than the later writings? And second, how are non-canonical writings, including hypothetical ones like Q, to be incorporated into the chronology? With respect to the first question, if earlier traditions are given more theological weight, the canon can potentially lose not only its cohesion as the Church's sacred anthology but its quality as a collection of equally inspired writings. Establishing one or some writings as a "canon within a canon" may be attractive hermeneutically since it is one way of establishing a theological coherence—and it has certainly been a habit throughout the history of Christianity—but it unfortunately leads to a minimizing and misinterpretation of those writings that are left in the shadows. Since there are no internal references to the superiority of some writings, or writers, over and against others, the selection process must be imposed from without. As is clear from the history of biblical interpretation, decisions about which parts of scripture should interpret (or overshadow) other parts have often been influenced by political factors.

If the reconstructed Jesus is the starting point and thus the hermeneutical key for the New Testament, we are faced with an additional problem. Since any reconstruction of Jesus' life and teachings is an external construct and not found within the New Testament, the result is a New Testament theology that does not begin with the New Testament itself. At this point, the potential danger is that reconstruction is fused with interpretation, fact is fused with meaning, and history is fused with faith. And in the process the authoritative interpretations of Jesus, which *is* the New Testament, are evaluated and interpreted in light of reconstructions, that is, revised interpretations of Jesus. In a sense, the new "canon within a canon" becomes a reconstruction based on the modernist optimism of the historical-critical method. This problem, once again, brings us back to Bultmann who, in recognizing the dangers, argued that the historical Jesus should be the *foundation*, but not a *part* of New Testament theology. Another way of shedding light on the problem is in the form of a question: Does the Christian faith go back to Jesus or is it the construct of the early church?

When we consider the second question (how are non-canonical writings, including hypothetical ones like Q, to be incorporated into the chronology?) a chronological structuring is problematic. On the one hand, a structure based on chronology has no internal means of excluding non-canonical Christian writing. Nor does it contain an internal mechanism that legitimizes a cut-off point in the chronology. One can posit that all the writings must be dated within the time frame of the canonical writings, but this too is arbitrary since the canon is a theologically based construct, and not one that is posited by the writings themselves. One can legitimately posit that they are Christian, but that is all. Even if the cut-off point is the first century, on what historical basis are first-century non-canonical Christian writings to be excluded from the chronology? And if they are not excluded, as the History-of-Religions school has argued, the term "New Testament theology" becomes a misnomer. Furthermore, earlier writings can legitimately be viewed as potentially conveying more theological weight than the later ones. On the other hand, if the canon is prioritized, and the writings it contains are given a different value than non-canonical writings, chronology is undermined since the notion of canon, hence divine inspiration, conveys an equally distributed authority despite the dating. In other words, theology trumps chronology.

The fourth problem is that reconstructions of the historical Jesus over the last two hundred years have not resulted in a consensus. Certainly the vast majority of scholars are agreed that the sayings attributed to Jesus in the Gospels are not necessarily exact quotations of what he said. While some sayings may well have come from Jesus, their placement within a narrative removes them from their original oral context and situates them within a representational narrative that necessarily reflects the context of the Gospel writers. Other sayings reveal editing by the Gospel writers. This is especially clear when sayings in Mark, the earliest Gospel, are compared to the same sayings (occurring in the same contexts) in Luke and Matthew, which most scholars believed used Mark. Still others reflect traditions that may well have circulated in the early church. Many of the sayings in John's Gospel, for example, are so different from those in the Synoptic tradition that they may well reflect the beliefs of the community. They appear to be expressions of faith that are fused with the "memories of Jesus". In other words, Jesus is made to say what the community of faith has come to believe. Not only was this commonplace in the early Christian use of scripture, but was also widespread in Greco-Roman and Jewish hermeneutics.

In attempting to isolate Jesus' sayings and actions, many scholars have proposed various criteria, such as the criterion of dissimilarity, the criterion of coherence, the criterion of multiple attestation and the criterion of embarrassment, all of which are discussed in most books on the historical Jesus.[11]

---

[11] A helpful discussion of these is found in John P. Meier, *A Marginal Jew: Rethinking the Historical Jesus* (New York: Doubleday, 1991) 167–95.

While these criteria are by no means appropriated by all historical Jesus scholars, among those who do find them useful they have yielded results. Unfortunately, the body of data has been too small for a thorough reconstruction. For example when the minimalist results of the Jesus Seminar are compared to the more optimistic results of John Meier, their use of similar criteria has only yielded a handful of authentic sayings, mainly on the kingdom of God.[12] Luke Timothy Johnson has argued that the diverse portrayals of Jesus by historians (e.g. rabbi, cynic, passive revolutionary, prophet, apocalyptic preacher) have left only tiny snippets of data, which render reconstructions futile. Instead, claims Johnson, we need to realize our limitations and return to the "real Jesus" of the Gospels where we find a person who defines his life and death as an existence that is measured by obedience, suffering, service and love.[13]

Mark as a historical source? A case study

A fifth problem has been the lack of a thoroughgoing sociological and literary analysis especially of the Gospel of Mark, which is widely believed to be the best source for reconstructing Jesus. If Mark is regarded as the earliest Gospel, historical Jesus scholars will need to incorporate sociological studies of collective memory in oral culture to appreciate better that the Jesus of Mark is more the Jesus of oral memory than the Jesus of factual history. Walter Ong's *Orality and Literacy* has served as a standard introduction to the psychodynamics of oral culture. As it pertains to historical Jesus research, the question of the meaning of history and how history was perceived in highly oral cultures is of first importance. Ong argues that the function of memory in oral cultures is oriented towards contemporary relevance. That is, analytical thought patterns are not exhibited, but instead memory functions in practical, situational patterns.[14] The events remembered may well have a high degree of historicity (i.e. an event that occurred, was committed to memory, and was eventually synthesized into a memorable pattern of speech so as to preserve it), but they are not ultimately preserved for their own sake in an exact manner. If, as Joanna Dewey argues, Mark was intended to be an oral performance, perhaps even repeated in varying forms prior to its composition, then the general principles of oral compositions may be helpful for historical purposes, which include (1) Jesus may be patterned after heroic figures which share common characteristics; (2) the most repeated teachings of Jesus are historically rooted; (3) much of Jesus' life was irrelevant (and thus lost) to the

---

[12] Robert W. Funk, Roy W. Hoover and The Jesus Seminar, *The Five Gospels: The Search for the Authentic Words of Jesus* (New York: Macmillan, 1993).
[13] Luke Timothy Johnson, *The Real Jesus* (San Francisco: HarperCollins, 1996) 167.
[14] Walter, J. Ong, *Orality and Literacy* (London: Routledge, 2002) 52–3.

Gospel audiences; and (4) easily remembered forms such as parables and aphorisms may have been accurately preserved.[15]

With regard to collective memory, the work of sociologist Maurice Halbwachs has been foundational in recent years for a handful of New Testament scholars.[16] One of Halbwach's key observations on the function of memory within religious frameworks, which is reiterated in more recent studies of social memory, is that recollections of the past are assimilated within the frameworks of the present. But the past is not completely lost to the present. While the past is continually (re)shaped and (re)collected so as to have meaning in the present, the present is continually informed and guided by the past, especially if the tradition is older, is adopted by a large number of adherents and is widespread.[17] Since collective memory is operative in the compositional history of Mark, the implications for historical Jesus research are only recently being realized. One of these implications is the loss of Jesus' (Galilean) "Jewishness" and his adherence to purity laws as he is remembered within Diaspora Jewish Christian and Gentile Christian communities.

Moving from the sociological to the literary sphere, the identity of Mark's genre is of crucial importance if the Gospel is to be used as a source for reconstructing the historical Jesus. Since there are no exact parallels among Greco-Roman and Jewish writings, of the several options that have been proposed, three stand out. First, during the rise of form criticism in the early part of the twentieth century, many began to view Mark as a *sui generis* (unique) writing, which constituted the creation of a new genre. Scholars like Rudolf Bultmann, argued that Mark is a passion narrative with an extended introduction and is to be viewed as the expansion and preservation of the *kerygma* (preaching) of the early church which focused on the death and resurrection of Jesus.[18] According to this view, Mark is a kind of anthology of stories and oral traditions about the life and teachings of Jesus. Since Mark was viewed more as the preservation of preaching developed within the creativity of the early church, as opposed to history, its value as a source for reconstructing Jesus was minimized. While some scholars still advocate that Mark is a unique genre, much more emphasis tends to be placed on the interconnection of theology and history in a more or less unified narrative—as opposed to simply a collection of early

---

[15] Joanna Dewey, "The Gospel of Mark as an Oral-Aural Event: Implications for Interpretation", in *The New Literary Criticism and the New Testament* (ed. E. McKnight and E. S. Malbon; Valley Forge: Trinity Press International, 1994) 145–63.

[16] Maurice Halbwachs, *On Collective Memory* (ed. and trans. L. A. Coser; Chicago: University of Chicago Press, 1992). On recent interaction with Halbwachs in historical Jesus research, see the essays in Alan Kirk and Tom Thatcher, eds, *Memory, Tradition, and Text: Uses of the Past in Early Christianity* (Semeia 52; Atlanta: Society of Biblical Literature, 2005).

[17] Halbwachs, *On Collective Memory*, 183.

[18] Rudolf Bultmann, *The History of the Synoptic Tradition* (rev. edn; Oxford: Blackwell, 1972) 374.

Christian traditions—that is viewed much more optimistically as a source for reconstructing Jesus. Most contemporary historical Jesus scholars fall into this category, referring to Mark as a new genre that contains elements of other genres, such as Greco-Roman biography.

As a second option, several scholars have compared Mark to Greco-Roman biographies, such as Plutarch, *Lives of the Noble Greeks and Romans*; Philostratus, *Apollonius of Tyana*; Tacitus, *Agricola*; and Suetonius, *Lives of the Twelve Caesars*. Richard Burridge has provided one of the most extensive treatments. Casting his net widely to include Classical Greek, Hellenistic and Roman biography, Burridge understands these ancient writings in a three-fold manner: (1) they are writings that naturally emerge within a group that has been formed around the teachings or leadership of a charismatic leader; (2) their main purpose and function is found in the context of didactic or philosophical polemic; and (3) they are flexible, allowing for adaptation and growth.[19] Burridge admits that on some levels the Gospels fall short of an exact parallel with any one biography—for they tell us nothing of Jesus' home life, how he spent his youth, his personality traits or physical appearance—but he concludes that there seems to be no other literature prior to the Gospels that we can point to with more similarity.

If Mark is taken to be a form of ancient biography, historians must be mindful of at least four characteristics that have implications for reconstruction. First, ancient biographers were interested in portraying their main characters as relatively constant throughout their lives, which is a major shift from modern biographers who emphasize change. Events and experiences were chosen not for a lesson in history, but to demonstrate the exemplary traits and the consistency of character through difficult obstacles. Ancient audiences would pay close attention to how characters not only acted and reacted to challenges, sometimes through impressive deeds, but how they carefully articulated their verbal responses. Great persons were believed to be born great, and they became models for others to imitate. Secondly, ancient biographers attempted to entertain their readers and often promoted the virtue and philosophy of (or through) their subject which posed a challenge to mainstream society. Thirdly, biographies of "holy men" or divine philosophers attributed divine qualities in varying degrees to their subjects. Some were characterized as sons of god(s), which implied divine parentage (e.g. Apollonius of Tyana and Pythagoras), whereas others were deemed godlike (e.g. Plotinus) because they were gifted beyond ordinary men, despite their human parentage.[20] Fourthly, although ancient biographers wrote with historical intentions, a certain amount of fiction

---

[19] Richard A. Burridge, *What are the Gospels? A Comparison with Graeco-Roman Biography* (SNTSMS 70; Cambridge: Cambridge University Press, 1992) 80–1.
[20] Patricia Cox, *Biography in Late Antiquity: A Quest for the Holy Man* (Berkeley: University of California Press, 1983) 30–44.

and exaggeration was commonplace. Data collection and verification of evidence cannot be compared to today's standards. Speeches and deeds, for example, followed consistent forms and were freely adapted to situations that would enhance the subject's traits and character, which was moulded to an established model. As Patricia Cox summarizes, "From its inception, biography was marked by its encomiastic tendencies to exaggerate a person's achievements and virtues, carefully selecting traits and deeds that lent themselves to idealization."[21] This may be why biographies for the ancient Greeks and Romans did not fall within the five major categories of historical writing, which were listed as genealogy or mythography, ethnography, history, horography or local history and chronography.[22] By the Imperial age, Plutarch (*Pompey* 8) makes a clear distinction between history and biography. Whereas history recalls the chronological account of one's life, biography provides a systematic treatment of character.[23] During this period, the lives of the emperors gained popularity as means not only of promoting Caesar, but also retelling and explaining events on a grander scale.[24] In the light of the function of these Roman biographies, Mark can be viewed as an alternative explanation on an even grander scale. David Potter claims that "Ultimately, the most powerful of these alternative narratives was that offered in the Christian gospels, and they in turn reshaped the world in which they were read."[25]

If Mark was considered to be a biography by the early Christians, it is not easy to determine which typecast would have emerged as dominant. Mark's portrayal of Jesus could be compared to that of the divine philosopher who likewise performed miracles, gathered disciples, demonstrated devotion and purity, challenged the establishment, and shared their knowledge of god. Craig Evans argues that another option is that the portrayal could be regarded as a subversive "apologetic that boldly challenges the emperor's claim to divinity and his demand for the absolute loyalty of his subjects".[26] A further option is that Jesus is portrayed as the "prophet-king" in the pattern of Philo's presentation of Moses in *On the Life of Moses*. Or in the end Mark may have woven together some kind of biographical amalgam.

As a third option, Mark's genre has been compared to Jewish novels. According to Michael Vines, Mark is a narrative in which God's intervention in human affairs is at the centre of the plot in much the same way

---

[21] Cox, *Biography in Late Antiquity*, 15.
[22] C. W. Fornara, *The Nature of History in Ancient Greece and Rome* (Berkeley: University of California Press, 1983) 1–3.
[23] Cox, *Biography in Late Antiquity*, 12–13.
[24] A. Momigliano, *The Development of Greek Biography* (rev. edn; Cambridge, MA: Harvard University Press, 1993) 99.
[25] David S. Potter, *Literary Texts and the Roman Historian* (Approaching the Ancient World. London: Routledge, 1999) 9.
[26] Craig A. Evans, *Mark 8.27–16.20* (WBC 34B; Nashville: Thomas Nelson, 2001) xi.

as God is depicted in Esther, Susanna, and Daniel 1–6.[27] Relying on the principles of Mikhail Bakhtin's poetics, Vines argues that genre needs to be distinguished from the form of a writing or its compositional features. Instead, genre, or "inner form", focuses on the presentation of various combinations such as time (past, present or future) and space (foreign or local) which create meanings, ideology, moods and discourse. Like Jewish novels, Vines argues that Mark creates a world open to divine intervention, even though the direct intervention usually does not occur, but is instead mediated through emissaries of God. One of the difficulties with Vines' proposal is that it is a generalization with little detailed exegetical support from Markan texts. Nevertheless, his careful examination of genre and critique of prior proposals require attention from historians. No historical Jesus studies, to my knowledge, have yet seriously interacted with Vines.

Implications of genre have been sorely lacking in discussions of the sources by Jesus scholars. What is common is that Mark is viewed as an integration of pre-Easter and post-Easter material. Reconstructions vary depending on where one places the emphasis and how one attempts to bridge the chasm. In using a narrative like Mark, which is written from the perspective of faith to an audience sharing in that faith, the historian must begin with a comparative examination of the nature and value of literary sources.

Author-by-author approach

Aim

This approach is less complicated because it is not dependent on the tenuous processes of determining the dating of writing and its provenance. Rather, as the heading indicates, it attempts to isolate the theology of each writer. Those who structure their New Testament theologies in this way strive to respect the terminology and context of each author. For example, the Matthean evangelist is not asked to answer questions that he himself does not ask. Instead of imposing dogmatic questions and categories onto Matthew—such as "What is Matthew's view of women in ministry?" or "What is Matthew's view of the Lord's Supper?"—most scholars will use categories common to the Gospel and ask related questions like "What does the Matthean Jesus mean by the 'kingdom of God?'" or "Who are the referents in the parable of the sower?" Since the main focus is the full scope of each writer's ideas within their literary and social contexts, the

---

[27] Michael E. Vines, *The Problem of Markan Genre: The Gospel of Mark and the Jewish Novel* (Society of Biblical Literature Academia Biblica 3; Atlanta: Society of Biblical Literature, 2002).

means of isolating their ideas has been historical criticism. Hence philology, grammar, syntax and first-century backgrounds have played a pivotal role. For the study of Matthew and Luke, redaction criticism has been the method of choice. While scholars have differed on backgrounds and the meaning especially of theologically loaded terms, like "reconciliation" in Paul, the "kingdom of God" in the Synoptics and "eternal life" in John, their results have commonly appeared within the same book. Thus a book might contain the title *New Testament Theology*, but its chapters may be devoted to the diverse ideas of each writer.

Also common has been the proliferation of books on the theology of only one writer. Given their narrow scope, these are not New Testament theologies, though they do follow the same principle and methods. One could say that these are like expansions of the chapters that are normally found in New Testament theologies of this sort. A recent example is James Dunn's massive *The Theology of Paul the Apostle*, which structures Paul's thought into categories that one might find in a systematic theology.[28]

Methodologically, this structuring has traditionally been dependent on historical criticism, but in recent years has benefited from research into ancient rhetorical practices (especially for Paul), social-scientific inquiry and narrative criticism. No one can deny that huge insights have been made into the theological ideas of individual New Testament writers through this kind of structuring.

Practitioners

I. Howard Marshall's historical-critical approach contains a twofold manoeuver that he terms "description" and "explanation".[29] Together they describe the task of New Testament theology. At the "descriptive" stage he attempts to lay out all the theological ideas that are contained in the New Testament. There is definitely an assumption in Marshall's work that the ideas can be understood through proper reconstruction of each author's intentions. At the root of these theological ideas is the authors' attempt to grasp God's relationship to the world. The writings are thus viewed as expressions of the authors' experiences in what Marshall calls a "piecemeal or a more systematic manner" and thus allows us to analyze and restructure them.[30]

This is followed by the "explanation" stage wherein he attempts "to show how these ideas developed and thus how one author's theology

---

[28] James D. G. Dunn, *The Theology of Paul the Apostle* (Grand Rapids: Eerdmans, 1998)
[29] I. Howard Marshall, *New Testament Theology: Many Witnesses, One Gospel* (Downers Grove: InterVarsity Press, 2004) 27–8. Marshall states that the only other New Testament theologian who uses this two-stage approach is Ferdinand Hahn in his two volume *Theologie des Neuen Testaments*.
[30] Marshall, *New Testament Theology*, 28

is related to that of another".[31] In recognizing the difficulty of unifying the diversity of theological ideas in the New Testament in the interest of formulating a theology, Marshall claims we are left with three options: (1) we leave the tensions unresolved and be content with New Testament *theologies*, (2) we attempt to find where opposing views might find some point of harmony, or (3) we find the unity of the New Testament on a deeper level of perception. Marshall opts for the third option, claiming that the diversity of theological views in the New Testament takes place within a common Jewish framework that views the world and its history as a narrative about God redeeming his people. Out of this framework, the New Testament writers give expression, albeit in different ways, to a common theme of redemption through mission, first by Jesus and then by his followers. Marshall summarizes the main theme of his New Testament theology as follows:

> Throughout the New Testament we are presented with a religion of redemption. The same four stages are common to all the writers: There is a situation of human need that is understood as sin that places sinners under divine judgment. There is a saving act by God that is accomplished through Jesus Christ, who is the Son of God manifested as a human being and whose death and resurrection constitute the saving act that must be proclaimed to the world, to Jews and to Gentiles. There is a new life for those who show faith in God and Jesus Christ, and this new life, mediated by the Holy Spirit, is experienced individually and as members of the community of believers. God will bring his redemptive action to its consummation with the parousia of Christ, final judgment and the destruction of evil, and the establishment of the new world in which his people enjoy his presence for evermore.[32]

Marshall should certainly be applauded for his sensitivity to the diversity of ideas in the New Testament, for his cautious recognition that his quest remains incomplete, and for his courage to find unity. In my estimation, however, his project does not escape the standard critiques directed against historical-critical attempts "objectively" to unify the theological ideas in the New Testament and within the canonical collection. His "history" is clearly theologically motivated and would understandably appeal to like-minded parishioners for whom perhaps he may be writing. For example, how much of his grand theme can be found in the Gospel of Mark? I find Mark neither addressing nor giving particular attention to (1) humanity under the bondage sin, (2) the incarnation of Jesus, (3) the Holy Spirit, (4) the establishment of a new world, (5) a post-resurrection universal mission

---

[31] Marshall, *New Testament Theology*, 27.
[32] Marshall, *New Testament Theology*, 717–18.

or (6) a salvific interpretation of Jesus' death. Instead, Mark concentrates on presenting Jesus, whose life and death is the *pattern* for the follower, as one who proclaims the kingdom of God.[33] Moreover, his claim that we need to find a deeper level of perception where the unification might be found at first sounds optimistic in the sense that one anticipates a discussion of the subjective element in all reading processes. But instead the so-called "underlying perspective" is disappointingly a quest for a common theme that, Marshall argues, emerges from careful historical study. In the end one is suspicious whether this grand theme actually *emerges* from the New Testament or whether it is *created* on the basis of prior assumptions. Finally, like other foundationalists who emphasize the historical component, Marshall admits that the New Testament has relevance for today's Christians, but in the end we are left with a high degree of uncertainly as to how his main theme finds meaning in our culture. Certainly much is implied, but an explanation is wanting.[34]

The final example is G. B. Caird's *New Testament Theology*, which provides an insightfully fresh angle to the author-by-author structure. Some, no doubt, might see Caird's structure as unique and would not even place it in this category. However, given that his goal is to let the New Testament writers speak for themselves, it seems fitting. Caird situates the New Testament writers within a hypothetical dialogue that he calls "the Apostolic Conference", modelled after Galatians 2 where Paul recalls his meeting with the established Christian leadership in Jerusalem. Caird does not say that the New Testament writers actually met with each other. What he means by "conference" is that it is "pictorial" in the sense that it is a reflection of what happens in the scholar's study when the canon provides the limits to a New Testament theology. For Caird, isolating the exact points of agreement emerging out of this first conference is foundational for his structuring of a unified New Testament theology—and he would even say the unity of the Church. The participants of the conference neither drew up a creed nor attained unanimity, but in spite of outstanding differences of opinion on a host of topics the apostolic group was unified in their common service to the same Christ. It has long been commonplace among New Testament scholars to point out the deep disagreements between Peter and Paul, but even though they went their separate ways, Caird writes that, "they could do this without any sense of radical division, because they had recognized that the same God was at work both in Peter's mission to the Jews and in Paul's mission to the Gentiles."[35] Later Caird goes on to claim that all the authors shared in the common belief that "Christ died

---

[33] See Thomas R. Hatina, *In Search of a Context: The Function of Scripture in Mark's Narrative* (JSNTSup 232; SSEJC 8; London: Sheffield Academic Press, 2002).
[34] Marshall, *New Testament Theology*, 43–6.
[35] Caird, *New Testament Theology*, 23–4.

for our sins."[36] This common recognition of mission in the service of the same Jesus, according to Caird, is the criterion for establishing the New Testament's unity. Caird spends a good portion of the book explaining how the New Testament writers understood Christ's atoning work on the cross as the pinnacle of history, which for them was indistinguishable from the biblical narratives. At this point, Caird's attempt to unify the New Testament into a coherent theology overlaps with the salvation-history approach, which is discussed in the next chapter.

Evaluation

The initial response that this structure elicits is positive because each writer appears to be treated equally and in his own right, without being made to conform to the ideas of his peers. As Caird comments, "It has the initial advantage of attempting the possible."[37] This structuring also conveys simplicity as a result of its focus on a single author. Aside from the need for comprehending an ancient writer's social background, the practitioner is primarily concerned with evidence that lies within a very small spectrum of material. There is also little need for reconstruction or for retrieving the various traditions in the compositional process since the context of the writing is the primary target.[38]

This simplicity, however, is also its primary weakness. The most common criticism that is levelled against this structure is that it does not adequately unify the theologies of the New Testament writers. Its primary contribution to New Testament theology is that it establishes and organizes well the accumulated data from the ancient writers; but it usually does not adequately interpret the data in a coherent manner. What we end up with is not a New Testament theology, but New Testament theologies. Certainly, in more recent attempts, scholars like Marshall and Caird have expressed sensitivity to this criticism, but has it been enough? For instance, does Caird's structure, based on the supposed common apostolic recognition of mission in the service of an agreed-upon Jesus, resolve the long-standing problem of unity? His allowance, on the one hand, for the individual voices of the New Testament writers to be heard, and his recognition, on the other hand, of the need for some kind of unity are certainly laudable, and in my opinion must be maintained, but in the end how does this advance the discipline of New Testament theology? The difficulty is that his criterion of unity is too broad. Belief in the so-called "same" Jesus and carrying out a mission for advancing this belief was tantamount to being called

---

[36] Caird, *New Testament Theology*, 74.
[37] Caird, *New Testament Theology*, 17.
[38] Caird, *New Testament Theology*, 17–18.

"Christian" in the first century, even for those that might today be called "aberrant" Christians.

Moreover, the last two hundred years of exegesis has made it exceedingly difficult to show that all of the New Testament writers share the same belief in the "same" Jesus. As was discussed earlier in the book, there is much diversity between John's portrayal of Jesus and that of the Synoptic tradition. Differences among the Synoptics abound, not to mention those between the reconstructed historical Jesus(es) and the Synoptics. Such omissions leave the reader with a perplexity that is well described by one reviewer in this way: Caird "delights in rejecting subjectivism, Gnosticism, form criticism, structuralism, deconstructionism. He shows no interest in the new quest for the Jesus of history since he never gave up on the old one." On the other hand, he rejects a "rigid confessionalism and dogmatic coersion".[39] If this is the case, where do we move from here?

Among those who attempt to bring some coherence to the diverse ideas of the New Testament writers, another problem arises. It is very easy in the structuring process for a major author in the New Testament corpus to dominate the others. Paul and John have typically been the dominant forces due to their literary bulk and theological content. While it is understandable that Paul might dominate much smaller writings, like Jude or 1 and 2 Peter, it is surprising that the author of Luke-Acts, who is responsible for the largest block of writing, has also remained in the shadows.

Despite the challenges, this approach is worth pursuing. Attempts at bringing coherence to, say, Jesus' preaching of the kingdom of God in Mark and Jesus' proclamation of eternal life in John can potentially only yield a better understanding of both. Comparing the ideas of different writers who are in geographical proximity to one another can also not only advance our understanding of their writings, but also the theological nuances and development of early Christian thought within a common region. By using the cosmopolitan port city of Ephesus as a locus for examination, for example, we can compare the ideas in the Gospel and Epistles of John, the letter to the Ephesians and Revelation.[40] From another angle, if those who strictly advocate a foundationalist approach conclude that theological coherence proves impossible to attain, the author-by-author approach will become a dominant structure for articulating at least New Testament theologies.

---

[39] Review of Caird's *New Testament Theology* by Paul Minear, *Journal of Biblical Literature* 115 (1996) 135.

[40] A recent example that uses location as a parameter for comparing and contrasting early Christian groups is Paul Trebilco, *The Early Christians in Ephesus From Paul to Ignatius* (WUNT 166; Tübingen: Mohr-Siebeck, 2004).

Conclusion

What is seen in both the chronological structures and the author-by-author structures are laudable attempts at forming a New Testament theology from the ground up. Both practices have been faithful to Gabler's founding principles. Both have contributed considerably to our knowledge of the cultural, linguistic, and literary backgrounds of the New Testament writings. Both have expanded our understanding of nascent Christianity and its origins. And both have significantly broadened our understanding of the theological ideas of the New Testament writers themselves. As far as the historical component of New Testament theology is concerned, gratitude is well deserved.

At the same time, the well-intentioned desire to remain historically faithful to the writings has not sufficiently dealt with the question of the how they might be relevant or normative. Relevance is certainly assumed by most foundationalists, but how exactly one bridges the gap between the past and the present has remained vague. In the next chapter, we shall see how dialectical structuring has attempted to solve the problem.

Discussion questions

1 What are the primary advantages and disadvantages of using structures in the development of New Testament theology?
2 Can a New Testament theology be formulated without structure?
3 What are the underlying assumptions within Christianity (as opposed to, say, Judaism) that tend always to lead to the systematization and unification of scripture?
4 Should the chronological structure begin with the historical Jesus and Q, both of which are reconstructions and not texts?
5 Is the author-by-author structure legitimate for the formulation of a New Testament theology?
6 How might we, or should we even, unify primary themes and concepts of the New Testament writings, such as "reconciliation" in Paul, the "kingdom of God" in the Synoptics and "eternal life" in John?

5

Dialectical structuring of New Testament theology

In contrast to the structures presented in the previous chapter, the ones discussed below coincide with the dialectical definition of New Testament theology. Once again, in Gerhard Ebeling's words, a dialectical approach understands New Testament theology as a discipline that is *"based upon* or *rooted* in the New Testament". Its formation begins from the top down. While it is a theology that attempts to be in accord with a historical understanding of scripture, it recognizes that its formulation, structuring and attempts at unifying the New Testament into doctrinal norms are highly influenced by external factors (e.g. cultural, existential, literary, social-scientific, biological, environmental or even theological systems) that continually intersect and contribute to our understanding of humanity and the world.

This chapter is an introduction to those practitioners who have used existentialist, dogmatic and salvation-history structures. Once again, my aim here is not to be comprehensive by including every practitioner, but to show through examples how a dialectical approach distinguishes reconstruction or exegesis from interpretation. To use literary categories, the interpretative authority in the dialectical process tends to be determined at the level of the reader, as opposed to the author or even the text.

The salvation-history approach

Aim

The salvation-history approach is an anomaly because it is the only structure in our survey that takes into account both the Old and New Testaments. Arising in nineteenth-century Germany Pietism where it was (and continues to be) called *Heilsgeschichte* ("salvation story"), the salvation-history approach was originally considered to be the second part of a twofold method of doing theology. In response to scholastic Protestantism, German Pietist scholars, most notably Johann Christian Konrad von Hofmann (1810–77), advocated a method that combined the Pietist construal of faith that was grounded in personal experience of God (called the "First Way") and historical criticism, which sought to uncover the totality of God's dealings with humanity (called the "Second Way").[1] The second initially presupposes the first. The two "ways" were believed by von Hofmann to ensure a scientific legitimacy to Christian experience by situating it within the story of humanity from the fall to the work of Christ to his return. The object of the "Second Way" was the historical study of the Bible that focused on discerning the eternal disposition of God. Predictably, the result was a salvation history of humanity, or the "'miracle' of holy history", which in turn served as the hermeneutical key not only for future exegesis, but future personal experience and the identity of the Church. The presentation of salvation in both the Old and New Testaments differed, but the former was believed to proceed towards a realization that is preliminarily achieved in the latter. Von Hofmann's understanding of the relationship between the Testaments has played an influential role for today's salvation-history approaches. Like his followers, von Hofmann viewed the relationship in two ways: (1) the life of Jesus is typologically related to the events in Israel's (biblical) history, and (2) interpretation is guided by a prophecy-fulfilment principle.[2] Like other influential thinkers, von Hofmann stood on the shoulders of his predecessors. In particular, it has often been argued that his influences stemmed from the views on spirituality and biblical revelation shared by figures like Friedrich Schleiermacher, Jacob Boehme and Friedrich Wilhelm Joseph von Schelling. All these thinkers saw the importance of welding personal faith experience with historical criticism in the formation of their theological systems.[3]

The basic aim of salvation-history, which has remained fairly constant for over a hundred years, is to show how the Bible is a grand narrative whose plot is God's redemption of humanity. In turn, the grand narrative becomes the paradigm, or the organizing principle, for both Old and New Testament theology. Since history becomes the sphere of God's salvation, exegesis is the means of retrieval.[4] As might be anticipated, this metanarrative of redemption has taken on a variety of plots, often resembling the

---

[1] Johann Christian Konrad von Hofmann, *Interpreting the Bible* (trans. Christian Preus; Minneapolis: Augsburg Press, 1959); translated from the German original *Weissagung und Erfüllung im Alten und im Neuen Testamente* (Nördlingen: C. H. Beck, 1841). On von Hofmann as the primary influence in the development of salvation-history, see Roy A. Harrisville and Walter Sundberg, *The Bible in Modern Culture: Theology and Historical-Critical Method from Spinoza to Käsemann* (Grand Rapids: Eerdmans, 1995) 131–54.
[2] Harrisville and Sundberg, *The Bible in Modern Culture*, 150.
[3] Harrisville and Sundberg, *The Bible in Modern Culture*, 146–7.
[4] B. S. Childs, *Biblical Theology of the Old and New Testaments: Theological Reflection on the Christian Bible* (Minneapolis: Fortress Press, 1992) 16–18.

theological position of its proponent. Another issue has been the meaning of "history". For some scholars, the history of God's redemptive work as it is reported in the Bible is constituted of factual events that do not differ from what might be called secular history. Most scholars, however, have argued that salvation-history is a subjective category that refers to a special kind of history wherein God reveals his plan of salvation and should not be intertwined with secular history. Another way of explaining this distinction is by asking the question, "What is the aim of history?" Those who make a distinction between salvation and secular history would answer the question differently depending on whether or not their guide is the Bible.[5] Scripture, they would say, provides an answer, whereas the probing of secular history or the sciences does not.

The death of Jesus brings out the distinction even more clearly. The historian interprets the arrest, suffering and death as the effect of social causes. Based on historical evidence, Jesus might be portrayed as a prophetic critic of the Jerusalem establishment. In order to ensure peace and set an example for Passover pilgrims, Jesus was arrested, tried and executed as an insurrectionist. He died as a martyr for his beliefs and posthumously became the founder of a new religion. From a salvation-history perspective, the Passion event is interpreted very differently. While it may incorporate the same historical reconstruction, the meaning is much broader and deeper. According to scripture, Jesus' death takes on a variety of theological meanings. Some writings, like Hebrews and John, clearly portray Jesus' death as a salvific event that brings redemption to humanity. Other writings, like Mark, portray his suffering and death as a pattern of obedience for all who follow. What is common to all the writings is that his death has meaning for humanity. A salvation-history approach incorporates that meaning into the larger biblical metanarrative of human redemption. The theologizing process is itself an interpretative move away from a literalist reading that considers writing and reality to be equivalent.

Practitioners

Arguably, the most well-known proponent of this structure is Oscar Cullmann whose three books, *Christ and Time*, *The Christology of the New Testament* and *Salvation in History*, have richly contributed to ongoing debate on the unity of the New Testament, even in Catholic circles.[6] Although these do not contain the title *New Testament Theology*, scholars have unanimously identified them as such. Cullmann understands

---

[5] Childs, *Biblical Theology of the Old and New Testaments*, 16–18.
[6] Translated from the original German as *Christ and Time: The Primitive Conception of Time and History* (trans. F. V. Filson; London: SCM Press, 1962, orig. 1946); *The Christology of the New Testament* (trans. S. C. Guthrie and C. A. M. Hall; Philadelphia: Westminster Press,

salvation-history as unfolding, or evolving, within secular history. Unlike many of his peers, Cullmann did not view the two histories separately running in parallel to one another. Instead, he understood salvation-history as a continuous hermeneutical activity that contemporizes the past. His distinction between the two histories is captured in this statement: "the thing that distinguishes history from salvation-history is the role played by revelation in salvation-history, both in the experiencing of events and facts, and in the appropriation of the accounts and their interpretation ('kerygma') through faith."[7] But salvation-history is not the sum of recognized saving events in the Bible. Instead, salvation-history is a complicated hermeneutical process whereby past saving events are corrected and reinterpreted in light of new events.[8] It often draws on the notion of the fulfilment of the past. At times the fulfilment is the *counterpart* to an earlier promise, whereas at other times it takes on the function of typology wherein the past *corresponds* to the present—all under the so-called "plan of God".

While Cullmann situates his method well within historical criticism, specifically the History-of-Religions school, he does not simply end with description, but advocates that all exegesis should be normative. In fact, the task of exegesis is to uncover the core belief common to all the New Testament writings and then to promote that core faith. He writes at the beginning of the second book that the centrality in the New Testament should be the centrality of modern Christian life.[9] The function of New Testament theology should lead to prescription. As we will see in the following discussion of Bultmann's existentialist structure, in principle there is agreement on the normative ends of exegesis. Both would agree that the driving question is "What is Christianity?"[10] And both would agree that the New Testament is relevant for today's Christian. But unlike Bultmann, Cullmann's exegesis is not dominated by an existentialist call to a decision of active faith. Instead, the relevance is that we, because of Christ, live in the same intermediate period before his second coming. Both practitioners rely on early Christian notions of eschatology, but each appropriates these very differently. Whereas Bultmann demythologized early Christian eschatological language and re-appropriated it in a way that the eschatological

---

1959, orig. 1957); and *Salvation in History* (trans. S. G. Sowers; London: SCM Press, 1967, orig. 1965).

[7] Cullmann, *Salvation in History*, 151–2.

[8] Cullmann, *Salvation in History*, 88–90. In his summary, Cullmann describes the process as containing three aspects: "first, the naked event [*nackte Ereignis*] to which the prophet must be an eye-witness and which is conceived by non-believers as well, who are unable to see any revelation in it; second, the revelation of a divine plan being disclosed in the event to the prophet with which he aligns himself in faith; third, the creation of an association with earlier salvation-historical revelations imparted to other prophets in the reinterpretation of these revelations" (p. 90).

[9] Cullmann, *Salvation in History*, xi–xii.

[10] Cullmann, *Salvation in History*, 19.

future is a decision for God, Cullmann retains the ancient eschatology as a central hermeneutical device that places the Church in the "middle of time" awaiting the final act of God in redemptive history. So what does Cullmann's exegesis uncover as the centrality of Christian faith? He argues that fundamental to both testaments is the perspective that God acts in history to save his people. Events throughout the Bible are interpreted by the early Christians as progressively leading towards a culminating salvific event, which Cullmann understands to be the Christ event. The early Christian notion of linear time is a foundational concept that guides his exegesis. For Cullmann, Christ was the centre of time, or the mid-point of time, when history (from the perspective of faith) reached its period of tension between the "already" and the "not yet".[11] Emphasis is placed on Paul's reinterpretation of select biblical narratives of Israel's history (especially Galatians 3–4, Romans 4, and 1 Corinthians 3) as early forecasts of the Christ event.[12] One is hard pressed, however, to find exactly how today's Christian benefits from his temporal schema.

In the wake of Cullmann, several comprehensive New Testament theologies have emerged. Two often-cited examples are George Eldon Ladd's *A Theology of the New Testament* and Leonhard Goppelt's two volume *Theology of the New Testament*.[13] With Ladd, who situates himself within the Evangelical tradition, we find a more restricted idea of salvation history. Unlike Cullmann, who views revelation as an ongoing event in believing communities through the process of reinterpreting earlier traditions of salvation history, Ladd understands salvation-history (which he calls "redemptive history") as a series of events recorded in the Bible where God reveals himself. For Ladd, each generation of believers cannot "correct" or "reinterpret" the New Testament so as to add more fullness in the advance of history because the revelation is fixed. What the church does is engage in preaching that recites, not retells, the salvific acts of God in history as they are contained in the Bible. The task of reinterpretation (as application) is left for the systematic theologian. Ladd argues that the task of the New Testament theologian is to reconstruct the theology of the New Testament in its historical setting. Predictably, Ladd relies on the historical-critical method. But as a salvation-history proponent, he recognizes its limitations, and at times he seems deeply ambivalent towards it. While he sees its usefulness in recovering how the early Christians understood the unfolding

---

[11] Cullmann, *Christ and Time*, 121–2.
[12] Cullmann, *Salvation in History*, 249–50.
[13] George Eldon Ladd, *A Theology of the New Testament* (Grand Rapids: Eerdmans, 1974); Leonhard Goppelt, *Theology of the New Testament. Volume 1: The Ministry of Jesus in its Theological Significance* (trans. John E. Alsup; ed. Jürgen Roloff; Grand Rapids: Eerdmans, 1981); idem, *Theology of the New Testament. Volume 2: The Variety and Unity of the Apostolic Witness to Christ* (trans. John E. Alsup; ed. Jürgen Roloff; Grand Rapids: Eerdmans, 1982).

history of God, he recognizes that it alone cannot address the divine plan or meaning of history. According to Ladd, historical criticism is restricted to a secular understanding of history as a closed continuum of causes and effects on the horizontal plain. It does not deal with the vertical reality expressed in scripture. In order to connect the divine reality with secular history, Ladd argues that prior to historical-critical investigation, the New Testament theologian must presuppose that God has revealed himself in another sphere of history, which is not observable in the secular historical. Ladd points to the resurrection of Jesus as a particularly vivid example of a divine act in history, writing, "From the point of view of scientific historical criticism, the resurrection cannot be 'historical' for it is an event uncaused by any other historical event.... God alone is the cause of the resurrection."[14]

Ladd arranges his book into six parts: the Synoptic Gospels, the Gospel of John, the "primitive church", Paul, the general epistles and Revelation. For each he surveys the scholarly discussion of their major themes, and selects one from each that appears to contribute to a universal theme. While the themes in the individual writings differ slightly, mainly due to their varied use of language, Ladd's focus on a universal theological theme in the New Testament unfortunately overshadows any inherent differences and nullifies his stated intent to preserve the diversity of thought among the New Testament writers.[15] Ladd's emphasis on unity dominates the book. For Ladd the overall theme of the New Testament emerges from his eschatological reading of the kingdom of God in the Synoptics which, he argues, synthesizes the redemptive work of God in Christ with the future apocalyptic consummation of that redemption at Christ's return. As with Cullmann's temporal schema, it is unfortunate that the ramifications of the Christian life, as it is lived today, during the "already" and "not yet" period of salvation history, are not developed.

Overall, Leonhard Goppelt's two volume *Theology of the New Testament* is closer to Cullmann's vision of a salvation-history approach than he is to Ladd's. However, some differences remain. Unlike Cullmann, Goppelt argues that the salvation schema drawn by his predecessor is not explicitly conveyed in the New Testament. All we have, according to Goppelt, are the correlations between promise and fulfilment that are expressed in varying ways. While he echoes Cullmann in saying that all the New Testament writers share the belief that Christ is the fulfilled promise given in scripture, a unified understanding of what this means is not conveyed. For Goppelt, salvation and secular histories are for the most part blurred. The main difference between the two is that salvation-history is a series of processes that are characterized by the promise-fulfilment schema, whereas

---

[14] Ladd, *A Theology of the New Testament*, 30.
[15] Ladd, *A Theology of the New Testament*, 33.

secular history is a series of causes and effects that convey no meaning. Like Cullmann, and in contrast to Ladd, Goppelt understands the task of New Testament theology as having both a descriptive and a normative task. At the historical-critical level, Goppelt sees the task as an excavation of related material on the significance of Jesus as the fulfilled promise. At the same time he is astute in recognizing that with any selective and interpretative process the results reflect the interests of the theologian, which convey an implied connection between the past and present. But the connection is more than implication. Unlike Ladd, who leaves normativity (except his own) to the systematic theologian, Goppelt calls for dialogue between the two, allowing for the New Testament scholar to express his or her ever-forming opinions.

Goppelt's two volumes are strategically divided. In the first volume Goppelt establishes the teaching and activity of the so-called "earthly" Jesus as the foundation for his New Testament theology. However, he does not rely on historical Jesus research, but on the developed reputation and the reporting about Jesus by his earliest followers, which for Goppelt is found in the four canonical Gospels. Since the Gospels assume a portrayal of Jesus that closely resembles his earthly life, the starting point for New Testament theology, argues Goppelt, should be the teaching and activity of Jesus. Unlike most Gospel critics over the last two hundred years, Goppelt makes little distinction between the so-called historical Jesus and the Christ of the canonical Gospels, or as it has often been called, the pre-Easter Jesus and the post-Easter Jesus. Yet his approach is not a return to a pre-critical reading. He clearly demonstrates an awareness and understanding of the modern divide. Goppelt's scepticism towards reconstructions of Jesus together with his assumptions of Gospel genre as accurate retellings of Jesus form his theoretical basis, which in turn leads him to the view that early Christian theologizing about Jesus *assumes* pre-Easter material in such a way that the salvation message of the early church is a reflection of the message of Jesus.

In his second volume, Goppelt describes how the Jesus tradition (established in the first volume) developed in the post-Pentecost period. Here he again departs from the conventional view which regards Easter, not Pentecost, as the demarcation point. Nevertheless, the principle that unifies the theological thinking of this period is the integration of the Jesus tradition with the resurrection event. The correlation between the two forms the basis for the preaching of the early church.

More recently, N. T. Wright, who has gained a considerable following in Evangelical scholarly circles, has provided a stimulating paradigm for reading the New Testament that can be placed into the salvation-history camp. Wright's firm planting of one foot in the Church (as an Anglican priest and former bishop of Durham) and the other in the academy, together with his engaging communication skills and a myriad of non-technical publications, has also earned him great popularity among the laity worldwide. Wright's thinking is intricately developed in his ambitious, yet incomplete, series entitled *Christian Origins and the Question of God*. At present, three of the projected five volumes have been published in the following order: *The New Testament and the People of God, Jesus and the Victory of God* and most recently *The Resurrection of the Son of God*.[16] These appear to be chronologically constructed whereby the first volume sets the hermeneutical platform and aim, the second attempts to reconstruct Jesus, and the third establishes Easter as the turning point in Christian origins. The much anticipated volume on Paul should be the next release. Although neither the series nor the volumes in it are entitled *New Testament Theology*, his overall attempt to unify early Christian theological thought in both a descriptive and a normative way has had many scholars situate his work within this discipline. In his first volume, Wright extensively develops a hermeneutical process rooted in an epistemology that he calls "critical realism", which he borrows from Ben Meyer.[17] The main idea espoused by critical realists is that all our knowledge about the reality around us can only be provisional because we as knowers can never divest ourselves of our subjectivity, which for Wright lies within our worldview or personal story.[18] But "provisional" does not mean "static". For Wright, knowledge is an ongoing dialectical process between the knower and the world around him or her. In the field of history, which Wright engages passionately, this means that while the past can never be accurately known, we can know selectively by placing past events into paradigms that can provide meaning.

Wright's overall task is ambitious. In attempting to juggle three grand approaches—Wrede's historicism, Bultmann's normativity and the postmodern focus on the text and reader—Wright sets out an integrative paradigm in studying early Christianity and Judaism, to which he refers as the literary/historical/theological approach. Wright summarizes, "The historian faces the question of Jesus; the theologian, the question of god. The literary critic… faces the question of the New Testament. What is to be done with it?"[19] Wright answers his question by addressing the need to read the New Testament faithfully, whereby its "overtones" and "fundamentals" are seriously considered. This means that the New Testament be read as a Jewish book that straddles the worlds of early Judaism and nascent Christianity. As a Jewish book it retells the story of Israel as the story of Jesus, and thereby subverts all competing stories that attempt

---

[16] N. T. Wright, *The New Testament and the People of God* (Christian Origins and the Question of God 1; Minneapolis: Fortress Press, 1992); *Jesus and the Victory of God* (Christian Origins and the Question of God 2; Minneapolis: Fortress Press, 1996); *The Resurrection of the Son of God* (Christian Origins and the Question of God 3; Minneapolis: Fortress Press, 2003).
[17] E.g. Ben F. Meyer, *The Aims of Jesus* (London: SCM Press, 1979); *Critical Realism and the New Testament* (Princeton Theological Monograph Series 17; Allison Park, PA; Pickwick, 1989).
[18] Wright, *The New Testament and the People of God*, 35-7, 124-5.
[19] Wright, *The New Testament and the People of God*, 469.

to provide meaning to the world. In this retelling, Jesus is the sovereign authority of the world, and in him God's plans culminate—in the first coming of Christ, the present age, and his final return. As a Christian book, the New Testament is infused with Israel's story, identity, ritual and hope, yet from the perspective that Jesus is the Christ who completes Israel's vocation to save the world. Thus, for Wright, the New Testament writings are not simply detached accounts of early Christian faith and practice, they are the expression of a new and subversive "people of God" within a specific worldview.

In a somewhat circuitous route, Wright's method for unifying early Christian thought in the New Testament begins with a comprehensive yet simple hypothesis which is verified by a selection of data from the ancient world that are consistent with the initial hypothesis. The method intentionally follows the natural sciences. While Wright claims that this is "how it has always been done" in New Testament studies,[20] more recent approaches to the historical Jesus, where the evaluation of sources precedes hypotheses, would suggest otherwise. For Wright, the hypothesis—defined as a story about, and explanation of, particular phenomena—is formed and verified by using the same three-tiered integrative paradigm, namely historical criticism, literary criticism and theology. In recognizing the built-in tensions between a hypothesis and data selection, Wright adds that the superiority of his hypothesis lies in its potential ability to explain or incorporate "other related areas".[21] At the root of the convergence lies the simplicity of his hypothesis, namely that the historical Jesus, the Gospel writers and Paul share a consistent worldview and message. As a result, individual passages, such as Jesus' kingdom sayings, are read (at times even allegorically) to fit the wider metanarrative of salvation history. Anyone who has seriously examined any one of these three fields may immediately disdain such an assumption since much scholarship in the last hundred years has rejected this approach; but, Wright claims, such rejection has come at the expense of simplicity.[22]

Wright's convergence results in the Christian retellings (or stories) of Israel's story of salvation, patterned after the "liberation from exile" motif, through the belief that "in the events of Jesus' death and resurrection Israel's god had finally vindicated his people."[23] The new "people of God", consisting of both Jewish and Gentile believers, are now grounded in the belief that their new familial relationship was the fulfilment of what it meant to be Israel. For Wright the new Israel is synonymous with the new people of God who are "in Christ". Since Jesus as Messiah brought Israel's history to its appointed end by obediently fulfilling the task of salvation—a

---

[20] Wright, *The New Testament and the People of God*, 103.
[21] Wright, *The New Testament and the People of God*, 100.
[22] Wright, *The New Testament and the People of God*, 101.
[23] Wright, *The New Testament and the People of God*, 446.

task in which national Israel failed—all who have united with the Messiah by faith share in the new life and identity of Israel. In other words, since national Israel failed in her mediating role to save the world, Jesus, the new Israel, took on the original role and fulfilled it obediently. The resurrection was the vindication of that obedience. In Wright's words,

> The motivating force behind the early Christian mission, as revealed in the stories that fan out across the spectrum of first-generation Christianity, is found in the central belief and hope of Judaism interpreted in the light of Jesus. The stories we have examined, and the praxis and symbol that went so closely with them, only make sense if the storytellers believed that the great Jewish story had reached its long-awaited fulfilment, and that now world history had entered a new phase, the final phase in the drama of which the Jewish story itself was only one part.... The widespread early Christian impetus towards what was often a risky and costly mission can only be explained in terms of the belief that Israel *had* now been redeemed, and that the time for the Gentiles had therefore come.[24]

Evaluation

One instructive point from all this is that attempts to unify the diversity of early Christian thought in the New Testament require the imposition of external paradigms, even if they are derived from the New Testament. However historical one wishes to remain, inevitably one part of the New Testament will serve as a hermeneutical key for another. An example of Wright's imposition is the allegorical reading of the kingdom parables in the light of Pauline theology, as it is expressed in Romans. Whatever literary and social distance may have existed between them has disappeared. Moving in the opposite direction, that is, from the reconstructed New Testament construct to its normative role in the present, we also encounter no distance. Wright's reconstructed salvation history is the salvation story in which the modern Christian also participates. In other words, despite his expressed caution to preserve a distinction between the ancient world and our own,[25] the apocalyptic worldview within which the New Testament was written is, perhaps unintentionally, fused with modern conceptions of the world. To say otherwise—that the modern Christian does not live out the story—would jeopardize the relevance of the scriptures for Wright. Unfortunately, Wright does not adequately engage Bultmann's contention that the relevance of scripture in the modern era requires demythologizing, given the vast difference between the first century and our own. When

---

[24] Wright, *The New Testament and the People of God*, 445.
[25] Wright, *The New Testament and the People of God*, 65–7.

we demythologize, argued Bultmann, we preserve the transcendence of God who is thus able to address every shift in culture. In Via's perceptive evaluation, Wright's own position can be itself categorized as myth, which needs to be demythologized. He sums up his evaluation by saying that Wright's story is "mythological in precisely the Bultmannian sense of myth. It identifies the transcendent—God's eschatological kingdom—with the finite—a *renewed* space-time universe, which is, nevertheless, *still* the *space-time* universe."[26]

Not surprisingly, one of the major criticisms that has been levelled against the salvation-history approach is that it is circular; in other words, the conclusions are assumed. While its past proponents have claimed that the redemptive plot of scripture can be demonstrated historically, in today's broad awareness of the subjective-objective problem, many critics have recognized that exegesis often contains an underlying theological aim, even if it is subconscious. The reality is that we still await a biblical plot that is unanimously accepted.

This criticism also raises the tangential problem of defining "history". Can exegesis, as historical criticism, accurately reconstruct the events of the past? And what is the "past"? Is it simply a collection of facts, which inherently do not contain meaning? If we try to bring meaning to "facts", which is what historians attempt to do, we necessarily engage in interpretation, and hence enter into subjectivity. My point is that the events in scripture that form the building blocks for a salvation-historical reading of the Bible must make the distinction between fact and meaning. In so doing, a historically verifiable biblical plot will prove to be much more difficult to establish than has been supposed. In the end, proponents might have to resign themselves to an overt subjective/theological starting point beyond von Hofmann's construal of personal faith, which uses exegesis as a means of support or explanation instead of verification. The result would still be a theologically unified Bible, but one could not argue that the unity is grounded in history. Von Hofmann and some of his followers were correct to see that personal faith is the preliminary step in biblical interpretation, but the anthropocentric starting point needs to be extended to its inevitable conclusion, namely the entire process of Christian life. Moreover, if personal faith is the foundation, then we must allow for the biblical plot to lie in the eye of the beholder, so to speak. This is exactly what we encounter in early Christian uses of scriptures where Christ serves as the hermeneutical key. Christ and the scriptures are unified in, one could say, a salvation-history, but not every New Testament writer understands the unification in the same way.

Another problem that has surfaced is the confusion between ancient hermeneutical practices and the "divine plan". While it is true that the Old

---

[26] Dan O. Via, *What is New Testament Theology?* (Guides to Biblical Scholarship; Minneapolis: Fortress Press, 2002) 91.

and New Testaments are filled with interpretations and reinterpretations of earlier biblical traditions (explicitly reshaping the past for contemporary purposes), it is quite another thing to conclude that these amalgamated processes of usage and meaning-making convey a "divine plan". In particular, Heikki Räisänen criticizes Oscar Cullmann because he confuses a modern phenomenological insight, namely that Israel's traditions were reinterpreted in the light of new events, with the assertion that all events are governed by a divine plan. The fact that the New Testament writers utilize quotations and allusions from the Old Testament to bring explanation and legitimacy to Christ does not mean that they were cognizant of a grand coherent plan of God. And assuming they were not cognizant of it, it is quite another thing to claim that the divine plan was operative "behind the scenes" as some kind of mechanism. Another problem is that since Cullmann does not view salvation-history in the Old Testament as either the actions of Yahweh in Israel's history or Israel's witness to those actions (since Israel was not cognizant of the Christ event), the so called great events in Israel's history, like the exodus, have no role.[27] Finally, despite Cullmann's eagerness to extend the function of exegesis to the present, his overall reading of the New Testament contains very little interpretation. Many scholars have assessed his two major books on salvation-history to be historical-critical studies, calling his approach descriptive or reconstructive. It has often been suggested that Cullmann was always cautious, perhaps overly so, in not letting his reading slip into existentialism, which for him imposed far too much on the text. The closest that Cullmann comes to interpretation is in saying that today's Christian participates in the "intermediate" period (i.e. the period of tension between the "already" and "not yet") that was initiated by the Christ. In this way, salvation-history is extended into the ongoing present until it reaches its completion in the Second Coming.[28]

This rather fragmented attempt at a connection between the past and the present is also a problem in Goppelt's well-intentioned appeal to normativity. The major structural difficulty in Goppelt's New Testament theology is the assumed unity between the Jesus of the Gospels, which Goppelt connects to the "earthly" Jesus, and the redemptive theology of Paul, who has very little to say about the walking and talking Jesus of Galilee in the late 20s of the first century.

The criticisms levelled against Ladd have been even more severe, extending to both his exegesis and his selection of unifying themes. Ladd's selective use of historical criticism has been a particular point of contention. While he sees it as a useful tool in some cases, such as his reconstruction

---

[27] Heikki Räisänen, *Beyond New Testament Theology: A Story and a Program* (2nd edn; London: SCM Press, 2000) 64–5.
[28] Cullmann, *Salvation in History*, 293.

of the kingdom of God, he is very clear about its secular assumptions and denials of God's actions in history.[29] In other places, such as his discussion of the historical Jesus, he completely abandons the method, offering no criteria for the selection process. Critics have also objected to Ladd's selection of the unifying themes that bring his New Testament theology together. While Ladd demonstrates an awareness of the options that have been proposed, his selection of one theme over other options is exegetically unsubstantiated. Ladd's overall theme and primary hermeneutic, namely the divine plan of redemption, may well prove to be a way forward in the formulation of a New Testament theology, but we cannot be content with Ladd's method. He is correct to say that all scholars begin with presuppositions, but these must be subject to some kind of testability, otherwise all New Testament theologies must be said to be of equal value. For example, how does one substantiate the claim that "God has been redemptively active in one stream of history in a way in which he is not active in general history"?[30] Or how does one effectively compare Ladd's grand theme with those proposed by, say, advocates for women's equality, gay and lesbian rights, economic injustice or broader concerns for social inequality like that of Paul Hanson, who argues that God's grand plan in the scriptures is to aid the oppressed, form an egalitarian and faithful society, and to live in the freedom of the spirit?[31] For Hanson the divine plan subverts religious institutionalism, social hierarchy and ritualistic structures that legitimize the oppression of the outsider.

Moreover, a salvation-history approach that does not address contemporary Christianity and its many expressions throughout the diverse cultures of the modern world is incomplete. A comparison of cultural expression of Christianity has the added benefit of recognizing that the so-called "redemptive history" of the Bible is highly conditioned by the cultural streams of its own day, especially the apocalypticism of the early Christians. Once again the problem seems to be a confusion of reconstruction and interpretation. On the one hand Ladd proposes that the task of New Testament theology is "primarily" descriptive and not interpretative, yet his means of description contains weighty interpretative baggage.

N. T. Wright has also not escaped criticism. One of the pressing issues in Wright's "hypothesis and verification" model is the process leading up to the formation of a hypothesis. The model begs us to back up a step. At the earliest stage, some evaluation of the data must take place. In the natural sciences, which Wright attempts to mimic, observable phenomena

---

[29] Ladd, *A Theology of the New Testament*, 173–80.
[30] Ladd, *A Theology of the New Testament*, 29.
[31] Paul D. Hanson, *Dynamic Transcendence: The Correlation of Confessional Heritage and Contemporary Experience in a Biblical Model of Divine Activity* (Philadelphia: Fortress Press 1978); idem, *The People Called: The Growth of Community in the Bible* (San Francisco: Harper & Row, 1986).

are subjected to repeated testing prior to the formation of a hypothesis. The hypothesis is then tested from a variety of angles before a theory is formulated, which in turn is subjected to continuous testing. In Wright's case, much more disclosure is needed in the process leading up to the formulation of a hypothesis. For example, what is the nature of the data in the Gospels? To what degree is the language about Jesus metaphorical, mythical, fictional or factual? What is the genre of the Gospels? What are the personal theological dispositions at work in the selection process? And what is the relationship between historiography and myth-making in the context of religion? In most historical Jesus research, the data are subjected to scrutiny prior to the formulation of a hypothesis.

Wright's second volume has often been criticized for fusing Mark's Jesus with the historical Jesus. Dan Via's assessment that "Wright's big picture of a highly messianic historical Jesus who intended, predicted, and theologically interpreted his death has overwhelmed appropriate critical decisions about individual elements" is not uncommon.[32] To have a historical Jesus that differs from the portraits of him in the Synoptics is a troubling prospect for Wright because it would mean that the Church must revise its faith. But does this not assume a much closer connection between fact and meaning than is warranted in the light of what we know today about ancient and modern hermeneutics, social memory, oral transmission and the imagination? In some places, Wright comes close to blurring the distinction between historical fact and theological meaning and opts for the latter as the "Procrustean bed", to use his metaphor, upon which the former lies, and in which it at times even seems embedded.[33] For example, in his discussion of the role of the historical Jesus in New Testament theology, Wright comments,

> It has been customary to say that the New Testament writers "did not think they were writing 'scripture'"; and though, as we shall see, that formulation may need to be revised..., it is certainly true to the extent that for them the place where Israel's god had acted decisively for the salvation of the world was not in their taking pen and ink to write the gospels, but in their god's taking flesh and blood to die on a cross. Their own work was conceived as derivative from and dependent upon that fact.[34]

What does Wright mean here by "fact"? Is he referring to the Gospel writers' assumptions that the incarnation was a fact? If this is the case,

---

[32] Via, *What is New Testament Theology?* 80–1. Via provides several examples where Wright's insistence on a rigorously "open-ended" (to use Wright's own words) study of history is compromised by theological presuppositions (Via, 80–93).
[33] Wright, *The New Testament and the People of God*, 22.
[34] Wright, *The New Testament and the People of God*, 23.

only John makes it clear. Or is he referring to his own assumption that the incarnation falls within the realm of historical fact? The latter seems more probable. Many can go along with Wright's insistence that Christian theology is rooted in history or that history matters to theology, but they cannot accept that theology matters to history. Via notes that "in historical work, the imaginative leap is *from fragmentary historical evidence to a coherent historical narrative*. It is *not from religious or theological beliefs to historical reconstruction*."[35] Moreover, Wright's fusion of history and theology needs to interact seriously with Rudolf Bultmann's discussion of myth, which was intended to preserve the transcendence of God.

Further, although Wright is certainly critical in his approach, the focus on a simple unifying hypothesis does not give fair consideration to the many scholars over the past two hundred years who have concluded that the historical method does not lead to the unification of the New Testament. For example, the Pauline paradigm has often been viewed as distinct from that of John or the historical Jesus. Instead of attributing such hypotheses to plausible ways of interpreting evidence, Wright (unfortunately) attributes fragmentation to peer pressure within the academic sphere. He writes,

> At this point in the historical study of the New Testament some pressure is regularly exerted within the guild to show how "critical" one's scholarship really is—i.e. to show whether or not one really belongs to the post-Enlightenment club of historical scholarship—by demonstrating one's willingness to jettison this or that saying or incident in the gospels, or this or that paragraph in Paul, in the interests of a particular hypothesis. This pressure acts (among other things) as a sort of guarantee that one is not after all a fundamentalist in disguise.[36]

As an example, Via points to Wright's opposition to those who would question that Jesus' final meal with the disciples was a Passover supper. Wright claims that these scholars are engaging in "radical scepticism". Likewise, any discussion of the church's involvement in reconstructing the actual supper and its Eucharistic sayings is regarded as "incredible".[37] John Dominic Crossan has pointed to other *ad hominem* statements, directed largely at himself, that are intended to show the inferiority of differing positions. While the passion for engagement at a deeper methodological level is exciting and can be passionate, diverting the focus onto peer pressure or personal attacks does not honestly help us to understand and even perhaps resolve deep interpretative differences.[38]

---

[35] Via, *What is New Testament Theology?* 82.
[36] Wright, *The New Testament and the People of God*, 105–6.
[37] Via, *What is New Testament Theology?* 81. Via cites Wright, *Jesus and the Victory of God*, 554–6, 558.
[38] See Crossan's criticism of Wright's bypassing of previous scholarship in John Dominic

Finally, while Wright's passion and conviction for his unifying structure certainly create enthusiasm within the field, they do so at the expense of competing options. Within the broad context of contemporary literary theory, Wright can certainly advocate a unified reading that is infused with a theological metanarrative. It is an entirely different matter, however, when that reading is repeatedly based on the intentionality of Jesus and the original authors of the New Testament.[39] This is where most of Wright's peers part company with his method for two major reasons. First, over the last half century or so, literary theorists have effectively disproved the view that an ancient author's intention can be retrieved and agreed upon, especially with narratives like the Gospels and Acts.[40] And second, historical critics, in whose company Wright finds allegiance, have repeatedly differed on their exegeses of passages that Wright uses as evidence to verify his grand five-act structure of salvation history.[41] One example is instructive. In order to preserve his larger salvation story, which climaxes in Jesus' announcement and activation of Israel's liberation from exile (i.e. national judgement), Jesus' warnings of final judgement are interpreted not as final judgement at all, but as another round of national judgement.[42] Those who do not accept Jesus' message of restoration are thus condemned to experience national judgement. This, however, raises serious problems. How does the message of restoration emerge out of the national judgement that Israel is supposedly experiencing at the time of Jesus' arrival? How does the warning of continued national judgement for those who reject Jesus correspond to the final judgement? How is it even possible for Jesus' contemporaries to understand a restoration message that differs from their traditional expectations of restoration? Wright interprets Jesus' message in the light of the Prophets, but they too equated restoration as the end of national judgement. Steven Bryan explains,

> Here is a problem: Jesus pronounces national judgement on his contemporaries for holding on to a hope of restoration which in many of its particulars—the defeat of Israel's oppressors, the re-establishment of a purified Israel in the Land focused on a renewed and glorious

---

Crossan, *The Birth of Christianity: Discovering What Happened in the Years Immediately After the Execution of Jesus* (New York: HarperCollins, 1998) 95–8.

[39] See also the criticisms in Via, *What is New Testament Theology?* 84.

[40] There are numerous anthologies of contemporary literary theorists on the market today. I particularly recommend David Lodge, ed., *Modern Criticism and Theory: A Reader* (London: Longman, 1988).

[41] Wright compares the biblical story to a five-act play: "Thus: 1-Creation; 2-Fall; 3-Israel; 4-Jesus. The writing of the New Testament—including the writing of the gospels—would then form the first scene in the fifth act, and would simultaneously give hints (Romans 8, 1 Corinthians 15, parts of the Apocalypse) of how the play is supposed to end (*The New Testament and the People of God*, 141–2)."

[42] Wright, *Jesus and the Victory of God*, 326–36.

Temple—sounds for all the world like traditions stemming from the prophets.[43]

Similarly, there are historical problems associated with Wright's reconstruction of the first-century Jewish worldview, which for Wright is a foundational concept in the formation of his salvation-historical narrative, and, of course, the exegeses of individual passages. Wright claims that during the Second Temple period a significant number of Jews viewed themselves as being in exile. Bryan agrees that there are texts expressing the restoration hope of some Jews living outside Palestine, but those tell us nothing about the worldview of the Jews living in Palestine under Roman rule. According to Wright, "exile" (understood as plight) was part of the national psyche, even for those living in Palestine,[44] despite its very different usage in Israel's scriptures where it is used as a reference for being "outside the Land". While the idea of captivity or bondage can be applied across the board, Wright's use of "exile" seems to mean nothing more than "non-restoration", which neuters the term "exile". In the end, Bryan's evaluation of Wright's reconstructed Jewish "exilic" worldview is quite forceful in showing that Second Temple Jews did not refer to their plight as "exile". The only texts that can potentially be used to support Wright's reconstruction are Tobit 14.5-7 and Baruch 3.6-8,[45] but these refer to Jews living outside the land of Palestine. Moreover, given the sparseness of texts, it is more accurate to say that most Jews living outside the Land did not view their condition as exilic.[46]

---

[43] Steven M. Bryan, *Jesus and Israel's Traditions of Judgement and Restoration* (SNTSMS 117; Cambridge: Cambridge University Press, 2002) 4–5. See also Bryan's response to the similar view that national judgement is part of the final judgement in first-century Jewish eschatology, argued by Scott McKnight, *A New Vision for Israel: The Teachings of Jesus in National Context* (Grand Rapids: Eerdmans, 1999).
[44] Wright, *The New Testament and the People of God*, 268–79.
[45] Tobit 14.5-7 reads "But God will again have mercy on them, and God will bring them back into the land of Israel; and they will rebuild the temple of God, but not like the first one until the period when the times of fulfilment shall come. After this they all will return from their exile and will rebuild Jerusalem in splendour; and in it the temple of God will be rebuilt, just as the prophets of Israel have said concerning it. Then the nations in the whole world will all be converted and worship God in truth. They will all abandon their idols, which deceitfully have led them into their error; and in righteousness they will praise the eternal God. All the Israelites who are saved in those days and are truly mindful of God will be gathered together; they will go to Jerusalem and live in safety forever in the land of Abraham, and it will be given over to them. Those who sincerely love God will rejoice, but those who commit sin and injustice will vanish from all the earth." Baruch 3.6-8 reads "For you are the Lord our God, and it is you, O Lord, whom we will praise. For you have put the fear of you in our hearts so that we would call upon your name; and we will praise you in our exile, for we have put away from our hearts all the iniquity of our ancestors who sinned against you. See, we are today in our exile where you have scattered us, to be reproached and cursed and punished for all the iniquities of our ancestors, who forsook the Lord our God."
[46] See the detailed evaluation in Bryan, *Jesus and Israel's Traditions of Judgement and Restoration*, 12–20. See also the discussion of God fearers and Diaspora Jews above in chapter 2.

Bryan's correlation between Jesus' message of restoration and his contemporaries' traditions and expectations is, in my opinion, on firmer historical and exegetical ground. For Wright to adopt Bryan's criticisms would mean a rethinking of his grand salvation-history narrative. It may even result in accepting a discontinuity between the expectations of the historical Jesus and the church's retelling of them in the light of Easter. If Jesus revised the national hopes and traditions of restoration in his own teachings, could not the church follow the same principle of revision in the light of their new context? In the light of Bryan's study, can we say that Jesus demythologized and then re-mythologized the hopes of his contemporaries, just as the church demythologized and then re-mythologized the pre-Easter Jesus?

The dogmatic or thematic approach

Aim

When the terms "dogmatic" and "thematic" are applied to New Testament theology there is very little methodological difference between them. Both structure New Testament theology according to pre-set theological categories. The main distinction is found in the kind of the categories that are used. The dogmatic structure is based on doctrinal categories that are representative of a particular Christian tradition or denomination, such as a specific view of the atonement, eschatology, or the Church. Proponents of thematic approaches structure their New Testament theologies on the basis of theological themes that tend to be derived from systematic theologies, such as sin, salvation, God, Christ, the sacraments, or the nature of humanity. While the advocates of both structures agree that the New Testament does not elaborate on any one of these theological themes or doctrines in the form of treatises, they do find that the structure can extract theological ideas from that New Testament that prove to be relevant to the modern reader. Moreover, this kind of structuring is a tool that is well suited to the development of a systematic or dogmatic theology. So in spite of Gabler's landmark division between biblical studies as a historically oriented discipline and dogmatic theology as a philosophically oriented discipline, practitioners of the dogmatic/thematic approach have remained unconvinced by his arguments for a divide. For most, Gabler's division resulted in an intolerable separation between the Bible and the Church. This objection to Gabler is not surprising given that most of the proponents of the dogmatic/thematic approach have strong ties to ecclesiastical traditions that are creedal and liturgical, such as Anglicanism and Catholicism. There is a clear recognition in this approach that interpretations of scripture matter to the faithful in the pews. Since they take scripture seriously, they likewise take its interpretation seriously. As Robert Morgan states, the interpretation of scripture is "a political act with consequences in the real world". Thus the pressure to achieve consistency between exegesis and an institution's theology becomes a never-ending struggle in the face of contemporary biblical scholarship.[47]

Methodologically, this structuring advocates that the New Testament be read in the light of these guiding themes or doctrines. Usually, there is no attempt to reconstruct the writings of the New Testament in order to uncover their potential influences or underlying syncretism that may have led to the formation of early Christian thought. Nor are there attempts to incorporate reconstructions of Jesus. Practitioners simply begin with the final form of the New Testament (or the whole Bible) and often assume that its writings are theologically unified on the basis of an assumed theory of divine inspiration. Normativity thus becomes the guiding principle of the exegesis process. In other words, the divide between "what it meant" and "what it means", to use Stendahl's terms, is fused. However, most practitioners are very careful in their exegesis not to commit the proof-texting mistakes for which so many systematic theologians over the years have been criticized.

Practitioners

In 1909 and 1910, Adolf Schlatter published his two-volume *The Theology of the New Testament*, which constituted a novel response to previous rationalist approaches. Surveyors of New Testament theologians have placed Schlatter in various categories. Some have seen his approach as novel, in a category by itself; while others have placed him within the salvation-history fold. His attention to the importance of dogma as prerequisite to the interpretation of the New Testament warrants his inclusion here. Dissatisfied with his predecessors who, in attempting to remain faithful to their historical method, left the New Testament in fragmented pieces with no unifying principle or theme, Schlatter recognized that if the New Testament is to serve as a sacred anthology for Christians, it must be theologically unified.[48] While he saw the importance of history, he also recognized that it alone does not provide meaning. To follow the lead of rationalists by entering into a quest for historical objectivity or neutrality

---

[47] Robert Morgan, "Can the Critical Study of Scripture Provide a Doctrinal Norm?" *Journal of Religion* 76 (1996) 232. See also the essays in Joel B. Green and Max Turner, eds, *Between Two Horizons: Spanning New Testament Studies and Systematic Theology* (Grand Rapids: Eerdmans, 2000).

[48] Adolf Schlatter, "The Theology of the New Testament and Dogmatics", in *The Nature of New Testament Theology* (trans. and ed. Robert Morgan; Studies in Biblical Theology 2.25; London: SCM Press, 1973) 115–25, 149–66.

was for Schlatter not only illusory, but constituted the betrayal of objectivity itself since such an approach was severely limited to only one part of reality within a closed system of causes and effects. Schlatter believed that this kind of quest for objectivity excludes faith and turns into a polemic against it.[49] History was important for the preservation of God's interaction with the world, but history alone as a closed system only results in a radical transcendence or no transcendence (or God) at all.[50] Schlatter argued that if the New Testament historian or theologian is to make sense of the scattered data, he or she needs to incorporate the study of doctrine, especially the doctrine of revelation, which in turn affects one's understanding of the nature of scripture. Schlatter was convinced that when the New Testament is viewed as an inspired text, revealing the divine will, the task of exegesis is affected. One of the major outcomes is that historical study is ordered towards theological unity of the writings. The underlying assumption is that God would not leave us with a fragmented anthology of sacred texts. Since God is one, so must his revelation be as well.[51]

Unlike Wrede, whose historical programme incorporated all early Christian texts, Schlatter limited the task of New Testament theology to the canonical writings, since only these contain the revelatory content that calls for a hermeneutic informed by faith. His chronological ordering of the New Testament and the Church was in opposition to that of the history-of-religions school. He saw the Church emerging out of the New Testament proclamation, and not the reverse.[52]

Alan Richardson has often been placed into this category. In his *An Introduction to New Testament Theology*, Richardson attempts to find a unified "Apostolic" theology preserved in the New Testament.[53] Although he occasionally relies on historical criticism, he is fully aware of its limitations, especially its inability to bring cohesion to the New Testament. For Richardson, unity of thought among the New Testament writers can be determined by placing their diversity of thought into predetermined categories based on broad theological themes or doctrines that are regularly used in systematic theology. The book contains sixteen chapters, each bearing a theological title, such as "Knowledge and Revelation", "The Holy Spirit", The Resurrection, Ascension and Victory of Christ" and "The Atonement Wrought by Christ". Richardson's approach is to take one such category/title, find all the key passages that refer to it, analyze each one independently of each other, and then look to see where the agreements lie. Note the methodological similarities with N. T. Wright's "hypothesis

---

[49] Gerhard F. Hasel, *New Testament Theology: Basic Issues in the Current Debate* (Grand Rapids: Eerdmans, 1978) 41.
[50] Hasel, *New Testament Theology*, 41–2.
[51] Schlatter, "The Theology of the New Testament and Dogmatics", 117–66.
[52] Hasel, *New Testament Theology*, 40
[53] Alan Richardson, *The Theology of the New Testament* (London: SCM Press, 1958).

and verification" model, despite the difference in the overall structure. Richardson describes the task of New Testament theology this way:

> Is it right to assume that the apostolic Church possessed a common theology and that it can be reconstructed from the New Testament literature? The only way to show that this question can be answered in the affirmative is to frame a hypothesis concerning the underlying theology of the New Testament documents and then to test the hypothesis by reference to the text of those documents in the light of all available critical and historical knowledge.[54]

Richardson calls for New Testament theologians to practise their craft from the perspective of faith. For without faith, meaning is inaccessible to the believer. To begin from alternative positions only leads to an improper understanding not only of Christian origins, but of the New Testament. Unlike many of his colleagues, Richardson does not regard New Testament theology as an end in itself, but as a first stage in the development of a broader theology. It is only the "theology of the Apostolic age". Moreover, as a historical discipline that continues to be reinterpreted in each generation, Richardson writes, "there can never be a final theology of the New Testament."[55]

The final example is Karl Hermann Schelkle's four volume *Theology of the New Testament*. Schelkle occupied the chair of New Testament Theology in the Catholic Theological Faculty at the University of Tübingen. In a discipline that was dominated by Protestant scholars, Schelkle's chair and four-volume work was certainly an anomaly. The volumes have the following titles in consecutive order: *Creation: World – Time – Man*; *Salvation History – Revelation*; *Morality*; and *The Rule of God: Church – Eschatology*. With almost no methodological preamble to his lengthy treatise, Schelkle briefly discloses his approach in the foreword: "My sketch is an attempt only to pursue more weighty words, concepts and themes through the New Testament, and to describe in systematic summarization what is to be thought of their actual formation and meaning in the individual writings and groups of writings which comprise the New Testament."[56] Throughout the volumes, Schelkle consistently expresses his underlying twofold assumption that guides his New Testament theology.

---

[54] Richardson, *The Theology of the New Testament*, 9.
[55] Richardson, *The Theology of the New Testament*, 12. See the varied discussion of Richardson in Leander Keck, "Problems of New Testament Theology", *Novum Testamentum* 7 (1964/65) 217–41 and A. K. M. Adam, *Making Sense of New Testament Theology: Modern Problems and Prospects* (Studies in American Biblical Hermeneutics 11; Macon, GA: Mercer University Press, 1995) 184–9.
[56] Karl Hermann Schelkle, *Theology of the New Testament. Volume 1: Creation—World, Time, Man* (trans. William A. Jurgens; Collegeville: The Liturgical Press, 1968) v.

First, he always begins with the belief that the Bible has much to teach us about ourselves and God, even if it is removed from us by space and time. And second, he was convinced that the Bible cannot simply be mined for its ancient meaning, despite its remote location. He writes, "That which has been handed on must always allow itself to be interrogated by a time which is ever new, prepared always to provide an answer to new questions."[57]

Evaluation

On the positive side, this structure attempts to incorporate several ingredients that every recipe for a New Testament theology should include. First, it seeks to unify the varied ideas found in the New Testament. Second, it attempts to establish a complementary relationship between the two Testaments. Third, like other dialectical approaches, it is explicit in maintaining the importance of both a descriptive and a normative perspective. The New Testament is viewed as a sacred text that is a witness to the purposes of God beyond itself and its own cultural context. It is agreed by the proponents that mere description is not equipped to make evaluations on the religious values conveyed in scripture. Thus a conceptual framework formulated within the collective body of believers that has proved itself relevant through the church's history is a necessary imposition onto the New Testament if the text is to continue to convey meaning. Another way of expressing this positive feature is that many proponents of this structure recognize the process of making meaning at the level of the reading community. And fourth, there is a clear recognition that one's presupposition about the nature of the New Testament—such its overall aim and theory of inspiration—affects how one practises New Testament theology. Unfortunately, this last ingredient has not been as developed as it should be. Even if theologians view the New Testament as an inspired text, the various theories of inspiration and nuances relating to how God "must have" intended the unity of the writings require much closer scrutiny.

So why has this structure not caught on? Simply put, the positive features have been overshadowed by historical concerns. Too often historians have criticized this structuring paradigm as an uncritical imposition of theology onto history. Whether it is a doctrine from outside the New Testament or a theme from within, the imposition of categories onto individual writings does not allow the variety of thought in the New Testament to emerge. Instead, those parts of the New Testament that do not fit the imposed moulds are too often omitted or misinterpreted for the sake of compatibility. Nor does it allow for each writing to be understood within its own cultural and literary context as this would run the risk of a reading that

---

[57] Schelkle, *Theology of the New Testament*, ix–x.

would be at variance with a theologically constrained text(s). One such problem is that the imposition of a grand theme or doctrine risks turning the entire New Testament corpus into a systematic theology, which itself is an Enlightenment category. It must not be forgotten that one of the assumptions of Modernism was that systematization or structure leads to objective truth.

Some have been more critical of the imposition of categories taken from systematic theology (e.g. sin, church or eschatology) as opposed to those taken from the New Testament itself (e.g. kingdom of God, eternal life, restoration). But an imposition is still an imposition. The major issue is not the kind of imposition, but the interpretative function of that imposition. All interpretations in the end require impositions, regardless of whether one believes that objective historical results can be achieved. Believing something does not make it so. Subjectivity is inescapable. In the next section of the book we will see how impositions are necessary not only in the quest for a unified theology, but for the preservation of a relevant New Testament.

Proposed doctrinal and thematic approaches have been too narrow in at least three ways. First, they have not addressed the contemporary social issues of our pluralistic North Atlantic Western culture, which is our frame of reference for identity. An informed identity leads to an informed hermeneutic. Second, and perhaps more importantly, they have not addressed the posture which individual Christians should take as they increasingly participate within a pluralistic world. For example, to what degree should religious and ethical tolerance be exercised and promoted within a democratic and pluralistic society? Orthodoxy seems always to overshadow orthopraxy. And third, they have not sufficiently addressed how the church is to view its identity and role within a much smaller and diverse world. For example, is there a place any longer for a triumphalist Christianity that sees itself as the only expression of divine revelation to humanity? Unfortunately too many of the past impositions within this structure of New Testament theology have had as their aim either the legitimization of the unity of the New Testament and/or the legitimization of a denominational statement of faith.

Another precaution that should be mentioned concerns the relationship between the discipline of systematic theology (or dogmatics) and that of New Testament theology. We have already discussed how a foundationalist approach can tend towards a displacement of systematic theology. A dialectical New Testament theology recognizes on the one hand its indebtedness to systematic theology for its pivotal role in canonicity, inspiration and related doctrinal formulations and, on the other hand, its reliance on exegesis; but it needs to find a complementary role that accommodates both. Since a competition between systematic theology and biblical theology is severely problematic because it inevitably results in negating both, a dialectical New Testament theology should probably play an intermediary role whereby it informs the broader field of systematic theology about how scripture is read by biblical scholars and interpreted among laypeople. As part of the dialectical process, this role can be easily extended to the history of biblical interpretation, which would provide additional insight into the relationship between culture, faith and the interpretation of scripture. If we understand systematic theology as a discipline that is ordered to the broadest possible unification of knowledge (and not just a narrow teaching about God), being informed by all known disciplines, then as John Macquarrie observes, New Testament theology should not be regarded as a branch of systematic theology, but as a special way of considering theological questions. Along with historical theology, it is for Macquarrie part of the first strand in theological studies. As the first strand, New Testament theology (along with Old Testament theology) provides systematic theology with material with which it can work in much the same way that other disciplines might contribute their material.[58]

The existentialist approach

The existentialist approach takes the quest for normativity outside the confines of the church and into the broader realm of anthropology by addressing the meaning of human self-understanding. Existentialism, which is an active rather than passive category, inquires about the individual's place, function and relationship to the world and to God (or lack thereof). It raises the question of how life can (or does not) have meaning through action. The chief proponent of this approach was Rudolf Bultmann (1884–1976) whose importance within the field of New Testament studies has already been mentioned. His interpretative approach has been the subject of hundreds of academic articles and books. A few scholars since Bultmann, like Hans Conzelmann,[59] have attempted to follow the existentialist hermeneutic, but considering Bultmann's enormous and ongoing influence, the following description and assessment of the existentialist approach is restricted to him.

As a student at the universities of Tübingen, Berlin and Marburg, Bultmann was saturated in the then thriving historical-critical method which served him well throughout an illustrious career that spanned six decades, most of which he spent at the University of Marburg. His use of the method, however, shifted considerably. During the earlier part of his career, Bultmann was a champion of the form-critical method, which was

---

[58] John Macquarrie, *Principles of Christian Theology* (2nd edn; New York: Charles Scribner's Sons, 1977) 40.
[59] Hans Conzelmann, *An Outline of the Theology of the New Testament* (trans. J. Bowden; New York: Harper & Row, 1969).

concerned with the recovery of the earliest Christian oral traditions prior to their incorporation into the Gospels.[60] The method was strictly descriptive. Bultmann eventually became displeased with historical criticism as the only tool for studying the New Testament because in and of itself it left the scriptures in the remote past and did not address their relevance. At the end of his New Testament theology, Bultmann summarizes the descriptive/normative divide:

> Since the New Testament is a document of history, specifically of the history of religion, the interpretation of it requires the labour of historical investigation.... Now such labour may be guided by either one of two interests, that of reconstruction or that of interpretation—that is, reconstruction of past history or interpretation of the New Testament writings. Neither exists, of course, without the other, and they stand constantly in a reciprocal relation to each other. But the question is: which of the two stands in the service of the other? Either the writings of the New Testament can be interrogated as the "sources" which the historian interprets in order to reconstruct a picture of primitive Christianity as a phenomenon of the historical past, or the reconstruction stands in the service of the interpretation of the New Testament writings under the presupposition that they have something to say to the present. The latter interest is the one for which historical labour is put to service in the presentation here offered.[61]

His unrelenting quest for a normative reading of scripture provided a formidable challenge to the History-of-Religions school and the so-called "liberalism" of his day, both of which advocated a rationalist historicism.

Bultmann's shift from a descriptive to a normative hermeneutic has been explained by means of three influential factors. First, although Bultmann's roots lay in the historical-critical method, his dissatisfaction with it in the 1920s attracted him to the dialectical theology of Karl Barth and Friedrich Gogarten.[62] His shift in thinking is already noticeable in his 1934 publication of *Jesus and the Word*, where he expresses the limitations of historical criticism, because "it misses the true significance of history. It must always question history solely on the basis of particular presuppositions, of its own method, and thus quantitatively it collects many new facts *out of* history, but learns nothing genuinely new *about* history and man."[63]

---

[60] Bultmann's most well-known work on form criticism is *The History of the Synoptic Tradition* (rev. edn; trans. J. Marsh; Oxford: Basil Blackwell, 1968; orig. 1921).
[61] Rudolf Bultmann, *Theology of the New Testament* (2 vols; trans. Kendrick Grobel; New York: Charles Scribner's Sons, 1951, 1955) 2.251.
[62] Hasel, *New Testament Theology*, 83.
[63] Rudolf Bultmann, *Jesus and the Word* (trans. L. Pettibone Smith and E. Huntress Lantero; New York: Charles Scribner's Sons, 1958; orig. 1934) 5.

Second, Bultmann's thinking was significantly altered by his experiences in the Second World War. The execution of his brother in a Nazi concentration camp, the first-hand observations of the regime's cruelty and injustice, and his active involvement in some of the churches that advocated anti-Nazi sentiment and action were important factors that led him to place a priority on acts of non-conformity in his method of interpreting ancient texts. The third factor was the influence of Martin Heidegger's existential philosophy wherein authentic human existence was understood as a life of action that is self-directed for the cause of the good and not one that is absorbed by the status quo of the world. Heidegger argued that (1) absorption results in everyone being the other, and not an authentic self; (2) absorption results only in the "they" and not the "I"; and (3) absorption results in continuity and not potentiality.[64] For Heidegger, the acknowledgement of death as the inevitability of life is the liberating realization that leads one away from a previous existence to an authentic existence.[65]

Heidegger's conception of existentialism as action led Bultmann to develop a hermeneutic that was based on the bifurcation of reality. One kind of reality was viewed as the sphere of human decision-making. Persons truly exist when they act on their freedom to make choices. Actions thus determine our identity. We fulfil ourselves only when we act. And when we act, we can be sure of our existence. Since action always allows for potential changes, this kind of existence is called "potentiality". The second kind of reality is the "world" which he called "actuality" because individuals by themselves cannot affect its change. It is the social constant. Bultmann called the "world" the realm that people have made into a power over them. This power is based on the past actions of the masses. It is more than complacency. It is an unwillingness to change when change is needed. Thus to live according to the "world" is to live in the past with no hope of change. The potential and actual realities are mutually exclusive, yet both are operative at the same time. As a result, the problem for humanity, as Bultmann saw it, is that true existence for the individual can only occur when one refuses to conform to the "world". Freedom is synonymous with nonconformity. Vice versa, to conform to the "world" is the denial of our existence and freedom.

Applying Christian language, Bultmann equated living according to the "world" with sin. Consequently, he equated living according to the

---

[64] The full expression of his existentialism appears in Martin Heidegger, *Being and Time* (trans. J. Macquarrie and E. Robinson; New York: Harper & Row, 1962, orig. 1927) 163–8. The integration of Heidegger is particularly evident in Rudolf Bultmann, *History and Eschatology: The Presence of Eternity* (New York: Harper & Row, 1962).
[65] See the lucid summary of Heidegger's existentialism in Via, *What is New Testament Theology?* 63–6. On the problems associated with the use of Heidegger in Christian theology, see Brian D. Ingraffia, *Postmodern Theory and Biblical Theology* (Cambridge: Cambridge University Press, 1995) 101–64.

potential for change with a life dependent on God. The latter was equated with authenticity, possibility, future and existence because it is a life that has been freed from the bondage of the world by the grace of God. One becomes a citizen of a different order of existence. The gospel frees the individual from the world because its origin is not from this world. For Bultmann, the event of Jesus Christ marked the pinnacle of the encounter between humanity and God. In Christ, we meet the revelation of the love of God and the love for God. In Jesus we find potential and true existence actualized which confronts and challenges each person to make a decision either for God or for the world. The one who decides to live for God lives to demonstrate the love of God to others. This is the life of faith. For Bultmann, the demonstration of love is a daily choice in daily encounters with the world. It can be expressed in simple acts of kindness or in acts of sacrifice that risk one's life.[66]

Bultmann's New Testament theology is based on a method that perceptively incorporates reconstruction and interpretation through an integrated two-stage process. In the first stage of the process, Bultmann leans on his expertise of the historical-critical method and History-of-Religions school to reconstruct early Christianity as a past phenomenon. For Bultmann, the historical-critical method was certainly vital, but its goal posed only two legitimate questions which Via summarizes as: "(1) What does the text tell me about the past? (2) What understanding of existence does it offer as a possibility for my existence?"[67] Bultmann opts for the latter. The aim of his reconstruction is to peel away the mythical constraints in order to disclose the authentic Christian *kerygma* (preaching), much like one peels a husk of corm to get at the kernels.

Bultmann appealed to the study of myth, which he understood as the language about the divine that is couched in cultural categories. In pre-scientific thought, Bultmann notes, such myths were taken literally. The confusion between the earthly and the divine needed to be unravelled. This is what Bultmann famously called *Entmythologisierung*, translated as "demythologization." He argued that when myth is literalized or historicized, the transcendence of God is undermined because it localizes the ubiquitous, temporizes the eternal, controls the uncontrollable, and exposes the hidden mystery which is only accessible through faith.[68] Bultmann's reconstructive process was guided by a negative answer to an insightful question that has caused discomfort ever since: Is the first-century apocalyptic worldview within which the New Testament writers lived and wrote necessarily Christian? To put it differently, on the one hand Bultmann

---

[66] See the lucid explanation of Bultmann's existentialism in Robert C. Roberts, *Rudolf Bultmann's Theology: A Critical Interpretation* (Grand Rapids: Eerdmans, 1976) chapters 1–3.
[67] Via, *What is New Testament Theology?* 60.
[68] Rudolf Bultmann, *Jesus Christ and Mythology* (New York: Scribner, 1958) 61–2.

believed that the Christian gospel (in the *kerygma*) is of universal import, but on the other hand he recognized that it was couched in a first-century worldview. Although he does not regard the mythical images and motifs as factual descriptions of the transcendent reality on which all existence is dependent, he does view them as expressions of human existence.[69]

In particular, Bultmann concentrated on Paul whom he regarded as the foundational Christian theologian. In his reconstruction, Bultmann argued that Paul's theology should be understood as anthropology in the sense that it focuses on the plight of humanity from sin to salvation, but not as a movement initiated by the need to be repentant. Instead, it was a movement towards a new human identity that finds its centre in the obedience of Christ to God. Through obedience to God the world is confronted. Paul's own conversion experience—which is likewise interpreted as a movement from inaction to action, from the world to Christ, from death to existence, or from stagnation to potential—serves as the climax from which his theology develops. In short, the Pauline gospel was itself an expression of change in the meaning of being or existence for the individual through an encounter with Christ in action that confronts the world. To emphasize this view, the individual and his or her own personal history is the locus of existential meaning, not the communal history of the church or, more broadly, humanity.[70] Bultmann always stresses the personal act of faith.

Once the layers have been removed—and the demythologizing has taken place—to reveal that early Christian (namely Pauline and Johannine) language about the divine is really language about human existence, the normative stage ensues. This second stage of his method brings (i.e. interprets) the rescued gospel into the present. Bultmann recognized, in the context of post-war Germany, that people could not accept the mythical character of the first century, but they could accept the gospel that was couched within it. Unlike some of his rationalist predecessors, Bultmann did not equate demythologization with the removal of first-century mythology. He recognized that just as Paul and John needed to communicate the gospel by first demythologizing the prior conceptions of the divine in their day, so contemporary Christians should follow in the process of demythologizing in order to communicate and, more importantly, to live out, the divine in their day. Relevance requires that impediments to faith need to be addressed in every generation.

Bultmann's presentation of the early *kerygma* is indebted to William Wrede and Wilhelm Bousset, who likewise make distinctions among its expressions in particular in Paul and John. Accordingly, in his *Theology of the New Testament*, Bultmann presents the theologies of Paul and

---

[69] Rudolf Bultmann, "The New Testament and Mythology", in *Kerygma and Myth* (ed. H.-W. Bartsch; trans. R. H. Fuller; London: SPCK, 1954) 1–4.
[70] Bultmann, *History and Eschatology*, 42–3.

John in the context of the Hellenistic Church. The book, originally published as two volumes, is divided into four parts. Part one, entitled "Presuppositions and Motifs of New Testament Theology", contains chapters on the eschatological urgency in Jesus' ministry and its interpretation in the "earliest church" and the "Hellenistic church, apart from Paul". Parts two and three, which are the focus of the book, tackle respectively humanity's plight from sin to faith in the theologies of Paul and John. Of these two, Paul predominates as the founder of Christian theology. The final part, entitled "The Development Toward the Ancient Church", addresses the doctrinal, administrative and ethical formulations in later generations. There is no preliminary theology of Jesus here as one finds in, say, Jeremias or Stephen Neill, who see Jesus' teachings and actions as the unquestionable content of New Testament theology.[71] For Bultmann, the message of the historical Jesus is not the content of New Testament theology, but its presupposition. This is made explicit in the first line of the book.[72]

Evaluation

The sheer volume of publications on Bultmann's hermeneutic makes it impossible to provide a comprehensive evaluation here. To emphasize the scope of the literature, Gerhard Hasel refers to a 1963 article that reviews some five hundred publications on Bultmann's theology and interpretative practice.[73] In the last forty-five years, the number of publications has surely multiplied. Reaction to Bultmann has come from every sector of scholarship and almost every ecclesiastical tradition. Gerhard Hasel has done a marvellous job in helping the student wade through the criticisms by dividing the reaction into three groups of critics.[74] The so-called "central" group, consisting primarily of Bultmann's students (often referred to as the "post-Bultmannians"), has proved to be the most formidable.[75] One of the major issues to which they took exception was Bultmann's bifurcation of the Jesus of history and the Christ of faith (or the Jesus of early Christian *kerygma*). For Bultmann, apart from sparse data, the historical Jesus was largely inaccessible. Many of the post-Bultmannians, with Ernst Käsemann's lead, attempted to repair that which Bultmann fragmented within the practice of New Testament theology.

---

[71] Joachim Jeremias, *New Testament Theology* (trans. J. Bowden; London: SCM Press, 1971); Stephen Neill, *Jesus Through Many Eyes. Introduction to the Theology of the New Testament* (Philadelphia: Fortress Press, 1976).
[72] Bultmann, *Theology of the New Testament*, 3
[73] Hasel, *New Testament Theology*, 84n. 61. Hasel refers to G. Bornkamm, "Die Theologie Bultmanns in der neueren Diskussion", *Theologische Rundschau* 29 (1963) 33–141.
[74] Hasel, *New Testament Theology*, 82–92.
[75] E.g. E. Käsemann, G. Bornkamm, J. M. Robinson, E. Fuchs, G. Ebeling.

Reaction from the so-called "right-wing" group, largely represented by Lutheran academics/clergy, was directed against Bultmann's de-historicizing of redemptive events in the Bible, such as the atonement, incarnation, resurrection, virgin birth and ascension.[76] His critics from the right either presupposed or sought to bring together knowledge that is acquired through the study of history and knowledge that is acquired through faith. For Bultmann, these lay in different spheres. Moreover, his critics noted that these redemptive events were arbitrarily subsumed within anthropology instead of Christology. In response, the assumption that objectivity could be reached was flatly rejected by Bultmann in his now well-known description of the interpretative (not reconstructive) process as the "hermeneutical circle". Bultmann argued that there is no interpretation of the text that does not at the same time include the exegete's interpretation of him or herself. This circularity occurs when one presupposes what one wants to prove. Despite his admonition that presuppositions cannot be avoided by the exegete, Bultmann maintained that this does not lead to the validity of all exegeses. Instead, he argued that presuppositions should be recognized as legitimate guides that determine what kind of knowledge one is seeking.[77]

Conservative Catholics were likewise distressed. From their perspective (which unites the message with the messenger) the discord between the demythologized "gospel" and the mythological Jesus—who is presented in the New Testament as the incarnate Son of God who died to expiate the sin of the world, rose from the dead, and ascended into heaven—results in a Christianity by name only. From the vantage point of the interpreter, the Catholic critic would also object to Butlmann's jettisoning of tradition, which in the end retains authority over the very scriptures he uses.[78]

Reaction from the so-called "left-wing" group focused on the incompletion of his demythologizing practice, especially in relation to his insistence that God was manifest in Christ. Gerhard Hasel cites three critics in particular: the Swiss theologian Fritz Buri, the German existentialist philosopher Karl Jaspers, and the American theologian Schubert M. Ogden. Both Buri and Jaspers fault Bultmann for an incomplete "de-*kerygma*tizing" of his belief that God was in Christ. While Bultmann relegates the redemptive interpretations of Jesus (e.g. atonement, incarnation, resurrection etc.) in the early church's *kerygma* to myth, Buri and Jaspers maintained that he does not extend the demythologizing to his existential premise that "God was in Christ." For God to be in Christ, in an objective sense, requires a link between the historical Jesus and the Christ of faith. Ogden questions Bultmann's basis for limiting the activity of God to Christianity or Jesus.

---

[76] E.g. Karl Barth, Joachim Jeremias, Hermann Diem, Julius Schniewind.
[77] Rudolf Bultmann, "The Problem of Hermeneutics", in *Essays: Philosophical and Theological* (trans. J. C. G. Greig; New York: Macmillan, 1955) 239–43.
[78] For a Catholic perspective, see L. Malevez, *The Christian Message and Myth* (trans. Olive Wyon; London: SCM Press, 1958).

Since the historical enterprise, to which Bultmann was committed, yielded only partial facts which in and of themselves could not be the basis for an objective claim that God was *only* in Christ, Ogden claimed that the possibility of other such manifestations has not been eliminated.[79]

A variety of other reactions have followed, such as critiques of Bultmann's anachronistic use of Gnosticism,[80] his omission of other writings in the New Testament, especially the Synoptic Gospels, and his understanding of the existential apart from social contexts.[81] Dan Via's summary of critiques is particularly helpful for students who have not wrestled with Bultmann. In his own assessment, Via criticizes Bultmann for not extending the personal existential dimension to the sociopolitical dimension so that the hermeneutic is guided by social as well as philosophical questions. Via is also helpful in recognizing, contrary to a number of critics, that Bultmann does not advocate a complete separation from the world. While Bultmann certainly gives much more attention to the act of detachment from the world than he does to his renewed *involved* detachment, a confrontational involvement with the world is nevertheless part of his thinking. Via puts it well when he writes that the detachment from the world should be viewed as a deliverance from "anxiety about whether the structures of the world can provide final security".[82]

What is particularly notable about Hasel's evaluation is his observation that none of the so-called post-Bultmannians went on to produce a New Testament theology, despite the continued interest in the topic.[83] The major problem which came to its full expression in Bultmann's work was the need to develop an adequate hermeneutic which is faithful both to the historical (or descriptive) and to the normative components in the formation of a New Testament theology. Bultmann's dialectical corrective to historical (i.e. foundationalist) approaches may have resulted in a unified New Testament theology, but his singular focus on existential meaning via Paul and John proved to be too narrow for many of his students.

So, if unity and meaning—two vital components of any New Testament theology—can only be attained by imposing subjective categories onto the New Testament, what constitutes as an adequate hermeneutical imposition? Where do we go after Bultmann if relevance requires external categories as hermeneutical keys? Those who saw the value in Bultmann's quest for

---

[79] The preceding three paragraphs are taken from Hasel, *New Testament Theology*, 87–90. See also the summary of critiques in Malevez, *The Christian Message and Myth*, 118–63.
[80] E.g. Craig A. Evans, *Word and Glory: On the Exegetical and Theological Background of John's Prologue* (JSNTSup 89; Sheffield: Sheffield Academic Press, 1993).
[81] E.g. Dorothee Soelle, *Political Theology* (trans. J. Shelley; Philadelphia: Fortress Press, 1974) 43–9; Gareth Jones, *Bultmann: Towards a Critical Theology* (Cambridge: Polity, 1991) 181–8.
[82] Via, *What is New Testament Theology?* 71. See also his *The Revelation of God and/as Human Reception* (Harrisburg, PA: Trinity Press International, 1997).
[83] Hasel, *New Testament Theology*, 94–6.

a normative New Testament theology retained the dialectical approach, but sought to replace his existentialist interpretation with alternatives. For example, James M. Robinson proposed a hermeneutic that is based not on anthropology, but on linguistic philosophy, which might allow the theological language of the New Testament to be placed into the categories of the modern world.[84] Another example is Norman Perrin's attempt to build a hermeneutic on the function of symbol as it was theorized in the work of Paul Ricoeur and Philip Wheelwright.[85] For Perrin, the unifying feature of the New Testament is the symbolizing or the imaging of Jesus based on post-Easter faith by the early Christians, which in and of itself was an act of normativity. Perrin has advocated that modern Christianity should follow in the same faith-imaging process, albeit in a way that is informed by the current study of language and particularly symbol. It is unfortunate that Perrin or Robinson did not write New Testament theologies, since their critiques of Bultmann beg the question of how their presentations of Paul and John's theologies would have differed from those of Bultmann.

Whether one adopts or shelves Bultmann's existentialist motif, it is indeed very difficult to be extricated from his broader normative method. What is common to Bultmann and his sympathizers is the recognition of a hermeneutical process already at work in the early church that concerned itself with normativity. As a result, the modern Christian is encouraged to follow the precedent established by the New Testament writers and engage in the same interpretative process whereby culture, worldviews and social issues are the starting point in the quest for relevance.

Conclusion

Bultmann continues to be influential. In the next section of the book, the same dialectical process is proposed for future formations of New Testament theologies, though not from an existentialist or linguistic perspective. Instead, I suggest a much broader approach that is rooted in the nature and function of religion and/or myth as social capital. In other words, I am guided by the problem of how the New Testament might speak to the so-called "big" issues of today in the public sphere, such as climate change, the war on terror, the UN declaration on Human Rights, economic ethics and inter-faith living. Bultmann's demythologizing is a

---

[84] James M. Robinson, "The Future of New Testament Theology", *Religious Studies Review* 2 (1976) 17–23.
[85] Norman Perrin, *Jesus and the Language of the Kingdom: Symbol and Metaphor in New Testament Interpretation* (Philadelphia: Fortress Press, 1976); "Paul Ricoeur on Biblical Hermeneutics", *Semeia* 4 (1975) 1–148. Perrin is indebted to Paul Ricoeur, *The Symbolism of Evil* (trans. E. Buchanan; Boston: Beacon, 1969); Philip Ellis Wheelwright, *Metaphor and Reality* (Bloomington: Indiana University Press, 1962).

key step in the normative process, but the ancient *kerygma* must find its expression in the modern myth, namely the modern stories or metanarratives we live by which attempt to unify "heaven and earth" through *our* own cultural forms. Likewise, Perrin and Robinson's focus on language is a vital component, but it too can be incorporated into a larger framework of how religion functions. Subjecting the New Testament to religion allows us to distinguish better the difference between what the German critics called *Historie* (the reconstructed past which is no longer relevant) and *Geschichte* (the reconstructed past which continues to inform the present). Viewing the faith of the New Testament writers through the prism of religion, before attempting to do theology, will in the next section be the mantra of normativity. This step is vital not only for understanding the Christian faith from a broader pluralistic perspective, which allows for a little more distance in the analytical process, but it is especially helpful in understanding the nature and function of the scriptures as writings that speak from faith to faith about faith.

A dialectical approach to New Testament theology requires us to embrace the importance of the subjective in the interpretative process. We necessarily bring our communal interests to texts, and especially so when they are authoritative texts such as scripture, constitutions, charters or policy statements. Interpretations are always guided by prior interests. In the legal field, this is just as obvious as it is in religion. As groups seek to legitimize themselves and their beliefs, they necessarily connect with past groups and their beliefs. Since the dialectic is never-ending in any quest for Truth (with a capital T), the hermeneutical key in the normative process should be one that resonates with what we call "human". In this sense, Bultmann's turn toward the anthropological (human existentialism) can never be ignored in quests for religious relevance. The theological becomes true only when it addresses our existential situation. At this point, all disciplines converge since all disciplines are necessarily imprinted with, and are ordered to, human existence.[86] Such a convergence raises the potential of theology either to take on its royal status once again, as the locus of unified human thought, or conversely can be theology's dethroning once and for all—but this is for another time.

When the scriptures are understood from the perspective of religion, the distance between past and present is narrowed considerably, language about God or the gods becomes language about human existence, and a more informed theologizing process can ensue. For Christians, the theological reading of the New Testament is the ultimate goal to which all the historical, social-scientific, philosophical, and literary tools contribute, as we shall see in the next section. As a point of departure, I make reference to a 1996 conference at the University of Chicago which resulted in a series

---

[86] Morgan, *The Nature of New Testament Theology*, 37–8.

of essays that called for a renewed interest in the theological reading of the Bible as it related to biblical theology and systematic theology. The following list is a summary of the proposals that were offered for future integration.[87]

(1) We need to recognize the collapse of modernity's dream of "objectivity" and its incessant assumption that facts can be retrieved from beliefs and values.

(2) We need to begin with a recognition that theological study need not compromise academic integrity. Theology has a place in the public domain.

(3) We need to recognize the detailed and time-consuming study of scripture is unjustifiable unless its findings somehow relate to broader and contemporary concerns and truth claims.

(4) We need to recognize that the subject matter of the New Testament and its implied reader are thoroughly theological in orientation, and so invite theological reflection.

(5) We need to recognize that the New Testament was always read canonically and, as such, unity was always preserved.

(6) We need to recognize that throughout the ages the reading of the Bible has taken place in the context of theology.

(7) We need to recognize that the role of the reader (in history and today) has blurred the distinction between exegesis and interpretation. Opportunity for a plethora of ideological and theological readings has opened up.

Discussion questions

1 Which of the five structures presented in the last two chapters is the best option? Why?

2 Is the overarching "biblical" narrative of a salvation-history structure imposed onto the Bible or is it derived from the Bible?

3 For some theologians the gap between the first century and today is closed by Jesus' preaching of the kingdom of God, in which the modern Christian allegedly participates. But after the bloodiest century in recorded history, what does it mean to participate in the kingdom of God?

---

[87] See the papers in John J. Collins, ed., "The Bible and Christian Theology", *Journal of Religion* 76 (1996) 167–348.

4 What role should established Christian doctrines play in the interpretation of the New Testament? And vice versa, what role should the New Testament play in critiquing established Christian doctrines? For example, are the doctrines of the canon and the inspiration of scripture a vital starting point in the formation of a New Testament theology?

5 Discuss Rudolf Bultmann's motive and method for making the New Testament relevant for today.

PART THREE

New Testament theology in a pluralistic age

6

Religion and theology: The new conversation

Given the perspective that has been offered at this point, it should be poignantly clear that normativity in New Testament theology requires that historical criticism, which cannot be abandoned, must be in conversation with methods that are ordered to meaning. Such a conversation with theology was observed in the salvation-history and dogmatic approaches. Bultmann and his followers have extended the conversation to the philosophy of language and being. What is needed in our age is a conversation that also includes religion. In the previous chapters, I stated several times that a dialectical New Testament theology which can potentially speak effectively to our pluralistic Western culture should include within it an understanding of religion prior to the act of theologizing. In addition to the benefit for establishing a common ground in pluralistic dialogue, I suggested that an understanding of religion can play a crucial role in what Augustine called "faith seeking understanding" and slow down the all-too-quick transition from scripture to theology. In the light of the woeful absence of engagement with the science of religion throughout much of the history of New Testament theology, this chapter is devoted to clarifying the differences and similarities between religion and theology, and how these may potentially contribute to the formation of a New Testament theology.

The confusion between religion and theology is more widespread than might initially be thought, especially among those who wrongly assume that the academic field of biblical studies is "sacred" instead of "secular". Such an assumption ignores the pursuits of the Enlightenment period when the modern academic study of the Bible began. In addition, it tends to confuse distinctions between faith and hermeneutics, which are essential for any kind of academic study of the Bible—even in contexts of faith. Given that New Testament theology is widely regarded today as a discipline (or sub-discipline of biblical studies) in and of itself, as opposed to simply the scattered or unified theological ideas in early Christian canonical writings, it is eye-opening to view it in relation to the larger field of religious studies, which likewise is a child of the Enlightenment, but is more oriented toward anthropology, sociology and comparative religions. The mainstream academy in North America has generally regarded New Testament theology as one small (even isolated) field of study under the overarching discipline of theology. Yet, somewhat paradoxically, it is taught in many North American confessional colleges and universities within "religious studies" departments.

The post-9/11 popularity of religion

Since the Enlightenment, and especially since the end of World War II, the public role of religion has steadily declined in Western culture. The Holocaust deeply impacted all subsequent discourse about God, his supposed relationship to history and humanity, and our ability to speak authoritatively about his character and will. Doubt, silence and the death of triumphalist religions seemed to have characterized the day for many who refused to deny the dignity of the victims of the Holocaust. After World War II, Christianized Europe was viewed by many academics to have run its course and lost.[1] Since both World Wars, Western culture has grown suspicious of traditional power structures, especially when they purport to speak for God, be they Muslim, Jewish or Christian. The prophetic words of writers like Friedrich Nietzsche and Albert Camus, who warned that final religious answers often result in final social solutions, were increasingly being realized in the post-war collective consciousness of the West, resulting in a much more private, subjective and tolerant practice of faith. Even the moral and theological authority of Evangelical fundamentalist leaders, be they clerical or political, have shown significant weakness within their own constituencies over the last fifty years, especially since the civil rights movement and the Vietnam War.[2] The so-called "traditional values" have been particularly criticized since the 1960s for their casting of stones from their glass houses. Today the foundations of the so-called moral high ground continue to erode. Let's face it, *The Simpsons*, *Family Guy* and *South Park* have won the day as mainstream icons, though they represent cultural shifts that occurred well before these shows aired. Gone are the days of *Leave it to Beaver* and its "Pleasantville" propaganda.

In academic circles, the shift has been profound. During the 1980s and 90s, we have seen the culmination of widespread perplexity regarding the value of the humanities. The result has been an unprecedented number of publications focused on the history and purpose of fields like sociology,

---

[1] J. Multmann, *God for a Secular Society: The Public Relevance of Theology* (Minneapolis: Fortress Press, 1999) 169–90.
[2] See the insightful discussion in Robert Jewett, *Mission and Menace: Four Centuries of American Religious Zeal* (Minneapolis: Fortress Press, 2008).

history and English; but none has received more vigorous scrutiny than the academic study of religion and theology. Dozens of books and scores of articles have commonly expressed discontent and uncertainty regarding the purpose and nature of university divinity schools, religious studies departments and seminaries.[3] This widespread concern should come as no surprise, given that religion, viewed as a cultural construct, has long ceased to be a major player in the appropriation and discernment of "the truth" in Western culture.

The terror of 9/11, however, has dramatically changed public interest in religion. Almost immediately, religion, especially Islam, gained widespread coverage in mainstream media and in academic circles. Popular primetime news shows like *60 Minutes* and *Dateline* ran numerous segments on Islam, its fundamentalist factions and its leaders. Questions concerning the relationship between religion and politics, religion and violence, and religion and social capital were at the forefront. Major secular universities began to advertize newly created positions in Islamic studies, and continue to do so. Although fundamentalist sectors of Islam, Judaism and Christianity have in the past received their share of coverage on network television and in major news magazines, from Middle East suicide bombings to the Branch Davidians to the polygamous cults, their coverage was short-lived and situational when compared to the intensity of ongoing interest in religion sparked by 9/11. For some who are intimately connected to the life of faith on both personal and professional levels, the connection drawn between terror and religion was immediate. In an interview with PBS's *Frontline*, Monsignor Lorenzo Albacete expressed one of the most sobering statements that captures the connection:

> From the first moment I looked into that horror on September 11, into that fireball, into that explosion of horror, I knew it. I knew it before anything was said about those who did it or why. I recognized an old companion. I recognized religion. Look, I am a priest for over 30 years. Religion is my life, it's my vocation, it's my existence. I'd give my life for it; I hope to have the courage. Therefore, I know it expressed a haunting admission about religion when the planes crashed into the towers.[4]

Public curiosity in religion, however, was not limited to its relationship with violence and politics, nor was it limited to Islam. More and more people, especially in the US and Canada, began to reflect personally on, and interact with peers about, religion and religious issues. Record numbers of people began to attend churches and other places of worship, though much of this rise in attendance was short-lived and can be accounted for

---

[3] W. Clark Gilpin, *A Preface to Theology* (Chicago: University of Chicago Press, 1996) ix–x.
[4] *Frontline*, "Faith and Doubt at Ground Zero", Winter, 2002.

by the existential anxiousness created by 9/11. For example, in the US, as opposed to Canada and the UK, Evangelicalism, which tends to be nationalistic, attracted considerable numbers. Explanations of increased public interest and curiosity about religion, however, cannot simply be limited to nationalism. Interest in personal spirituality, which had already been on the rise before 9/11, continues to increase. A Canadian sociologist has shown that despite the slow decline of attendance and membership in institutional places of worship in Canada over the last few decades, public interest in spirituality is steadily increasing.[5] The Canadian scene seems to reflect the broader trends in Western culture. The same cannot be said for the US, where attendance in Evangelical churches appears to be on the rise.

The post-9/11 context, which has contributed to an increased interest and curiosity in religion on the one hand and contributed to discrimination and sometimes persecution of non-Christian religions (especially Islam) on the other, should have an impact on how New Testament theology is understood and practised today. As a result of a keener public awareness of the relationship between religious devotion and violence, not to mention politics and economics, more scholars and clergy, and probably laypersons, have a heightened sensitivity to the social-scientific dynamics in their own readings of the Bible. The religious intensity and fervour on display in some sectors of Islam, which is frequently captured in the media, and the war in Iraq and Afghanistan initiated by George W. Bush who identifies as an Evangelical, undoubtedly caused many people to reflect on the problematic nature of organized or institutionalized religion in modern society. Participation in organized religion is still culturally respected, but one wonders about the ability of large religious organizations, like the former Moral Majority—which has traditionally been associated with the Republican Party—to wield the same unified and powerful voice as it once did. Too many people regard the religious quest as a subjective and private experience that counteracts modern technical and bureaucratic structures, which are poor generators of values and meaning.[6] The subtle cultural protest happening in the business world is reflected in religious practice. Individuals serve institutions but do not trust them because institutions are viewed as self-serving—they neither love nor relate. Out of all this we are forced to wrestle with questions like this: in such an anxious and sceptical climate, how is New Testament theology to be understood, practised, and applied as a vehicle of hope, restoration and peace, both inside and outside the Christian community?

---

[5] Peter C. Emberley, *Divine Hunger: Canadians on Spiritual Walkabout* (Toronto: HarperCollins, 2002).
[6] Bryan R. Wilson, *Religion in Social Perspective* (Oxford: Oxford University Press, 1982) 49.

"Religion" is not a dirty word: New Testament theology inside and outside the faith community

It is common knowledge that words derive their meanings from the contexts in which they are found. "New Testament theology" is no exception. It is safe to say that most Christians would have no problem in understanding what is meant by the "New Testament", even if they do not know or cannot recall its specific features—such as its authors, the date of the writings, or even the number of writings it contains. Christians generally understand that it is a collection of early Christian writings that focus on the ministry, death and resurrection of Jesus. And even if they cannot immediately find the words to describe it, many have at one time read the New Testament, whether in whole or in part. This same degree of understanding, however, cannot be said of the word "theology". Despite its common use in Christian settings, for many lay people the term is an enigma when a definition is requested. There is a general understanding that it has something to do with the study of God, the Church, doctrines and the Bible; but beyond that it remains a nebulous, albeit important, category. The difficulty is compounded when the term "religion" is raised in the same breath. What is the difference between "religion" and "theology"? Are they the same? If we can speak of a New Testament theology, can we synonymously speak of New Testament religion?

New Testament theologies usually do not include such delineations. Many simply begin with a definition of New Testament theology or with issues concerning method. The audience, and in some ways the culture, is assumed to be monolithic in its broad religious or worldview convictions. But in an increasingly pluralistic Western culture where religious ideas are bumping up against each other all the time, especially in urban centres, there is a great need to understand how Christianity, and more specifically the New Testament, corresponds to the multidimensionality that is all around us. Living in a major Canadian urban centre, religious pluralism is unavoidable. I encounter it in local media, at the shopping centres, in personal academic pursuits, at the local ice rinks where I coach hockey, and occasionally in deeper dialogues at my favourite café. My experiences have been overwhelmingly positive in the sense that they have been respectful, educational and often affirming of human dignity. It pains me to say that similar kinds of interactions in church contexts have not always yielded such tolerance, respect and genuine interest in the views of the other. Taking a posture where human dignity precedes personal beliefs is certainly worth pondering.

My point in all this is that an awareness of our multicultural/multi-faith contexts is indispensable if the theological ideas of the New Testament are to be brought into the current marketplace, lest Christian groups become sectarian or isolationist. My working assumption is that the discipline of New Testament theology can be practised and discussed in the public square where "religion", not "theology", is the operative term. Respect and a fair hearing of what lies in these early Christian writings can only be expected in a pluralistic culture if the same consideration is offered to those of other faiths or those of no faith, no matter how certain the Christian is of the truth of his or her faith convictions. Since the Bible is increasingly sharing more cultural space with other sacred writings, Christians must recognize that the theology found in the New Testament represents one religious tradition among many, and each equally claims the Truth.[7]

Referring to Christianity as a religion in the marketplace of daily life should not be looked upon with disparagement by Christians, as it sometimes is. Christians tend to look at other faiths as "religions", but not their own. What is sometimes heard in conservative Christian settings is the claim that Christianity is "not a religion, but a relationship". The terms "religion" or "religious" tend to suffer negative connotations, much like we have seen with the term "myth". I have even heard a few pastors telling their congregations that the Pharisees and Sadducees were religious, but Jesus, Paul and the disciples were not. Over the centuries, this distinction has been part of Christian anti-Semitic rhetoric.[8] In a multi-faith context, this kind of sentiment connotes inferiority of all other religions since it is assumed that they (with perhaps the exception of Judaism) originate with humankind or are counterfeits, whereas Christianity alone is believed to originate from God. Of course, such bifurcation betrays not only a gross misunderstanding of the general category "religion" and specifically of world religions, but unnecessarily erects boundaries and defensive mechanisms, and thereby severely limits any function of New Testament theology outside the Christian context as a legitimate voice in the marketplace of religious ideas. Furthermore, if Christianity is not regarded as a religion, it begs the question of what it is, especially since its characteristics and main themes overlap with other so-called religions, many of which also promote a loving relationship with the transcendent. The posture should instead be one that embraces "religion" as terminology that fosters common ground. New Testament theology as a discipline studied and practised in the contemporary world must be interactive on the world stage if it is to be relevant to Christians and engaging to non-Christians. In short, New Testament theology must be viewed as operative under the contemporary category of religion when it is brought outside the context of the Christian faith

---

[7] On claims to truth among religions, see Keith Ward, *Religion and Revelation: A Theology of Revelation in the World's Religions* (Oxford: Clarendon Press, 1994).
[8] One need only cite the blemished history of the Church's treatment of Jews in James Carroll, *Constantine's Sword. The Church and the Jews: A History* (Boston: Mariner Books, 2001).

community. If New Testament theology is positioned under the umbrella of religion, then logically it must somehow be permitted to interact with the broad field within which it is situated.

Having said this, the study of New Testament theology in the context of the Christian faith community does not require it to be viewed in this way. For Christians the New Testament is rightly viewed as a collection of sacred writings that reveal the truth for faith and morals. Within this boundary there is less need or pressure for the Christian theologian to present and to study the New Testament as one scripture among others. Spiritual identification or theological commonness between the theologian and his or her audience allows and indeed requires scriptural interpretation to be motivated by spiritual and/or ecclesiastical concerns. The same principle is true for theologians of other faiths wherein their own scriptures play an authoritative role. However, the Christian who is engaged in modern society ought to become familiar with the major beliefs of other religions, especially those that are in his or her social sphere. One's understanding of one's own Christian faith can be tremendously informed intellectually and emotionally by understanding foreign beliefs and practices. So ideally my proposed process for doing New Testament theology—that is, the movement from scripture to religion to theology—can apply to a lifelong growth in the Christian faith. In short, while the study of other religions is not a necessity for laypersons seeking a devout Christian life, it can be very illuminating in the context of "faith-seeking understanding".

In reality, Western culture is post-Christian and increasingly pluralistic. In summary, therefore, New Testament theology finds itself positioned facing two directions. The first is the broader pluralistic culture where it is operative as one voice among many. The second direction is the "in-house" or ecclesiastical sphere where it has no such competitors. This is not to discount competing traditions vying for supremacy which continue to be operative within Christianity. At this stage, my aim is simply to sort out these two broad contexts. At the heart of the difference between them is the distinction between the study of religion and the study of theology. In what follows, I will first examine the general meaning of "religion" and "theology" and then explain how each is studied. Both of these aspects are important, for as in the study of other disciplines, such as the natural sciences, one cannot truly understand their nature and scope without having some knowledge of their methodologies. Finally, I will attempt to provide some complementary proposals.

What is religion?

If, at the most basic level, theology is defined as thinking about questions initiated by and about religion, then the definition of religion must be primary.[9] "Religion" is one of those all-encompassing words in our popular parlance that we assume we understand. And one need not be religious to understand the general meaning of religion. When a person is said to be "religious", or when we say, "religion and politics should not mix", we often have a good idea of what is being communicated, even if it is usually at a superficial level. Like the term "theology", the general complacency in the popular use of the term is quickly realized when an explanation of the term is requested. We immediately realize that it is one of the those broad terms, perhaps like "love" or "justice", which we frequently use, but rarely attempt to describe and understand. The breadth of the term is simply overwhelming.

The problem becomes acute when we attempt to catalogue all the world's religions, ancient and modern, with their varied rituals, beliefs, deities, experiences and structures. How does one take into account all the differences within a single definition? It is no wonder that psychologist and philosopher William James (1842–1910), who attempted a similar endeavour over a century ago, simply put it this way, "... the very fact that they are so many and so different from one another is enough to prove that the word 'religion' cannot stand for any principle or essence, but is rather a collective name."[10] Even at what may seem to be the most basic level, a definition lacks precision. For example, the average North American equates someone who is religious with a belief in God and regular church attendance. While this definition works (in part) for Christianity, it is not broad enough. For instance, Buddhism has no parallel requirement for belief in God. Judaism, as well as many tribal religions, is largely defined by its ethnicity, and not membership in an institution. Even if, as a starting point, we were to limit our description of religion to a familiar religion like Christianity, inevitable disagreement would ensue. Christianity does not mean the same thing to all who call, or have called, themselves "Christian".

Religion is a social universal. Sociologists and anthropologists generally agree that there is no past or present culture tht lacks religious traditions. The problem is its diversity. The imprecision of language and its cultural relativism compounds the difficulty in the search for a comprehensive definition. It is estimated that today there are between four and five billion people, from every culture, who participate in a world religion.[11] Since religion is not an entity apart from culture, the language of one culture can only inadequately express the religion of another culture. While temples, artifacts or ceremonies can be observed and pose no problem in translation, the significance of religion lies at the unseen level: the level of imagination,

---

[9] On this elementary definition, see David Ford, *Theology: A Very Short Introduction* (Oxford: Oxford University Press, 1999) 17.
[10] William James, *Varieties of Religious Experience* (London: Longmans, Green, 1902) preface.
[11] Ford, *Theology*, 3.

idea and inner life. For example, Western religious and philosophical notions of "will", "truth" or "evil" differ extensively from those of Eastern cultures. Language can also be imprecise within the context of the same culture. Take the word "supernatural", for instance. Many people think that the supernatural realm is a key component within a definition of religion. Aside from the question whether or not religious belief demands belief in the supernatural, the meaning of the term "supernatural" as something beyond the "natural" or normal series of events fluctuates depending on one's starting point. If a person believes that God audibly speaks to humans on a regular basis, the hearing of the divine voice should no longer be considered supernatural, but an expected (hence "natural") event. The cause of the voice is not explained psychologically, but as God's normal interaction with humans.[12]

Given the variations among religions, most scholars have opted for a series of characteristics or dimensions instead of a single definition. Depending on the characteristics, a few scholars allow for ideologies, like Marxism or humanism, to be incorporated into the category "religion" since for some people they serve as contemporary replacements for traditional religions.[13] Most religion scholars, however, include characteristics that would exclude these ideologies, as is the case here. Many books on religion include characteristics that overlap.[14] These have been masterfully surveyed and synthesized in Richard Warms, James Garber and Jon McGee's *Sacred Realms*, which is a widely used textbook on religion in university undergraduate courses across North America. The authors point to seven characteristics that are shared by almost all religions:[15]

1. Religions are composed of stories that have been transmitted in the language of the culture over long periods of time from one generation of devotees to another. These stories are regarded as revelations of profound truths about the invisible world that provide explanations/meanings for the present life in the physical world. Most religions have stories about the origins of the world, evil, humanity, the afterlife, salvation, the religion's founder(s), heroes and gods. These stories have often been called "myths".

---

[12] Richard Warms, James Garber and Jon McGee, "What is Religion?" in *Sacred Realms: Essays in Religion, Belief, and Society* (ed. Richard Warms, James Garber and Jon McGee; New York: Oxford University Press, 2004) x.
[13] For a helpful survey of religious theories, see Daniel L. Pals, *Eight Theories of Religion* (2nd edn; Oxford: Oxford University Press, 2006).
[14] Many scholars still point to the helpful series of characteristics offered in Ninian Smart, *The Religious Experience of Mankind* (New York: Charles Scribner's Sons, 1969) 6–12. For Smart, religion is composed of six dimensions: the ritual, the mythological, the doctrinal, the ethical, the social and the experiential.
[15] Warms, Garber and McGee, "What is Religion?" xi–xvi. Also recommended is the introduction by Malory Nye, *Religion: The Basics* (2nd edn; London: Routledge, 2008).

To reiterate, the term "myth" in this context should not to be equated with a belief system that is false. Terms like "myth" or "mythological" are neutral categories as far as the historicity of a story is concerned. Some myths are religious re-enactments or retellings of actual historical events, like the crucifixion of Jesus. It is a historical event; but it is also a story that concerns the invisible world. The religious meaning of the crucifixion is not found in the fact of the event, as important as it is, but in the interpretation of it. Interpretations require narratives, which is where we encounter the mythological dimension as a key feature in a cosmic drama concerning salvation, evil and restoration of the cosmos. Hence the purpose of these myths, or sacred stories, is that they communicate meaning that transcends the historical event and a single generation of devotees.

2. Religions posit the existence of supernatural beings, powers, states and qualities. Though the diversity in these is immense, there is commonality in the postulation of a reality that transcends the physical realm. And since that reality is not limited to the material world, it cannot be proved or disproved by scientific methods. For example, the existence of God, spirits, ancestors, heaven and hell cannot be subjected to empirical testing. In order to legitimize transcendent reality, religion scholars have sometimes pointed to other non-material realities such as beauty or love as analogies. While most religion scholars and philosophers would argue that the existence of God, gods or spirits cannot be measured scientifically, some, like Phillip Wiebe, continue to pursue that goal. Wiebe attempts to show that a cautious phenomenological study of alleged encounters with the spiritual realm yields empirical data that can be used to assess such claims.[16]

3. Religions use symbols and symbolism. Symbols, which are developed within a collective consciousness, have critical functions in religious systems. One of these functions is that symbols encapsulate religious ideas that cannot be described literally. Take, for example, the ideas of the afterlife or eternity. Since the meaning of language is based on comparison of one thing with another, we cannot speak in the same way (i.e. literally) about eternal realms, eternal existence or beings like God. Given that there is no direct frame of reference in the physical and temporal world that we live in, religious language necessarily employs symbol, along with analogy and metaphor. In addition, religion's attempt to unite "heaven and earth" necessarily requires symbol.

---

[16] Phillip H. Wiebe, *God and Other Spirits: Intimations of Transcendence in Christian Experience* (Oxford: Oxford University Press, 2004).

4   Religions include rituals. Although much of life includes ritual, from getting up in the morning to getting ready for a good night's sleep, religious ritual is different because it is oriented toward interaction with the transcendent or supernatural. Ritual practitioners usually regard their role in the ritual as participation in a greater reality or in *the* reality. The events that comprise the ritual are regarded as real and effective. They are believed truly to effect change, be it communication with an ancestor, cleansing from sin, or taking on another identity.

   The repetition of religious rituals (along with ceremonies) serves to preserve collective memory. Events are often re-enacted in rituals so as not to lose the community's connection (i.e. identity) with the past. Through ritual, the community recalls the divine origins of the world, the problem of evil in the world, the defeat of evil, and the hope of an afterlife. Sin or wrongdoing in many religions can be narrowed down to forgetting the ritual of the religious life, namely that human existence is a result of divine creation. It is ritual, like sacrifice, which in turn restores the memory. Mircea Eliade recalls the important connection between ritual and memory in the following rite:

   > For example, among the Wemale the Moon is a dema-divinity; it is believed to have a menstrual period at the new moon and to remain invisible for three nights. This is why menstruating women are isolated in special huts. Any infraction of this interdict requires an expiatory ceremony. The woman brings an animal to the cult house, where the influential men are gathered, confesses her guilt, and goes away. The men sacrifice the animal, roast it and eat it. This killing rite is a commemoration of the first blood sacrifice, that is, of the primordial murder. "The sacrilege of *not having remembered* is logically expiated by *remembering with special intensity*. And because of its original meaning, blood sacrifice is a particularly intense 'reminder' of this sort."[17]

5   Religions have clerics who are responsible for preserving the religion and/or practising the rituals on behalf of the other members of the community. Anthropologists have divided clerics into shamans and priests. Although no specific definition is agreed upon, priests tend to derive their authority not from within themselves, but from the institution they serve. When they are at great variance

---

[17] M. Eliade, *Myth and Reality* (trans. W. R. Trask; San Francisco: Harper & Row, 1963) 107. Elidae quotes Adolf E. Jensen, *Mythes et cultes chez les peuples primitifs* (trans. M. Metzger and J. Goffinet; Paris, 1954) 225.

with the institution they represent, they can be dismissed from their priestly duties. A shaman, on the other hand, does not represent an institution and does not hold an office. His supernatural abilities such as healing, predicting the future or communicating with ancestors are believed to come directly from a divine source. Often these abilities are believed to be inherited.

6   Religions make frequent use of altered states of consciousness. In every religion there are people who testify to having experiences of a transcendent reality, which can include visions, hearing of voices, or uncontrollable physical activity such as writhing on the ground or unintelligible speech. These people, and others within the same religious community, usually regard such experiences as divine verification of their core beliefs. According to sociologist Peter Berger, since the human being is ultimately an empirical animal, personal experience is always the most convincing evidence.[18] Historians of religion, such as Mircea Eliade, view religious experiences as phenomena that presuppose the bipartition of the world into an interplay and mutual transformation (not dualism) between the sacred and the profane.[19] Such experience can today be measured scientifically through neurological analyses during the time of the experience, and are thus termed "altered states of consciousness"; but there is no way of measuring objectively whether the soul encounters the supernatural. Anthropologists, along with other social scientists, observe that religious experiences are usually dependent on the context wherein they occur. Contexts provide for expectations and boundaries. For example, *glossalalia* ("speaking in tongues") usually occurs in Pentecostal churches and not in Baptist churches. Uncontrollable dancing or hallucinations occur in tribal religions, but not in Eastern Orthodoxy, and so forth.

7   Religious belief and practice change over time. Although the archetypical aspects of religions rarely change, interpretations of those archetypes frequently do, especially at the popular level of religious practice. One of the major reasons for change has to do with the close connection between religion and culture. Usually changes in culture, which are themselves complicated, effect changes in religious belief and practice. Religions require relevance. On a macro scale, modernity has had a particularly challenging impact on world religions because of their pre-modernist roots and their

---

[18] Peter L. Berger, *The Heretical Imperative: Contemporary Possibilities of Religious Affirmation* (New York: Doubleday, 1979) 30.
[19] Mircea Eliade, *The Quest: History and Meaning in Religion* (Chicago: The University of Chicago Press, 1969) 133.

inherent continuity with the past.[20] Numerous changes are also observable on a micro scale. Take, for example, the fairly rapid change in eschatological perspective from that of Mark's Gospel written probably during the Jewish war (CE 66–70) and that of Luke's Gospel written some 15–20 years later. Mark portrays Jesus from an apocalyptic perspective as one who announces the imminence of the Son of Man's return for the purpose of judgment and restoration. The context of the war undoubtedly causes Mark to situate Jesus at the end of history, as Mark understands it. Luke, however, does not portray Jesus at the end of history (literally "end of the age"). He instead situates him in the middle of history, so to speak. For Luke and his Gentile audience, the war has no impact. Changes such as these are repeated throughout the Bible. The history of the Christian Church is filled with change in practice and belief. One need not go any further than denominational variances in Protestantism. The same is true for all religions—one of the most notable for its flexibility is Hinduism which has perhaps accommodated itself the most to changes in culture, personality types and the stages of life. As a final example, the destruction of the Temple in CE 70 had a profound impact on Judaism. In this case, experience is much more than simply emotion (as Smart defines the term), but is grounded in an external event that caused a reinterpretation of a religion.[21]

What these characteristics reveal is that religions cannot simply be reduced to sets of universal principles in varying cultural garb. Religions are not identical to ideologies. And religions are not just ethical guidelines, contrary to traditional rationalistic claims.[22] Religions are rather closer to organisms that have a life of their own—including a beginning, dynamics of change, maturity, and in some cases eventual death.[23] Another observation from these characteristics is that religion, in Peter Berger's words, is "the human enterprise by which a sacred cosmos is established".[24] Even in the use of "religion" as a singular term, the significance should always be the plurality of religions. If religions retreat into an introverted ideological and defensive posture, misunderstanding

---

[20] Ford, *Theology*, 9.
[21] Heikki Räisänen, "Tradition, Experience, Interpretation: A Dialectical Model for Describing the Development of Religious Thought", in *Challenges to Biblical Interpretation: Collected Essays 1991–2001* (ed. H. Räisänen; Biblical Interpretation Series 59; Leiden: Brill, 2001) 253.
[22] Huston Smith, *The World's Religions: Our Great Wisdom Traditions* (3rd edn; New York: HarperCollins, 1991) 3.
[23] On religion as organism, see Smart, *The Religious Experience of Mankind*, 8.
[24] Peter Berger, *The Social Reality of Religion* (Harmondsworth: Penguin, 1993) 34.

and antagonism would surely overshadow any attempt toward humility, mutual understanding and hope for peace.[25]

One final observation: at the heart of every religion lies a mysticism: a profound experience of, or connection with, a transcendent reality. Among mystics, it is sometimes identified as an epistemology that goes beyond the senses and the intellect, achieving insights through rigorous disciplines like prayer and fasting. And it is this profundity of experience that also lies at the core of early Christian beliefs as they are represented in the New Testament. Mysticism should be a pivotal component in the dialectical process because it introduces a search for the transcendent, not a search for propositions or reconstructions. As such, it may well prove to be an important external unifying component in formulations of New Testament theology.

What is theology?

The characteristics that are attributed to religion can also be extended to theology—though only to a point. Like religion, theology tries to systematize, bring coherence to and intellectually control these characteristics. And like religion, theology is more concerned with communities of faith than the private experiences of individuals. No religion or theology was ever based on a unique private experience, even when dreams or claims of supernatural experiences of the individual profoundly affect a community. Tradition has always served as the foundation of the community's acceptance and eventual practice of individual experiences, even if their source is a shaman, priest or prophet. Some kind of shared experience is required for authentication and acceptance to occur, and for religious experience to be transformed into an expression of the larger community. Sanctioned participation among its adherents is crucial.

Unlike religion, theology's main concern is with divine disclosure to humanity, through natural and/or special revelation. The former assumes that God can be known through nature and our humanness, while the latter assumes that God can only be known by direct divine disclosure. Whatever the case, theology assumes that God (or whatever label we attribute to transcendent being and/or reality) exists and can be known though only to a limited degree. However, theology is not simply interested in the primordial revelation in the history of a religious community, but also in its renewal in subsequent generations. Theology is consumed with this interplay between the past and the present. The balance between the two is often struck by means of so-called "formative factors" such as experience, scripture, tradition, culture and reason, all of which function in an integrative manner

---

[25] Keith Ward, *The Case for Religion* (Oxford: Oneworld, 2004) 5.

for constructing and evaluating Christian theologies.[26] Depending on the tradition or denomination, these factors in various combinations may also be regarded as vehicles of divine revelation that bring ongoing understanding to the ultimate revelation in Christian theology, which is Christ. In bringing understanding and clarity, theology has no choice but to use the language of the culture in which it finds itself.

On the most basic level theology is a second-order activity because it begins with a predisposition to the superiority of one religious tradition over and sometimes against all others. John Macquarrie has helpfully described it in these terms: "Theology may be defined as the study which, through participation in and reflection upon a religious faith, seeks to express the content of this faith in the clearest and most coherent language available."[27] What Macquarrie is saying, and he is not alone in this, is that when one examines the characteristics of religion from a theological perspective, one does so as a so-called "insider" who existentially identifies with his or her community of faith and its practices. The key difference is that theology is concerned with the understanding and practice of a given religion. In this regard, faith precedes theology. Theology, however, is not faith; but the thoughtful religious expression of a collective faith that leads to the highest possible intelligibility and consistency.

The modern study of religion and theology

In the first part of this chapter I have tried to provide a social context for understanding the contemporary state of religious pluralism in the Western world. I have also tried to make sense of the broad categories of "religion" and "theology". I now turn from definitions to the contemporary study of religion and theology. In so doing, I will present five characteristics of the study of religion and see where they differ from, and potentially intersect with, the modern study of Christian theology.

As one surveys the contemporary study of religion and theology, the modernist chasm that was dug between confessional and secular study, which continues to be observed at many institutions, is slowly attempting to be bridged by individuals on both sides. The strongest impediment to progress at the moment seems to lie ironically at the academic institutional level where self preservation, self-identity, fear, politics, economic factors

---

[26] Theologians vary on the exact number of these factors. John Macquarrie (*Principles of Christian Theology* [2nd edn; New York: Charles Scribner's Sons, 1977] 4), for instance, adds revelation as a sixth factor. Others simply follow the so-called Wesleyan Quadrilateral, which includes only experience, scripture, tradition and reason.

[27] Macquarrie, *Principles of Christian Theology*, 1.

and especially entrenched methods and theories provide fierce resistance to theology at secular institutions and to religion at confessional ones.

Postmodern reflections on hermeneutics and the notion of truth are slowly allowing for renewed dialogue about the role of theology in the secular educational context, far from the Church's reach.[28] If we are to move forward beyond the political divide and indeed the tarnished past, confessional institutions will have to allow religious studies research (not by name only) to take place alongside theology; and conversely, secular institutions will have to accept theology as a vital complement, as has been the tradition in British and European universities. Postmodernity may potentially open a way forward since it allows epistemological and methodological paradigms (secular and sacred) mutually to co-exist without reverting to positions of superiority, power and control over the other.

Some scholars advocate that the two disciplines must borrow from each other if each is to remain a viable field of study. Religious Studies is hard pressed if it cannot interact with centuries of theological discourse in all the major world religions. Congruently, theology must interact with and incorporate the insights of religious studies if it is to be relevant to an increasingly pluralistic world.

The modern study of religion has its roots in the social sciences, and like them it is a fairly young discipline. One of the earliest and most influential attempts to understand the nature and development of religious thought was that of Sir Edward Burnett Tylor's *Primitive Culture*, published in 1871.[29] The novelty of Tylor's treatment was found in his attempt to understand the development of religious thought through the study of cultures.[30] Those who immediately followed after him shared his observation that religion was not only a human universal, but that it plays a vital role in the development and structuring of society. Many of these early pioneers were well known social scientists who were preoccupied with the origin and development of religion, and shared the belief that it is in some way rooted in humanity, as opposed to the divine. These early studies of religion were products of their modernist environment and thus used the tools and rules of evidence that were commonplace in the social sciences of the day. For example, Émile Durkheim concluded that religion is the product of social conditions and not individual minds. Karl Marx argued that religion is a political phenomenon that functions to uphold social order and the positions of the privileged and powerful. Max Weber tried to explain the

---

[28] See the varied viewpoints in L. E. Cady and D. Brown, eds, *Religious Studies, Theology, and the University: Conflicting Maps, Changing Terrain* (Albany: State University of New York, 2002).

[29] Edward Burnett Tylor, *Primitive Culture: Researches into the Development of Mythology, Philosophy, Religion, Language, Art, and Custom* (London: John Murray, 1871).

[30] Warms, James Garber, and McGee, "What is Religion?" x.

rise of modern capitalism as a product of Protestantism. And Sigmund Freud understood religion from a psychoanalytic perspective as a way to cope with the universal obsessive neurosis of insecurity and fear.

The following series of distinctions in the modern study of religion and the study of theology are intended to reflect the general tendencies in each field, so that the reader can acquire an initial foothold, and appreciate the need to move forward in our thinking about future formulations of New Testament theology.

Inclusive vs. exclusive

The early quests of the nineteenth and early twentieth centuries, while certainly proving influential, should not however be equated with today's formal study of religion. Much of the study of religion in the English-speaking world up until the 1960s, when departments of Religious Studies began to emerge in many universities, were concerned with "the history of religion(s)", "the comparative study of religion", "the sociology of religion", and so forth. These approaches were generally single-dimensional and sometimes double-dimensional. The former focuses only on description, whereas the latter attempts to add an explanation (usually theoretically based) to the description. For example, Mircea Eliade's single-dimensional comparative approach yielded fascinating similarities—everything from the importance of creation myths in ritual practices for understanding the present to the role of mythical ancestors who constitute absolute values or paradigms for all human actions.[31] Eliade's explanations of the similarities, however, are often tentative and not subjected to social-scientific theories. Although Eliade occasionally advocated the rediscovery of the existential dimension of religion for contemporary Western society, his broader normative intent was not clear. In short, his work was primarily descriptive and is therefore single-dimensional.

An example of a double-dimensional approach, and one that may be familiar to lay readers, is found in the work of Joseph Campbell whose series of television interviews with Bill Moyers in 1988, entitled *The Power of Myth*, popularized the comparative study of religion. Campbell carried the comparative approach a step further by seeking to understand the similarities among religions in the light of Carl Jung's theory of "archetypal images" which are deeply seated basic images of ritual, mythology and vision found throughout time and across cultures.[32] Again, it is this attempt not only to describe, but also to provide an explanation that deems

---

[31] E.g. Eliade, *Myth and Reality*; idem, *The Myth of the Eternal Return or Cosmos and History* (trans. W. R. Trask; Princeton: Princeton University Press, 1954).
[32] E.g. Joseph Campbell, *The Hero with a Thousand Faces* (2nd edn; Princeton: Princeton University Press, 1968). Eliade was also influenced by Jungian analysis, but did not utilize it

this kind of approach double dimensional. According to Campbell, there is a basic saviour *mythos*, a "monomyth", which is found in all stories of a saviour-hero, even within the contemporary quest for identity and meaning. As interesting and informative as Campbell's comparisons and explanations may be, his assessments have been viewed as reductionist in the sense that they excluded numerous differences.

Although the current study of religion has made great strides in synthesizing the historical and the comparative approaches and has certainly become much more sensitive to the differences in addition to the similarities in religious thought, it has not departed from its social-scientific roots. As Ninian Smart puts it, the modern study of religion (i.e. since the 1960s) "was created out of a blend of historical studies, comparative expertise and the social sciences, with a topping of philosophy of religion and the like".[33] A methodological theme, or overriding rationale, which emerges from this historical overview is that the modern study of religion is at its roots comparative and thus inclusive.

By contrast, the study of Christian theology has traditionally excluded serious consideration of other faiths because, as with other exclusivist religions, it has operated with the assumption of superiority with regard to divine revelation. The religion of ancient Israel and early Judaism, however, have been exceptions for obvious reasons, though modern Judaism has rarely entered into the study of Christian theology. Today, one finds a wide spectrum of opinion among Christian theologians with regard to the legitimacy of religious claims in other faiths, ranging from complete rejection to full acceptance. While most books on Christian theology still omit serious discussion of other faiths, there is increasing interest in more inclusive and comparative approaches that are directly influenced by religious studies. This is part of the early bridge-building to which I referred above. The works of Hans Küng, David Tracy, Keith Ward and Wilfred Cantwell Smith are thought-provoking examples of Christian theologians who take seriously the truth claims of other faiths. Ward, for example, even refers to his approach as "comparative theology" in contrast to the traditional designation "comparative religion".[34] The potential for narrowing the gap between the traditional categories "religion" and "theology" appears positive, and it is no wonder that some have speculated that the next millennium of theological study will be consumed with similar comparative and inclusive approaches.

---

methodologically in the way that Campbell did. Campbell clearly conveys his intention for engaging in comparative study.
[33] Ninian Smart, "Forward", in *Approaches to the Study of Religion* (ed. P. Connolly; London: Cassell, 1999) ix.
[34] Ward, *Religion and Revelation*.

Nonpartisan vs. partisan

The study of religion tries to be nonpartisan in its comparisons and faith assumptions, while at the same time recognizing that complete objectivity cannot be achieved. In matters of comparison, no single tradition is intentionally dominant in relation to another. This is where a postmodern study of religion has recognized and also tended to resist a Western culture-bound approach that has operated, though sometimes unintentionally, with its own set of value judgments. For example, Matthew's and Luke's accounts of the miraculous birth of Jesus are not assumed to be the touchstone for similar stories in other religions, such as the typical Native American stories of young women who conceive from the rays of the sun, or the birth of the Buddha, or the birth of the Hindu saint Vyasa, or Alexander the Great, to name but a few. Even if in the end the truth claims of religion cannot be settled, religion scholars clearly show that comparisons are vital for stimulating thought and theories concerning religious experience, concepts, language, social implications and a host of other important issues.

By contrast, the study of Christian theology in the West has tended to assume the inferiority of non-Western cultures partly because other cultures are dominated by non-Christian religions. If one begins with the assumption that other religions are inferior, then it is easy to see how one can assume the same with regard to other cultures within which they are practised. This is no surprise since religion and culture are intrinsically linked. While much sensitivity towards cross-cultural communication has been raised, especially by missiologists, it is difficult to be completely removed from deep-seated prejudices that are ubiquitous in cultures that export "their" religion to other cultures. Rome, Canterbury and American Evangelicalism, which are evangelistic centres, are all culturally Western. At present, the reigns of theological power still remain in the northern hemisphere, but a tectonic shift of the loci of religious authority seems to be occurring.[35] For example, there are currently more Anglicans in Africa than in Canada, Europe and Australia combined. If shifts in ecclesiological and theological power follow, then culturally laden theological language, expression and method will not be far behind.

Since the study of religion is a broadly diverse and inclusive discipline that resists religious affiliation, it is practised by scholars of both genders, various faiths and ethnic backgrounds. Unlike the traditional study of theology, which has typically had a particular ecclesiastical affiliation and creedal identity, the study of religion as a social science does not have the same tradition.[36] Both modernist and postmodernist approaches to

---

[35] See Philip Jenkins, *The Next Christendom: The Coming of Global Christianity* (Oxford: Oxford University Press, 2007).
[36] Eric J. Sharp, *Comparative Religion: A History* (2nd edn; London: Duckworth, 1986) xiii.

the study of religion have resulted in an enormous knowledge pool and incorporated a variety of methods, divergent strategies and competing interests. While a synthesis of knowledge seems out of reach, the breadth of cultural representation has been a valuable contribution.

By contrast the study of Christian theology has tended to be dominated by white Western males, which is the residual effect of centuries of the patriarchal academic and ecclesiastical hierarchies in the West. One certainly does not expect substantial contributions to Christian theology by scholars of other faiths, any more than other faiths expect contributions by Christian theologians. With respect to ethnicity and gender, studies in Christian theology have a long way to go if they are to meet the same level of representation found in religious studies. Having said that, there is some progress. Christian theology has benefited enormously from contributions by women and members of diverse ethnic groups, and their impact is slowly being seen at the cultural level. However, American Evangelicalism along with Catholicism has lagged considerably in ethnic and gender diversity. A survey of Evangelical publishing houses clearly demonstrates that books on theology and biblical studies are still dominated by white males, and the same can be said for professors teaching at Evangelical colleges and universities. It would be very interesting and telling, I believe, to compare the ratio of men to women professors in religious studies (or theology) departments at confessional and non-confessional schools. If publications are any indication, I would venture to guess that non-confessional schools reflect a much broader representation.

Cross-disciplines vs. doctrines

Modern comparative approaches tend to exploit the multidimensional character of religion on individual and social levels. This is sometimes called the "dimensional theory" of religion because the focus is not so much on doctrinal or theological development as past historical approaches to Christianity tended to be, but on the impact of religion in various dimensions of life (i.e. experience, ritual, legal, economic, ethical). In order to meet the growing desire to depict religions more accurately, a variety of (often complementary) approaches are pursued, such as anthropological and sociological, feminist, phenomenological, philosophical and legal.[37] While the advancements made through a multiplicity of approaches are well recognized, according to a growing number of religion scholars the future study of religion must resist traditional academic divisions, along with their accompanying methodologies.[38] Otherwise the study of religion

---

[37] See for example Peter Connolly, *Approaches to the Study of Religion* (London: Cassell, 1999).
[38] Smart, "Forward," xi–xii.

could easily be fragmented and potentially become the "property" of other disciplines.

The study of theology inherently seeks to unify knowledge. Traditionally it has interacted with and adopted numerous philosophical structures and terms. However, since the Enlightenment, it has all too often lost touch with, and at times been adverse to, the rise of the social sciences. With the onset of the epistemological rift between faith and reason, the study of theology has today often become compartmentalized and even esoteric. In contrast to the hard sciences, it is unfortunately left in the position of validating its role in mainstream academic culture. It is not a stretch to say that over the last several hundred years, theology has been dethroned as the queen of the sciences and relegated to the basement. Although theology has always relied on philosophy (especially Platonic and Aristotelian) for its expression and continues to do so in many Christian traditions, it is challenged in some circles by the sciences. In the social sciences, religious phenomena are approached and explained from the perspective of observable or deduced causes and effects without appeals to the supernatural. For example, in psychology, religious experiences are being examined in the light of neuroscience which can duplicate a feeling of oneness with God or the universe in the laboratory by stimulating certain parts of the brain. In sociology, the study of power structures, socio-economic organization and nationalism has overshadowed the social significance of religion. In the field of history, reconstructions of Jesus in his rural Jewish context and reconstructions of early Christianity in its urban Hellenized context have resulted in conflicts with some theological reconstructions and doctrines. Mainstream historians have, for example, argued that the historical Jesus as a Jewish peasant would not have claimed to be God; that Jesus would have had siblings born to Mary; and that he would not have envisioned his own death as an atonement for the sins of the world. The modern challenge to theology, and especially its own understanding of revelation, from other disciplines is certainly weighty, but not insurmountable. A few postmodern theologians have been particularly attuned to the challenge of the nature of truth as something other than an objective rational goal. What is interesting to observe among these theologians is a tremendous respect for the methods and conclusions in the sciences. Some, for example, would view biblical and historical studies as preliminary activities which provide material for the theologian.[39] Unfortunately, at the popular level of Christianity, the Enlightenment rift is still widely evident in producing a dualism between "a Sunday mentality and an everyday mentality".[40] It is akin to the difference between Prometheus (our every day mentality) who is his own authority by caring nothing for Zeus even when punished, and Job (our Sunday

---

[39] Macquarrie, *Principles of Christian Theology*, 33.
[40] Macquarrie, *Principles of Christian Theology*, 21.

mentality) who in the midst of divinely sanctioned suffering prostrates himself before Yahweh and admits his own inadequacy even when his questions are not answered.

Non-(a)theism vs. (a)theism

In contrast to the study of theology that presupposes that a knowledge of God is possible, the modern study of religion tends to be methodologically what I would call non-(a)theistic in its epistemology. What I mean by this is that it leaves the question of the human knowledge of God as an object of critical study. But it does not necessarily reject the existence of God. A religion scholar may personally believe in God or the gods. This is not the issue. The important point for the religion scholar is to evaluate all claims critically and equally. Claims of knowledge about God are evaluated socially, anthropologically and psychologically, not apologetically or evangelistically. In other words, the science of religion does not attempt to evaluate which claim is correct. At the same time, it should not make sweeping statements that all such claims are false. It simply does not have the tools to make such evaluations. It is widely acknowledged that a fair representation is much more difficult to achieve if one begins with an overt commitment to a particular religious tradition. Although biases emerge and will continue to do so, religious studies are not formally oriented toward conclusions that are value judgments whereby one tradition is pitted over and against another. Put another way, the study of religion is not ordered to finding the "best" religion. When the issue of value is raised, it has more to do with the positive and/or negative role of religion—whatever the religion might be—in relation to individual and social life. For example, is religion x more inclusive of women? Is religion y more consistent with democracy? Or is a certain stream of religion z prone to violence? This is why terms like "theistic", "atheistic" or "agnostic" are often not useful for understanding the perspective from which religious studies begin. Such terms also carry unnecessary value judgments about individual belief systems and can overshadow the benefits that the science of religion can offer. A non-(a)theistic vantage point is important for understanding the methodological approach to data in the social sciences, and is necessary if religion scholars are to compare religions fairly.

The study of religion, however, has not always operated from a non-(a)theistic perspective. Throughout its short history, the study of religion has contained streams that have been atheistic and overtly hostile towards all religions by denying the existence of transcendent beings, supernatural events, and explaining all religious experience as psychologically induced. The views, for example, of Sigmund Freud and Karl Marx have been synonymous with this kind of hostility, claiming that religion as an irrational activity is incapable of being identified as objective knowledge and thus is not worthy of scientific study. Many of these ideas continue to be regurgitated in popular form.[41] By contrast, non-(a)theism is much more open to academic inquiry because it allows for religion to be studied as social capital and a valuable contributor to our understanding of human behaviour.

Bridging the divide

Phenomenology

My use of "non-(a)theism" as a broad category incorporates what has been called the "phenomenology of religious experience", which began not so much as a method, but as a means for legitimizing the scientific study of religion. Its impact, stemming from the works of James, Eliade, Campbell and others, continues to be widely felt. Phenomenology has proven to be very helpful in the study of religion because it is oriented towards the pursuit of empathetically walking in the shoes of people of different faiths. This is a significant development in our ability to understand better religious belief and practice among different ethnic groups, social classes, age groups, genders and a host of minorities without making *a priori* value judgments.

From a phenomenological perspective, religion is understood as a phenomenon (or a series of phenomena like ritual, myth, doctrine, ethics, social structure and experience, to use Ninian Smart's categories) through which life, the world and the cosmos makes sense to religious devotees. Yet religion is not viewed as its own entity, somehow separate from culture. Another way of stating it is that religion is a vehicle that generates meaning(s) from within the devotee's cultural context. Such awareness requires a certain degree of cultural deconstruction on the part of the researcher who needs to be aware of unconscious cultural prejudices. An example of phenomenological criticism is found in the work of Edward Said who has powerfully demonstrated how Arab and Islamic identity is classified by Western scholars from the perspective of the so-called Western myth of imperial supremacy. In Western portrayals, Arab and Islamic identity is regarded as the "other" or the "alter-ego" of the West's self-image.[42] Said's critique significantly helps to reduce distortions of Western

---

[41] Two recent examples are Christopher Hitchens, *God is Not Great: How Religion Poisons Everything* (New York: Twelve, 2007); Richard Dawkins, *The God Delusion* (Boston: Houghton Mifflin, 2006).
[42] Clive Erricker, "Phenomenological Approaches", in *Approaches to the Study of Religion* (ed. P. Connolly; London: Cassell, 1999) 94; Edward Said, *Orientalism* (London: Routledge Keegan Paul, 1978).

religious epistemology and typological classifications of non-Western religions.

There is no question that phenomenological inquiry, which is still unfolding, has contributed to our understanding not only of religion, but also of the religion scholar. However, the problem that emerges is whether or not epistemological empathy can truly be attained. As postmodern philosophers repeatedly caution, phenomenological approaches can easily slip into being governed by ideological and value-laden assumptions of modernity, imperialism and colonialism. So if completely "objective" or "precise" empathy is impossible, surely some connection with, and appreciation for, religious groups can only benefit the researcher. Even the postmodern philosopher must admit—for fear of being misunderstood himself—that a process of empathetic contact contributes to knowledge and aids in reducing misunderstanding, prejudice, intolerance and fear. So we speak instead of *sufficient empathy* that may take the form of standard sociological enquiry such as questionnaires, interviews or a limited participation within the group being studied. While valuable data can be collected, the success often depends on the personal capacities (e.g. sympathy, intuition, adaptability) of the embedded researcher and his or her ability to attain a balance between the simultaneous identification with the subjects and the distance from them.[43] On the one hand, since religion elicits such deep emotion in devout people, empathetic dispassion, which sounds like an oxymoron, should be the target. On the other hand, if a researcher has a strong prior religious commitment or is an apostate, negative emotions must be kept in check. For example, if the researcher has a prior personal commitment to a religious tradition such as Evangelicalism, can he or she adequately study Jehovah's Witnesses dispassionately and empathetically if he or she assumes that the object of study is heretical? Or if a researcher was emotionally wounded by a given religion, can he or she do justice to the study of that religion? These are just a few challenges that beset a phenomenological approach. What is clearly evident in such enquiry is the need for the researcher to maintain a sufficient balance between empathy and distance. Methodologically, the potential breadth of religious enquiry requires some kind of epistemological non-(a)theism if all the data are to be equally heard and evaluated.

By contrast, the study of theology begins with a faith conviction that revelation has taken place and that this revelation can be understood. In the study of Christian theology the content of the conviction differs widely, but is always set forth in the language of symbol or image. As many theologians in the past and present have realized, temporal and physical language is incapable of describing fully the true essence of revelation. Collective ascent

---

[43] Bryan R. Wilson, *The Social Dimensions of Sectarianism: Sects and New Religious Movements in Contemporary Society* (Oxford: Clarendon Press, 1992) 14–15.

to liturgy, creeds, doctrines and confessions of faith have always been the means through which revelation is given expression—such as a triune God, the fallen nature of humanity, the salvific role of Jesus, the religious authority of scripture, a purpose for history and an overall unifying truth. So unlike an epistemological non-(a)theism in the science of religion, theology begins with an epistemological theism which attempts to balance on the one hand the believed knowledge in a transcendent and immanent God who has revealed himself and on the other hand the tools of rational enquiry with all of their limitations.

Unlike the study of religion, the study of theology must not seek its own end lest it degenerate into a strictly academic pursuit whose goal is speculation and description instead of encounter and prescription. In this sense, it is perhaps more overtly circular than the study of religion. This is not to say that theology is uninterested in the speculative and descriptive, for methodologically it must begin with these. Beginning with a faith conviction does not mean that attention to method is somehow relegated to a subordinate position or is excluded altogether. Every theological question presupposes the need for a method. Take, for example, questions concerning revelation: What is revelation? How does one validate a claim to revelation? How is scripture revelatory? Or how are ancient revelations relevant today? Answers to such questions may begin with a faith conviction, but they require a consistent method at the outset. The method, however, cannot precede the questions, but is formulated through the process of prior theological problems. In other words, method in theology is a flexible enterprise that is shaped by a spiralling and experimental process over time.

Once again, John Macquarrie's approach to theology, which co-ordinates three major strands, serves as a helpful example.[44] As in the study of religion, Macquarie assigns an important role to description through the aid of phenomenology, whose advantages we discussed above. As a first strand, it allows the theologian to direct his or her attention to the phenomena that are being studied, without appealing to inherited theological presuppositions and ideas to the extent that they prevent the theologian from not facing the phenomena. The second strand is interpretation. Since the primordial revelation is mediated through scripture and tradition, which is a product of the past, the revelation needs to be continually reinterpreted. Understanding cannot take place without interpretation because theology is a dialectical process on a constant search for relevance, which not only incorporates current experiences, contemporary culture and the motivations of the interpreter, but also the nature of history from where it receives its inheritance and identity. I would also add to this strand the necessity of a working theory of language. Too often text-centred or exegetical, methods have completely bypassed theories of texts, be these written or otherwise.

---

[44] Macquarrie, *Principles of Christian Theology*, 34–8.

The final methodological strand is application. As theology originates within a community of faith, so its ultimate goal is to bring clarity and coherence back to that community. The goal is not simply intellectual, but one that orders the life and illumines the self-understanding of that community.

In addition to the contrasts between the study of theology and religion, there is an important similarity that requires mention. Phenomenological approaches to religion have had a direct bearing in some sectors of theological studies in recent years. Aside from the agnostic/theistic methodological difference discussed above, theology and religious studies are on a parallel course in these sectors of the discipline. Several theologians, such as the above-mentioned Hans Küng, David Tracy, Keith Ward and Wilfred Cantwell Smith, have tried to bypass the long-established divisions among religions by trying to understand them empathetically on their own levels. In the last ten years, new types of inclusive theological approaches have emerged, such as *theologies of religions*, which are separate theologies attempting to understand different religious traditions from a phenomenological perspective, *comparative theologies of religion*, which examine theological attitudes within particular religious traditions toward other religions, *theology of religion*, which attempts to formulate a universal theology of religion through transcendent categories, and *global theology of religions*, which begins with the complexity of human affairs in the world today and in turn seeks to formulate a theology arising from various religious traditions.[45] In the field of New Testament studies, Luke Timothy Johnson has successfully applied phenomenological inquiry to the study of early Christian religious experience.[46]

Although seminal contributions have been made, we are still at an early stage of research. The dissemination of research at the popular level, given the complexity and breadth inherent to these emerging approaches, is even further away. In keeping with the theme that theology is to be informed by religion, the body of data that has been amassed over the last fifty years which shows similarities of experience, ritual, use of metaphor and belief across the religions clearly warrants the expansion of theological study beyond traditional confines.

A cautiously optimistic future and the academy

Despite some recent criticisms, phenomenologists have not been swayed. Instead, phenomenological approaches have in fact been responsible for

---

[45] For an introduction to theological approaches to religion, see F. Whaling, "Theological Approaches", in *Approaches to the Study of Religion* (ed. P. Connolly; London: Cassell, 1999) 226–69.

[46] Luke Timothy Johnson, *Religious Experience in Earliest Christianity: A Missing Dimension in New Testament Studies* (Minneapolis: Fortress Press, 1998).

a growing optimism in the study of religion. The critiques levelled against phenomenological approaches over the last few decades have tended to be aimed at its hesitance and even omission in formulating an epistemological theory that can validate empathetically oriented research by a practitioner who is a devout participant of the religion being studied. While its temporizing posture has left it open to such critique, it has at the same time legitimized its importance by recognizing its own limitations. Moreover, it has been demonstrated over the last century of comparative study that one need not be a devotee of a religion to gain an understanding and appreciation of it.[47] Both the limitation and optimism are well expressed by Huston Smith who acknowledges that while we will never quite understand the religions which are not our own, the study of religion must nevertheless by taken seriously and empathetically. He writes,

> And to take them seriously we need do only two things. First, we need to see their adherents as men and women who faced problems much like our own. And second, we must rid our minds of all preconceptions that could dull our sensitivity or alertness to fresh insights. If we lay aside our preconceptions about these religions, seeing each as forged by people who were struggling to see something that would give help and meaning to their lives; and if we then try without prejudice to see ourselves what they see—if we do these things, the veil that separates us from them can turn to gauze.[48]

In the long run, however, it remains to be seen whether the empathetic approach that Smith and so many other religion scholars advocate will inevitably be the demise of organized religions as we know them. I do not intend for this to be a value judgment, just speculation. Outside of the scholarly realm the implications are immense. For once religious devotees begin to view their own faith as one of many religious options, and empathetically try to understand the other beyond the basic level of description, can organized religion function as a medium for ultimate meaning any longer? While the quest for meaning would undoubtedly remain since religion is part of our humanness, long-held symbols of belief and practice may well erode. Ideologies that bump against one another must soften if power plays driven by fear and control are to be averted. Though it is unconceivable that myths would ultimately be eradicated; they will simply form into other myths more fitting with the times. Yet with the dismantling of prejudicial barriers (not distinctives) that often emerge from unfounded fears, perhaps a peace among religions (not an assimilation) can effect one level of peace in the world. Another way of looking at this

---

[47] Smart, *The Religious Experience of Mankind*, 4–5.
[48] Smith, *The World's Religions*, 11.

impasse is to speculate, like Jacques Derrida, that since religious devotees cannot sufficiently step outside of their convictions (otherwise they are not devotees of that religion), religious tradition will continue to pull its adherents insatiably into itself well into the foreseeable future, while causing little in the way of true understanding and empathy towards the other. At the moment, peace on this level is nowhere on the horizon. To put it simplistically, the impasse seems irresoluble: either sacrifice personal religious bliss for the sake of peace among religious traditions; or sacrifice peace among world religions for the sake of personal religious bliss.

The study of theology has traditionally likewise been optimistic, but in a very different sense. Christian theology has always included a strong eschatological dimension in its understanding of the meaning of history. Despite all of the tragedies of history, the underlying belief that God is sovereign and that he will bring history to a close in accordance with his will is inherited from the Jewish scriptures. The belief in the atoning death of Christ and his resurrection is the basis for an optimism that the restoration of all things has already begun. Thus the optimism is not one of peace among religions, but a victory over all that is considered evil, which for some Christian groups even includes other religions. Therefore theology in many Christian traditions begins with an inherent eschatological optimism that bifurcates the fate of the "righteous" and the fate of the "wicked", to use biblical language. The optimism that arises in the community is directed back at the community. The challenges which this traditional exclusivist position faces today, even by Christian theologians who argue for a universalistic eschatology, are numerous and weighty. One such challenge is the criticism that exclusivist positions must necessarily incorporate violence, even if deemed "righteous", as a means to achieving restoration, but that card has been played all to often throughout Christian history with devastating results. Religious exclusivism is increasingly becoming a hard sell in the academy, given that we live in a time that has just emerged from the bloodiest century in history, a time that is filled with constant media exposure of religiously motivated and sanctioned violence. Another challenge which traditional theology faces is the relevance of the first-century apocalyptic worldview that is assumed in a number of the New Testament writings. Rudolf Bultmann's question remains: Is the apocalyptic worldview, which radically criticizes culture and civilization and presumes that an evil world is beyond human remedy, necessarily Christian?[49] The challenging question of Bultmann as to what the kernel of Christianity truly is, if it is not the first-century worldview, remains a thorn in the side of those Christian groups who tend to be more literalist in their reading of scripture. As optimistic as eschatology can be, it presents us with the

---

[49] John Dominic Crossan, *Jesus: A Revolutionary Biography* (New York: HarperCollins, 1994) 52–3.

proverbial fork in the road. It is in the writing of New Testament theologies that the roads begin to be paved. Once again it is not whether one believes in the sacredness of the New Testament text; it is rather in how that text is interpreted which can make the difference between peace and violence.

The Christian university seems ideally suited for welcoming a phenomenological approach to religion, provided that its ideology is inclusive. Its commitment to and experiential understanding of its own religion in its broadest expression should position it to be much more empathetic in the study of other faiths. This is necessary if religion and theology are to survive and benefit each other. By now it should be quite clear that Christianity must be viewed as a religion and not some entity that is non-religious. Once Christianity is perceived as a religion by its adherents, sacrosanct statements of faith—which can potentially clash with scholarly discoveries that inhibit creativity and freedom—can be understood sociologically as protective boundaries which keep more people out than they let in.[50] In a pluralistic culture, sectarianism is always tempting for more fundamentalist devotees, that is those who are vehemently resistant to social change. Theologically, exclusionary measures and statements must even be reconciled with the broad call to unity in Christ (e.g. John 17). The second hurdle is to attribute the same meaning and significance it finds in its own faith commitment to those who share different faith commitments. This is not only common sense if Christians expect to be heard and treated with respect in a pluralistic culture, but it is also consistent with the ethic of loving one's neighbour.

In one of the most insightful, yet relatively unknown, treatments of love, Russian philosopher and mystic Vladimir Solovyov defines love as the transference of all one's interests in life from oneself to another.[51] Love is not a feeling, but an act of the will that shifts the centre from the self to the other. Solovyov is particularly fond of describing love as the abrogation of egoism, which is the ascribing of absolute significance to oneself while at the same time denying it for the other.[52] Love affirms that one is a particle in a universal whole that is connected to everything else, and participates in everything else. For Solovyov, love allows one to *be* in the truth, not just to be conscious of it. Authentic love preserves individuality because it recognizes and affirms that the other is also an individual.[53] In much of what Solovyov says, the posture of love comes to appreciate truly everything that is *other*. If Solovyov's understanding of love is correct and reflects the character of God's love for all that is other, then are not Christians

---

[50] Jaroslav Pelikan, in a series of lectures at Vancouver School of Theology (Vancouver, BC), argued that the rise of Christian statements of faith during the Reformation have done more to exclude other Christians than to include them.
[51] Vladimir S. Solovyov, *The Meaning of Love* (trans. T. R. Beyer Jr.; Hudson, NY: Lindisfarne Press, 1985) 41.
[52] Solovyov, *The Meaning of Love*, 42–3.
[53] Solovyov, *The Meaning of Love*, 68.

challenged to view people of other faiths with the same authentic love? This would require that the study of religion be not only enthusiastically welcomed, but approached with the same empathy that one would want Christianity to be presented and studied by non-Christians.

While secular universities have advanced the study of religion in tremendous ways, theoretically the same level of empathy has been much more difficult to achieve due to the prevailing modernist conceit in the social sciences. Religions tend to be objectified and their devotees tend to be studied from a distance. Professors who hold faith convictions privatize their experiences, some willingly and some out of peer pressure. In my experiences in secular institutions, it has been fascinating to see that the privatization of faith has usually occurred among professors who held Christian beliefs. Perhaps the same is true for devout Muslim professors in progressive Muslim countries and devout Jewish professors in Israel. I don't know. Nevertheless, if religion as a lived experience is neutered and artificially removed from the very context that actually makes it what we call "religion", the net effect is that the educational process becomes sterile and minimalist. Students become the losers. An encouragement of a little autobiographical disclosure and loosening on the part of both professors and students in the classroom goes a long way in developing not only mutual respect, but also an understanding of the impact that religion plays in people's lives and on the world scene. It is intellectually and emotionally freeing to foster a respectful authenticity. Surely this can done without proselytizing. This widespread problem in religious studies departments has been articulated recently by C. T. McIntire, professor of history and religion at the University of Toronto, in *Academic Matters*, which is the official publication of the Ontario Confederation of University Faculty Associations. McIntire most aptly writes,

> By behaving as a first-set item, religious studies plays a trick on itself. The effect is either to privilege the tendency to reduce religions to something like merely societal, cultural, economic, psychological, social-controlling or power-driven phenomena, or to force the removal of religions to the stratosphere as other-worldly phenomena concerned with transcendent spirits, gods and heroes. Either way religious studies fails to see religion as a dimension of human existence and the religions as ways of life for people who live them. In so far as this happens, religious studies neglect or distort the religiousness of the religions as practised and witnessed by the people studied. ... scholars in religious studies are neutral and blank, and, with appropriate academic criticism, they produce objective results independent of their personhood, that is, detached from their gender, race, class, ethnicity, sexuality, wealth, relationship with power, politics, morality and above all religion.[54]

---

[54] C. T. McIntire, "How Religious Studies Misunderstands Religion", *Academic Matters* December (2007) 11–12

Conclusion

It should be fairly clear at this point that the science of religion operates with different presuppositions and towards different ends than does the study of theology. Nevertheless, the divide that has been present for so long in the theological enterprise is not necessary. The two fields can be complementary and can advance each other. Theology can inform religion about the existential dimension of human existence, to use McIntire's phrase. Since the study of theology is much older than the science of religion, it can likewise be highly informative historically. In turn, as I have mentioned earlier, the modern study of religion can provide a broader perspective that brings attention to the role of cultures, psychological propensity towards the human need for meaning, the nature of religious language, and the importance of myth and mythmaking, to name but a few. More specifically, in a dialectical New Testament theology that aims to provide provisional answers from the scriptures to contemporary questions, religion serves as the common ground in a pluralistic society. And within the Christian community, it is one way of looking at Augustine's dictum of "faith seeking understanding". The study of religion helps the faithful to understand the nature and importance of belief, ritual, worship, formulations of creeds, religious language like symbol and metaphor, and interpretative presuppositions, to name but a few, within the broader world context.

As we attempt to formulate New Testament theologies within our pluralist Western culture, we are caught in a dialectic between reconstruction and interpretation. On the one hand, faithfulness to the text's initial meaning must be maintained; yet on the other hand, the text must be freed to speak to our times. I have proposed that this dialectic must incorporate the science of religion before we deem any such formulation "theology". But the science of religion is admittedly an enormous undertaking and not a simple intermediary pathway to normativity. In New Testament studies, it has certainly been a road less travelled. That being the case, future ventures in this direction will require considerable effort in clearing the dense underbrush. But I am confident that the effort is worth it for two general reasons. First, if New Testament theology is to have a respected voice that can contribute to our understanding of what it means to be human and what that humanness looks like as it strives to live it out responsibly in the complexities of our times, it needs to take the posture of humility by recognizing that we live in a post-Christian culture where a plurality of religious voices seek to be heard. Relevance requires an understanding of the present. Listening needs to precede speaking, and watching needs to precede "seeing". Without this posture, I do not see how New Testament theology can be welcomed, let alone respected. And second, dialectic with the science of religion can be very instructive for understanding the Christian faith itself. To mention a few places where this can happen: It reveals the nature of religious language. It helps us to evaluate religious experiences. It reveals a common human quest for meaning and identity. It can disclose the mystical heart of the religious life. It can reveal the negative side of religion. It can show how institutionalism can take hold. It can reveal how ideologies emerge. It can show how and why authorities develop. It can reveal how and why varied interpretations of sacred texts occur. And it can show how religious life corresponds with the secular.

In the final chapter, I move beyond the introductory material that has been covered up to this point in the book and perilously stick my proverbial neck out by proposing an approach to a normative New Testament theology that incorporates insights from that part of religious studies known as myth theory. My aim is to generate the dialogue—to start clearing the dense underbrush, hoping to construct a path that leads to relevance.

Discussion questions

1. How would you assess the current state of religion (and even the quest for spirituality) in Western culture today?
2. Discuss the warning issued by some twentieth-century philosophers that final religious answers can lead to final social solutions.
3. Should a New Testament theology extend beyond the confines of the Church?
4. Compare the popular definition of religion with the one offered above by James Garber and Jon McGee in *Sacred Realms*.
5. In the attempt to demonstrate the relevance of the New Testament for today's world, should the theologian incorporate the study of religion? Or, more broadly, should the study of theology be informed by the study of religion?

7

New Testament theology as a dialectical process: An exercise in mythmaking

At this point it may not be too bold to state that a dialectical approach is better suited than the foundationalist approach if we seek a New Testament theology that is culturally relevant and engaging. Though there is no consensus today regarding the specific structure and theme within the dialectical process, we can draw from the insights of the discipline's predecessors and offer a series of informed considerations in the hope that the next round of formulations of New Testament theologies can become contributing voices in our pluralistic age.

We have seen that the aim of a dialectical New Testament theology is to *understand* the New Testament theologically, but we have also seen that when we burrow below the surface to define "understanding," we run into complications. Understanding, or insight, comes to all of us since the human mind is ordered to it, no matter what our culture or education.[1] But how that understanding is achieved and why interpretations differ so widely is another matter. As we mentioned in the first chapter, a dialectical approach is not oriented towards a *final* or *complete* theology, such as a doctrine or creed. Instead, the aim is dialogue or what Joachim Gnilka has called a continuous process,[2] which alone can bring an understanding and appreciation of differing points of view, be it dialogue between exegesis and doctrine, the past and present, the sacred and the secular, or the theological and the religious. Moreover, since the search for understanding the New Testament can never be removed from the self-understanding of the exegete, it is a continuous dialogue between the subject and object. As

---

[1] See Bernard J. F. Lonergan, *Insight: A Study of Human Understanding* (3rd edn; New York: Philosophical Library, 1970).
[2] Joachim Gnilka, *Theologie des Neuen Testaments* (Freiburg: Herder, 1994); Hans Hübner, *Biblische Theologie des Neuen Testaments* (3 vols; Göttingen: Vandenhoeck und Ruprecht, 1990–5).

each generation of Christians wrestles with its humanness in the face of new issues and their challenges, it necessarily engages in a conversation that is very old and very broad. It is a conversation that wrestles with identity, meaning and legitimization. It is, in short, the conversation of religion. But for the Christian, the scriptures are a constant in the conversation even if their answers to ever-new questions are only provisional. The dialectic must continue if the scriptures are to remain relevant in a rapidly changing world. To use a relevant truism, the journey (of a dialectic) is the destination. There is also a warning here: history has shown that dialectic or conversation about scripture leads to more positive, though perhaps insecure, ends; whereas final interpretative answers, where alternatives are in principle denied, have all too often led to final social solutions. Living without certainty can have benefits.

Readers shaping texts

From a dialectical perspective, the overriding task is not so much descriptive, but prescriptive, attempting to answer the question: How is the New Testament relevant today? This is clearly an open-ended question that begs for answers from every social and psychological direction in every generation. As with preceding generations of scripture readers, I would argue that the interpretative process is determined by the current context of the reader, be it a community or an individual. As a dialectical partner, New Testament theology cannot be reduced to an apologetic or a series of proof texts in support of doctrinal formulations, otherwise its strength as a discipline that offers theological accountability and creativity is compromised. It must be free enough to challenge and even dissent from prevailing theological views. While cognitive dissonance is usually discouraged and even punished by power structures, advancements in human achievement and the knowledge of our identity is contingent upon it, lest creativity is curtailed. Even the power structures which are currently in place owe their success to dissent that occurred somewhere down the line.[3] Christianity would never have emerged without it. Dissent is also bound up with relevance, which is the attempt to be sensitive to the social issues of our day. I say "social" because, as a religious text, the New Testament addresses the foremost of social issues, namely our human identity and interaction. Stagnation is the surest way for a social movement, even if it is religious, to become obscure at the cultural level of society.

Thus New Testament theology need not only serve the church, despite its indebtedness to it. It should play a role in the broader culture, especially

---

[3] See Cass R. Sunstein, *Why Societies Need Dissent* (Cambridge: Harvard University Press, 2003).

as more and more people today, despite their pursuit of spiritual fulfilment, distance themselves from religious institutions and authorities. But in contrast to Wrede who thought that the exegete must be independent of the church, New Testament theology must recognize its connection to the church lest the discipline be reduced to a description of early Christianity. How we understand the "connection" requires ongoing attention. At a minimum, the church necessarily remains one of the key dialectical partners. But the exegetical and hermeneutical task of New Testament theology must remain at arm's length so that it can freely instruct and be instructed by the church. This approach is consistent with what scholars like Heikki Räisänen, David Tracy and Hans Küng have called a "global perspective" or truly "ecumenical" ethos for biblical study which aims to benefit (as all disciplines should) all humankind, though they may seek less ecclesiastical "intrusion" for fear of its potential dominance in the dialectic.[4] Nevertheless, the point that Räisänen (as an example) makes is legitimate, for "the traditional interests of the churches, which are still often assumed in an authoritarian and aprioristic way, cannot provide the orientation for a synthesis. A non-ecclesiastical synthesis has to be comprehensible and give guidance to understanding to anybody, independently of faith and worldview."[5] The posture required is that of fairness and tolerance in the evaluative process so as not to subordinate rival religious or non-religious views to one's own. New Testament theologians have traditionally been particularly guilty of caricaturing and subordinating not only their rival theologians, but also rival belief systems contemporary with the Christianities found in the New Testament, such as the various Judaisms, Gnosticisms and mystery religions.[6] Once again, the way forward is first to gain an understanding of religion as the common ground (e.g. language, myth, ritual and power structures), prior to the theologizing process. This does not preclude, as I mentioned in the introduction, that one begins with a blank slate. If we begin with the belief that the New Testament is authoritative or has a role to play in our culture, we ultimately begin with a faith position. So the pathway leads from the experience of faith to an understanding of religion, and then to theologizing.

In general, this kind of external imposition onto the text, be it ideological or otherwise, is not novel, but is consistent with the history of biblical

---

[4] Heikki Räisänen, *Beyond New Testament Theology: A Story and a Program* (2nd edn; London: SCM Press, 2000) 155. E.g. David Tracy, *The Analogical Imagination: Christian Theology and the Culture of Pluralism* (London: SCM Press, 1981); Hans Küng, *Theology for the Third Millennium: An Ecumenical View* (trans. P. Heinegg; New York: Doubleday, 1988).
[5] Räisänen, *Beyond New Testament Theology*, 156. In providing a supportive example, Jesus' call to love God and neighbour in the context of his kingdom sayings comes immediately to mind. While ecclesiastical interpretations can (and should) provide an important voice to understanding the act of love, its universality as a human need transcends any one religion.
[6] See Räisänen, *Beyond New Testament Theology*, 158–9.

interpretation.[7] N. T. Wright has perceptively noted that subjectively oriented postmodern readings share a certain affinity with pietistic readings since each is concerned with the text's personal meaning.[8] I would extend his comparison much further (and beyond Christianity). Whether it was the Protestant response to Roman Catholicism, the Pietist response to Protestant Orthodoxy, or the nascent Christian response to early Judaism, readers and reading groups have always attempted to understand the meaning of scripture for their own day. In comparison, the rationalist-historical tendency in traditional Evangelical interpretation is an anomaly. A dialectical approach to New Testament theology can be informed by the history of biblical interpretation as another sounding board that helps us to understand the mechanisms and motivations of interpretation. In a real sense, it is a way of understanding ourselves as searchers for meaning, identity and legitimization. Yet at the same time the discipline of New Testament theology cannot be equated with the history of biblical interpretation. While New Testament theology is certainly consistent with the posture of scriptural critique throughout the history of Christianity (whereby new ideas/groups critique established ones), it is much more deliberate in maintaining a distinction. For example, one cannot strictly speak of a Patristic or scholastic New Testament theology (or biblical theology) just because their novel biblical interpretations challenged the *status quo*.[9] Most Protestant biblical scholars who have engaged in New Testament theology have been very deliberate in their structuring and systematizing techniques, which has set this discipline apart.

Texts shaping readers

At the same time a dialectical approach must be informed by critical exegesis and its ancillary disciplines, such as literary, social-scientific, rhetorical and linguistic study. Here, I depart from the positions of, say, A. K. M. Adam and Francis Watson, who for fear of attributing interpretative authority to modernism, limit the proven advancements that we have been made over the last two hundred years. And in turn they limit opportunities for an effective dialectic to take place. But as was mentioned in previous chapters, since the New Testament writings are historically bound and

---

[7] Steven J. Kraftchick, Charles D. Myers, Jr., and Ben C. Ollenburger, eds, *Biblical Theology: Problems and Perspectives. In Honor of J. Christiaan Beker* (Nashville: Abingdon, 1995) 8.
[8] N. T. Wright, *The New Testament and the People of God* (Minneapolis: Fortress Press, 1992) 60.
[9] Contra, for example, Kathleen McVey, "Biblical Theology in the Patristic Period: The Logos Doctrine as a 'Physiological' Interpretation of Scripture", in *Biblical Theology: Problems and Perspectives. In Honor of J. Christiaan Beker* (ed. Steven J. Kraftchick, Charles D. Myers and Ben C. Ollenburger; Nashville: Abingdon, 1995) 15–27.

attest to a historical revelation, historical inquiry is an inevitable result, whatever the method (such as social-scientific, rhetorical or literary). Even the most advanced hermeneutical (mis)readings which the Fathers, the Reformers, the Pietists or the postmodernists have mustered cannot escape the allure of the historical quest even if confidence in its "assured" results has waned. I do not believe that the question "What happened?" is necessarily modernist. Although our "rules" for investigating the past have changed and our optimism about objective results have waned, the question has always been part of our search for identity.

When it comes to understanding the New Testament, we must respect its "otherness" or "distance" before appropriating it for our time. We would want nothing less from those who appropriate our own writings or even our lives as examples in the service of their own interests. Likewise, advocates of a strict hermeneutical approach still insist that their position be understood and not misread. The distance is real. Texts shape readers as much as readers shape texts. Sometimes readers are even surprised by their readings. The text is a catalyst that cannot be stripped of its causal role.[10] The New Testament requires philology, lexicography and semantics for a hermeneutical reading even to begin. It requires attention to the study of ancient genres lest we reduce them to propositions and proof texts. It requires textual criticism lest we fail to determine what the text actually is. It requires attention to the study of rhetoric lest we bypass the actual means of argumentation. And it requires social-scientific study lest we confuse cultures.

Dan Via provides a helpful summary of several postmodern critics who have recognized the necessity of historical scholarship in the development of their own literary/ideological (mis)readings of texts.[11] It is well-recognized among postmodern critics that facts and texts have historical causes that stem from their cultural cradles, but what they are not prepared to admit is that these contribute to a larger narrative that we call history. The narratives that historians construct are likewise products of cultural causes. To put it rather simplistically, postmodernism has not so much disputed facts, but it has exposed the subjectivity of making meaning from those facts. And the making of that meaning is usually attributed to the reading agent who cannot avoid intertextual links.

---

[10] Wesley A. Kort, *Take, Read: Scripture, Textuality, and Cultural Practice* (University Park Pennsylvania State University Press, 1996) 66–70.
[11] Via, *What is New Testament Theology?* chapter 7. Via discusses Hayden Whyte, Hans Kellner, Fredric Jameson and Jacques Derrida.

Texts and readers in a dialectical dance

With one ear tuned to the hum of contemporary culture and the other trained on the voices from the historical context of scripture, the New Testament theologian's task is to speak to the life of faith as it wrestles with contemporary complexities, such as human identity, human rights, poverty, global warming, terrorism, imperialism and racial inequality. But this interplay between the past and present is more easily said than done. Both the foundationalist and dialectical positions wrestle with the age-old problem of a valid connector. As we have seen in the previous section of our study, reconciling early Christian beliefs, which were expressed in the language of a foreign worldview (i.e. Jewish apocalypticism or Roman imperialism), with those of our own continues to be an enormous challenge.

I have found this problem especially pronounced in popular Christianity. Without intending to generalize, by far most of the sermons I have heard in Evangelical churches have attempted to be exegetical on the one hand and relevant on the other, yet the connector between the two has often been missing. Often the relevance is understood as "correct" belief about salvation as it is connected with one's "personal relationship with Jesus", which is consistent with a deeply seated dualism rooted in the principle of what Marcus Borg has called "believing today for the sake of heaven later".[12] I use the term "attempted" deliberately since well-intentioned historical interpretations have often failed to consider properly issues of genre, rhetoric, social-scientific criticism and religion. While the exegete attempts to be historical, he or she is hurried by propositional aims. In other words, the focus has been on what the text meant with attached "application" portions that attempt to transfer ancient religious beliefs and ethical principles to today as quickly as possible within the confines of Western individualism. One example is the language of the "personal relationship with Jesus". This individualistic expression, though not found in the Gospels, has undoubtedly emerged from texts that speak of belief, faith and faithfulness to Christ. When "applied" to the life of faith within an individualistic culture, the result is a solitary pilgrimage accompanied by Jesus and the Bible. Social implications tend to recede. Even during heightened social and political awareness, such as global terrorism, homelessness in the inner cities, genocide in Rwanda, famine in Darfur, climate change and economic injustice in globalization, I have rarely heard how the scriptures can be read today in ways that shed some theological light on the Christian response to these and many other contemporary social challenges.

My experience of sermons in the mainline traditions, especially Anglicanism, has been the reverse. While the challenges of contemporary

---

[12] Marcus J. Borg and N. T. Wright, *The Meaning of Jesus: Two Visions* (New York: Harper Collins, 1999) 239–40.

life take on the central role, I have found the exegetical aspect wanting. Yet I am forced to admit that it is the focus on the contemporary instead of the historical that has tended to effect more social change, even at the expense of careful exegesis. One example is the civil rights movement in the United States. Sermons were largely issue-oriented, dealing with obvious racial inequality and oppression, and New Testament texts were read through the lenses of injustice. The relevance of the sermons filled the African-American churches of the American South and mobilized a powerful movement. We can say the same about Liberation Theology, which has attempted to empower the oppressed in Latin America through Marxist readings. I have found the so-called "historical" readings of its theologians such as Segundo and Sobrino wanting, but their overall theme of social justice, which found its way into more Gospel texts than might be warranted, nevertheless proved socially effective.[13] More recently, in the American political scene, one of George Bush's religious mantras during his tenure had been that God wants all peoples to be politically free and all nations to be democratic. Apart from whatever one thinks of his administration's policies, the mantra itself, coming from a self-proclaimed "born-again" Christian, is an illuminating example of how a current political ideal serves as an interpretative lens. In the New Testament, which Bush regards as sacred and authoritative, there is variance. On the one hand, the Gospel of Mark can be viewed as a writing that subverts the Emperor, as one who brings peace and salvation, with Jesus. On the other hand, in those sections where Paul discusses the role of the Roman government, albeit tangentially, he endorses its imperialistic and authoritarian practices, since they are believed to be sanctioned by God (Rom. 13). Elsewhere, not only is political freedom and democracy not advocated as the "will of God", but slavery is simply accepted as a normal way of life. All that the Pauline tradition advocates is that masters treat their human property justly and fairly (Col. 4.1), and that slaves obey their masters with "fear and trembling" (Eph. 6.5). There is no opening in the religious-political language of Pauline tradition for revolution against existing political powers or for the abolition of slavery. History is replete with examples of scripture being used to support the ideologies of the powerful whether it is ultimately for the good, such as the social justice movements, or evil, such as the Inquisition and the Holocaust.

Those who are familiar with Heikki Räisänen's recent writings will notice considerable parallels in my description of a dialectical approach. Like Räisänen, I see New Testament theology playing a role in our culture through the advocating of universal human dignity, justice and peace. Also, like Räisänen, I draw attention to the necessity of developing a connector between the work of the exegete and that of the theologian.

---

[13] Juan Luis Segundo, *Jesus of Nazareth Yesterday and Today* (3 vols; Maryknoll, NY: Orbis, 1984–86); Jon Sobrino, *Christology at the Crossroads* (Maryknoll, NY: Orbis, 1978).

Though he has received his share of criticism, especially from conservative New Testament theologians, for fragmenting the canon and carrying on Wrede's programme, Räisänen's observations of current practices that theologize too quickly need to be heard and reiterated. He is not opposed to reading the ancient texts in the light of modern issues (contrary to the assessment of some critics), but he is concerned that the problems that typically confront the exegete are not addressed with scholarly vigour. Too often, for the sake of preserving theological unity, the problems are denied, harmonized or drowned out by a boisterous theistic God-talk.[14] In short, I share Räisänen's observation that the gap between the ancient text and modern life is real. The way forward, as he suggests, is not by separating the theological task from the historical, but by keeping them distinct so each can be in dialogue with the other. This is how I understand dialectic at its most basic level.

As a complement to Räisänen's exegetical efforts, I steer the direction more towards a New Testament theology as social capital by advocating an approach that is dialectical, but with an emphasis on the side of the hermeneutical instead of the historical. Since ideologies precede any interpretative work, their role in New Testament theology must be prioritized, recognized and honestly shared. As Räisänen states, "It is quite impossible to build a theology on the Bible alone."[15] The history of Christianity testifies to the ideologically driven interpretative agendas. After almost two thousand years of Christian anti-Semitism, centuries of religious warfare in Europe, genocides committed by Christianized states in the last century and the recent foreign policies of injustice in the Middle East sanctioned by the "Christian" American administration, to name but a few, the moral high ground has been eroded. Clearly, a new posture for reading sacred texts is needed. The old hermeneutical lenses, which were fallaciously perceived as providing 20/20 vision, are in need of a new prescription. Too many have died, been maimed, dehumanized and treated unjustly in the cause of "right" belief. And too often the value placed on the "other" is determined by belief instead of our common humanness.

Discrimination is not only found in the realms of race, gender and age, but is alive and well in the sphere of religion. So a hermeneutic which is rightly suspicious of the negative side of religion—one that leads to control and power over others—not only makes sense from a global perspective on relevance, but is well-rooted in the portrayals of Jesus in the Gospels.[16] Where I would further advance Räisänen's approach is in the prioritizing of religion over theology in the hermeneutical process. Although he advocates the study of early Christian religion as a vital component

---

[14] Räisänen, *Beyond New Testament Theology*, 2–8.
[15] Räisänen, *Beyond New Testament Theology*, 7.
[16] Charles Kimball, *When Religion Becomes Evil: Five Warning Signs* (revised edn; New York: HarperCollins, 2008).

of a New Testament theology, I believe that the prerequisite should be an understanding of religion in general—its nature, language, ritual and systems of belief—prior to theologizing.

Dancing the three-step

As in all interpretations, we must begin somewhere, and beginning with the traditional belief that the New Testament is canonical, surely passes for legitimacy in the postmodern understanding of intertextuality, which advocated the intersection of all things in human experience. It is just as legitimate as starting with an assumption that there is no canon.[17] Such distinctions among starting points—namely which constitute knowledge and evidence in the disciplines—should be ably informed by the field of epistemology.[18] Räisänen's epistemology, which calls for an exegesis that is not informed by faith, is perilously close to traditional modernism and hence borders on excluding his study from the field of New Testament theology altogether, despite his intentions.[19] Starting with a personal faith position, provided that it is not equated with a rationalist certainty, can lead to an effective New Testament theology that is faithful to both the historical and hermeneutical sides in the dialectic.

Faith

For most who study the Christian scriptures, the initial step in the formulation of a New Testament theology is the raw faith experience, which resides in the emotional life. This is what Ninian Smart has called "empathetic objectivity, or if you like a neutralistic subjectivity".[20] I also find it helpful at

---

[17] The term "experience" in the science of religion conveys a variety of nuances. I follow Ninian Smart's general description: "A religious experience involves some kind of 'perception' of the invisible world, or involves a perception that some visible person or thing is a manifestation of the invisible world." Taken from his *The Religious Expereince of Mankind* (New York: Charles Scribner's Sons, 1969) 15.
[18] A helpful discussion that extends knowledge into the realm of imaginative and creative faculties is found in Michael Polanyi, *Personal Knowledge: Towards a Post-Critical Philosophy* (Chicago: University of Chicago Press, 1974); Michael Polanyi and Harry Prosch, *Meaning* (Chicago: University of Chicago Press, 1977). A helpful introduction to the role of reason and religion is found in Ninian Smart, *The Phenomenon of Religion* (New York: Herder and Herder, 1973); Keith Ward, *The Case For Religion* (Oxford: Oneworld, 2004).
[19] Yet elsewhere he writes (*Beyond New Testament Theology*, 200), "Thus, the dialectical interaction between tradition (symbolic universe), experience and interpretation governs the way in which the world is perceived and interpreted by groups and individuals." His hesitation that this model "is hardly a universal key that opens every lock" does not detract from his softening of Wrede's agenda.
[20] Smart, *The Phenomenon of Religion*, 6.

this point to adopt Peter Berger's distinction between the propositional (as reflective and secondary) and experiential (as mystical encounter, emotional and primary) aspects of faith.[21] Like Smart's "empathetic objectivity", Berger's experiential component refers to encounter with a "fuller" reality, which may be unwanted or even take the subject by surprise. Wilfred Cantwell Smith's understanding of the relationship between inherited tradition and personal faith experience is likewise helpful.[22] For Smith, faith is personal, experiential and always dynamic. While it can change (or be adjusted) every day, it is tied to the meaning one gives to the universe in the light of an inherited tradition. By the "rawness" of faith I refer to Smart, Berger and Smith's notion of a faith experience that is not informed or structured by an institutionalized theology, though it often uses the language of a host religious community. It is simply raw encounter emerging out of a community and influenced by the community's language and concepts. For example, the experiences of a new convert, which are raw, are almost always consistent with the host community's established parameters that give expression to conversion experiences. The new convert will use the language of the community, especially when he or she describes the experience to other members of the community. When the description of the experience corresponds to that of the community, it is deemed authentic. But there is another dimension of expression today. Since we live in an age when religious communities are subcultures subsumed within the broader dominant culture, raw faith experience can also be informed by the cultural traditions within which one regularly participates. Non-partisan language of spirituality, for example, has become very popular outside religious communities. Our cultural symbols and language are interwoven with what we experience and how we interpret that experience. Even when the experience challenges a tradition, it is framed within familiar language and pre-existent interpretative structures.

Religion

The second step in the sequence is to understand the raw faith experience in the context of religion. There is much debate about whether religion is a helpful category in understanding faith, but it seems to me that attempts to use other terms or more holistic approaches have not actually advanced our understanding of the phenomenon. This step is often omitted by New Testament theologians, but is vital because it grounds individual and group experiences in the broader context of the collective human experience,

---

[21] Peter L. Berger, *The Heretical Imperative: Contemporary Possibilities of Religious Affirmation* (New York: Doubleday, 1979) 50–2.
[22] Wilfred Cantwell Smith, *The Meaning and End of Religion: A New Approach to the Religious Traditions of Mankind* (New York: New American Library, 1964) 141–68.

which in turn allows for both understanding and accountability in the evaluative process. As a result, I devote considerable attention to it. One of the most important benefits is that it allows us to understand how language functions in describing our experiences and beliefs in transcendent realities. Recognizing similar attempts to use language in other religions for describing transcendent reality in narrative form establishes a broader human context for understanding how faith experiences have been, and are, conveyed. Breadth is a prerequisite for any search for truth—which, as an aside, I would loosely define as the totality of human experience.

Räisänen has shown well how theological positions (i.e. the canon of the New Testament) *can* distort exegesis. However, he has not shown that theological positions *always do* lead to distortions. Nor has he demonstrated that a non-adherence to the canon results in a more objective exegesis. This potentially debilitating issue can be bypassed if we first start by reading the canonical books in the light of the science of religion. At this stage, we can begin with the canon, but there is no pressure to unify the ideas conveyed in it. Nor is there a need to impose doctrinal content onto the writings. Religion, as a middle step, allows us to understand comparatively what the writings convey in their earliest contexts and how they have continued to be appropriated in the subsequent changing contexts of faith. Furthermore, the science of religion allows us to compare the Christian canon with the canons of other religions. Christianity and Judaism are not the only religions that claim a divine inspiration for their canons. A vast majority of Muslims and Hindus, for example, also claim that their scriptures are revelatory and inspired. Such an inter-faith communication is not only illumined by the science of religion, but may play a role in understanding the practice of exegesis.

Enter the problem of unbiased comparison, which presents us with a delicate situation that requires the suspension, not the abandonment, of faith conviction at the intellectual level. But is it at all possible for a person of faith to present a fair comparative assessment? Answering this question requires much more discussion than I can offer here. However this may be developed, the starting point should always be self-reflection. An inventory of attitude can control, or at least mitigate, prejudices that inhibit comparison. For example, the tacit conviction among many Christian scholars concerning the uniqueness of the Christ-event may preclude any serious discussion of comparison because all other religious events in all other religions are potentially scrutinized by the Christian standard.[23] What is needed is not for the Christian scholar no longer to be a Christian. That would be absurd. Instead, what is needed is a theory of religion that can establish a common ground. Echoing Jonathan Z. Smith, without

---

[23] See Jonathan Z. Smith, *Drudgery Divine: On the Comparison of Early Christianities and the Religions of Late Antiquity* (Chicago: The University of Chicago Press, 1990) 36–53.

parity with non-Christian materials, comparative research cannot begin. It is its prerequisite.[24]

A vivid example from personal experience may prove helpful. Consider the claim by devout Christians that the Bible is the word of God. The claim is usually based on a deep emotional attachment to the scriptures because they are believed to convey divine revelation, aside from the particularities of interpretation. Undoubtedly some of my readers will identify with this faith position without even knowing how it was formed. They may have been raised with the belief or they may have adopted it upon conversion. It is simply a foundational aspect of the raw faith experience. Without any counterclaims and especially direct exposure to alternative faith experiences, one can easily relegate the scriptures of other religions to non-revelatory status. Within the confines of a single faith the pathway to truth is very short, leading from the raw faith experience to theologizing. But a very interesting thought process occurs when one encounters people of other faiths expressing the same, or perhaps even more intense, emotional devotion to their own scriptures. I have frequently encountered events like this, but one stands out as particularly vivid. In the summer of 2005 I took several students on an archaeological study trip to Turkey, Greece and Rome. During a visit to the Topkapi Palace in Istanbul we encountered several Muslim women intensely weeping and praying as they stared at a copy of the Qur'an in the museum. Since we were in close proximity to the women, their devotion was not only mesmerizing, but created a feeling of empathy shared by several of my students. Surprisingly, some of them felt that the women's devotion narrowed the cultural and religious gap between "us and them". The discussion afterwards was reflective of how such an empathetic encounter can lead to questions of comparison and the nature of religion. I still remember some of the reflective comments by my mostly Protestant Christian students: "maybe God is bigger than Christianity", "culture effects our theologies", "maybe the world's scriptures are anthologies of human devotion, and not direct revelations", "all scriptures are revelations to some degree" and "my faith is really challenged by the women's deep devotion." All the comments had a common theme that advocated the need of people of faith to interact and understand each other's spiritual journey as it is shaped within the cultures in which they participate. It was nothing short of a realization that faith calls for an understanding that includes an empathetic comparison of religions. The students' remarks reminded me of Max Müller's famous dictum written about a hundred and forty years ago: he who knows only one religion, knows none.[25] Müller's sentiments are well summarized by Daniel Pals:

---

[24] Smith, *Drudgery Divine*, 87.
[25] F. Max Müller, *Lectures on the Science of Religion* (New York: Charles Scribner and Company, 1872) 11.

He [Müller] reminded his listeners that the words which the poet Goethe once wrote about human language could also be applied to religion: "He who knows one, knows none". And if that is so, he continued, then perhaps it was time for a new and objective look at this very old subject. Instead of following the theologians, who wanted only to prove their own religion true and all others false, the time had come to take a less partisan approach, seeking out those elements, patterns and principles that could only be found uniformly in the religions of all times and places.[26]

An understanding of religion is an important step in the process of what Augustine famously called "faith seeking understanding", though admittedly I cast my net of understanding beyond his. This kind of understanding cannot simply be achieved by analysing the scripture texts. While historical criticism has yielded huge benefits in the collection of data from the ancient world and contributed significantly to reconstructions, it has not produced an adequate theoretical framework that is capable of conveying meaning.[27] Armin W. Geertz perceptively remarks that

> *the study of religion is significantly more than reading and analyzing texts*. The study of religion is a theoretical project exploring an academic construction called "religion", which is informed by empirical evidence perceived in terms of a whole range of ideas and assumptions. These ideas and assumptions often turn on the nature of human beings, their origins, cognition and psychology, their cultural and social needs, and so on.[28]

The current reign of the historical-critical method, which so often illicitly transforms raw data into theological meaning, has indeed become a methodological trap for the exegete, rather than a tool to be used, challenged, modified or even abandoned. Rita M. Gross incisively argues that

> the most critical and liberating thing to be said about methodology is that it is a tool... Methodology often turns from tool to trap because aspects of a scholar's personal interest and identity become tangled up with supposedly neutral scholarly methods... Beliefs about religion are at stake, no matter how neutral their proponents claim to be... *Such*

---

[26] Daniel L. Pals, *Seven Theories of Religion* (Oxford: Oxford University Press, 1996) 3–4.
[27] See Elisabeth Schüssler Fiorenza, *Jesus and the Politics of Interpretation* (New York: Continuum, 2000).
[28] Armin W. Geertz, "Cognitive Approaches to the Study of Religion", in *New Approaches to the Study of Religion* (ed. Peter Antes et al.; Religion and Reason, 42–3; 2 vols; Berlin: Walter de Gruyter, 2005) 2.354–5.

doctrinal adherence to an already accepted methodology is usually what bars further advances in the field.[29]

These two quotations are representative of a considerable number of religion scholars today, but they are rarely heeded among New Testament theologians. There are, I believe, at least three reasons for the absence of theoretical discussions. First, New Testament theologians have been reluctant to perform critical self-reflection, which is to say, they lack a clearly articulated purpose. As motivations for scholarship tend to be either apologetic and defensive or antagonistic and offensive, methods become self-serving tools. The methods employed for these interests are rarely the object of debate and cannot be so unless the apologetic task is first abandoned, a risky prospect for those whose own identities are linked with the results of their scholarship.[30] As Jonathan Z. Smith writes, "Lacking a clear articulation of purpose, one may derive arresting anecdotal juxtapositions or self-serving differentiations, but the disciplined constructive work of the academy will not have been advanced, nor will the study of religion have come of age."[31]

Second, New Testament theologians remain largely uninterested in, or unaware of, theories of religion developed in other disciplines, such as cultural anthropology, comparative religion, evolutionary biology or cognitive psychology, to name but a few. The theory of religion in New Testament theology is, by and large, a Christian theory of religion which, even if subconsciously, serves as a standard by which all other belief structures are measured, and inevitably found lacking. This model, which emphasizes personal experience and divine moments of transformation, sustains a theory of religion that, even after comparative efforts (if any), promotes Christianity to be unique and superior.[32] Burton Mack articulates the problem in the following way:

---

[29] Rita M. Gross. "Methodology—Tool or Trap?" in *How to do Comparative Religion? Three Ways, Many Goals* (ed. René Gothóni; Religion and Reason, 44; Berlin: Walter de Gruyter, 2005) 154. Emphasis is mine.

[30] This became startlingly apparent to me when, during a recent guest lecture at my institution, a prominent New Testament scholar argued that the kernel of nascent Christianity was more or less equal to that of later orthodox Christianity. This may be so, but a validation process was omitted. After I asked him to reveal what method he was using to make such assertions, he responded candidly by announcing that he did not have one. He went on to say that he simply read the text and observed. This upfront admission reminds me of what Nietzsche called the "myth of immaculate perception" (*Zarathustra* 2.15, taken from Smith, *Drudgery Divine*, 51). Are we to believe that the results of his passive observations and their reinforcement of orthodox Christianity are merely a sensational coincidence? Surely, as this example illustrates, investigation into the aims and methods of New Testament scholars is paramount.

[31] Smith, *Drudgery Divine*, 53.

[32] See Burton Mack, *The Christian Myth: Origins, Logic, and Legacy* (New York: Continuum, 2001) 64–6. See also Smith, *Drudgery Divine*, 36–53.

...since the discipline does not demand expertise in the fields of comparative religions, cultural anthropology, and religious studies, it has not seemed necessary to venture beyond the history of Christianity to look for a general theory of religion. Familiarity with the Christian religion has taken the place of theoretical discussion, and Christianity has provided the categories that are used to name and explain early Christian phenomena.[33]

Third, if the reason is lack of interest, then it may stem from today's common sentiment that general theories of religion, as with all holistic endeavours, have resulted in numerous debates and few cohesive and conclusive ends, as several recent studies demonstrate.[34] However, if this is the case, it should not discourage New Testament theologians from participating in the ongoing debate.[35] As Robert Segal has perceptively stated, "Being sceptical of the universality of any theory is one thing. Being able to sidestep theorizing altogether is another."[36]

Theology

The final step in the sequence of formulating a New Testament theology is the theologizing stage. This is the stage at which New Testament theologies are written. Unfortunately, too many New Testament theologians have omitted the intermediate stage and moved from faith and text to theology without understanding the nature of religion. In this regard Räisänen's concerns are valid. But if we include an understanding of religion as the middle step, Räisänen's concerns might be abated. His claims that the canon cannot "be the starting point in exegesis oriented on society"[37] proves inadequate if we introduce the intermediate step and look at the canon as a religious phenomenon common to other religions. Beginning with a raw faith position that the New Testament writings are scripture does not invalidate the kind of historical work that Räisänen calls for because

---

[33] Mack, *The Christian Myth*, 65.
[34] Antes, *New Approaches to the Study of Religion*; Willi Braun and Russell T. McCutcheon, eds, *Guide to the Study of Religion* (London; New York: Cassell, 2000); Gothóni, *How to do Comparative Religion?*; Robert Segal, ed., *The Blackwell Companion to the Study of Religion* (Malden, MA: Blackwell Publishing, 2006).
[35] Some exceptions include the Christian Origins Project whose work is published in *Redescribing Christian Origins* (ed. Ron Cameron and Merrill Miller; Atlanta: Society of Biblical Literature, 2004); Gerd Theissen, *A Theory of Primitive Christianity* (trans. John Bowden; London: SCM Press, 2003); and Heikki Räisänen, *Marcion, Muhammad and the Mahatma: Exegetical Perspectives on the Encounter of Cultures and Faiths* (London: SCM Press, 1997).
[36] Robert A. Segal, *Myth: A Very Short Introduction* (Oxford: Oxford University Press, 2004) 10.
[37] Räisänen, *Beyond New Testament Theology*, 187.

the intermediate step allows one to evaluate comparatively the nature of faith and scripture prior to making theological prescriptions. To put it in different words, raw faith experiences that lead directly to the formulation of theology are inadequately informed and thus require a degree of deconstruction so as to maintain the posture of "faith seeking understanding". In my estimation all theologizing processes—be they dogmatic, historical, or biblical—have fallen victim to our culture's neurotic obsession with instantaneous results. If we are to take theology seriously, the process from faith to theology takes years, lifetimes and even centuries to develop. In Catholic teaching, for example, it is a development that has been ongoing since the "fall of man". Theologizing of any kind needs to be more guarded and even "feared" because, unlike the previous two steps, it is prescriptive and inherently dangerous since its proponents make demands on people's lives.

The dialectical process and mythmaking

Results of a dialectical New Testament theology, no matter how provisional, recast the ancient stories, events, and preaching in ways that address contemporary life. Some portions of the ancient texts may be overshadowed by others, some may be neglected altogether, and some may be given prominence. This process of attaining currency and legitimization of meaning has taken place in all religions since our distant ancestors sat around their evening fires recalling stories of the day's hunt. The past has always given meaning to the present, just as the present has always given meaning to the past. In the field of religion, the process has been variously called myth, mythmaking, or mythopoesis. I find the dialectical formulations of New Testament theology no different. As was mentioned in the opening chapter, the question of how New Testament theology is to be understood and done is essentially a hermeneutical one, meaning that it is a product of particular interpretative methods, structures and sets of assumptions that stem from the one who attempts to formulate a New Testament theology. When we read the New Testament, we do not find a New Testament theology in it. We find theological language, reflection and faith conviction, but no unified theology or theological structure. To reiterate, New Testament theologies are books written by modern scholars attempting to describe and/or prescribe the religious teaching in the New Testament, as they see it or want to see it. Mythmaking, as it is understood in the field of religion, is a useful category for understanding the process in formulations of New Testament theologies because, as we shall see below, they share as their constitutive elements the dialectic between past and present, the assumption of a transcendent reality, and most importantly the need for ideological legitimacy.

Applying the term "myth" in the field of New Testament studies runs the risk of being identified with the History-of-Religions schools that gained prominence in the nineteenth century through the influential work of figures like David Friedrich Strauss (1808–74) who read the Gospels as history interpreted through myth. Strauss added immensely to the growing recognition among scholars that the "Jesus of history" cannot be identified with the "Jesus of faith". For Strauss, the Gospels were mythical retellings of Jesus often interpreted in the light of the prototypes, structures and themes of the Old Testament. In his influential, and at the time controversial, two-volume *The Life of Jesus Critically Examined*, Strauss called for an objectively critical historical reconstruction of Jesus by peeling back early Christian mythical retellings.[38] While it is commonplace today among historical Jesus scholars not to view the Gospels as history, the publication of Strauss' book caused such an outrage that he was dismissed from his position at the University of Zurich. As has been covered in chapter five, about a century later the demythologizing of the Gospels (particularly John) came to its culmination in the work of Rudolf Bultmann who sought to uncover, not the historical Jesus, but the "kernel" of Christian preaching (the *kerygma*). For Bultmann, the central Christian message, which he wanted to make relevant for a post-war Europe, was encapsulated in the New Testament, but was obscured by the mythical content and language of the first century world. Bultmann sought to peel back, or demythologize, the first century worldview that gave shape to the Christian writings like one peels the husk of corn. Deep within the New Testament, he argued, lies the untainted existential message, calling individuals to "exist" for the sake of the other. While a number of the historical assumptions and conclusions that Bultmann reached are no longer accepted, his theological questions raised in the attempt to make the New Testament relevant are still with us.[39]

My attention to myth in relation to New Testament theology is an indirect response to the History-of-Religions school, but it is specifically oriented towards contemporary formulations of New Testament theology. Similar to the History-of-Religions approach, which sought to bifurcate the historical from the mythical with little attention paid to the biases of the "bifurcator", so it is today with the formulations of theologies based on the New Testament. The vast majority of New Testament theologians would never consider relegating their constructs produced by careful exegesis to the realm of myth, any more than their modernist predecessors would have considered their meticulously crafted historical reconstructions in the same way. The common denominator is that "myth" in New Testament scholarship continues to be used to convey the negative side of the bifurcation,

---

[38] David Friedrich Strauss, *The Life of Jesus Critically Examined* (3 vols; trans G. Eliot; London: Chapman, 1846; reprinted: P. C. Hodgson, ed., Lives of Jesus Series; Philadelphia: Fortress, 1972/London: SCM Press, 1973).
[39] Reginald H. Fuller, "New Testament Theology", in *The New Testament and its Modern Interpreters* (ed. E. J. Epp and G. W. MacRea; Philadelphia: Fortress Press, 1989) 567.

be it as a reference to the non-historical or as a reference to competing religious traditions and/or conclusions. The (usually orthodox) Christian or so-called "biblical" view is not regarded as mythic by Christians, while non-Christian beliefs, such as paganism, are usually regarded as mythic. One of the clearest examples of this is Matthew and Luke's Infancy Accounts, which, in contrast to numerous similar stories of supernatural births in Greco-Roman literature (not to mention the stories in Muslim, Hindu and Buddhist traditions, among others), are rarely regarded as myth.[40] It is reminiscent of Joseph Campbell's popular definition of myth as "someone else's religion". Judging from Michael Fishbane's observations in his illuminating work on Rabbinic mythmaking, the sentiment seems to be no different in the study of the Jewish scriptures. Fishbane writes, "A striking feature of contemporary attempts to differentiate ancient Israel from myth thus often depends upon constructions that first define myth in terms of polytheistic paganism, and then juxtapose this definition to features of biblical monotheism – concluding thereby that 'myth' is absent from the latter."[41]

I have argued that the formulation of a New Testament theology requires preliminary attention being paid to the nature of religion, which in turn necessarily requires a carefully developed theory of comparison that is sensitive to the tendency towards an assumed superiority and uniqueness of one's own belief system over and against another. Such a theory would have the benefit of placing all formulations of New Testament theologies on an equal plane so that the comparative programme could begin. Enter myth. When understood ideologically, myth and mythmaking serve as non-threatening collective categories within which New Testament theologies (and all other religious constructs) can be located. When a formulation of any New Testament theology is scrutinized hermeneutically for its legitimization tendencies, its mythmaking programme is disclosed.

As an aside, evaluating any book on New Testament theology as mythmaking should not be alarming provided that the category is sufficiently broad to incorporate what we do on a regular basis when merging the past with the present for the purpose of attaining meaning. This seemingly natural human tendency is poignantly conveyed in Bill Moyers' interview of Kathleen Hall Jamieson, Director of the Anneberg Public Policy Center at the University of Pennsylvania.[42] Two decades previously, Moyers

---

[40] See, for example, John P. Meier, *A Marginal Jew: Rethinking the Historical Jesus. Volume 1: The Roots of the Problem and the Person* (New York: Doubleday, 1991) 221; Guus Labooy, "The Historicity of the Virginal Conception. A Study in Argumentation", *European Journal of Theology* 13 (2004) 91–101, esp. 98.

[41] Michael Fishbane, *Biblical Myth and Rabbinic Mythmaking* (Oxford; Oxford University Press, 2003) 4–5.

[42] Taken from transcript of "Bill Moyers Journal", n.p. [Cited 8 February 2008]. Online: www.pbs.org/moyers/journal/02012008/transcript3.html.

hosted the now famous video series on PBS in which he interviewed Joseph Campbell on the subject of mythology.[43] The interview with Jamieson also dealt with the topic of myth, although this time in a very different way. In contrast to Campbell's Jungian notion of myth as an expression of the unconscious, Jamieson used the term in a much more "verbal" sense. In the interview, Jamieson speaks on the 2008 presidential candidates' evocation of past figures in United States history:[44]

> MOYERS: Two ghosts kept floating across the screen this week. John F. Kennedy and Ronald Reagan. How do you explain their reincarnation?
> JAMIESON: Each side mythologizes its own past. And so, when the Republicans invoke Ronald Reagan, and, you know, Ronald Reagan was the presence in the room and is the presence in the room through much of this Republican debate ...
> ... What are we invoking with the legacy of John Kennedy? It was Caroline Kennedy's endorsement ad for Senator Obama, with Edward Kennedy's impassioned speech and impassioned speeches. We're invoking the mythic past the same way that we're invoking the mythic past of Ronald Reagan on the Republican side.
> MOYERS: Mythic.
> JAMIESON: Mythic. It's a construction ...
> ... [T]hey select the pieces that they want you to remember. And they feature those pieces. And to some extent, people who haven't lived through those times, and a large part of the electorate hasn't lived through those times, are now being invited to see a part of the past without seeing its full historical context. At a certain point, we're substantially misrepresenting the historical whole.
> MOYERS: But that's always the case in our in American politics, isn't it?
> JAMIESON: That's always the case.
> MOYERS: You bring the past forward to tell—to give it your meaning.
> JAMIESON: And the question is, do we in the process lose some meanings that would help inform our understanding of the present?

This interview is an apt representation of a process that takes place in the formation of New Testament theology. While its practitioners are usually much more critical in their historical assessments than politicians, the process of utilizing the past for the sake of the present nevertheless takes place. Jamieson's point is that the political storytellers of United

---

[43] The interview series is found in Joseph Campbell, *The Power of Myth* (New York: Doubleday, 1988).
[44] See also, B. Jackson and K. H. Jamieson, *UnSpun: Finding Facts in a World of Disinformation* (New York: Random House Trade Paperbacks, 2007).

States history mythologize their own past in order to create a new meaning for the present. Inevitably this involves excluding or overshadowing some data of the past in order to centralize or highlight other features; it includes a synthesis of the selected data; and it includes a contemporizing of the data. This process, however, is not sequential. Jamieson's notion of myth contains three salient features that may be useful for understanding the formations of a dialectical New Testament theology. First, New Testament theology is not defined by its substance, but rather by its *function*. Rather than an object to be studied, it is a form of argumentation. Its intent is to convey and persuade what the faith is and how it is to be practised. Second, the strategy of mythologizing the past is concerned first and foremost with pronouncing and defending a *new meaning* in the present context. And third, new figures or symbols are mythologized to *embody the past*, which is to say that a dialectical New Testament theology pronounces and substantiates a believer's *identity* by connecting it with the past. One's own connection with certain figures or symbols is a mythmaking strategy designed to establish and validate the authority of the symbol or figure and those associated with it. This third salient feature, namely the legitimizing of identity, is myth's central function.

Myth theory

At a popular level, myth is usually defined as a story or belief that is false in contrast to stories and beliefs that are considered to be true or factual. In broad academic discourse, the meaning of the term has become a source of considerable debate. The lack of agreement, however, has not detracted from its use.[45] In fact, it has even seen a resurgence over the last ten years, judging by the number of books published on myth, mythology and myth theory.[46] Consequently it is vital that myth be adequately defined prior to its usage, even if this is only a working definition. In what follows, I survey several theories of myth and attempt to establish a plausible definition that elucidates the function of mythmaking in the formative process of New Testament theology. In short, it is an attempt to answer the

---

[45] Robert Ellwood ("Is Mythology Obsolete?" *JAAR* 69 [2001] 673–86, 685) even suggests replacing the word *myth* "with new language to indicate an entirely new approach, as increasingly scholars are doing with a another four letter word, *cult*". In scholarship myth has become "almost inextricably bollixed up in debates like those about Indo-Europeanism and anti-Semitism with which [Robert Segal and Bruce Lincoln] have dealt".

[46] See, for example, Fishbane, *Biblical Myth and Rabbinic Mythmaking*; Richard G. Walsh, *Mapping the Myths of Biblical Interpretation* (Playing the Texts 4; Sheffield: Sheffield Academic Press, 2001); Glen Robert Gill, *Northrop Frye and the Phenomenon of Myth* (Toronto: University of Toronto Press, 2006); Eric Csapo, *Theories of Mythology* (Oxford: Blackwell Publishing, 2005).

underlying question: What happens when we construct a New Testament theology? Associating New Testament theology with mythmaking may seem problematic to some New Testament scholars, and may invite disagreement from conservative laypeople who are committed to a literalist reading of the New Testament. Yet among my colleagues in the English and Philosophy departments, it may sound more appropriate. In order to alleviate a potential misunderstanding, I will try to elucidate the mythmaking process as a natural human attempt to make sense of religious experience.

Rationalist and romantic approaches

Religion scholars have traditionally classified theories of myth into two principal categories: rationalist and romantic.[47] The rationalist pioneers of myth theory, Edward Burnett Tylor (1832–1917) and James G. Frazer (1854–1941), defined myth as the primitive counterpart to science.[48] Instead of science, so-called primitive cultures relied on myths to explain the origins, mechanisms and even destiny of the physical world. Robert Segal summarizes the distinction in early rationalist theories this way: "Myth and science are not merely redundant but outright incompatible: myth invokes the wills of gods to account for events in the world; science appeals to impersonal processes like those of atoms."[49] For early rationalists, myth was therefore inferior to modern thought; science replaced myth as a means of explaining the natural world. One of the most well known of the rationalist approaches is that of the structural anthropologist Claude Lévi-Strauss. As a variation on Tylor, Lévi-Strauss argued that primitive mythology should not be regarded as unscientific if we take into consideration that modern thinking is abstract while primitive mythic thinking is concrete.[50] In its attempt to explain the physical and social world, Lévi-Strauss viewed the function of myth as a coping mechanism of society that mediates contradictions and thereby relieves deep social anxieties that are usually expressed in binary oppositions such as life/death, male/female, clean/unclean.[51] For example, mediators of the life/death binary may be expressed as follows: Life ↔ Agriculture ↔ Herbivores ↔ Carrion Eaters ↔ Hunting ↔ Predators ↔ War ↔ Death.

---

[47] See, for example, Robert Segal, *Theorizing About Myth* (Amherst: University of Massachusetts, 1999); Hans Blumenberg, *Work on Myth* (Cambridge, MA: MIT Press, 1985).
[48] Edward Burnett Tylor, *Primitive Culture* (2 vols; London: Murray, 1871; 5th edn reprint: New York: Harper, 1958); James G. Frazer, *The Golden Bough* (3rd edn; 12 vols.; London: Macmillan, 1907–15).
[49] Robert Segal, "Myth and Politics: A Response to Robert Ellwood," *JAAR* 70 (2002) 611–12.
[50] Segal, *Theorizing About Myth*, 29–30.
[51] E.g. Claude Lévi-Strauss, *Structural Anthropology* (trans. C. Jacobson and B. G. Schoepf; Handsworth: Penguin, 1978; orig. 1958); Segal, *Theorizing About Myth*, 114.

In this binary, the mediators make sense of the process, relationship and purpose of the life cycle. They have no independent meaning. Without death there can be no life, and vice versa. In some North American indigenous myths, the mediator between life and death, often the trickster within the story, is usually a raven or coyote, i.e. a carrion eater.[52] The coyote's character as a mediating figure is indecipherable without knowledge of the totalizing structure.

Romantic theorists, by contrast, do not interpret myths as explanations of the physical or social worlds. Myth, for theorists like Carl Jung, Joseph Campbell and Mircea Eliade, is a phenomenon that expresses psychological or metaphysical realities.[53] Many critics have noted that romantic theorists divide the mythic source (as an external entity or agency) from the consciousness upon which the mythic "other" acts. Eliade argues that the interplay between the sacred and profane is considered to be the objective reality to which myth speaks. Myth is ultimately a means to an experiential encounter with the divine.[54] For Jung, assumed archetypes exist in an abstract state in the collective unconscious and (without explanation) make the transition into the conscious sphere. In other words, in our quest for holistic meaning, myth links the collective unconscious and the external world.[55] And for Campbell, the assumption of a grand *monomyth*, namely a single metaphysical reality, unifies all the particulars, though often with little attention paid to their differences.[56] Religions can obstruct

---

[52] See Eric Csapo, *Theories of Mythology* (Malden, MA: Blackwell Publishing, 2005) 226–8. Even in unrelated cultures, mediators may serve the same function. Csapo writes: "Clothing is a mediator between culture and nature: naked we are all children of nature; clothed we are fully products of culture; by clothing we manifest all cultural differences: status, rank, nationality, gender, profession etc... rats, lice and other vermin mediate between culture and nature in many societies, since they are unwanted products of nature, but they breed in the midst of the human community, and most prolifically where the population is most dense" (Csapo, *Theories of Mythology*, 228). For a recent application of Strauss, see Andre Van Dokkum, "Belief Systems about Virgin Birth: Structure and Mutual Comparability", *Current Anthropology* 38.1 (1997) 99–104. Van Dokkum shows how myth resolves inconsistencies by comparing the male role of conception in the Trobriand Islanders to the belief in the virgin birth held by Australian Christians. See also the critique of Van Dokkum by Mark S. Mosko, "On 'Virgin Birth', Comparability, and Anthropological Method", *Current Anthropology* 39.5 (1998) 685–7.
[53] See the summaries of their ideas in Gill, *Northrop Frye and the Phenomenon of Myth*.
[54] Segal, *Myth*, 56. On Eliade, see Robert Baird, *Category Formation and the History of Religion* (The Hague: Mouton, 1971) 74–89; Guilford Dudley, *Religion on Trial: Mircea Eliade and His Critics* (Philadelphia: Temple University Press, 1977); Bryan S. Rennie, *Reconstructing Eliade: Making Sense of Religion* (Albany: State University of New York Press, 1996).
[55] See Robert Segal, ed., *Jung on Mythology* (Princeton, NJ: Princeton University Press, 1998) 88–94; Eric Gould, *Mythical Intentions in Modern Literature* (Princeton: Princeton University Press, 1981) 21–3; J. J. Clarke, *In Search of Jung: Historical and Philosophical Enquiries* (London: Routledge, 1992).
[56] See William Kerrigan, "The Raw, The Cooked, and the Half-Baked", *Virginia Quarterly*

the experience of this reality because they often turn the poetic metaphor, which is the "mask of God through which eternity is to be experienced", into literal prose.[57] Speaking with Bill Moyers in the aforementioned interview series, Campbell clarifies:

> The psychologist Jung has a relevant saying: "Religion is a defence against the experience of God." The mystery has been reduced to a set of concepts and ideas, and emphasizing these concepts and ideas can short-circuit the transcendent, connoted experience. An intense experience of mystery is what one has to regard as the ultimate religious experience.[58]

In sum, the differences between rationalist and romantic approaches are considerable. Most prominently, rationalist theorists have tended to interpret myth literally and thus as no longer relevant for modern, "scientific" society; whereas romantic theorists have focused on the symbolic, and hence ongoing, value of myth in human experience. Both, however, share at least one conviction: myth is understood substantially and thus defined by its content.[59]

Ideological approaches

As an alternative to the previous theories, Russell McCutcheon, following Roland Barthes, argues that myth should be understood in a formal rather than a substantial way. McCutcheon writes:

> ... a shift in perspective allows us to suggest (1) that myths are not special (or "sacred") but ordinary human means of fashioning and authorizing their lived-in and believed-in "worlds", (2) that myth as an ordinary rhetorical device in social construction and maintenance makes *this* rather than *that* social identity possible in the first place and (3) that

---

Review 51 (1975) 651–5; Walter B. Gulick, "The Thousand and First Face", in *Paths to the Power of Myth: Joseph Campbell and the Study of Religion* (ed. Daniel C. Noel; New York: Crossroads, 1994) 29–44.
[57] Campbell, *The Power of Myth*, 73.
[58] Campbell, *The Power of Myth*, 261.
[59] Surprisingly, in a recent important work on biblical myth and mythmaking, Michael Fishbane (*Biblical Myth and Rabbinic Mythmaking*, 11) opts for a content-oriented definition of myth. He writes, "we shall understand the word 'Myth' to refer to (sacred and authoritative) accounts of the deeds and personalities of the gods and heroes during the formative events of primordial times, or during the subsequent historical interventions or actions of these figures which are constitutive for the founding of a given culture and its rituals." Fishbane unfortunately minimizes interaction with more widely held ideological approaches, and instead relies on the dated view of myth in Lauri Honko, "Der Mythos in der Religionswissenschaft", *Temenos* 6 (1970) 36–67.

a people's use of the *label* "myth" reflects, expresses, explores and legitimizes their own self-image.[60]

Barthes, who is one of the first to apply an ideological hermeneutic to the study of myth, argues that "myth is not defined by the object of its message, but the way it utters this message: there are formal limits to myth, there are no 'substantial' ones."[61] In its most basic sense, myth is understood as "a type of speech". For Barthes, as well as McCutcheon, the real power of myth lies in its ability to parade as a self-evident truth.[62] This understanding is rooted in Barthes theory of how language functions as a semiological system, that is, a system of signs and referents.[63] In language, the meaning of any given sign is defined not by the literal referent, but by the sign and its relationship to other signs within the total language system. As a formal equation, the signifier (acoustic sound) + the signified (mental image) = the sign (which may be a picture, painting, ritual etc.). The mythological sign has no literal referent, but acquires meaning from the cultural system to which it belongs. Consider Barthes' well-known example of a black boy in a French uniform saluting on the cover of *Paris-Match*. Initially, it is literally a picture of a boy in a uniform gazing slightly skyward and saluting. But when it is viewed within its cultural system (from which meaning is always initiated), it signifies that "France is a great Empire, that all her sons, without any colour discrimination, faithfully serve under her flag, and that there is no better answer to the detractors of alleged colonialism than the zeal shown by this Negro in serving his so-called oppressors."[64] With reference to this same example, Eric Csapo concludes that

> ... mythology is indistinguishable from a particular ideological function, mystification, and a particular operation claimed to be especially characteristic of bourgeois ideology, namely naturalization (concealing the constructed nature of the "myth" but making the myth sit invisibly upon the seemingly unassuming and matter-of-fact linguistic sign).[65]

In recent years, McCutcheon has not been the only theorist to have made the shift from a substantial to a formal understanding of myth. Bruce Lincoln, who has become an important voice in the field, views myth as

---

[60] Russell T. McCutcheon, "Myth", in *Guide to the Study of Religion* (ed. Willi Braun and Russell T. McCutcheon; New York: Cassell, 2000) 200.
[61] Roland Barthes, *Mythologies* (trans. Annette Lavers; New York: The Noonday Press, 1972; orig. 1957) 109.
[62] McCutcheon, "Myth", 201.
[63] Barthes, *Mythologies*, 114.
[64] Barthes, *Mythologies*, 116.
[65] Csapo, *Theories of Mythology*, 278.

ideology represented in narrative form.⁶⁶ Like Lincoln, Csapo suggests that "myth is a function of social ideology... and we should not insist on certain contents and context but rather use these as evidence for the existence of the mythic function."⁶⁷ It is this ideological approach to myth—as a form of social argumentation—which is most useful in understanding the formation of New Testament theologies. As such, the primacy of the investigation falls upon *discourse*, that is, the rhetorical intent of the New Testament theology, instead of the *language*, which is content driven.⁶⁸ Since ideology aims to convince, its orientation is towards a holistic goal that will be adopted by others. Ideology's uses of mythic or imaginary elements, which are often historicized, are likewise employed for a unifying function. In Terry Eagleton's words, the mythic and imaginary elements aim to resolve contradictions by employing such strategies as "unification, spurious identification, naturalization, deception, self-deception, universalization and rationalization".⁶⁹ Unlike structuralism's abstractions and homogenous approach to language, an ideological approach to myth regards language and semiotic systems as conflicted, practical and non-autonomous components in a social structure. Both approaches, however, attempt to resolve conflicts and offer solutions to oppositions in the social sphere.⁷⁰

The "practical" feature of the ideological approach concerns social formation, which assumes that humans naturally form groups that have common social interests. Even subgroups within a larger social body tend toward common ends and interests such as the collection of food in the formation of group identity. Mythmaking plays a crucial role in the social process because it legitimizes or authorizes a group's identity in relation to other groups. In Robert Ellwood's words, "Myth and mythmaking assimilate collectivities of people to a single leader or hero and reduce complicated struggles to the war of the children of light against the children of darkness."⁷¹ In this regard, mythmaking may be used either to reinforce or confront dominant power groups. It is the stage for ideological confrontation and reinforcement, always bound to social interests and group identity.

---

⁶⁶ Bruce Lincoln, *Theorizing Myth: Narrative, Ideology, and Scholarship* (Chicago: University of Chicago Press, 1999) xii, 147.
⁶⁷ Csapo, *Theories of Mythology*, 9.
⁶⁸ Terry Eagleton, *Ideology: An Introduction* (London: Verso, 1991) 223.
⁶⁹ Eagleton, *Ideology*, 222.
⁷⁰ Csapo, *Theories of Mythology*, 298–9. See also Eagleton, *Ideology*, 194.
⁷¹ Ellwood, "Is Mythology Obsolete?" 680. On social formation and mythmaking, see also Burton Mack, "Social Formation", in *Guide to the Study of Religions* (ed. Willi Braun and Russell T. McCutcheon; London and New York: Cassell, 2000) 292; William Arnal and Willi Braun, "Social Formation and Mythmaking: Theses on Key Terms", in *Redescribing Christian Origins* (ed. Ron Cameron and Merrill Miller; Atlanta: Society of Biblical Literature, 2004) 459–68.

Northrop Frye and myth as a perennial search for identity

A more inclusive theoretical starting point for understanding the mythmaking process is Northrop Frye's concept of myth as it was originally articulated in his *Fearful Symmetry* and later developed in *Words With Power*.[72] Not only does Frye incorporate the ideological understanding of mythmaking as identity formation and legitimization, he also recognizes myth's poetic and imaginative features. As such he subtly incorporates a degree of content (namely, type of speech) into the formal (or ideological) view of myth. Recently, Glen Gill and Robert Ellwood have argued that unlike the rationalist and romantic theories of his contemporaries in the middle of the twentieth century, Frye's theory does not suffer from poststructuralist criticism that points to the problem of ontological or metaphysical prioritization, to which I have referred as an external entity or agency acting on a collective consciousness.[73] The missing insight in each case, according to Gill, is "an oversight of the essentially phenomenological or imaginative condition of consciousness, of which all thought and reality is a function, and myth the perennial expression".[74] In Frye's theory there is no gap between the archetype's origin and its occurrence in consciousness, and hence expression in language, because the archetypes are the structures in language. Since Frye is leery about an "unconscious" that is somehow known, the separation between the physical body and mind is more of a distinction whereby the physical is at the same time the ground of language and the source of archetypal form.[75]

Frye's conception of myth is rooted in the unification of sense perception, which is at times called "the literal", and consciousness, which constitutes "the imagination". Another way of putting it is that it is an integration of material and spiritual aspects of a culture. The whole of life is a single mental form that attempts to transform the totality of human experience into symbol or art. Another way of saying this is that we all instinctively seek to make sense of all of our experiences. In so doing, we attempt to unify or harmonize in the quest for truth. For Frye, this single mental form is the drama of life, which is the archetype of all prophecy and art, even if each only reveals and transforms reality in pieces. Myth is this single mental form that seeks to make sense of a unified reality. As Frye puts it, myth is

---

[72] Northrop Frye, *Fearful Symmetry: A Study of William Blake* (Princeton: Princeton University Press, 1947); idem, *Words With Power: Being a Second Study of 'The Bible and Literature'* (Toronto: Penguin, 1992).
[73] Gill, *Northrop Frye and the Phenomenology of Myth*; Robert Ellwood, *The Politics of Myth: A Study of C. G. Jung, Mircea Eliade, and Joseph Campbell* (Albany: State University of New York Press, 1999).
[74] Gill, *Northrop Frye*, 172.
[75] Gill, *Northrop Frye*, 187.

"the end of the journey of our intellectual powers".[76] In *The Critical Path*, the cultural or societal function of myth is further developed by showing myth's cohesive function, at least as far as words have the power to do so. Myth as cultural or societal cohesion is a socially established truth and reality, though not necessarily tied to or derived from evidence or reason. Truth is that which a society does and believes. It is, as Frye puts it, "the language of belief" out of which literature and art are existentially commissioned and received.[77] Where Frye differs from other mythologists is in his unification schema, which moves beyond a comparison of rituals and the subconscious commonness of mythopoeic dreams. These he regards as crude art forms or rough drafts of the artist.[78] A spiral pattern of mythic development occurs from individual (rough drafts) to community and back again. Frye explains:

> In time the communal myth precedes the individual one, but the latter focuses and clarifies the former, and when a work of art deals with a primitive myth, the essential meaning of that myth is not disguised or sublimated or refined, but revealed. A comparative study of dreams and rituals can lead us only to a vague and intuitive sense of the unity of the human mind; a comparative study of works of art [including literature] should demonstrate it beyond conjecture.[79]

When understood as an artistic process, this is no different from what we see in the early Christian use of the Jewish scriptures, which are regularly used in the formation of earliest theological thinking. Like the Irish ollaves, the legendary Druid bards, the pre-Homeric figures such as Orpheus or the Hebrew prophets, the evangelists are the poets of their communities who retell the past in the light of the present, and vice versa, selecting the mythological information that their communities needed to know.[80] The poet's connection with the past, through various means of retelling, allusion or quotation, is a manoeuvre that garners authority by a kind of osmosis, whereby the old accepted wisdom, be it in Homer or the evangelists, finds both a new context and a new veracity in the present. Thus, the poet's particular attribute is not so much a knowledge of *style*, but a broad knowledge of *data* stemming from an understanding of what we might call a mythopoeic history. In the cycle, individuals break with accepted ideology and are freed (and instinctively compelled) to create their own. To put this into more of a popular context, when one's ear is trained to pick up on this

---

[76] Frye, *Fearful Symmetry*, 340.
[77] Northrop Frye, *The Critical Path: An Essay on the Social Context of Literary Criticism* (Bloomington: Indiana University Press, 1971) 36.
[78] Frye, *Fearful Symmetry*, 424.
[79] Frye, *Fearful Symmetry*, 425.
[80] Frye, *Words with Power*, 54.

process, a particularly clear expression is heard today in American politics where past presidents like Abraham Lincoln, John F. Kennedy and Ronald Reagan are invoked and reinterpreted for purposes of legitimizing identity and social formation, be it a candidate, a party or a nation.[81]

Frye also distances himself from theological language because it must rely on subjects and objects even when speaking of God as immanent or transcendent, and this leaves language in a very limiting state. Whenever humans are the subject and God is the object the distance seems unbridgeable even in the use of analogy. Instead of analogy, Frye finds more cohesion in *identity*, which is the principle behind metaphor and imagination, and ultimately myth. Thus paradoxical claims that two different things are the same, such as "God is man" or "Christ is a lamb", are at the heart of both religious and poetic language, which resist habitual thinking, expand the mind and incline towards the imaginative. Frye concisely writes, "I think the real conception 'God' must start in typological metaphor: God is the existential reality of the 'all one body we' metaphor."[82] Identity as the principle of myth is clearly seen in the earliest stories of creation and redemption wherein the gods were identified with the particulars of a created order, such as the sun, the moon, rivers, oceans, plants, and the cycle of life and death. These stories allowed for the identification of individuals and people groups with the world and its life cycle. The identification process in myth occurs within the historicizing of the stories. In other words, we are who we are because of events that have happened in a distant past. The present and the past are brought together in myth, though never apart from the universal human narrative whose plot extends from creation to apocalypse.[83]

Since myth is eschatological and all encompassing, and attempts to incorporate the totality of human experience, its medium can only be symbol; and in this way it surpasses, though still includes, ideology. Thus Frye's view is broader than that of more recent mythologists, such as Bruce Lincoln's ideology in narrative form.[84] Frye would most likely have incorporated this notion into a wider realm of human consciousness that seeks to bring ideologies into more eternal or transcendent perspective through imagination and art—the real forms of myth. Ideology, for Frye, is subordinated to myth, not the reverse. Mythology creates ideology, which

---

[81] See, for example, the varied remembrances of Lincoln in the last one hundred years in Barry Schwartz, *Abraham Lincoln and the Forge of National Memory* (Chicago: University of Chicago Press, 2000).

[82] Robert D. Denham, ed., *Northrop Frye's Notebooks and Lectures on the Bible and Other Religious Texts* (Collected Works of Northrop Frye, Volume 13; Toronto: University of Toronto Press, 2003) 350.

[83] Robert D. Denham, *Northrop Frye: Religious Visionary and Architect of the Spiritual World* (Charlottesville: University of Virginia Press, 2004) 9; Northrop Frye, *Myth and Metaphor: Selected Essays, 1974–1988* (ed. Robert D. Denham; Charlottesville: University of Virginia Press, 1990) 115.

[84] Lincoln, *Theorizing Myth*.

in turn selects, adapts, historicizes and applies myth in the formation of a social belief system. Myth in this context provides an identity and a shared knowledge proclaiming what must be known.[85] The belief is akin to adherence, obedience and at times even fact, and is often reinforced by a power structure. Since ideology, according to Frye, is monological and exclusive, it is very guarded in permitting competing ideologies to be dialogue partners. To restrict dialogue that potentially challenges existing ideologies is for Frye a controlling tendency that is authoritative and aggressive. The mythological underpinnings become especially visible when an ideology is enforced or advanced in extreme ways.[86]

The breaking with the dominant ideology also has political consequences at the institutional level. Myth is potentially threatening to the foundations of societal structure because it elicits new visions of reality. G. S. Kirk has well articulated how in the ancient world (particularly Mesopotamian culture) nature gods developed into city gods and in the process re-established the natural and social order. At its root is a questioning of the relationship between nature and culture.[87] Development of and/or dissention from the institution frequently results in a new, perhaps synthesized, institution. Nascent Christianity fits well within the process of institutional separation and replacement as it broke from its Jewish moorings through a Christological hermeneutic of scripture.

Protestantism, which (to reiterate) is the cradle of New Testament theology, shares an affinity with this kind of re-mythologizing of a prior religious tradition. Like many of the early Jewish Christians, a shift in authority (e.g. temple, ritual, interpretation, sect) and identity (believers in Jesus as the Christ) was intertwined with a need for social legitimization. As this legitimization intensified, mythmaking subtly turned to ideology until the next round of mythmaking occurred. Like nascent Christianity, Protestantism's break with Roman Catholic structure created a vacuum wherein the mythmaking process could restart. Since Protestantism has no established interpretative authority structure (i.e. inspired scripture has no inspired interpreter), it has allowed the ideal conditions for the mythmaking process to flourish in virtually endless directions. The last five hundred years have testified to the countless attempts by groups to re-identify themselves, on the basis of scripture, with respect to what it means to be Christian—and the legitimizing of identities shows no signs of abating. Every time a New Testament theology (which is concerned with relevance) is written, it participates in the mythmaking process because it inevitably engages in

---

[85] Frye, Words with Power, 31
[86] Frye, Words with Power, 23-4.
[87] G. S. Kirk, Myth: Its Meaning and Functions in Ancient and Other Cultures (Sather Classical Lectures, 40; London: Cambridge University Press; Berkeley: University of California Press, 1970) 253.

making sense of the past in the light of the present and vice versa, all the while wrestling with the Christian identity that lies at its foundation.

One of the challenges with which Protestantism has been faced when it is viewed from the perspective of mythmaking is that in many cases denominations have shifted from belief to ideology far too quickly. This is understandable given that most denominations have emerged out of schisms and as splinter groups. The result is that the legitimizing of the new identity has turned religious language into history or reality, which has unnecessarily been a major factor in the unfortunate divide between religion and science. Once again, we are back to the necessity of understanding the nature of religion before we theologize. Jacques Derrida's famous dictum that texts do not represent, but replace, the unattainable reality may well be a helpful corrective to ponder.[88] Derrida's dictum may be indicative of one of the major problems with the premise of Protestantism, and hence many New Testament theologies. Are we attempting to legitimize so much in formulations of New Testament theologies that we treat the biblical text as a representation of reality instead of a replacement? If so, the current reality we experience will always be under pressure to conform to the biblical "representation", which has the potential to obscure an open and fair dialectical process. There is much to learn here from the Orthodox and Catholic traditions where reality and its symbols are much broader, including the long tradition of experience and multivalent interpretative approaches, and where the "replacement of the unattainable reality" is more welcomed as part of a long mythmaking developmental process.

Discussion questions

1 Should the aim of New Testament theology be the formation of a *final* or *complete* theology, such as a doctrine or creed? Or should the aim be dialogue (or what Joachim Gnilka has called a continuous process), which can bring an understanding and appreciation of differing points of view—be it dialogue between exegesis and doctrine, the past and present, the sacred and the secular, or the theological and the religious?

2 How might the study of religion and religious language affect the interpretation of the New Testament?

3 Discuss Max Müller's well-known dictum: "He who knows one [religion], knows none."

---

[88] Petri Merenlahti, *Poetics for the Gospels? Rethinking Narrative Criticism* (Edinburgh: T and T Clark, 2002) 9.

4 Is the formation of a New Testament theology an exercise in mythmaking?
5 Is the survival of Protestantism dependent on the viability of a New Testament theology?
6 Should the early Christian re-mythologizing of prior religious traditions serve as a model for modern biblical interpretation?

CONCLUDING REFLECTIONS

New Testament theology and Protestantism

The search for relevance has guided the discipline of New Testament theology since its inception. It is simply inherent in it. Whether we subscribe to a foundationalist theory or a dialectical one, when we regard the New Testament writings as sacred we attribute to them a quality that transcends other texts—much like devotees of other faiths attribute an unparalleled value to their own sacred texts. Likewise, whether we hold the view that these texts' sacredness is dependent on us as devotees and readers, or that they are somehow independent of us, does not change their value. The point is that unlike other kinds of writing—ancient and modern—which can also instruct us about our humanness, the quality of sacredness alone conveys a revelatory dimension where it is believed that the divine meets the human. As a result, the New Testament begs the question of meaning. While all three of the great traditions of Christianity have wrestled with the meaning of scripture, the struggle in the Protestant tradition has been especially intense. At the risk of an oversimplification, the main reason for this is that, in contrast to Catholicism and Orthodoxy, Protestantism has bypassed an authoritative interpreter. From its beginnings in the Reformation, Protestantism's incessant appeal to the Bible as the locus of revelation unfortunately did not adequately foresee that the text is only one part of the hermeneutical process. It left the inspired text, so to speak, without an inspired interpreter who can ascribe authoritative meaning to the text. The fragmented history of the Protestant experiment speaks for itself. It is replete with divisions that are legitimized on the principle of going "back-to-the-Bible", but all the while the lingering question remains: "Who decides on a method and its unifying structure?" We live in a time when the text can no longer be divorced from the interpreter. For good reason, our time has been called an era "after theory". We can no longer get away with legitimizing our theology by saying, "That's what the Bible says!"

The problem for Protestantism was compounded when it reacted against the Catholic Church's polysemous interpretations in favour of only one—the one, of course, that was considered to lie in the text itself. When the interpretation of the New Testament was dependent on the Church's traditions and doctrines, unification was not an issue. Discrepancies could be harmonized through allegory or through a kind of *sensus plenior* ("fuller sense" intended by God) approach that saw paradoxical texts as less developed in meaning, yet containing the germ of a broader and fuller meaning. By shedding a polysemous approach, Protestantism found itself in a position that required a new kind of theological unification of the scriptures, but it did not have adequate tools to achieve this. Early Reformers still relied on some Catholic traditions and Church Fathers in their exegeses, but the shift was clearly towards the historical meaning of the New Testament. The development of the historical-critical method in the Enlightenment period provided a powerful tool for reconstructing and describing early Christian thought, but the tool in and of itself was neither equipped to unify nor was it able to provide a normative meaning to the scriptures. New Testament theology as a discipline emerged in this context. With this new focus, it attempted to extricate the New Testament from the established ecclesiastical authorities in an attempt to arrive at a pure theology that was based solely on the Bible.

It is worth pondering how closely New Testament theology (and biblical theology as a whole) is linked to Protestantism. If Protestantism is rooted in the principle that underlies New Testament theology—that scripture is the sole basis for theology, that there is one meaning, and that through proper method we can find it—does it continue to have an intellectual/theological basis if a coherent and unified New Testament theology proves unattainable? And if the New Testament cannot be unified historically, contrary to the beliefs of the Reformers and their followers, must we impose a unifying principle from outside the New Testament itself? If so, are we not in principle undermining the "protest" of Protestantism?

New Testament theology on the intellectual map: From modernity to postmodernity[1]

We have come a long way to get to these questions. While the quest for relevance in the scriptures is not new, the line of questioning that began in the Enlightenment was. The locus of truth was wrenched from the Church and placed within the individual, and the historical assumptions of the previous 1,600 years were challenged through the method of radical doubt. With the advent of Rationalism, and its concomitant social ascendance over the truth claims of the Christian church, came the reshaping of European philosophy, politics, religion and individual identity. Seeking to defend

---

[1] I would like to extend my appreciation to my former graduate student, Mike Kozowski, for his help in the writing of this subsection.

themselves in a new intellectual climate, Christian thinkers who were uneasy with the intellectual changes attempted to respond with the aid of the tools of rationalistic inquiry, hoping to apprehend and articulate a creditable Christian faith.

Rationalistic inquiry, as expressed through the historical-critical method, developed primarily from the polemical efforts of white, educated, European men who were socially located within a period now infamous for its racial, gender, Christian-based assumptions, and overarching commitment to colonialist expansion and empire building. Historical criticism provided a means by which ancient authors could be understood within their own cultural contexts. Since the authors' intentions were believed to be accessible, they were believed to be holders of the "true" interpretation of their own writings. If the right kind and quantity of data could be utilized through the application of proper method, an accurate portrayal could be adduced of any historical artifact or event. Objectivity, like a "pure" New Testament theology, was considered to be attainable.

These endeavours constituted the main approach to New Testament theology until the middle of the twentieth century. While the historical-critical approach by no means died, it had to contend with the accumulated weight that was stacked against methods that claimed objectivity in their results. The epistemological glasshouse was shattered by, among other factors, the two world wars, the Holocaust in a Christianized nation, the purges and gulags of Lenin and Stalin, the Cold War and the threat of global nuclear annihilation, the civil rights movements, and overall discontent with institutional and other power structures. Once the dust settled, millions of people lost their lives as a result of the social products engineered through the philosophical and technological achievements of modernism. By the 1960s, progressive optimism was dead or dying. Its promise of ideological and material progress was devastated by a scale of human atrocities unimagined in the pre-industrial, pre-critical world. The steady, self-perceived march towards human actualization and fulfilment had floundered, and new answers to old questions were sought.

The consensus did change, and philosophical systems came to question seriously the foundational assumptions of modern methods. What had been certain was now suspect and, much like the Church at the beginning of the Enlightenment, yesterday's orthodoxies became today's anachronisms. The intellectual life of the West had moved on, and where the prior interpretations of history and search for meaning had been located in the past (the author and his world), the new locus of meaning was firmly centred in the present. The historical constructs of the past, such as formulations of foundationalist New Testament theologies, were exposed as being derived from the assumptions and expectations of the modern interpreters' philosophical agendas and social locations. Many scholars began to question its approach to linguistic media. Saussure's semiotics and the development of Structuralism eventually led to an understanding of written communication that revealed the actual locus of authority to be the individual reader. Linguists, literary theorists and philosophers of language increasingly showed that when a reader engages with a text, the interpretation of that text is a derivative of the world of the reader, who can never extricate him- or herself. Borrowing from the final line of The Eagles' *Hotel California*, "You can check out any time you like, but you can never leave." A one-to-one correspondence from subject to object was viewed as impossible, and room had to be made for a new understanding of reading as a shared encounter between past and present. With scholarly attention drawn to the reader, and away from modernist assumptions about authorial intent, Structuralism developed into Post-structuralism, and a postmodern epistemology gained a firm foothold. Roland Barthes showed the signifier-to-signified progression could move in both directions, so meaning was no longer univocal. Truth was not a static quantity to be apprehended through the right application of foundational principles, but was a polyvalent quality residing in the experience of the individual. In a sense, truth became a semiotic event, duly shown through Post-structuralism to be derived from the perspective and social location of the subject. The object does not, indeed cannot, exist solely in and of itself; its contemporary existence is to some measure a derivative of the subject's assessment and assimilation of the object as a quantifiable event. Like an astronomical singularity, the object is known only indirectly through its event "horizon".

There is great sense to be gained here, as Cornell West forthrightly describes postmodern epistemology as "antifoundational, antitotalizing and demystifying".[2] Overt charges of relativism foisted by historical critics leave its core arguments untouched, and dissatisfaction with the concomitant loss of certainty and control is likewise inappropriately put at the feet of its proponents. The fatal flaw in historical criticism is its own responsibility, and postmodern ideological critics cannot reasonably be blamed for pointing out the elephant in the room. Ultimately the historical-critical method identified certainty and truth in a manner that was at the expense of the disenfranchised. By revealing that the real locus of meaning was within the interpreter and his or her social location, and by demonstrating that the modernist claims to "truth" were often mythic constructs, postmodern ideological criticism turns its considerable efforts to an examination of modern social locations and the organs of enfranchisement which are served by contemporary interpretative communities. Elisabeth Schüssler Fiorenza's publications have been magnificent in denouncing the ongoing modern endeavours that continue to legitimize particular readings as "factual" when their results are predicated by their own vested social interests and

---

[2] From West's lectures at Yale, as cited in A. K. M. Adam, *What is Postmodern Biblical Criticism?* (Minneapolis: Fortress Press, 1995) 5.

perspectives.³ Though her polemic can appear resentful, it is nonetheless full of insight and demands a serious response. The longstanding hegemonic politics of Western nation-building and colonialism, the repressive laws and practices in "developed" nations which denied egalitarian social rights to others based on race, gender, age and other social "legitimacies", and the implicit collusion with conservative social protectionism by the academy, have all led to an overt praxis of suspicion. The conservative endeavour to curtail the polyvalence of meaning(s), and to legitimize their own peculiar delimitation of data, are inadequate to the task. Post-structuralist interpretations both actively and openly seek alternative readings and cheerfully sanctioned boundaries between closed systems of interpretation and alternate meanings. The stable door is open, the horses are all gone, and the poor farmer is left scratching his head. But the horses are free, and to the ideological critic that is precisely the point.

Of course, there are significant problems. Just as the accusations by historical-critical scholars directed toward postmodern relativism miss the point, so postmodern denunciations of all metanarratives may miss an equally important point.⁴ Ultimately they may both be seen to derive from the same modernistic assumption. What defines the experiment of Rationalism is the foundational nature of the system. *It is a closed system positing the delimitation and containment of all data.* In this sense postmodernism is a product of the same foundation for it has to posit a closed, albeit an immensely larger, system as well. In other words, it is an anti-foundational modality engineered from a systemically defined foundation that presumes the delimitation of all data. The final problem of Rationalism is its programmatic and paradigmatic certainty that our own existence, of necessity, constrains possibilities; and in this same sense Post-structuralism, the wellspring of postmodern epistemology, is built upon the same foundation. Therefore postmodernism is, in a sense, the logical extension of modernism. They fired the farmer, but kept the farm intact.

The problem of the Christian engagement with the Enlightenment is that there are still modern Christian intellectuals who fail to understand

---

³ E.g. Elisabeth Schüssler Fiorenza, *Jesus and the Politics of Interpretation* (New York: Continuum, 2001).

⁴ In terms of Jean-François Lyotard's "incredulity toward metanarratives", and its probative use by scholars in dismissing the Christian story, see the compelling statements of Merold Westphal which carefully distinguish between grand narratives, or "meganarratives", and Lyotardian *philosophical* metanarratives. "*A metanarrative is a metadiscourse in the sense of being a second-level discourse not directly about the world but about a first-level discourse.*" Lyotard was rightly identifying (and rejecting) metanarratives as second level discourses, and was not necessarily addressing narratives, such as the biblical narrative, which are first level discourses. Merold Westphal, *Overcoming Onto-Theology: Toward A Postmodern Christian Faith* (New York: Fordham University Press, 2001) xiii; Jean-François Lyotard, *The Postmodern Explained* (trans. and ed. Julian Pefanis and Morgan Thomas; Minneapolis: University of Minnesota Press, 1993).

the crux of the discussion. As streams of meaning are (rightly) shown to be polyphonic and not univocal, so *frames* of meaning, or systemic algorithms, are not closed and constrained, but open and pliable. While this may obviate, or at least complicate, our ability to delimit and define what is ultimately true, it also means that the transcendental tension cannot be honestly dismissed or ignored. The farm is not the farmer's domain alone; and while self-governing, the farmer is not really self-employed; he is not the master of his own fate. So the hierarchical dominions of power about which Fiorenza is so justly and wisely outspoken can be engaged as artificial constructs of a social and fideistic megalomania. The danger of postmodernism's corrective to modern orthodoxies is that it would simply replace them with un-orthodoxies. This fails to address the real problem. The modernistic "pool" is stagnant and must be open to that which is outside and beyond itself. If postmodernism fails to initiate this, it will over the long term be seen as simply another failed expression of the modernist experiment. If it does break this artificial ceiling of possibility, it will be the herald of a new epistemology that is both fresh and urgently needed, albeit terrifying for many.

Therefore an even greater breadth is required in our approach to biblical studies and theological meaning-making. An inordinate abandonment of the benefits of the historical-critical movement would be a poor choice. Yet an uncritical adoption of historical-critical theories and their methods of interpretation would lead to the same discursive results. However, a precipitous adoption of a postmodern hermeneutic of suspicion may make no real progress either. In keeping with Fiorenza's recommendation of a truly democratic process, I am reminded of G. K. Chesterton's comment that in a true democracy a voice would be given to all its members, including those who had lived before us. I wonder what methodological constraint/direction could be utilized as we welcome the larger ecclesial voice of the believing community through the millennia. While it is certainly true that the past is not fully accessible, it is just as plain that neither is it fully inaccessible. To extend the possibilities further, I wonder how a phenomenological engagement with the mystical aspects of the world's great religions might benefit a new method. I also agree entirely with Fiorenza that theological meaning-making without contemporary social engagement is unbiblical, if not obscene, and has no place in our supposed "orthodoxies". The hermeneutical endeavour must be informed by a clear assessment of the social location, practices and assumptions within which the interpreter works. Finally, the matrix of interpretative possibilities must admit into its stream of meaning of the Other that which is transcendent; an algorithm of significance of that which is both unquantifiable and "unrealistic". For ultimately, in the words of Rowan Williams, "The questioning involved here is not our interrogation of the data, but its interrogation of us."[5] A

---

[5] Rowan Williams, *The Wound of Knowledge: Christian Spirituality from the New Testament to Saint John of the Cross* (Cambridge, MA: Cowley Publications, 1979, 1990) 11.

postmodern understanding of intertextuality, which posits a limitless interaction between texts (written and non-written) and subjects, is a helpful concomitant.

Benefits of New Testament theology

If indeed a unified New Testament theology proves unattainable, the past efforts should not be viewed negatively. Looking back at its two-hundred-year run, New Testament theology has been a valuable experiment in religious autonomy. It has freely taken on various definitions, methods, structures and aims. Most of these have followed Gabler's programme insofar as the practice of exegesis and theological formulation was performed outside ecclesiastical controls. Although some have argued that it has been a failed experiment, most biblical scholars today would urge that a call for termination is too premature. Whatever position one holds, it cannot be denied that New Testament theology's overall impact on biblical scholarship has been intellectually positive. Since scholarship was emancipated from the Church, individuals have become free to be creative and critical. This has allowed for much broader social representation in research, from which we have benefited. Under strict ecclesiastical control, interpretation of the Bible was dominated by white, middle-aged, even elderly, celibate Italian men. Breadth has brought much needed accountability. Emancipation from the Church, however, brought an uncertainty about the faith because it tended to rely on the latest historical reconstruction of the New Testament. But this has proven to be a relative consequence, since uncertainty became liberation for some and a crisis for others. Both structure and autonomy have proven to be beneficial as well as detrimental in intellectual and spiritual development and vitality. Although we have not arrived at a New Testament theology that is unanimously accepted, we have made incredible strides forward in trying to do so. And in doing so, New Testament theologians have had the opportunity to contribute in a variety of ways.

First, over the last two hundred years our historical knowledge of the individual writings in the New Testament has increased exponentially. Despite varied opinions, we have much more knowledge about dating, provenance, authorship, audiences, opponents, social background, genre, rhetorical practices, compositional development and structuring, use of the Jewish scriptures, mythmaking and text-critical history.

Second, the search for a "pure" theology has placed New Testament theologians at the forefront of the discussion on the relationship between faith and reason (or theology and history). Historical-critical approaches to the New Testament opened up the world of the first century and allowed scholars for the first time to reconstruct the writings critically. The reconstructions not only left the New Testament writings fragmented, but created an interpretative vacuum. The issues with which the earliest Christians dealt were not the issues of modernity or postmodernity. Ancient meanings were no longer confused with current meanings. Once history dominated the study of the New Testament, the call for its relevance closely followed.

Third, New Testament theology has contributed to our understanding of the relationship between scripture and doctrine (and systematic theology). Although there is disagreement on how this relationship should be achieved, our knowledge of the issues and processes involved in proposing a connection has allowed scholars to interact on theoretical and methodological levels instead of political ones.

Fourth, New Testament theology has contributed to our understanding of the relationship between the two Testaments. The rise of historical criticism has broadened the study of the Old Testament. Instead of reading it allegorically as a Christian book, in the light of the New Testament and received ecclesiastical traditions, scholars could for the first time study it in its own right as an anthology of Jewish writings within the context of the ancient Near East. While this approach was deemed valuable, it inevitably raised the question of the relationship between the Jewish Bible and the Christian Testament. How can the historical study of the Old Testament be of value to Christianity and our understanding of the Christ event?

Fifth, New Testament theology has contributed immensely to our understanding of the varieties of Christian ideas in the New Testament writings themselves. Again, because of the advancements made through historical criticism, New Testament theologians have had to wrestle with diverse interpretations of Jesus in their attempt to formulate a unified theology. As a result, our understanding of early Christianity as a multidimensional faith has led to varied dialectical approaches that might accommodate the diversity.

Sixth, New Testament theology has contributed to our understanding of the relationship between the historical Jesus and the New Testament. Not all scholars see the relationship in the same way. For example, some regard the historical Jesus as the topic of New Testament theology, whereas others see him as the presupposition of it. Nevertheless, given that Jesus is the basis of Christian faith, we are all the richer from continued discussions on early Christian interpretative method, historiography and myth-making—all of which attempt to provide meaning to Jesus.

And finally, New Testament theology has contributed to our understanding of the relationship between the text and interpreter. While most of the insights continue to come from the fields of literary theory, hermeneutics and philosophy, New Testament theologians continue to grapple with this relationship. In many ways, New Testament theology, like biblical studies, has by and large remained a very traditional discipline rooted in modernist presuppositions. Sooner or later, however, it will have to interact more deliberately with adjacent disciplines if it is to force the hermeneutical questions to the forefront. Since it is engaged in history, written texts, religious ideas and interpretation, it needs to engage, for example, in historiography, philosophy of language, comparative religions, and literary and hermeneutical theories. Engagement is occurring, but the pace is slow.

The posture of the New Testament theologian

As we try to keep up with a rapidly changing world, the relevance of New Testament theology is in part dependent on a humble, creative and fair posture of its practitioners. Humility often requires listening before talking, and reading before writing. Unfortunately, theology has over the years received an unflattering reputation due to its defensive and/or dogmatic disposition. The reputation has at times unfairly preceded changes in the field, but overall it has been a fair assessment. This is not surprising, though. Unlike any other field, it has sought to convey a unified understanding of God and his relation to the world. Such attempts at grandiose unifications of intellectual knowledge and spiritual experience impact every sphere of individual and social life at the deepest of levels. Unification is not the problem, since our minds tend towards it. The problem is social in the sense that theological systems can be powerful tools for control. Conversion can be imperialism. And final interpretations can lead to final solutions. In our intellectually free society that has become very leery of power plays, detractors are not far behind the latest system or apology. I think of Krister Stendahl's observation that apologetics is often the lowest form of theology and activates in us the least-creative energies for mutual understanding and peace. There is a touch of arrogance in defending God. In Swedish wit, "it is pathetic to hear mosquitoes cough."[6] Even problematic biblical texts which today cause offence, such as those that demean other groups, should be faced head on and acknowledged as no longer instructive. By the same token, this does not mean capitulation to the latest social fads, but it does requires the right demeanour of listening and passion for the dignity of humanity, respect for culture and the environment—no less than the Golden rule, or Micah's summarized admonition to love mercy, to act justly, and to walk humbly with God, or Jesus' command to love God and neighbour, or the Johannine call (contra Gnostic) to adopt a posture of love and respect for all that is physical as it is metaphorized in the incarnation.

Confrontation or defensiveness is not the way forward. Each often emerges out of a sense of fear and a loss of control. The posture of humility in scholarship demands a focused listening to alternative views, a cautious evaluation, and what Elisabeth Schüssler Fiorenza has called "critical self-reflexivity", which is an ongoing reflection that reveals our deepest ideological goals. She asks, what does our hermeneutic serve? Does it have emancipatory aims or does it serve to maintain or protect the status quo?

---

[6] Stendahl, *Reading the Bible in the Global Village*, 61–2

A particularly challenging example of where more humility can be exercised is in the relationship between New Testament theology and science. If the accepted conclusions of science—say in biology, physics, chemistry, paleontology and geology—are incorporated into a theological paradigm, it would allow us to isolate more easily those portions of the New Testament that cannot be proved or disproved by modern scientific method. These portions we could deem as religious. If a distinction is drawn between religious and non-religious portions, a complementary relationship between the two is possible. Different perceptions of knowledge can coincide. Yet this is by no means a return to rationalism, since science is not privileged in the relationship.

Another example of a complementary relationship is one with the social sciences. We might ask, using contemporary categories: How might we understand the New Testament in the light of modern insights into human behaviour, addiction, gender, mental illness, marriage, sexuality, human rights and dignity, the brain/mind relationship, religious experience, political power and democracy, and other religions? The benefit in showing how different first-century culture is from our own—particularly how a two-thousand-year-old science and social science—would challenge modern readers of the Bible to distinguish between reconstruction and interpretation. Such recognition would most likely lead to a more metaphorical reading of the New Testament and thus preserve its relevance in an ever-changing world. This approach does not minimize the value of the Bible, but it situates it in the realm of the religious. Instead it frees it to be integrated within modern life in a non-sectarian manner. Theologically speaking, it allows the truths of special revelation in Christ and the scriptures to be integrated with the ever-unfolding truths of natural revelation.

A final example where humility can be exercised is in the relationship between New Testament theology and literary studies. Since the New Testament is comprised of written texts, how might our understanding of those texts be enhanced by modern theories of language and its relationship to reality? And, how might these theories benefit our self-understanding as interpreters? Metaphor often emerges in attempts to answer such questions because it is often viewed as the language of religion, which bridges consciousness and nature. Metaphor, symbol and myth are essentially unifying categories that can bring together history, science, social science and religion. These categories appear to be the way forward, given their exploratory, rather than explanatory, function.[7] What also emerges is the recognition that we play language as much as it plays us. Interpretation is not the sole property of any group or individual. Its life-changing impact

---

[7] W. Taylor Stevenson, "Myth and the Crisis of Historical Consciousness", in *Myth and the Crisis of Historical Consciousness* (ed. Lee W. Gibbs and W. Taylor Stevenson; Missoula: Scholars Press, 1975) 9.

upon us must be preserved for our children. They too have the right to let all literature speak afresh to them. There is a paradox here in that any final "solution" to meaning may be the end of literature itself. Italo Calvino in his Norton Lectures stated, "Literature remains alive only if we set ourselves immeasurable goals, far beyond all hope of achievement."[8] Northrop Frye envisioned it in a similar way when he argued that the aim of interpretation is absolute experience, instead of absolute knowledge, where things may not agree, but they mirror each other.[9]

---

[8] Northrop Frye, *Words With Power: Being a Second Study of "The Bible and Literature"* (Toronto: Penguin, 1992) xxiii.
[9] Robert D. Denham, *Northrop Frye: Religious Visionary and Architect of the Spiritual World* (Charlottesville: University of Virginia Press, 2004) 46–7.

BIBLIOGRAPHY

Achtemeier, P. J. *Inspiration and Authority: Nature and Function of Christian Scripture* (Peabody: Hendrickson, 1999).
Adam, A. K. A. *Making Sense of New Testament Theology: Modern Problems and Prospects* (Studies in American Biblical Hermeneutics 11; Macon, GA: Mercer University Press, 1995).
—*What is Postmodern Biblical Interpretation?* (Guides to Biblical Scholarship; Minneapolis: Fortress Press, 1995).
—ed., *Handbook of Postmodern Biblical Interpretation* (St. Louis: Chalice Press, 2000).
Allison, D. C. *Jesus of Nazareth: Millenarian Prophet* (Minneapolis: Fortress Press, 1998).
Argall, R. A., B. Bow and R. A. Werline, eds, *For a Later Generation: The Transformation of Tradition in Israel, Early Judaism, and Early Christianity* (Harrisburg, PA; Trinity Press International, 2000).
Arnal, W and W. Braun, "Social Formation and Mythmaking: Theses on Key Terms" in *Redescribing Christian Origins* (ed. R. Cameron and M. Miller; Atlanta: Society of Biblical Literature, 2004), 459–68.
Baird, R. *Category Formation and the History of Religion* (The Hague: Mouton, 1971), 74–89.
Balla, P. *Challenges to New Testament Theology: An Attempt to Justify the Enterprise* (Peabody: Hendrickson, 1997).
Barr, J. *Holy Scripture: Canon, Authority, Criticism* (Philadelphia: Westminster Press, 1983).
—*The Concept of Biblical Theology* (Minneapolis: Fortress Press, 1999).
Barrett, C. K. *The Acts of the Apostles* (ICC; Edinburgh: T & T Clark, 1994).
Barthes, R. *Mythologies* (trans. A. Lavers; New York: The Noonday Press, 1972).
Barton, J. "Biblical Theology: An Old Testament Perspective," in *The Nature of New Testament Theology* (ed. C. Rowland and C. Tuckett; Oxford: Blackwell Publishing, 2006), 18–30.
Bauckham, R. *Jesus and the Eyewitnesses: The Gospels as Eyewitness Testimony* (Grand Rapids: Eerdmans, 2006).
Bauer, G. L. *Biblische Theologie des Neuen Testaments* (2 vols; Leipzig: Bengandschen, 1800–2).
Bauer, W. *Orthodoxy and Heresy in Earliest Christianity* (trans. Philadelphia Seminar on Christian Origins; ed. R. A. Kraft and G. Krodel; Philadelphia: Fortress Press, 1971).
Baur, F. C. "[ET] The Christ Party in the Corinthian Church, The Conflict Between Petrine and Pauline Christianity in the Early Church, the Apostle Peter in Rome," *Tübinger Zeitschrift für Theologie* 4 (1831), 61–206.

—*The Church History of the First Three Centuries* (trans. A. Menzies; 3rd edn; London: Williams and Norgate, 1878; original German publication in 1853).
Bennett, C. *In Search of Jesus: Insider and Outsider Images* (New York: Continuum, 2001).
Berger, K. *Hermeneutik des Neuen Testaments* (Güttersloh: Gütersloher Verlagshaus G. Mohn, 1988).
—*Theologiegeschichte des Urchristentums* (Tübingen: Francke, 1994).
Berger, P. L. *The Social Reality of Religion* (Harmondsworth: Penguin, 1993).
—*The Heretical Imperative: Contemporary Possibilities of Religious Affirmation* (New York: Doubleday, 1979).
Bingham, D. J. *Irenaeus' Use of Matthew's Gospel in* Adversus Haereses (Traditio Exegetica Graeca 7; Leuven: Peeters, 1998).
Blumenberg, H. *Work on Myth* (Cambridge, MA: MIT Press, 1985).
Boers, H. *What is New Testament Theology?* (Guides to Biblical Scholarship; Philadelphia: Fortress Press, 1979).
Borg, M. J. *Conflict, Holiness and Politics in the Teachings of Jesus* (Harrisburg, PA: Trinity Press International, 1998).
Bornkamm, G. "Die Theologie Bultmanns in der neueren Diskussion," *Theologische Rundschau* 29 (1963), 33–141.
Braun, W. and R. T. McCutcheon, eds, *Guide to the Study of Religion* (London and New York: Cassell, 2000).
Brown, R. E. *The Community of the Beloved Disciple: The Life, Loves, and Hates of an Individual Church in New Testament Times* (New York: Paulist Press, 1979).
—*The Birth of the Messiah: A Commentary on the Infancy Narratives in the Gospels of Matthew and Luke* (2nd edn; New York: Doubleday, 1993).
Broz, J. "From Allegory to the Four Senses of Scripture Hermeneutics of the Church Fathers and of the Christian Middle Ages," in *Philosophical Hermeneutics and Biblical Exegesis* (ed. P. Pokorny and J. Roskovec; WUNT 153; Tübingen: Mohr Siebeck, 2002), 301–9.
Brueggemann, W. *Theology of the Old Testament: Testimony, Dispute, Advocacy* (Minneapolis: Fortress Press, 1997).
Bryan, S. M. *Jesus and Israel's Traditions of Judgement and Restoration* (SNTSMS 117; Cambridge: Cambridge University Press, 2002).
Bultmann, R. *The History of the Synoptic Tradition* (rev. edn; trans. J. Marsh; Oxford: Basil Blackwell, 1968 [orig. 1921]).
—*Jesus and the Word* (trans. L. P. Smith and E. H. Lantero; New York: Charles Scribner's Sons, 1958 [original 1934]).
—*Theology of the New Testament* (2 vols; trans. K. Grobel; New York: Charles Scribner's Sons, 1951, 1955).
—"The New Testament and Mythology," in *Kerygma and Myth* (ed. H.-W. Bartsch; trans. R. H. Fuller; London: SPCK, 1954), 1–44.
—"The Problem of Hermeneutics," in *Essays: Philosophical and Theological* (trans. J. C. G. Greig; New York: Macmillan, 1955), 234–61
—*Jesus Christ and Mythology* (New York: Scribner, 1958).
—*History and Eschatology: The Presence of Eternity* (New York: Harper, 1962).
Burridge, R. A. *What are the Gospels? A Comparison with Graeco-Roman Biography* (SNTSMS 70; Cambridge: Cambridge University Press, 1992).
Burton-Christie, D. *The Word in the Desert: Scripture and the Quest for Holiness in Early Christian Monasticism* (Oxford: Oxford University Press, 1993).

Büsching, A. F. *Dissertatio inauguralis exhibens epitomen theologiae e solis literis sacris concinnatae* (Göttingen, 1756).
—*Epitome Theologiae* (Lemgo, 1757).
—*Gedanken von der Beschaffenheit und dem Vorzug der biblisch-dogmatischen Theologie vor der scholastischen* (Lemgo, 1758).
Byrne, J. M. *Religion and the Enlightenment: From Descarte to Kant* (Louisville: Westminster John Knox Press, 1997).
Cady, L. E. and D. Brown, eds, *Religious Studies, Theology, and the University: Conflicting Maps, Changing Terrain* (Albany: State University of New York, 2002).
Cadzow, H. "New Historicism," in *The Johns Hopkins Guide to Literary Theory and Criticism* (ed. M. Groden and M. Kreiswirth; Baltimore: Johns Hopkins University Press, 1994), 534–40.
Caird, G. B. *New Testament Theology* (ed. L. D. Hurst; Oxford: Clarendon Press, 1994).
Calinescu, M. *Five Faces of Modernity: Modernism, Avant-garde, Decadence, Kitsch, Postmodernism* (Durham: Duke University Press, 1987).
Cameron, R. "Thomas, Gospel of," in *Anchor Bible Dictionary* (ed. D. N. Freedman; New York: Doubleday, 1992), 6.535–40.
Cameron, R. and M. Miller, eds, *Redescribing Christian Origins* (Atlanta: Society of Biblical Literature, 2004).
Campbell, J. *The Hero with a Thousand Faces* (2nd edn; Princeton: Princeton University Press, 1968).
—*The Power of Myth* (New York: Doubleday, 1988).
Capel Anderson, J. and S. D. Moore, eds, *Mark and Method: New Approaches in Biblical Studies* (Minneapolis: Fortress Press, 1992).
Carroll, J. *Constantine's Sword. The Church and the Jews: A History* (Boston: Mariner Books, 2001).
Casey, M. *Sacred Reading: The Ancient Art of Lectio Divina* (Liguori: Triumph, 1996).
Childs, B. S. *Biblical Theology of the Old and New Testaments: Theological Reflection on the Christian Bible* (Minneapolis: Fortress Press, 1992).
Clarke, J. J. *In Search of Jung: Historical and Philosophical Enquiries* (London: Routledge, 1992).
Collins, J. J., ed., "The Bible and Christian Theology," *Journal of Religion* 76 (1996), 167–348.
Connolly, P. *Approaches to the Study of Religion* (London: Cassell, 1999).
Conzelmann, H. *Acts of the Apostles* (trans. J. Limburg, A. T. Kraabel and D. H. Juel; Hermeneia; Philadelphia: Fortress Press, 1987).
—*An Outline of the Theology of the New Testament* (trans. J. Bowden; New York: Harper & Row, 1969).
Cousins, M. "The Practice of Historical Investigation," in *Post-Structuralism and the Question of History* (ed. D. Attridge et al.; Cambridge: Cambridge University Press, 1989), 126–36.
Cox, P. *Biography in Late Antiquity: A Quest for the Holy Man* (Berkeley: University of California Press, 1983).
Crossan, J. D. *The Historical Jesus: The Life of a Mediterranean Jewish Peasant* (New York: HarperCollins, 1991).
—*Jesus: A Revolutionary Biography* (New York: HarperCollins, 1994).

—*The Birth of Christianity: Discovering What Happened in the Years Immediately After the Execution of Jesus* (New York: HarperCollins, 1998).

Crossan, J. D. and J. L. Reed, *In Search of Paul: How Jesus's Apostle Opposed Rome's Empire with God's Kingdom. A New Vision of Paul's Words & World* (New York: HarperCollins, 2004).

Csapo, E. *Theories of Mythology* (Oxford: Blackwell Publishing, 2005).

Cullmann, O. *Christ and Time: The Primitive Conception of Time and History* (trans. F. V. Filson; London: SCM Press, 1962 [original 1946]).

—*The Christology of the New Testament* (trans. S. C. Guthrie and C. A. M. Hall; Philadelphia: Westminster Press, 1959 [original 1957]).

—*Salvation in History* (trans. S. G. Sowers; London: SCM Press, 1967 [original 1965]).

Dawkins, R. *The God Delusion* (Boston: Houghton Mifflin, 2006).

Deissmann, A. *Light from the Ancient East: The New Testament Illustrated by Recently Discovered Texts of the Graeco-Roman World* (trans. L. R. M. Strachan; New York: George H. Doran Co., 1927 [reprinted by Hendrickson, 1995]).

de Lubac, H. *Medieval Exegesis. Volume 1: The Four Senses of Scripture* (trans. M. Sebanc; Grand Rapids: Eerdmans, 1998).

Denham, R. D. *Northrop Frye: Religious Visionary and Architect of the Spiritual World* (Charlottesville: University of Virginia Press, 2004).

—ed., *Northrop Frye's Notebooks and Lectures on the Bible and Other Religious Texts* (Collected Works of Northrop Frye, Volume 13; Toronto: University of Toronto Press, 2003).

Derrida, J. *Speech and Phenomena* (trans. D. Allison; Evanston: Northwestern University Press, 1979).

—*Of Grammatology* (trans. G. C. Spivak: Baltimore: Johns Hopkins University Press, 1980).

Dewey, J. "The Gospel of Mark as an Oral-Aural Event: Implications for Interpretation," in *The New Literary Criticism and the New Testament* (ed. E. S. Malbon and E. V. McKnight; JSNTSup 109; Sheffield: Sheffield Academic Press, 1994), 145–63.

Di Berardino, A. and B. Studer, eds, *History of Theology 1: The Patristic Period* (trans. M. J. O'Connell; Collegeville, MN: Liturgical Press, 1997).

Digeser, E. D. *The Making of a Christian Empire: Lactantius and Rome* (Ithaca: Cornell University Press, 2000).

Donahue, J. R. "The Changing Shape of New Testament Theology," *Theological Studies* 50 (1989), 314–35.

—"The Literary Turn and New Testament Theology: Detour or New Direction?" *Journal of Religion* 76 (1996), 250–75.

Dostoevsky, F. *The Brothers Karamazov* (trans. R. Pevear and L. Volokhonsky; Everyman's Library 70; New York: Alfred A. Knopf, 1992).

Drake, H. A. *Constantine and the Bishops: The Politics of Intolerance* (Ancient Society and History; Baltimore: Johns Hopkins University Press, 2000).

Dudley, G. *Religion on Trial: Mircea Eliade and His Critics* (Philadelphia: Temple University Press, 1977).

van Dülmen, R. *The Society of the Enlightenment: The Rise of the Middle Class and Enlightenment Culture in Germany* (trans. A. Williams; Cambridge: Polity Press, 1992).

Dungan, D. L. *Constantine's Bible: Politics and the Making of the New Testament* (Minneapolis: Fortress Press, 2006).
Dunn, J. D. G. *Unity and Diversity in the New Testament: An Inquiry into the Character of Earliest Christianity* (2nd edn; London: SCM Press, 1990).
—*The Theology of Paul the Apostle* (Grand Rapids: Eerdmans, 1998).
Eagleton, T. *Ideology: An Introduction* (London: Verso, 1991).
—*The Illusions of Postmodernism* (Oxford: Blackwell, 1997).
Ebeling, G. "The Meaning of 'Biblical Theology'," *Journal of Theological Studies* 6 (1955), 210–25 [Reprinted in *Word and Faith* (London: SCM Press, 1963), 79–97].
Ehrman, B. D. *The New Testament and Other Early Christian Writings: A Reader* (Oxford: Oxford University Press, 1998).
—*Jesus: Apocalyptic Prophet of the New Millennium* (Oxford: Oxford University Press, 1999).
—*The New Testament: A Historical Introduction to the Early Christian Writings* (4th edn; Oxford: Oxford University Press, 2008).
Eliade, M. *The Myth of the Eternal Return or Cosmos and History* (trans. W. R. Trask; Princeton: Princeton University Press, 1954).
—*Myth and Reality* (trans. W. R. Trask; San Francisco: Harper & Row, 1963).
—*The Quest: History and Meaning in Religion* (Chicago: The University of Chicago Press, 1969).
Ellwood, R. *The Politics of Myth: A Study of C. G. Jung, Mircea Eliade, and Joseph Campbell* (Albany: State University of New York Press, 1999).
—"Is Mythology Obsolete?" *JAAR* 69 (2001), 673–86.
Emberley, P. C. *Divine Hunger: Canadians on Spiritual Walkabout* (Toronto: HarperCollins, 2002).
Erricker, C. "Phenomenological Approaches," in *Approaches to the Study of Religion* (ed. P. Connolly; London: Cassell, 1999), 73–104.
Esler, P. F. *New Testament Theology: Communion and Community* (Minneapolis: Fortress Press, 2005).
Evans, C. A. *Word and Glory: On the Exegetical and Theological Background of John's Prologue* (JSNTSup 89; Sheffield: Sheffield Academic Press, 1993).
—*Mark 8:27–16:20* (WBC 34B; Nashville: Thomas Nelson, 2001).
—*Ancient Texts for New Testament Studies: A Guide to the Background Literature* (Peabody: Hendrickson, 2005).
Fiorenza, E. S. *In Memory of Her: A Feminist Theological Reconstruction of Christian Origins* (New York: Crossroad, 1983).
—*Jesus and the Politics of Interpretation* (New York: Continuum, 2000).
Fish, S. *Is There a Text in the Class: The Authority of Interpretive Communities* (Cambridge, MA: Harvard University Press, 1980).
Fishbane, M. *Biblical Myth and Rabbinic Mythmaking* (Oxford: Oxford University Press, 2003).
Fitzmyer, J. A. "The Interpretation of the Bible in the Church," in *The Pontifical Biblical Commission Document: Text and Commentary* (Rome: Pontifical Biblical Commission, 1995).
Ford, D. *Theology: A Very Short Introduction* (Oxford: Oxford University Press, 1999).
Fornara, C. W. *The Nature of History in Ancient Greece and Rome* (Berkeley: University of California Press, 1983).

Fowl, S. E. "The Role of Authorial Intention in the Theological Interpretation of Scripture," in *Between Two Horizons: Spanning the New Testament and Systematic Theology* (ed. J. B. Green and M. Turner; Grand Rapids: Eerdmans, 2000), 71–87.
Frazer, J. G. *On Golden Bough* (3rd edn; 12 vols; London: Macmillan, 1907–15).
Frontline, "Faith and Doubt at Ground Zero," PBS; Winter, 2002.
Frye, N. *Fearful Symmetry: A Study of William Blake* (Princeton: Princeton University Press, 1947).
—*The Critical Path: An Essay on the Social Context of Literary Criticism* (Bloomington: Indiana University Press, 1971).
—*Myth and Metaphor: Selected Essays, 1974–1988* (ed. R. D. Denham; Charlottesville: University of Virginia Press, 1990).
—*Words With Power: Being a Second Study of "The Bible and Literature"* (Toronto: Penguin, 1992).
Fuller, R. H. "New Testament Theology," in *The New Testament and its Modern Interpreters* (ed. E. J. Epp and G. W. MacRea; Philadelphia: Fortress Press, 1989), 565–84.
Funk, R. W. and R. W. Hoover, and The Jesus Seminar, *The Five Gospels: The Search for the Authentic Words of Jesus* (New York: Macmillan, 1993).
Gamble, H. Y. *The New Testament Canon: Its Making and Meaning* (Philadelphia: Fortress Press, 1985).
—*Books and Readers in the Early Church: A History of Early Christian Texts* (New Haven: Yale University Press, 1995).
Geertz, A. W. "Cognitive Approaches to the Study of Religion," in *New Approaches to the Study of Religion* (ed. Peter Antes et al.; Religion and Reason, 42\3; 2 vols; Berlin: Walter de Gruyter, 2005).
Gill, G. R. *Northrop Frye and the Phenomenon of Myth* (Toronto: University of Toronto Press, 2006).
Gilpin, W. C. *A Preface to Theology* (Chicago: University of Chicago Press, 1996).
Gnilka, J. *Theologie des Neuen Testaments* (Freiburg: Herder, 1994).
Goppelt, L. *Theology of the New Testament. Volume 1: The Ministry of Jesus in its Theological Significance* (trans. J. E. Alsup; ed. J. Roloff; Grand Rapids: Eerdmans, 1981)
—*Theology of the New Testament. Volume 2: The Variety and Unity of the Apostolic Witness to Christ* (trans. John E. Alsup; ed. Jürgen Roloff; Grand Rapids: Eerdmans, 1982).
Goodacre, M. *The Synoptic Problem: A Way Through the Maze* (The Biblical Seminar 80; London: Sheffield Academic Press, 2001).
Gothóni, R., ed., *How to do Comparative Religion? Three Ways, Many Goals* (Religion and Reason, 44; Berlin: Walter de Gruyter, 2005)
Gould, E. *Mythical Intentions in Modern Literature* (Princeton: Princeton University Press, 1981).
Gradel, I. *Emperor Worship and Roman Religion* (Oxford Classical Monographs; Oxford: Clarendon Press, 2002).
Green J. B. and M. Turner, eds, *Between Two Horizon: Spanning New Testament Studies and Systematic Theology* (Grand Rapids: Eerdmans, 2000).
Greenblatt, S. J. *Renaissance Self-Fashioning: From More to Shakespeare* (Chicago: University of Chicago Press, 1980).

—*Learning to Curse: Essays in Early Modern Culture* (London: Routledge, 1990).
Grelot, P. *The Language of Symbolism: Biblical Theology, Semantics, and Exegesis* (trans. C. R. Smith; Peabody: Hendrickson, 2006).
Grentz, S. J. and R. E. Olson, *20th-Century Theology: God and the World in a Transitional Age* (Downers Grove: InterVarsity, 1992).
Gross, R. M. "Methodology—Tool or Trap?" in *How to do Comparative Religion? Three Ways, Many Goals* (ed. R. Gothóni; Religion and Reason, 44; Berlin: Walter de Gruyter, 2005).
Guelich, R. A. *Mark 1–8:26* (WBC 34A; Dallas: Word, 1989).
Gulick, W. B. "The Thousand and First Face," in *Paths to the Power of Myth: Joseph Campbell and the Study of Religion* (ed. D. C. Noel; New York: Crossroads, 1994), 29–44.
Gundry, R. H. *Matthew: A Commentary on His Handbook for a Mixed Church under Persecution* (2nd edn; Grand Rapids: Eerdmans, 1994).
Habermas, J. *Philosophical Discourse of Modernity: Twelve Lectures* (trans. F. Lawrence; Cambridge, MA; The MIT Press, 1987).
Hafemann, S. J., ed., *Biblical Theology: Retrospect and Prospect* (Downers Grove: InterVarsity Press, 2002).
Hahn, F. *Theologie des Neuen Testaments* (2 vols; Tübingen: Mohr Siebeck, 2002).
Halbwachs, M. *On Collective Memory* (trans. and ed. L. A. Coser; Chicago: University of Chicago Press, 1992).
Hanson, A. T. *The Living Utterances of God: The New Testament Exegesis of the Old* (London: Darton, Longman and Todd, 1983).
Hanson, P. D. *Dynamic Transcendence: The Correlation of Confessional Heritage and Contemporary Experience in a Biblical Model of Divine Activity* (Philadelphia: Fortress Press 1978).
—*The People Called: The Growth of Commnity in the Bible* (San Franciso: Harper & Row, 1986).
Harrisville, R. A. and W. Sundberg, *The Bible in Modern Culture: Theology and Historical-Critical Method from Spinoza to Käsemann* (Grand Rapids: Eerdmans, 1995).
Hasel, G. F. *New Testament Theology: Basic Issues in the Current Debate* (Grand Rapids: Eerdmans, 1978).
Hassan, I. *The Postmodern Turn: Essays in Postmodern Theory and Culture* (Columbus: Ohio State University Press, 1987).
Hatina, T. R. *In Search of a Context: The Function of Scripture in Mark's Narrative* (JSNTSup 232; SSEJC 8; London: Sheffield Academic Press, 2002).
Hays, R. B. *The Moral Vision of the New Testament: A Contemporary introduction to New Testament Ethics* (New York: HarperCollins, 1996).
Heidegger, M. *Being and Time* (trans. J. Macquarrie and E. Robinson; New York: Harper & Row, 1962 [original 1927]).
Hennecke, E. and W. Schneemelcher, eds, *New Testament Apocrypha* (rev. edn; 2 vols; trans. R. McL. Wilson; Louisville: Westminster John Knox, 1991–2).
Hens-Piazza, G.*The New Historicism* (Guides to Biblical Scholarship; Minneapolis: Fortress Press, 2002).
Hillerbrand, H. J. *The Protestant Reformation* (New York: Harper & Row, 1968).
Hitchens, C. *God is Not Great: How Religion Poisons Everything* (New York: Twelve, 2007).

von Hofmann, J. C. K. *Interpreting the Bible* (trans. Ch. Preus; Minneapolis: Augsburg Press, 1959); translated from the German original *Weissagung und Erfüllung im Alten und im Neuen Testamente* (Nördlingen: C. H. Beck, 1841).
Honko, L. "Der Mythos in der Religionswissenschaft," *Temenos* 6 (1970), 36–67.
Hübner, H. *Biblische Theologie des Neuen Testaments* (3 vols; Göttingen: Vandenhoeck und Ruprecht, 1990–5).
Ingraffia, B. D. *Postmodern Theory and Biblical Theology* (Cambridge: Cambridge University Press, 1995).
Jackson, B. and K. H. Jamieson, *UnSpun: Finding Facts in a World of Disinformation* (New York: Random House Trade Paperbacks, 2007).
James, W. *Varieties of Religious Experience* (London: Longmans, Green, 1902)
Jameson, F. *Postmodernism, or, The Cultural Logic of Late Capitalism* (Post-Contemporary Interventions; Durham, NC: Duke University Press, 1991).
Jefferson, T. *Thomas Jefferson's Life of Jesus: Bicentennial Edition* (Springfield: Templegate, 1975).
Jenkins, P. *The Next Christendom: The Coming of Global Christianity* (Oxford: Oxford University Press, 2007).
Jeremias, J. *New Testament Theology: The Proclamation of Jesus* (trans. J. Bowden; London: SCM Press, 1971).
—*The Parables of Jesus* (trans. S. H. Hooke; New York: Scribner, 1963, rev. 1972).
Jewett, R. *Mission and Menace: Four Centuries of American Religious Zeal* (Minneapolis: Fortress Press, 2008).
Johnson, L. T. *The Real Jesus* (San Francisco: HarperCollins, 1996).
—*Religious Experience in Earliest Christianity: A Missing Dimension in New Testament Studies* (Minneapolis: Fortress Press, 1998).
Jones, G. *Bultmann: Towards a Critical Theology* (Cambridge: Polity, 1991).
Juel, D. *Messianic Exegesis: Christological Interpretation of the Old Testament in Early Christianity* (Philadelphia: Fortress Press, 1988).
Käsemann, E. *Essays on New Testament* Themes (trans. W. J. Montague; London: SCM Press, 1964).
Keck, L. "Problems of New Testament Theology," *Novum Testamentum* 7 (1964/65), 217–41.
Kelsey, D. H. *The Use of Scripture in Recent Theology* (Philadelphia: Fortress Press, 1975).
Kermode, F. *The Genesis of Secrecy: On the Interpretation of Narrative* (Cambridge, MA: Harvard University Press, 1979).
—"Institutional Control of Interpretations," in *The Art of Telling* (ed. F. Kermode; Cambridge, MA; Harvard University Press, 1983), 168–84.
Kerrigan, W. "The Raw, The Cooked, and the Half-Baked," *Virginia Quarterly Review* 51 (1975), 651–5.
Kimball, C. *When Religion Becomes Evil: Five Warning Signs* (rev. edn; New York: HarperCollins, 2008).
Kirk, A. and T. Thatcher, eds, *Memory, Tradition, and Text: Uses of the Past in Early Christianity* (Semeia 52; Atlanta: Society of Biblical Literature, 2005).
Kirk, G. S. *Myth: Its Meaning and Functions in Ancient and Other Cultures* (Sather Classical Lectures, 40; London: Cambridge University Press; Berkeley: University of California Press, 1970).

Kort, W. A. *Take, Read: Scripture, Textuality, and Cultural Practice* (University Park Pennsyvania State University Press, 1996).
Koester, H. "Apocryphal and Canonical Gospels," *Harvard Theological Review* 73 (1980), 105–30.
Konstan, D. "The Invention of Fiction," in *Ancient Fiction and Early Christian Narrative* (Society of Biblical Literature Symposium Series 6; ed. Ronald F. Hock, J. Bradley Chance and Judith Perkins; Atlanta: Scholars Press, 1998), 3–17.
Kraemer, R. and M. Rose D'Angelo, eds, *Women and Christian Origins* (Oxford: Oxford University Press, 1999).
Kraftchick, S. J., C. D. Myers, Jr. and B. C. Ollenburger, eds, *Biblical Theology: Problems and Perspectives. In Honor of J. Christiaan Beker* (Nashville: Abingdon, 1995).
Krentz, E. *The Historical-Critical Method* (Guides to Biblical Scholarship; Philadelphia: Fortress Press, 1975).
Kümmel, W. G. *The New Testament: The History of the Investigation of Its Problems* (Nashville: Abingdon, 1972).
—*The Theology of the New Testament According to its Major Witnesses: Jesus-Paul-John* (trans. J. E. Steely; Nashville: Abingdon, 1973).
Küng, H. *Theology for the Third Millennium: An Ecumenical View* (trans. P. Heinegg; New York: Doubleday, 1988).
Labooy, G. "The Historicity of the Virginal Conception. A Study in Argumentation," *European Journal of Theology* 13 (2004), 91–101.
Ladd, G. E. *A Theology of the New Testament* (Grand Rapids: Eerdmans, 1974).
Lévi-Strauss, C. *Structural Anthropology* (trans. C. Jacobson and B. G. Schoepf; Handsworth: Penguin, 1978 [original 1958]).
Lonergan, B. *Method in Theology* (Toronto: University of Toronto, 1990).
Lonergan, B. J. F. *Insight: A Study of Human Understanding* (3rd edn; New York: Philosophical Library, 1970).
Luz, U. *Studies in Matthew* (trans. R. Selle; Grand Rapids: Eerdmans, 2005).
Lyotard, J.-F. *The Postmodern Explained* (trans. and ed. Julian Pefanis and Morgan Thomas; Minneapolis: University of Minnesota Press, 1993).
Mack, B. "Social Formation," in *Guide to the Study of Religions* (ed. W. Braun and R. T. McCutcheon; London; New York: Cassell, 2000), 283–96.
—*The Christian Myth: Origins, Logic, and Legacy* (New York: Continuum, 2001).
Macquarrie, J. *Principles of Christian Theology* (2nd edn; New York: Charles Scribner's Sons, 1977).
Malevez, L. *The Christian Message and Myth* (trans. O. Wyon; London: SCM Press, 1958).
Marcus, J. *The Way of the Lord: Christological Exegesis of the Old Testament in the Gospel of Mark* (Louisville: Westminster John Knox Press, 1992).
Marsh, C. "Quests of the Historical Jesus in New Historicism," *Biblical Interpretation* 5 (1997), 403–37.
Marshall, L. H. *New Testament Theology: Many Witnesses, One Gospel* (Downers Grove: InterVarsity Press, 2004).
Matera, F. J. "New Testament Theology: History, Method, and Identity," *Catholic Biblical Quarterly* 67 (2005), 1–21.
McCutcheon, R. T. "Myth," in *Guide to the Study of Religion* (ed. W. Braun and R. T. McCutcheon; New York: Cassell, 2000), 190–208.

McIntire, C. T. "How Religious Studies Misunderstands Religion," *Academic Matters* December (2007), 9–13.
McKnight, S. *A New Vision for Israel: The Teachings of Jesus in National Context* (Grand Rapids: Eerdmans, 1999).
McVey, K. "Biblical Theology in the Patristic Period: The Logos Doctrine as a 'Physiological' Interpretation of Scripture," in *Biblical Theology: Problems and Perspectives. In Honor of J. Christiaan Beker* (ed. S. J. Kraftchick, C. D. Myers and B. C. Ollenburger; Nashville: Abingdon, 1995), 15–27.
Meier, J. P. *A Marginal Jew: Rethinking the Historical Jesus. Volume 1: The Roots of the Problem and the Person* (New York: Doubleday, 1991).
Merenlahti, P. *Poetics for the Gospels? Rethinking Narrative Criticism* (Edinburgh: T & T Clark, 2002).
Metzger, B. M. *The Canon of the New Testament: Its Origin, Development and Significance* (Oxford: Clarendon Press, 1987).
Meyer, B. F. *The Aims of Jesus* (London: SCM Press, 1979).
—*Critical Realism and the New Testament* (Princeton Theological Monograph Series 17; Allison Park, PA; Pickwick, 1989).
Momigliano, A. *The Development of Greek Biography* (rev. edn; Cambridge, MA: Harvard University Press, 1993).
Moore, S. D. "History After Theory? Biblical Studies and the New Historicism," *Biblical Interpretation* 5 (1997), 289–99.
Morgan, R. "Introduction: The Nature of New Testament Theology," in *The Nature of New Testament Theology* (ed. Robert Morgan; Studies in Biblical Theology 2.25; London: SCM Press, 1973), 1–67.
—"The Historical Jesus and the Theology of the New Testament," in *Studies in Christology in Memory of G. B. Caird* (ed. L. D. Hurst and N. T. Wright; Oxford: Oxford University Press, 1987), 187–206.
—"Can the Critical Study of Scripture Provide a Doctrinal Norm?" *Journal of Religion* 76 (1996), 206–32.
Morris, L. *New Testament Theology* (Grand Rapids: Academie Books, 1986).
Mosko, M. S. "On 'Virgin Birth', Comparability, and Anthropological Method," *Current Anthropology* 39.5 (December 1998), 685–87.
Müller, F. M. *Lectures on the Science of Religion* (New York: Charles Scribner and Company, 1872).
Müller, M. "Neutestamentliche Theologie als Biblische Theologie: Einige grundsätzliche Überlegungen," *New Testament Studies* 43 (1997), 457–90.
Muller, R. A. "Biblical Interpretation in the Era of the Reformation: The View From the Middle Ages," in *Biblical Interpretation in the Era of the Reformation: Essays Presented to David C. Steinmetz in Honor of His Sixtieth Birthday* (ed. R. A. Muller and J. L. Thompson; Grand Rapids: Eerdmans, 1996), 3–22.
—"The Hermeneutic of Promise and Fulfillment in Calvin's Exegesis of the Old Testament Prophecies of the Kingdom," in *The Bible in the Sixteenth Century* (ed. D. C. Steinmetz; Second International Colloquy on the History of Biblical Exegesis in the Sixteenth Century; Durham, NC: Duke University Press, 1990), 68–82.
Multmann, J. *God for a Secular Society: The Public Relevance of Theology* (Minneapolis: Fortress Press, 1999).
Neill, S. *Jesus Through Many Eyes. Introduction to the Theology of the New Testament* (Philadelphia: Fortress Press, 1976).

Neill, S. and T. Wright, *The Interpretation of the New Testament, 1861–1986* (Oxford: Oxford University Press, 1988).
Nickelsburg, G. W. E. *Ancient Judaism and Christian Origins: Diversity, Continuity, and Transformation* (Minneapolis: Fortress Press, 2003).
Noll, M. "Evangelicals. Creation and Scripture: Legacies from a Long History," *Perspectives on Science and Christian Faith* 63.3 (September 2011), 147–58.
Nolland, J. *Luke 1–9:20* (WBC 35A; Dallas: Word Books, 1989).
Nye, M. *Religion: The Basics* (2nd edn; London: Routledge, 2008).
O'Keefe, J. J. and R. R. Reno, *Sanctified Vision: An Introduction to Early Christain Interpretation of the Bible* (Baltimore: Johns Hopkins University Press, 2005).
Ollenburger, B. C. "What Krister Stendahl 'Meant'—a Normative Critique of 'Descriptive Biblical Theology,'" *Horizons in Biblical Theology* 8 (1986), 61–98.
Ong, W. J. *Orality and Literacy: The Technologizing of the Word* (London: Routledge, 2002 [1982]).
Pagels, E. *Beyond Belief: The Secret Gospel of Thomas* (New York: Random House, 2003).
Pals, D. L. *Eight Theories of Religion* (2nd edn; Oxford: Oxford University Press, 2006).
Perkins, P. *Introduction to the Synoptic Gospels* (Grand Rapids: Eerdmans, 2007).
Perrin, N. *Rediscovering the Teaching of Jesus* (New York: Harper & Row, 1967).
—"Paul Ricoeur on Biblical Hermeneutics," *Semeia* 4 (1975), 1–148.
—*Jesus and the Language of the Kingdom: Symbol and Metaphor in New Testament Interpretation* (Philadelphia: Fortress Press, 1976).
Polanyi, M. *Personal Knowledge: Towards a Post-Critical Philosophy* (Chicago: University of Chicago Press, 1974).
Polanyi, M. and H. Prosch, *Meaning* (Chicago: University of Chicago Press, 1977).
Potter, A. "Respect All and Trust No One: Life in a Multi Culti World," *Maclean's* (27 November, 2006), 13.
Potter, D. S. *Literary Texts and the Roman Historian* (Approaching the Ancient World; London: Routledge, 1999).
Räisänen, H. *Marcion, Muhammad and the Mahatma: Exegetical Perspectives on the Encounter of Cultures and Faiths* (London: SCM Press, 1997).
—*Beyond New Testament Theology: A Story and a Program* (2nd edn; London: SCM Press, 2000).
—"Comparative Religion, Theology, and New Testament Exegesis," in *Challenges to Biblical Interpretation: Collected Essays 1991–2001* (ed. H. Räisänen; Biblical Interpretation Series 59; Leiden: Brill, 2001), 209–25.
—"The New Testament in Theology," in *Challenges to Biblical Interpretation: Collected Essays 1991–2001* (ed. H. Räisänen; Biblical Interpretation Series 59; Leiden: Brill, 2001), 227–49.
—"Tradition, Experience, Interpretation: A Dialectical Model for Describing the Development of Religious Thought," in *Challenges to Biblical Interpretation: Collected Essays 1991–2001* (ed. H. Räisänen; Biblical Interpretation Series 59; Leiden: Brill, 2001), 251–62.
Reill, P. H. *The German Enlightenment and the Rise of Historicism* (Berkeley: University of California Press, 1975).
Reiss, T. J. *The Discourse of Modernism* (Ithaca: Cornell University Press, 1982).

Rennie, B. S. *Reconstructing Eliade: Making Sense of Religion* (Albany: State University of New York Press, 1996).
Richardson, A. *The Theology of the New Testament* (London: SCM Press, 1958).
Ricoeur, P. *The Symbolism of Evil* (trans. E. Buchanan; Boston: Beacon Press, 1969).
—"Biblical Hermeneutics," *Semeia* 4 (1975), 29–148.
Roberts, R. C. *Rudolf Bultmann's Theology: A Critical Interpretation* (Grand Rapids: Eerdmans, 1976).
Robinson, J. A. T. *The Priority of John* (London: SCM Press, 1985).
Robinson, J. M. "The Future of New Testament Theology," *Religious Studies Review* 2 (1976), 17–23.
Roof, W. C. *Spiritual Marketplace: Baby Boomers and the Remaking of American Religion* (Princeton: Princeton University Press, 1999).
Rorty, R. "Lofty Ideas that May be Losing Altitude," *The New York Times* (B 13:3, 1 November, 1997).
Rosenberg, B. "Historicizing the New Historicism: Understanding the Past in Criticism and Fiction," *Modern Language Quarterly* 50 (1989), 375–92.
Said, E. *Orientalism* (London: Routledge Keegan Paul, 1978).
Sandys-Wunsch, J. *What Have They Done to the Bible? A History of Modern Biblical Interpretation* (Collegeville: Liturgical Press, 2005).
Sandys-Wunsch, J. and L. Eldredge, "J. P. Gabler and the Distinction Between Biblical and Dogmatic Theology: Translation, Commentary, and Discussion of his Originality," *Scottish Journal of Theology* 33 (1980), 133–58.
Scharlemann, R. P., ed., *Theology at the End of the Century: A Dialogue on the Postmodern* (Studies in Religion and Culture; Charlottesville: University Press of Virginia, 1990).
Schelkle, K. H. *Theology of the New Testament. Volume 1: Creation—World, Time, Man* (trans. W. A. Jurgens; Collegeville: The Liturgical Press, 1968).
Schillebeeckx, E. *The Understanding of Faith: Interpretation and Criticism* (London: Sheed & Ward, 1974).
—*Interim Report on the Books Jesus and Christ* (New York: Crossroad, 1981).
Schlatter, A. "The Theology of the New Testament and Dogmatics," in *The Nature of New Testament Theology* (trans. and ed. R. Morgan; Studies in Biblical Theology 2.25; London: SCM Press, 1973), 115–25, 149–66.
Schmidt, J. "Introduction: What Is Enlightenment? A Question, Its Context, and Some Consequences," in *What Is Enlightenment? Eighteenth-Century Answers and Twentieth-Century Questions* (ed. J. Schmidt; Berkeley: University of California Press, 1996), 1–44.
Schmithals, W. *The Theology of the First Christians* (trans. O. C. Dean Jr.; Louisville: Westminster John Knox, 1997).
Schnelle, U. *Antidocetic Christology in the Gospel of John: An Investigation of the Place of the Fourth Gospel in the Johannine School* (trans. L. M. Maloney; Minneapolis: Fortress Press, 1992).
—*Theology of the New Testament* (trans. M. Eugene Boring; Grand Rapids: Baker Academic, 2009)
Schwartz, B. *Abraham Lincoln and the Forge of National Memory* (Chicago: University of Chicago Press, 2000).

Schweitzer, A. *The Quest of the Historical Jesus: A Critical Study of Its Progress from Reimarus to Wrede* (3rd edn; trans. W. Montgomery; London: Adam & Charles Black, 1954).
Segal, R. A., ed., *Jung on Mythology* (Princeton, NJ: Princeton University Press, 1998).
—*The Blackwell Companion to the Study of Religion* (Malden, MA: Blackwell Publishing, 2006).
—*Theorizing About Myth* (Amherst: University of Massachusetts, 1999).
—"Myth and Politics: A Response to Robert Ellwood," *Journal of the American Academy of Religion* 70 (2002), 611–20.
—*Myth: A Very Short Introduction* (Oxford: Oxford University Press, 2004).
Segundo, J. L. *Jesus of Nazareth Yesterday and Today* (3 vols; Maryknoll, NY: Orbis, 1984–6).
Sharp, E. J. *Comparative Religion: A History* (2nd edn; London: Duckworth, 1986).
Simonetti, M. *Biblical Interpretation in the Early Church: An Historical Introduction to Patristic Exegesis* (trans. J. A. Hughes; Edinburgh: T & T Clark, 1994)
Smart, N. *The Religious Experience of Mankind* (New York: Charles Scribner's Sons, 1969).
—*The Phenomenon of Religion* (New York: Herder and Herder, 1973).
—"Forward," in *Approaches to the Study of Religion* (ed. P. Connolly; London: Cassell, 1999), ix.
Smith, C. *Moral, Believing Animals: Human Personhood and Culture* (Oxford: Oxford University Press, 2003).
Smith, H. *The World's Religions: Our Great Wisdom Traditions* (3rd edn; New York: HarperCollins, 1991).
Smith, J. Z. *Imagining Religion: From Babylon to Jonestown* (Chicago Studies in the History of Judaism; Chicago: University of Chicago Press,1988).
—*Drudgery Divine: On the Comparison of Early Christianities and the Religions of Late Antiquity* (Chicago: The University of Chicago Press, 1990).
Smith, W. C. *The Meaning and End of Religion: A New Approach to the Religious Traditions of Mankind* (New York: New American Library, 1964).
Sobrino, J. *Christology at the Crossroads* (Maryknoll, NY: Orbis, 1978).
Soelle, D. *Political Theology* (trans. J. Shelley; Philadelphia: Fortress Press, 1974).
Solovyov, V. S. *The Meaning of Love* (trans. T. R. Beyer Jr.; Hudson, NY: Lindisfarne Press, 1985).
Soskice, J. M. *Metaphor and Religious Language* (Oxford: Clarendon Press, 1985).
Stegemann, E. and W. Stegemann, *The Jesus Movement: A Social History of Its First Century* (trans. O. C. Dean, Jr.; Minneapolis: Fortress Press, 1999).
Stein, R. H. *The Synoptic Problem: An Introduction* (Grand Rapids: Baker, 1987).
Steinmetz, D. C., ed., *The Bible in the Sixteenth Century* (Second International Colloquy on the History of Biblical Exegesis in the Sixteenth Century; Durham, NC: Duke University Press, 1990).
Stendahl, K. *Meanings: The Bible as Document and as Guide* (Philadelphia: Fortress Press, 1984).
—"Method in the Study of Biblical Theology," in *The Bible in Modern Scholarship* (ed. J. P. Hyatt; Nashville: Abingdon Press, 1965), 196–216.

—"Biblical Theology, Contemporary," in *The Interpreter's Dictionary of the Bible* (ed. G. A. Buttrick; Nashville: Abingdon Press, 1962), 1.418–32.
Stevenson, W. T. "Myth and the Crisis of Historical Consciousness," in *Myth and the Crisis of Historical Consciousness* (ed. L. W. Gibbs and W. Taylor Stevenson; Missoula: Scholars Press, 1975), 1–18.
Strauss, D. F. *The Life of Jesus Critically Examined* (3 vols; trans. G. Eliot; London: Chapman, 1846 [Reprinted: P. C. Hodgson ed., Lives of Jesus Series; Philadelphia: Fortress, 1972/London: SCM Press, 1973]).
Strauss, L. *Spinoza's Critique of Religion* (New York: Schocken Books, 1965).
Strecker, G. *Theology of the New Testament* (trans. M. E. Boring; Louisville: Westminster John Knox Press, 2000).
Stuhlmacher, P. *Biblische Theologie des Neuen Testaments* (2 vols; Göttingen: Vandenhoeck und Ruprecht, 1992, 1999).
Sunstein, C. R. *Why Societies Need Dissent* (Cambridge: Harvard University Press, 2003).
Talbert, C., ed., *Reimarus: Fragments* (trans. R. S. Fraser; Lives of Jesus Series; Philadelphia: Fortress, 1970).
Tambiah, S. J. *Magic, Science, Religion, and the Scope of Rationality* (Cambridge: Cambridge University Press, 1990)
Taylor, C. *A Secular Age* (Cambridge, MA: Belknap Press, 2007).
Thielman, F. *Theology of the New Testament: A Canonical and Synthetic Approach* (Grand Rapids: Zondervan, 2005).
Theissen, G. *The Religion of the Earliest Churches: Creating a Symbolic World* (trans. J. Bowden; Minneapolis: Fortress Press, 1999).
—*A Theory of Primitive Christianity* (trans. J. Bowden; London: SCM Press, 2003).
Toland, J. *Christianity Not Mysterious* (reprint; London: Routledge, 1995).
Torjesen, K. J. *When Women Were Priests: Women's Leadership in the Early Church and the Scandal of Their Subordination in the Rise of Christianity* (San Francisco: HarperCollins, 1993).
Tracy, D. *The Analogical Imagination: Christian Theology and the Culture of Pluralism* (London: SCM Press, 1981).
—"Theology and the Many Faces of Postmodernity," in *Readings in Modern Theology: Britain & America* (ed. R. Gill; Nashville: Abingdon Press, 1995), 225–35.
Trebilco, P. *The Early Christians in Ephesus From Paul to Ignatius* (WUNT 166; Tübingen: Mohr-Siebeck, 2004).
Tuckett, C. "Does the 'Historical Jesus' Belong within a 'New Testament Theology'?" in *The Nature of New Testament Theology: Essays in Honour of Robert Morgan* (ed. C. Rowland and C. Tuckett; Oxford: Blackwell, 2006), 231–47.
Tylor, E. B. *Primitive Culture: Researches into the Development of Mythology, Philosophy, Religion, Language, Art, and Custom* (London: John Murray, 1871).
—*Primitive Culture* (2 vols; London: Murray, 1871; 5th edn reprint: New York: Harper Collins, 1958).
Van Dokkum, A. "Belief Systems about Virgin Birth: Structure and Mutual Comparability," *Current Anthropology* 38.1 (1997), 99–104.
Vanhoozer, K. J. *Is There Meaning in this Text? The Bible, The Reader, and The Morality of Literary Knowledge* (Grand Rapids: Zondervan, 1998).

—*First Theology: God, Scripture and Hermeneutics* (Downers Grove: InterVarsity Press, 2002).
Via, D. O. *The Revelation of God and/as Human Reception* (Harrisburg, PA: Trinity Press International, 1997).
—*What is New Testament Theology?* (Guides to Biblical Scholarship; Minneapolis: Fortress Press, 2002).
Vines, M. E. *The Problem of Markan Genre: The Gospel of Mark and the Jewish Novel* (Society of Biblical Literature Academia Biblica 3; Atlanta: Society of Biblical Literature, 2002).
Walsh, R. G. *Mapping the Myths of Biblical Interpretation* (Playing the Texts 4; Sheffield: Sheffield Academic Press, 2001).
Ward, K. *Religion and Revelation: A Theology of Revelation in the World's Religions* (Oxford: Clarendon Press, 1994).
—*The Case For Religion* (Oxford: Oneworld, 2004).
Warms, R., J. Garber and J. McGee, "What is Religion?" in *Sacred Realms: Essays in Religion, Belief, and Society* (ed. R. Warms, J. Garber and J. McGee; New York: Oxford University Press, 2004).
Watson, F. *Text and Truth: Redefining Biblical Theology* (Edinburgh: T & T Clark, 1997).
Westphal, M. *Overcoming Onto-Theology: Toward A Postmodern Christian Faith* (New York: Fordham University Press, 2001).
Whaling, F. "Theological Approaches," in *Approaches to the Study of Religion* (ed. P. Connolly; London: Cassell, 1999), 226–69.
Wheelwright, P. E. *Metaphor and Reality* (Bloomington: Indiana University Press, 1962).
Wiebe, P. H. *Visions of Christ: Direct Encounters from the New Testament to Today* (New York: Oxford University Press, 1998).
—*God and Other Spirits: Intimations of Transcendence in Christian Experience* (Oxford: Oxford University Press, 2004).
Wilkins, U. *Theologie des Neuen Testaments* (5 vols; Neukirchen-Vyuyn: Neukirchener, 2002–).
Williams, R. *The Wound of Knowledge: Christian Spirituality from the New Testament to Saint John of the Cross* (Cambridge, MA: Cowley Publications, 1979, 1990).
Wilson, B. R. *Religion in Social Perspective* (Oxford; Oxford University Press, 1982).
—*The Social Dimensions of Sectarianism: Sects and New Religious Movements in Contemporary Society* (Oxford: Clarendon Press, 1990).
Wilson, S. *The Magical Universe: Everyday Magic and Ritual in Pre-Modern Europe* (London: Hambledon & London, 2004).
Wollheim, R., ed., *Hume on Religion* (New York: Meridian, 1963).
Wood, S. K. *Spiritual Exegesis and the Church in the Theology of Henri de Lubac* (Edinburgh: T & T Clark, 1998).
Wrede, W. "The Task and Methods of 'New Testament Theology,'" in *The Nature of New Testament Theology* (ed. Robert Morgan; Studies in Biblical Theology 2.25; London: SCM Press, 1973), 68–116.
Wright, N. T. *The New Testament and the People of God* (Christian Origins and the Question of God 1; Minneapolis: Fortress Press, 1992).
—*Climax of the Covenant: Christ and the Law in Pauline Theology* (Minneapolis: Fortress Press, 1993).

—*Jesus and the Victory of God* (Christian Origins and the Question of God 2; Minneapolis: Fortress Press, 1997).
—*The Resurrection of the Son of God* (Christian Origins and the Question of God 3; Minneapolis: Fortress Press, 2003).
Yovel, Y. *Spinoza and Other Heretics* (Princeton: Princeton University Press, 1989).

AUTHOR INDEX

Achtemeier, P. J. 60
Adam, A. K. M. 15, 16, 27, 36, 37, 38, 39, 47, 51, 53, 54, 159, 212, 244
Allison, D. C. 29, 56, 146
Anderson, J. C. 16
Antes, P. 221, 223
Argall, R. A. 70
Arnal, W. 233
Attridge, D. 18, 48

Baird, R. 230
Balla, P. 14, 28
Barr, J. 18, 44, 60
Barrett, C. K. 55
Barthes, R. 27, 32, 46, 47, 231, 232, 244
Barton, J. 9
Bartsch, H. W. 34, 166
Bauckham, R. 74
Bauer, G. L. 117
Bauer, W. 65, 66
Baur, F. C. 65
Bennett, C. 111
Berger, K. 15, 63
Berger, P. L. 188, 189, 218
Bingham, D. J. 49
Blumenberg, H. 229
Boers, H. 13
Borg, M. J. 29, 50, 214
Boring, M. E. 15
Bornkamm, G. 167
Bousset, W. 122, 166
Bow, B. 70
Braun, W. 223, 232, 233
Brown, D. 192
Brown, R. E. 67, 74, 88
Broz, J. 93, 94, 97
Brueggemann, W. 63

Bryan, S. M. 154, 155, 156
Bultmann, R. 22, 33, 34, 35, 36, 43, 51, 59, 80, 126, 129, 142, 146, 148, 149, 153, 162, 163, 164, 165, 166, 167, 168, 169, 170, 171, 173, 177, 204, 225
Buri, F. 168
Burridge, R. A. 130
Burton-Christie, D. 93
Büsching, A. F. 103, 115
Byrne, J. M. 105, 108, 112

Cady, L. E. 192
Cadzow, H. 46
Caird, G. B. 8, 23, 120, 135, 136, 137
Calinescu, M. 16, 17
Cameron, R. 78, 223, 233
Campbell, J. 193, 194, 199, 226, 227, 230, 231
Camus, A. 187
Carroll, J. 182
Casey, M. 97
Chance, J. B. 90
Chesterton, G. K. 246
Childs, B. S. 8, 20, 140, 141
Clarke, J. J. 230
Collins, J. J. 172
Connolly, P. 194, 196, 199, 202
Conzelmann, H. 55, 162
Coser, L. A. 129
Cousins, M. 18, 48
Cox, P. 130, 131
Crossan, J. D. 29, 50, 71, 78, 153, 154, 204
Csapo, E. 228, 230, 232, 233
Culler, J. 37
Cullmann, O. 28, 141, 142, 143, 144, 145, 150

D'Angelo, M. R. 76
Dawkins, R. 199
Deissmann, A. 70, 122
De Lubac, H. 95, 98, 100
De Man, P. 46
Denham, R. D. 236, 251
Derrida, J. 46, 56, 204, 213, 238
Dewey, J. 49, 128, 129
Di Berardino, A. 93
Digeser, E. D. 77
Donahue, J. R. 33, 35, 36, 38, 47, 51
Dostoevsky, F. 108
Drake, H. A. 77
Dudley, G. 230
Dungan, D. L. 64
Dunn, J. D. G. 50, 66, 133

Eagleton, T. 16, 17, 233
Ebeling, G. 18, 19, 21, 64, 119, 139, 167
Ehrman, B. D. 29, 58, 77
Eldredge, L. 116
Eliade, M. 187, 188, 193, 199, 230
Ellwood, R. 228, 233, 234
Emberley, P. C. 3, 180
Epp, E. J. 225
Erricker, C. 199
Esler, P. F. 52
Evans, C. E. 61, 79, 86, 98, 131, 169

Fish, S. 27, 32, 46, 52, 53
Fishbane, M. 226, 228, 231
Fitzmyer, J. A. 97
Ford, D. 184, 189
Fornara, C. W. 131
Foucault, M. 27, 32
Fowl, S. E. 99
Frazer, J. G. 229
Freedman, D. N. 78
Frye, N. 95, 228, 230, 234, 235, 236, 237, 251
Fuller, R. H. 225
Funk, R. W. 128

Gabler, J. P. 116, 117, 138, 156, 247
Gadamer, G. 27, 46
Gamble, H. Y. 64, 78
Garber, J. 185, 192
Geertz, A. W. 221

Gerhardsson, B. 122
Gibbs, L. W. 250
Gill, G. R. 228, 230, 234
Gill, R. 16
Gilpin, W. C. 179
Gnilka, J. 15, 209, 238
Goodacre, M. 72, 125
Goppelt, L. 19, 83, 143, 144, 145, 150
Gothóni, R. 222, 223
Gould, E. 230
Gradel, I. 55
Green, J. B. 99, 157
Greenblatt, S. J. 46, 47
Grelot, P. 52
Grentz, S. J. 106
Gross, R. M. 221, 222
Guelich, R. A. 48
Gulick, W. B. 231
Gundry, R. H. 87

Habermas, J. 17
Hafemann, S. J. 9
Hahn, F. 15, 133
Halbwachs, M. 129
Hanson, A. T. 85
Hanson, P. D. 151
Harrisville, R. A. 57, 59, 140
Hasel, G. F. 83, 103, 116, 117, 124, 158, 163, 167, 168, 169
Hassan, I. 17
Hatina, T. R. 98, 135
Hays, R. B. 22
Heidegger, M. 37, 46, 164
Hennecke, E. 77
Hens-Piazza, G. 47
Hillerbrand, H. 101
Hitchens, C. 199
Hock, R. F. 90
Hodgson, P. C. 225
Honko, L. 231
Hoover, R. W. 128
Horsley, R. 50
Hübner, H. 15, 209
Hume, D. 107
Hurst, L. D. 23, 124

Ingraffia, B. D. 164

AUTHOR INDEX

Jackson, B. 227
James, W. 184, 199
Jameson, F. 45, 213
Jamieson, K. H. 226, 227
Jaspers, K. 168
Jefferson, T. 110
Jenkins, P. 195
Jensen, A. E. 187
Jeremias, J. 21, 28, 49, 123, 124, 167, 168
Jewett, R. 178
Johnson, L. T. 128, 202
Jones, G. 169
Juel, D. 90

Käsemann, E. 56, 167
Keck, L. 159
Kelsey, D. H. 57
Kermode, F. 51, 52, 88
Kerrigan, W. 230
Kimball, C. 216
Kirk, A. 129
Kirk, G. S. 237
Koester, H. 78
Konstan, D. 90
Kort, W. A. 213
Kraemer, R. 76
Kraft, R. A. 66
Kraftchick, S. J. 62, 212
Krentz, E. 34, 93, 105, 106, 109, 112, 113
Krodel, G. 66
Kümmel, W. G. 110, 122, 123, 124
Küng, H. 194, 202, 211

Labooy, G. 226
Ladd, G. E. 57, 143, 144, 145, 150, 151
Lawrence, F. 17
Léonard, A. 56
Lévi-Strauss, C. 229
Lincoln, B. 228, 232, 233, 236
Lodge, D. 154
Lonergan, B. F. J. 8, 209
Luz, U. 68
Lyotard, J.-F. 46, 245

Mack, B. 222, 223, 233
Macquarrie, J. 31, 162, 164, 191, 197, 201

MacRea, G. W. 225
Malbon, E. S. 49, 129
Malevez, L. 168, 169
Marcus, J. 98
Marsh, C. 47
Marshall, I. H. 24, 25, 133, 134, 135, 136
Matera, F. J. 44
McCutcheon, R. T. 223, 231, 232, 233
McGee, J. 185, 192
McIntire, C. T. 206, 207
McKnight, E. V. 49, 129
McKnight, S. 155
McNamara, M. 87
McVey, K. 212
Meier, J. 50, 127, 128, 226
Merenlahti, P. 51, 238
Metzger, B. M. 64, 187
Meyer, B. F. 146
Miller, M. 223, 233
Minear, P. 137
Momigliano, A. 131
Moore, S. D. 16, 47, 62
Morgan, R. 17, 21, 83, 124, 157, 171
Morris, L. 60, 61
Mosko, M. S. 230
Moyers, B. 193, 226, 231
Müller, F. M. 220, 221, 238
Müller, M. 9
Muller, R. A. 101, 102
Multmann, J. 178
Myers, C. D. 62, 212

Neill, S. 59, 167
Nickelsburg, W. E. 70
Nietzsche, F. 178, 222
Noel, D. C. 231
Noll, M. 112
Nolland, J. 71
Nye, M. 185

Ogden, S. M. 168, 169
O'Keefe, J. J. 94, 113
Ollenburger, B. C. 30, 62, 212
Olson, R. E. 106
Ong, W. 32, 48, 128

Pagels, E. 68
Pals, D. L. 185, 220, 221

Pelikan, J. 64, 205
Perkins, J. 90
Perkins, P. 74
Perrin, N. 51, 123, 170, 171
Pokorny, P. 93
Polanyi, M. 217
Potter, A. 45
Potter, D. S. 131
Prosch, H. 217

Räisänen, H. 25, 26, 50, 63, 83, 150, 189, 211, 215, 216, 217, 219, 223
Reed, J. L. 71
Reill, P. H. 111
Reiss, T. J. 17
Rennie, B. S. 230
Reno, R. R. 94, 113
Ricoeur, P. 46, 51, 170
Richardson, A. 158, 159
Roberts, R. C. 165
Robinson, J. A. T. 125
Robinson, J. M. 43, 167, 170, 171
Roloff, J. 19, 83, 143
Roof, W. C. 6
Rorty, R. 17, 46
Rosenberg, B. 47
Roskovec, J. 93
Rowland, C. 9, 124

Said, E. 199
Sandys-Wunsch, J. 116, 117
Scharlemann, R. P. 17
Schelkle, K. H. 159, 160
Schillebeeckx, E. 35, 99
Schlatter, A. 157, 158
Schmidt, J. 104, 105, 108, 109, 118
Schmithals, W. 15
Schneemelcher, W. 77
Schnelle, U. 15, 68
Schüssler Fiorenza, E. 37, 50, 76, 113, 221, 244, 245, 246, 249
Schweitzer, A. 19, 31, 50
Segal, R. A. 223, 228, 229, 230
Segundo, J. L. 35, 215
Sharp, E. J. 195
Simonetti, M. 94, 95
Smart, N. 185, 189, 194, 196, 199, 203, 217, 218

Smith, C. 48
Smith, H. 189, 203
Smith, J. Z. 6, 27, 65, 70, 219, 220, 222
Smith, W. C. 194, 202, 218
Sobrino, J. 35, 215
Soelle, D. 169
Solovyov, V. 205
Soskice, J. M. 55, 56
Stein, R. H. 74
Steinmetz, D. C. 101
Stendahl, K. 18, 30, 157, 249
Stevenson, W. T. 250
Strauss, D. F. 225
Strecker, G. 15, 23
Struder, B. 93
Stout, J. 37
Stuhlmacher, P. 15, 20
Sundberg, W. 57, 59, 140
Sunstein, C. R. 210

Talbert, C. H. 111
Tambiah, S. J. 5
Taylor, C. 4, 5
Taylor, E. B. 192
Thatcher, T. 129
Theissen, G. 18, 223
Thielman, F. 25, 26, 27
Thompson, J. L. 101
Toland, J. 111
Torjesen, K. J. 76
Tracy, D. 16, 194, 202, 211
Trebilco, P. 137
Tuckett, C. 9, 124
Turner, M. 99, 157
Tylor, E. B. 229

Van Dokkum, A. 230
Van Dülman, R. 105
Vanhoozer, K. J. 51
Via, D. O. 2, 14, 15, 17, 19, 27, 28, 38, 39, 149, 152, 153, 154, 164, 165, 169, 213
Vines, M. E. 131, 132
Von Hofmann, J. C. K. 140, 149

Walsh, R. G. 228
Ward, K. 182, 190, 194, 202, 217
Warms, R. 185, 192

Watson, F. 9, 14, 212
Werline, R. A. 70
West, C. 244
Westfall, M. 245
Whaling, F. 202
Wheelwright, P. E. 51, 170
Wiebe, P. H. 91, 186
Wilkins, U. 15
Williams, R. 246
Wilson, B. R. 103, 180, 200
Wilson, S. 5

Wollheim, R. 107
Wood, S. K. 98, 100
Wrede, W. 14, 17, 18, 20, 22, 25, 26, 27, 28, 31, 37, 43, 146, 158, 166, 211, 216, 217
Wright, N. T. 50, 57, 58, 59, 114, 124, 145, 146, 147, 148, 149, 152, 153, 154, 155, 156, 158, 212, 214

Yovel, Y. 105

SCRIPTURE INDEX

Old Testament

Genesis
2.2 85
2.2 (LXX) 85
17.14 86
22.9-10 87
41.45 86

Exodus
12.46 88

Deuteronomy
26.12 85
26.12 (LXX) 85
30.11-14 89
30.12-14 89

Leviticus
24.7 85
24.7 (LXX) 85

Isaiah
40.3 98

Habakkuk
1.4 89
1.6 89

Daniel
1–6 132

Apocrypha

Tobit
14.5-7 155

Wisdom
10.10 86

Baruch 3.6-8 155

Targums

Genesis
Neofiti 22.10 87

Dead Sea Scrolls

1QpHab
1.10–13 89
2.10–15 89

New Testament

Matthew
1.18-25 73
2.1 73
2.11 73
2.23 74
4.5-11 73
4.13 74
5–7 86
6.24 73
11.14 75
17.10-13 75
19.21 93
27 72
27.46 111
28.16-20 68

Mark
1.1 61
1.3 98
1.4 61
1.9-11 61
1.15 98
7 86
8.27-30 75

11.18 74
14 72
14.12 74
15.34 61, 111
15.39 61

Luke
1.17 75
1.26-27 73
1.56 73
4.5-13 73
7 72
8.2 72
11.28 99
16.13 73
24.27 91

John
1.21 75
1.41 75
4.24 93, 94
5.39 20, 91
5.46 91
6 75
10.30 94
12 72
14–16 91
17 205
18.28 74, 88
19.14 74, 88
19.36 88
20.28 66

Acts
1 55
5.27-29 77

Romans
1.27-28 22
4 99
10.5-9 90
10.6-8 89
13 215
13.1-2 76

1 Corinthians
5.7 88

15 125
15.3-4 91

Ephesians
4.25 93
6.5 215

Philippians
2 125
2.5-11 125, 126

Colossians
4.1 215

1 Timothy
3.16 68

2 Timothy
3.16 60

Hebrews
11 99

James
1.22-25 99

Non Canonical Literature

Church Fathers

Athanasius

De Sententia Dionysii
15 94

Basil

Adversus Eunonium
3.3 94

De Spiritu Sancto
18.47 94
19.48 94

Eusebius

Ecclesiastical History 3.39.15 48

Origen

De Principiis
1.1.1–2 94
4.1.6 94

Commentary on John
13.21–23 94

Tertullian

Adversus Praxean
7.8 94

8.4 94
9.2 94

Roman Sources

Plutarch

Life of Pompey
8 131

www.ingramcontent.com/pod-product-compliance
Lightning Source LLC
Chambersburg PA
CBHW050136240426
43673CB00043B/1689